GENEALOGICAL RESOURCES
IN
ENGLISH REPOSITORIES

GENEALOGICAL RESOURCES

IN

ENGLISH REPOSITORIES

by

JOY WADE MOULTON

HAMPTON HOUSE
COLUMBUS, OHIO

To Ned

Hampton House, P.O. Box 21534, Columbus, Ohio, 43221
© 1988 by Joy Wade Moulton
Published 1988
Printed in the United States of America
Library of Congress Catalog Card Number 87–082876
ISBN 0-944485-00-6

CONTENTS

PART I: GREATER LONDON REPOSITORIES

PART II: COUNTY REPOSITORIES

PART III: LONDON BOROUGH REPOSITORIES

ACKNOWLEDGMENTS

A work of this nature is possible only with the cooperation and assistance of many individuals. It is with pleasure that the author recognizes their contributions to this volume.

The early encouragement given by Anthony J. Camp, Director of the Society of Genealogists, of my idea for such a guide was the catalyst for developing the format for the original survey. As my genealogical mentor, his wise counsel and delightful wit have provided great encouragement.

I am indebted to the archivists, librarians, and others responsible for collections in the surveyed repositories. Their contribution of time and their patience in responding to my queries was essential to the publication of this volume. Special acknowledgment is given to J.M. Farrer, County Archivist for the County Record Office, Cambridge; Annette M. Kennett, City Archivist for the Chester City Record Office; Dr. Dorothy M. Owen, Keeper of Manuscripts Emeritus at Cambridge University Library; Timothy Padfield of the Public Record Office, Kew; and Richard Samways, Archivist for the Greater London Record Office, for their thoughtful critiques of the survey in its earlier stages.

My appreciation is extended to Paul L. Smart, Supervisor of the British Reference Section of the Family History Library in Salt Lake City, for providing current information about holdings in the British Collection at the Library. Dean Hunter, Supervisor of Collections Development for the British Isles at the Family History Center, was extremely helpful in providing details about the microfilm program of the Genealogical Society of Utah as well as the microfilm holdings of the Family History Center.

For the advice and assistance given by Kip Sperry, Supervisor of United States and Canadian Collection Development at the Family History Library, J. Michael Armstrong, Publisher of *Family Tree Magazine*, and Richard Moore, Chairman of the Federation of Family History Societies, I am most appreciative. Netti Schreiner-Yantis and Carl Boyer, III have been extremely helpful in providing information relating to the production of this publication.

For permission to use the maps of the Pre-1974 and Post-1974 Counties of England and Wales, I am indebted to F.C. Markwell and Pauline Saul, the authors of *Enquire Within*, and to its publisher, the Federation of Family History Societies. Permission for use of the map of the Post-1965 London Boroughs, originally published in *London Cemeteries and Crematoria* by the Society of Genealogists, was granted by Anthony J. Camp.

The expertise in computer formatting of Dean Roush, his original street maps for repositories in Part I, and his painstaking editing have been key to the completion of this work. I am especially appreciative of his patience throughout. My appreciation is also extended to Nancy Gallagher, who typed most of the original draft.

And to my husband, Edward, and children Jennifer, Charles, David and Alison, I am deeply grateful for their encouragement of my professional career, and understanding of the time commitment involved in the completion of this publication.

Joy Wade Moulton

December 1987

INTRODUCTION

Five centuries ago the recording of an English family's history, aside from personal registers, was limited to a single document – the pedigree chart. Used exclusively for nobility and gentry, this elemental form originally included the lord of a manor, the name of his manor, and given names of his descendants for several generations. The ancestral charts kept by genealogists and family historians today, while more comprehensive, still retain the basic component of that early form – a graphic description of the relationship of one generation to another. While early pedigrees were based on the oral enumeration of living descendants of the lord of a manor, recorded information about present-day ancestors is based primarily on evidence found in manuscript records, as well as printed, transcribed and microform sources.

Any library or record repository in England will have some useful resources. However, genealogists and family historians should have more effective results with searches in county and city record offices, libraries which are depositories for specific classes of records, and libraries with specialized genealogical and family history collections.

PURPOSE

This volume is designed to provide genealogists and family historians with up-to-date information on resources in the key repositories of England. It categorizes manuscript records, as well as printed, transcribed and microform materials, with respect to their contents, and in most instances, lists covering dates.

With this guide, family tracers should be able to identify sources most likely to contain genealogical information within a given time period. In the event one of the more commonly used resources no longer exists, or does not contain the desired information, researchers can quickly determine other manuscripts or printed, transcribed and microform materials which might be examined. The book also provides researchers with an opportunity to utilize numerous documents in attempting to establish an individual's location, the date of a specific event, or the relationship of family members based on a preponderance of the evidence.

This volume is basically a "where to find" reference guide. Originally conceived as an aid to Americans searching for British ancestors, it soon became apparent that the book would be useful to anyone researching English ancestry.

SCOPE

A survey was taken of genealogical holdings in the county record offices, repositories with major genealogical collections, denominational historical societies, and libraries in the thirty-two London Boroughs. Additionally, district archives and designated district libraries in the six former metropolitan counties were surveyed. Information received from the archivists, librarians and others responsible for collections was then compiled into the present format, with minor exceptions.

Resources listed for most libraries in the category "Other Repositories" were taken from the original survey of the county record offices and include only those items noted in the survey or in the literature provided by those repositories.

The major categories of holdings of the LDS Family History Centres (formerly called Branch Genealogical Libraries) was obtained from the Family History Library (formerly called the Genealogical Library) in Salt Lake City. Information about resources microfilmed by the Genealogical Society of Utah was obtained through the Family History Library Catalog at the Family History Center, Reynoldsburg, Ohio, and from the Supervisor of Collection Development for the British Isles at the Family History Library in Salt Lake City.

Names and addresses of correspondents for the respective Family History Societies were provided by the Federation of Family History Societies, and were verified through correspondence with secretaries of the individual societies.

Resources in the survey were selected on the basis of the information which they contained. Some include vital information as well as evidence of family relationships for individuals at a specific time and location. Others give only the name of an individual in a locality on a given date. Some are original records, others microform copies, transcriptions or printed sources. While some extend back into the medieval period, a majority of the resources pertain to the period between 1538 and the present time. Some are readily available, while others are located only at the specified repository.

NOTES ON THE REPOSITORIES

The book is divided into three parts. Part I (Greater London Repositories) includes record offices and libraries in that geographical area, which have resources relating to various segments of the general population of the country. It also includes repositories which hold records of different religious denominations, the (ancient) City of London, and the British overseas. The repositories in this part are listed in alphabetical order for the convenience of readers. A street map is shown for each repository indicating its location in relation to the nearest subway or British rail station. Since the types of records in Part I are so varied, no attempt was made to standardize the format of repositories which hold resources for only a limited segment of the population.

Part II (County Repositories) includes county record offices and other repositories within each of the present geographical counties. In addition, there is a listing for those counties which were abolished at the time of the reorganization of local government in 1974, as well as for Middlesex County and the County of London, which were eliminated in the reorganization of the Greater London area in 1965. For each county listed, there is a description of the changes in geographical boundaries and administrative jurisdiction since 1888. (Since records remain with the county where they originated, it is important for researchers to note the date of any changes.) The incorporation of Boroughs and the designation of Municipal Boroughs is also given, since in most instances Boroughs were granted some jurisdiction independent of the county in which they were located. Separate records will be found wherever both the county and borough had separate authority, e.g., Rates, Quarter Ses-

sions, Justices of the Peace. Cities were occasionally designated as a "county of a city" or "County Corporate." In those
instances the city had been granted authority equal to and
separate from the county in which it was geographically
located. This, too, should be noted, for records of such cities will
be separate from those of the county.

When the metropolitan county councils were abolished
1 April 1986, responsibility for the administration of archival
repositories in each county was assigned to the councils of the
districts which made up the respective counties. The arrangement of these county repositories and their records in the book
reflects the variation in their administration.

In Part II a section is devoted to each of the present counties.
Designated county record offices and/or archive services, and
Church of England diocesan depositories are listed first.
Current address, telephone number and hours are given for
each repository, followed by a general statement of its holdings.
A list of specific resources with covering dates then follows. A
second category (Other Repositories) includes county and city
libraries which have genealogical information. This was
originally added at the request of several county archivists so
that resources held by local history or local studies libraries
housed in the same building or nearby would be clearly
identified as under a separate authority, for example, Census
Returns, International Genealogical Index, Postal and Trade
Directories, Newspapers, and Poll Books. It also includes
repositories in a county which have sizeable genealogical collections, but have not been officially designated as a county
record office, county archives service, or diocesan depository.
The LDS Family History Centres in England (formerly called
Branch Genealogical Libraries) are also included in this
category, since English resources filmed by the Genealogical
Society of Utah have been specially noted in the book. A third
category, Genealogical and Family History Societies,
completes the section for each county. Member societies of the
Federation of Family History Societies have been included, and
for each, the address of the correspondent is listed along with the
name of the society's quarterly journal or newsletter. (A majority of towns in England now have local historical societies

which may also have valuable information useful to genealogists and family historians. The addresses of these societies
can normally be obtained from the appropriate county record
office or borough library. No effort was made to include these
groups in this publication.)

Part III (London Borough Repositories) includes the principal libraries which house archival materials and local
study/history collections in each of the thirty-two London
Boroughs. There is considerable variation in the extent and
type of holdings in these repositories. A number have some
original documents such as the Estate and Family Papers of
prominent families in the area, one or more Parish Registers
and other Parish Records for Church of England parish
churches and some Registers of Nonconformist churches
within the area. All of the repositories listed in this part have
printed sources relating to their areas. The format in listing
resources for the London Borough repositories is the same as for
County Repositories. The LDS Family History Centres in the
Greater London area are listed at the end of Part III along with
Genealogical and Family History Societies in the London
Boroughs.

N.B. The addresses, telephone numbers, hours, and admission fee policies are current as of this printing. Since these
items are continually subject to change, supplements are
planned to update the information.

NOTES ON THE RESOURCES

Two categories of resources have been established for most
repositories: 1) those which will only identify an individual
with a specific location, and 2) those which may additionally
provide vital data and/or proof of family relationships. This
format was selected so that readers can readily identify the type
of information a specific resource is likely to provide. The
source materials within each category are listed in alphabetical
order, and do not reflect in any way the usefulness of one
resource over another. While the category "Sources that may
Provide Vital Data and/or Proof of Family Relationships" is

listed second, sources within that category should be utilized first if at all possible.

The first letter in the title of each resource has been capitalized for the convenience of readers (e.g., Parish Register). Also, the original spelling of records has been used throughout.

Within each category the following specific resources have been grouped together under the institution or court which has or had original jurisdiction. Borough Records include documents pertaining to those municipalities which had been incorporated. Many pre-twentieth-century boroughs had their own Quarter Sessions, while most normally had authority to acquire and hold lands, and to collect rates. Church of England diocesan records (e.g., Bishops' Transcripts, Marriage Licences, and Probate Records) are identified separately from the Church of England parish records (e.g., Parish Registers, Vestry Minutes, Churchwardens' Accounts). Although the Parish Poor Law Records were under jurisdiction of the Church of England, they have been listed separately in this publication to emphasize their importance as a resource.

The Court of Quarter Sessions records for a county or borough include Judicial Records, and in addition, documents registered with the Clerk of the Peace to 1888 (e.g., Lists of Jurors, Lists of Freeholders, Registration of Papists' Estates).

The various types of manorial records (e.g., Court Baron Rolls, Rentals and Surveys) are grouped together without specific notation. Nonconformist Records include all Protestant dissident denominations (i.e., Baptist, Congregational/Independent, Bible Christian, Bretheren, Huguenot, Church of Jesus Christ of Latter-day Saints (Mormons), Moravian, Presbyterian/Unitarian, and Society of Friends (Quakers). Jewish and Roman Catholic records, however, have been listed separately.

Inclusive dates are given for most resources. In a few instances, however, the dates are actually outside covering dates for the entire record group. Therefore, where several classes of records are listed within the group (e.g., Borough Records, Parish Poor Law Records), the dates given may not be representative of the individual classes of records. Similarly, there may be large gaps in dates for the record classes of Estates and

Family Papers, Manorial Records, and Title Deeds, especially in the early period.

It should be noted that the resources listed do not necessarily reflect a complete series of manuscript records or printed materials, either with respect to the geographical areas within a county or borough, or with respect to the time period.

MICROFORMS, PRINTED SOURCES AND TRANSCRIPTIONS

This publication is designed for use by researchers who visit repositories as well as those who seek information through correspondence and by use of printed, transcribed or microform copies of original documents. An attempt has been made to note such copies of resources wherever possible, as they may be available in other repositories or through an interlibrary loan service.

Most microfilming has been undertaken by the Genealogical Society of Utah, an arm of the Church of Jesus Christ of Latter-day Saints. In addition to the vast collection of microform and printed sources in Salt Lake City, copies of some microfilmed records are available in a number of county record offices and libraries in England, some of the Greater London repositories, and London Borough libraries. Most LDS microfilms are also available on interlibrary loan though the 1,000-plus Family History Centers located worldwide. Microfiche copies of the International Genealogical Index can also be found at many of these repositories.

Over the years the Genealogical Society of Utah has filmed records in repositories which did not have original jurisdiction, as well as resources which pertain to other areas. Poll Books and Directories, for instance, were filmed at the Society of Genealogists, which has an extensive collection for the whole of England. Hearth Tax Assessments, Estate (Death) Duty Registers and Nonconformist Registers are some of the records filmed at the Public Record Office which apply to all counties. Likewise, Protestation Returns for all of England were filmed at the House of Lords Record Office. Some years ago the pre-1858 Wills held at Somerset House were microfilmed before those documents were returned to the respective diocesan depositories. It has been estimated that 95 per cent of all pre-1858 Wills are on microfilm. Filming at the National Library of Wales has included records pertaining to some English counties as well. Denominational records of Nonconformist churches may also have been filmed at a denominational historical society, for example, the Presbyterian Historical Society of Pennsylvania.

Every effort has been made to identify material which has been filmed by the Genealogical Society of Utah. It should be noted, however, that films of English records are continually being added to their collection. The actual filming takes about thirty days, and in addition there is approximately a six-month period from the time filming is completed until the microfilm copies will be available for use. It is possible to make a request to the Genealogical Society of Utah to have manuscript or printed sources in the Family History Library microfilmed for use in the Family History Centers, provided the material is considered to have widespread interest and has no restrictions.

Not all filming has been done by the Genealogical Society of Utah, however. The General Register Office in London has also filmed the Indexes to Births, Deaths, and Marriages for England and Wales. The latter filming covers the period from 1837 to 1980. A few record offices and libraries have obtained the films to 1912 for either their own region, or for all of England. In addition, a few record offices and libraries have filmed the Parish Registers deposited at their respective repositories in order to preserve the original records.

Prior to the era of microfilms, damaged records or those too old for constant use were often transcribed. Personal documents of individuals have also been copied, so that others may have access to the information. Some are still in handwritten form, while others have been printed. A number of Parish Registers are available in both forms. Handwritten transcriptions were many times made by a vicar or rector, while printed editions have appeared in the publications of the various societies in England. Bible Records, Pedigree Charts and many early documents have been published in various journals and serials. It should be remembered that in instances where a manuscript has been transcribed, there is a chance for error. Whenever possible, original documents or microfilm copies should be consulted once the transcribed version is deemed to have pertinent information.

CORRECTIONS

With the tremendous amount of data contained in this volume, it is inevitable that some errors will be present. Every effort has been made to minimize the number, as well as the omission of information listed on the survey sheets. It is hoped that such occurrences will have minimal impact on the reader's success in searching for ancestors.

If such information comes to the attention of the reader, please inform the author, through the publisher, so that it may be corrected in a future edition.

LIST OF ABBREVIATIONS

A.D.	Anno Domini	e.g.	*exempli gratia*, for example
am	ante meridiem		
Admin.	Administrative	etc.	*et cetera*, and so forth
Admon.	Administration (Letters of)	ext.	extension
Apr.	April	F	Friday
Archd.	Archdeaconry	God'r	Godmanchester
Attn.	Attention	H'don	Huntingdon
Av.	Avenue		
		i.e.	*id est*, that is
B.C.	before Christ	Inv.	Inventory
Beds	Bedfordshire	Ire.	Ireland
Berks	Berkshire		
Bish.	Bishop	Jan.	January
Bucks	Buckinghamshire	Lancs	Lancashire
		LB	London Borough
C	century	LDS	Latter-day Saints
c.	*circa*, approximately	Leics	Leicestershire
Cambs	Cambridgeshire	Lincs	Lincolnshire
Ches	Cheshire		
Cumbld	Cumberland	M	Monday
co.	county	M.M.	Monthly Meeting
Comm.	Commissary	Mar.	March
comp.	compiler	Middx	Middlesex
Const.	Consistory	mo.	month
cont.	continued		
ct.	court	N	North
		NE	Northeast
Dec.	December	Norf	Norfolk
Derbys	Derbyshire	Northants	Northamptonshire
Durh	Durham	Nthbld	Northumberland
		Notts	Nottinghamshire
E.	East	NW	Northwest
ed.	editor, edition	NYCRO	North Yorkshire County Record Office
edn.	edition		

xxxiii

Oct.	October	Stat.	Statute
O.S.	Ordinate Survey	stn.	station
Oxon	Oxfordshire	SW	Southwest
p.	pence	T	Tuesday
Pl.	Place	Tel.	Telephone
pm	post meridiem	Th	Thursday
pp.	pages	UDC	Urban District
PRO	Public Record Office		Council
pt.	part	UK	United Kingdom
QS	Quarter Sessions	US	United States
		USA	United States of
rev.	revised		America
Rutl	Rutland	W	Wednesday
S	Saturday	W.	West
SE	Southeast	Warws	Warwickshire
Sept.	September	Wstmld	Westmorland
Shrops	Shropshire	Wilts	Wiltshire
Soms	Somerset	Worcs	Worcestershire
Sq.	Square		
St.	Street	Yorks	Yorkshire

LIST OF SYMBOLS

⚓	British rail station	c/o	in care of
⊖	subway station	#	number
⇌	British rail terminal	1st	first
£	pound sterling	2nd	second
		3rd	third
		4th	fourth

PART I

GREATER LONDON

REPOSITORIES

RECORD OFFICES

BAPTIST CHURCH HOUSE
4 Southampton Row, London WC1 4AB
Tel. (01) 405 9803

Hours: M-F 9-5; closed S

Admission free

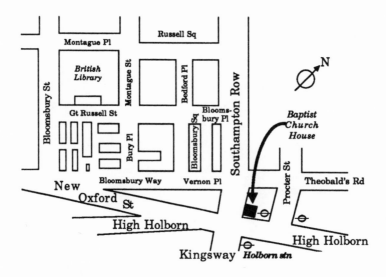

HOLDINGS

Repository for materials of the Baptist Union of Great Britain and Ireland. Includes church yearbooks beginning in 1832, obituaries and memorials of Baptist Ministers throughout England; Baptist Quarterlies.

(Most Baptist churches keep their own membership records or have deposited them in the appropriate county record offices. Minutes of a few local churches, some membership lists, and published church histories formerly held at Baptist Church House were transferred to Angus Library at Regent's Park College, Pusey Street, Oxford OX1 2LB.)

Church Year Books*   1832–
    (includes obituaries and memorials
    of Baptist ministers throughout England)

*Baptist Quarterlies** (full run)   1922/3–

(Addresses of Baptist County Associations available)

---

*Printed or transcribed

BRITISH LIBRARY, DEPARTMENT OF MANUSCRIPTS
Great Russell Street, London WC1B 3DG
Tel. (01) 636 1544 ext. 7508, 7520

Hours: M-S 10-4:45
(closed annually for stocktaking one week in
late October or early November)

Admission: By Reader's Ticket upon application with accompanying recommendation or letter of introduction from someone of recognized status.

List of record searchers available upon request[†]
(The staff does not undertake searches)

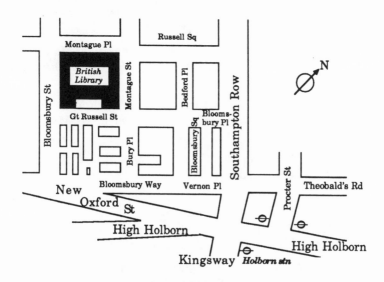

HOLDINGS

Vast collections of European manuscripts and charters dating from the third century B.C. to the present. Areas of most interest to (advanced) family tracers include British topography, heraldry, transcripts of public records (originals in the

---

[†]For additional information send 2 Postal Reply Coupons or 31 pence of English postage for reply to North America; 34 pence to Australia and New Zealand.

Public Record Office) and materials pertaining to the American colonial and federal periods.

The Library contains the largest heraldic collection of manuscripts outside the College of Arms. It includes Register Books of Heralds' Visitations 1530–1686 for all counties, pedigrees of nobility and gentry (including abstracts of deeds, charters and family settlements, coats of arms and inquisitions post mortem), monumental inscriptions, and lists of coats of arms.

PUBLICATIONS

C.M. Andrews and F.G. Davenport, *Guide to the Manuscript Materials for the History of the United States to 1783 in the British Museum* (1908)

G. Gatfield, *Guide to Printed Books and Manuscripts Relating to English and Foreign Heraldry and Genealogy* (1982)

M.A.E. Nickson, *The British Library: Guide to the Catalogues and Indexes of the Department of Manuscripts* (1978)

A. Payne, *Views of the Past: Topographical Drawings in the British Library* (1987)

R. Sims, *A Manual for the Genealogist, Topographer, Antiquary and Legal Professor* (1856). (contains a list of Heralds' visitations for all counties and the repositories where they were deposited in that year)

Sir A.R. Wagner, *A Catalogue of English Mediaeval Rolls of Arms*, Harleian Society, Visitations 100 (1950)

C.E. Wright, *English Heraldic Manuscripts in the British Museum* (1973)

Catalogue of Heralds' Visitations... in the British Museum, 2nd ed. (1825)#

#Microfilm copy available at the LDS Family History Library in Salt Lake City, Utah, and through the LDS Family History Centers.

BRITISH LIBRARY
INDIA OFFICE LIBRARY AND RECORDS
197 Blackfriars Road, London SE1 8NG
Tel. (01) 928 9531

Hours: M-F 9:30-6:00, S 9:30-1:00

Admission free, without prior appointment

Searches by Staff for a fee — Ecclesiastical Returns only
List of research agents available upon request[†]

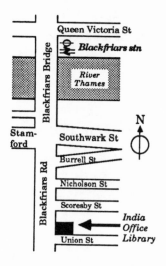

HOLDINGS

The archives of the East India Company and the India Office, comprising material on the British presence in pre-1947 India (including Burma) and related areas outside South Asia such as St. Helena, Persian Gulf, Indonesia and China.

[†]For additional information send 2 Postal Reply Coupons or 31 pence of English postage for reply to North America; 34 pence to Australia and New Zealand.

BIOGRAPHICAL SOURCES

Ecclesiastical Returns# births/baptisms, marriages and deaths/burials of European and Eurasian Christians, all denom- inations, official and non-official	1698–1947
Appointment papers, service records and family information for civil, military and naval servants of the East India Company and the India Office	17C–1947
Wills, administrations and estates Wills, etc.	1618–1950, 1710–1936#
Private papers Newspapers*	 late 18C–

PUBLICATION†

Ian A. Baxter, *A Brief Guide to Biographical Sources* (1979)

#Microfilm copy available at the LDS Family History Library in Salt Lake City, Utah, and through the LDS Family History Centers.
*Printed or transcribed
†For additional information send 2 Postal Reply Coupons or 31 pence of English postage for reply to North America; 34 pence to Australia and New Zealand.

BRITISH LIBRARY
NEWSPAPER LIBRARY
Colindale Avenue, London NW9 5HE
Tel. (01) 323 7353

Hours: M-S 10-4:45 (last order 4:15);
(Closed annually for stocktaking one week either in
late October or early November)

Admission: By Reader's Ticket only, obtained at either the
British Library Newspaper Library or the British Library
Reader Admissions Office, Great Russell Street.

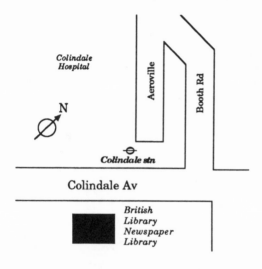

HOLDINGS

National collection of English, Welsh, Scottish and Irish
newspapers, numbering approximately 575,000 volumes and
parcels plus 230,000 rolls of microfilm. Includes primarily
daily and weekly newspapers and periodicals for London from
1801; English provincial, Welsh, Scottish and Irish newspapers
(from about 1700), and a large collection of Commonwealth and
foreign newspapers. The United Kingdom collection since 1840
includes nearly all published newspapers within the U.K.

excepting those volumes destroyed in World War II. The years affected include 1896–98 and 1910–12. Many of these gaps, however, have been filled with microfilm copies of the newspapers.

PUBLICATION†

Newspapers in the British Library (1987)

---

†For additional information send 2 Postal Reply Coupons or 31 pence of English postage for reply to North America; 34 pence to Australia and New Zealand.

COLLEGE OF ARMS
Queen Victoria Street, London EC4V 4BT
Tel. (01) 248 2762

ADMISSION

The College is open Monday through Friday from 10am to 4pm, when the Officer of Arms on duty will attend to inquiries made in person, by letter, or on the telephone gratis.

SEARCHES

If in order to answer a question, research in the records of College is necessary, search and report fees are charged. The amount in each case being quoted before research is undertaken.

ACCESS

The Record Room and Library of the College are *not* open to members of the public, but by arrangement, particular records and documents can be viewed in the presence of a member of the

College of Arms. From time to time a visiting party, no greater than twenty in number, can be conducted under the aegis of an Officer of Arms.

HOLDINGS

Armorial Bearings officially registered and genealogies of numerous families, most of English extraction which have been approved for entry, as well as a large collection of pedigrees, genealogical evidences and the like, compiled by Officers of Arms during the last five hundred years and by Heralds since the College's foundation in 1484.

RELEVANT PUBLICATIONS

Hubert Chesshyre and Adrian Ailes, *Heralds of Today* (1986)

Walter H. Godfrey *et al.*, *The College of Arms, Queen Victoria Street, Being the Seventh and Final Monograph of the London Surety Committee* (1963)#

Sir Anthony R. Wagner, *The Records and Collections of the College of Arms* (1952)

#Microfilm copy available at the LDS Family History Library in Salt Lake City, Utah, and through the LDS Family History Centers.

CORPORATION OF LONDON RECORD OFFICE
Guildhall, London EC2P 2EJ
    (Located in the North Office Block, Rm. 221
    second floor, immediately behind the Guildhall;
    Entrance is from Basinghall Street)
Tel. (01) 606 3030 ext. 1251; (01) 260 1251 (direct dial)

Hours: M-F 9:30-4:45; closed S

Admission free

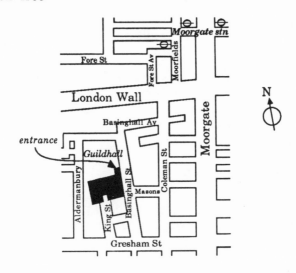

HOLDINGS

    Civic records, including Quarter Sessions and other resources pertaining to the Corporation of the (ancient) City of London.

SOURCES THAT IDENTIFY AN INDIVIDUAL WITH A SPECIFIC LOCATION

Assessments (lists of inhabitants   1663/4–1698;
    compiled for tax purposes)   some 18C–19C

Bridge House	12C–20C
Deeds	12C–20C
Rentals	14C–20C
City Lands	16C–20C
Rents and Rentals	17C–20C
Leases (mainly)	1666–20C
French Protestant Refugee Account Books	1681–1717/18
Licence Books	1750–1845
Lord Mayor's Waiting Books	1624–25/26,
	1660–1706
(inclusive details of emigrants)	1682–1692
Lists of Freemen	1681–1915
Prisons	17C–19C
Registers of Electors*	1872–
Sessions of Peace	1605–1971
Hair Powder Tax	1795–1798
Lists of Papists	1736–1745
Sessions of Gaol Delivery	1568,
(gaps)	1603–1834
Transportation Bonds	1667–1775

SOURCES THAT MAY ADDITIONALLY PROVIDE VITAL DATA AND/OR PROVE FAMILY RELATIONSHIPS

Apprenticeship Indentures††	17C
Court of Husting‡‡ (Index#)	1252–1717
Deeds (enrolled)	
Wills	
Emigration and Transportation of Convicts to America	17C–18C
Common Serjeant's Books# (Orphans' Records)	16C–18C

---

*Printed or transcribed

††See also Freemen's Lists above.

‡‡Records mainly in Latin or French except for the Commonwealth period; relatively few entries after 1534.

#Microfilm copy available at the LDS Family History Library in Salt Lake City, Utah, and through the LDS Family History Centers.

School Records	19C–20C
Title Deeds	17C–20C

PUBLICATIONS†

D.J. Johnson, *Southwark and the City* (1969)
xiv + 441 pp. + map

P.E. Jones, *Calendars of Plea and Memoranda Rolls,*
1437–1458 (1954)
1458–1482 (1961)
(all other volumes out of print)

P.E. Jones, *The Fire Court-Calendar to the Decrees of the Court of Judicature on disputes as to rebuilding after the Great Fire,*
1667–1668, I (1966)
1667–1668, II (1970)

R.R. Sharpe, *Calendar of Coroners' Rolls of the City of London, A.D. 1300–1378* (London, Richard Clay and Sons, 1913)

R.R. Sharpe, *Calendar of Wills Proved and Enrolled in the Court of Husting, London, A.D. 1258–1688*
Part I, A.D. 1258–1358 (London, J.C. Francis, 1889)
Part II, A.D. 1358–1688 (London, J.C. Francis, 1890)

---

†For additional information send 2 Postal Reply Coupons or 31 pence of English postage for reply to North America; 34 pence to Australia and New Zealand.

GENERAL REGISTER OFFICE
ST. CATHERINE'S HOUSE
10 Kingsway, London WC2B 6JP
Tel. (01) 242 0262

Hours: M-F 8:30-4:30; closed S

Admission free

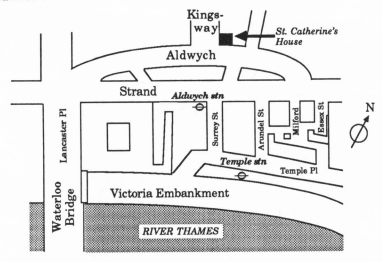

HOLDINGS

Civil Registration of Births, Deaths, and Marriages for all of England and Wales since 1837.

Quarterly Indexes to the births, deaths, and marriages for each year, arranged alphabetically by name. (There is no separate index by geographical location.) The public *cannot* view the actual Birth, Death and Marriage Records, *only* the printed Indexes. The Indexes are on microfilm at other repositories.[#§]

[#]Microfilm copies (1837-1906) available at the LDS Family History Library in Salt Lake City, Utah, and through the LDS Family History Centers.

[§]Microfilm copies (1837-1980), filmed by the General Register Office, are available at some county record offices and other repositories for either all of England or for their respective geographical areas, for either part or all of the time period.

Consular Returns of Births, Marriages, and Deaths	1849–
Marine Register (births and deaths at sea)	1837–
	(1854–1890#)
Regimental Returns (births, deaths and marriages while serving in the Army)	1761–1924
Adoption Registers	1927–

By prior appointment:

South African War Deaths	1899–1902
World War I Deaths	1914–1921
World War II Deaths	1939–1948

(Death returns of English men and women serving abroad, and members of their families living abroad)

Charges: Fee for copy of record when applied for in person
(currently £5 for long form)
Fee for copy of record when applied for by post
(currently £10 for long form; part of fee returned if record not found)

PUBLICATION†

General Register Office: Abstract of Arrangements respecting Registration of Births, Marriages and Deaths in the United Kingdom and the other countries of the British Commonwealth of Nations, and in the Irish Republic (1952) (OOP)

#Microfilm copy available at the LDS Family History Library in Salt Lake City, Utah, and through the LDS Family History Centers.

†For additional information send 2 Postal Reply Coupons or 31 pence of English postage for reply to North America; 34 pence to Australia and New Zealand.

GREATER LONDON RECORD OFFICE
40 Northampton Road
London EC1R 0HB
Tel. (01) 633 6851

Hours: M, W, Th, F 10-4:45; T 10-7:30; closed S
Records for use on T evening must be
ordered in advance
(Closed 3rd and 4th weeks of October for stocktaking)

Admission free

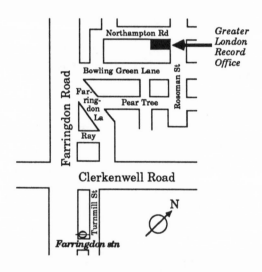

HOLDINGS

Church of England diocesan records for the Archdeaconry
of Middlesex, Diocese of London: some Bishop's Transcripts,
Wills, Tithe Apportionments: Archdeaconry of Surrey, Diocese
of Winchester; Bishop's Transcripts, Marriage Licence Bonds
and Allegations; Wills for the Consistory Court of London;
parish records including deposited Parish Registers for more
than 380 churches in the former county of Middlesex (excepting
the City of London, City of Westminster and borough of Hammersmith), the areas of Deptford, Greenwich, and Woolwich

formerly in Kent, and Battersea, Bermondsey, Camberwell, Lambeth, Southwark, and Wandsworth previously in Surrey; local government records including Quarter Sessions for the former county of Middlesex and for the City of Westminster; other resources pertaining to the Greater London area.

SOURCES THAT IDENTIFY AN INDIVIDUAL WITH A SPECIFIC LOCATION

Church of England (diocesan)		
Tithe Apportionments§		19C
Church of England (parish)		
Churchwardens' Accounts		17C–19C
Directories* (some#)		1780's–
Enclosure Awards (Middlesex)		1781–1862
Maps		
Parish Poor Law Records		17C–1834
Parish Poor Rates (some#)		
Poll Books* (some#)		
(Middlesex)	(few)	18C
(City of Westminster)	(periodic)	1749–1820
Quarter Sessions (Middlesex)		
Judicial Records		1689–1889
Hearth Tax Assessments		1664,
		1669–1674
Land Tax Assessments		1767,
		1780–1832
Lists of Freeholders		1696–1889
Plantation Indentures		1683–1684
Recusants		1675–1764

Registers of Electors*
  Ancient County of Middlesex   1847–1889
  London   1890–1965
  Admin. County of Middlesex   1889–1965
  Greater London Area   1905–
Registers of Jesuits   1829
Quarter Sessions (City of Westminster)
  Judicial Records (some#)   1620–1844
  Hearth Tax Assessments   1664, 1672–1674
  Land Tax Assessments   1767, 1781, 1797–1832
  Freeholders' Books   1728, 1792
  Recusants   1657–1722
Quartering Soldiers   (periodic) 1697–1837
Rates (periodic)
  Commissioners of Sewers   19C (to 1847)
  Metropolitan Commission of Sewers   1848–1855
  Metropolitan Board of Works   1855–1889
Return of Aliens   1798

SOURCES THAT MAY ADDITIONALLY PROVIDE VITAL DATA AND/OR PROVE FAMILY RELATIONSHIPS

Church of England (diocesan)
  Bishops' Transcripts   1660–19C
    (part Middx; Surrey)
  Marriage Licence Bonds   1604–20C
    and Allegations (Surrey)
  Wills, Admon, Inven.
    Archd. Middx#   (gaps) 1608–1858
    Archd. Surrey#   1480–1858
    Const. Ct. London#   1467–1858
    Comm. Ct. Bshp. Winchester#   1662–1857

*Printed or transcribed
#Microfilm copy available at the LDS Family History Library in Salt Lake City, Utah, and through the LDS Family History Centers.

Church of England (Parish)
    Parish Registers (some#)   1538–
        Middlesex: all except City of
        Westminster and Hammersmith;
        Kent: only Deptford, Greenwich,
        Woolwich, Lewisham; Surrey: only
        Battersea, Bermondsey, Camberwell,
        Lambeth, Southwark, Wandsworth
Estate and Family Papers (some#)   15C–
Manorial Records (some#)   13C–1937
Middlesex (County) Deeds Registry††   1709–1938
    Indexes   1709–1919#,
                                 1920–1938
Monumental Inscriptions
Nonconformist Registers   1850–c. 1960
    Congregational   1850–c. 1960
    Methodist
Newspapers*
Parish Poor Law Records   17C–1834
    Apprenticeship Indentures
    Examinations
    Removal Orders
    Settlement Papers (some#)
Poor Law Union   1834–1929
    Workhouse Records
School Records (some#)   18C–
Title Deeds   12C–

#Microfilm copy available at the LDS Family History Library in Salt Lake City, Utah, and through the LDS Family History Centers.
††Postal inquiries not accepted.
*Printed or transcribed

PUBLICATIONS[†]

K. Goodacre and E. Doris Mercer, *Guide to the Middlesex Sessions Records 1549–1889* (1965)

Ida Darlington, *Guide to the Records in the London County Record Office, Part I* (1962)

Leaflets:
Summary Description of Holdings
Parish Register Summary Guides
The Middlesex Deeds Registry 1709–1938

[†]For additional information send 2 Postal Reply Coupons or 31 pence of English postage for reply to North America; 34 pence to Australia and New Zealand.

GUILDHALL LIBRARY
Aldermanbury, London EC2P 2EJ
Tel. (01) 606 3030

Hours: M-S 9:30-4:45

Admission free

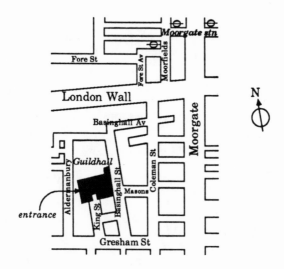

HOLDINGS

Church of England parish records including parish registers deposited for 106 churches within the (ancient) City of London; some Church of England diocesan records for the Diocese of London; some civil records and other resources pertaining to the City of London.

(Some Church of England diocesan records – Diocese of London – for the former county of Middlesex are located at the Greater London Record Office.)

SOURCES THAT IDENTIFY AN INDIVIDUAL
WITH A SPECIFIC LOCATION

Church of England (diocesan)[††]		
Tithe Assessments		17C–20C
Church of England (parish)		
Churchwardens' Accounts		15C–20C
Directories*#		
(City of London, suburbs,	(gaps)	17C–
districts,some provincial towns)		
Genealogies*		
Lists of Inhabitants		17C–20C
Local Histories*		
London Livery Companies (some#)		
Freemen Lists		16C–20C
London Rate Assessments		16C–20C
Periodicals*		
Poll Books*#	(periodic)	17C–19C
Poor Law Records#		
Parish Poor Rates		17C–20C
Protestation Returns*#		1641
Registers of Electors* (City of London)		1832–
Sessions Records, Old Bailey*		1684–1913

SOURCES THAT MAY ADDITIONALLY PROVIDE VITAL
DATA AND/OR PROVE FAMILY RELATIONSHIPS

Burial Ground Registers#	18C–20C
Census‡# (City of London)	1841–1881

---

††Some diocesan records for the City of London are also located at the Greater London Record Office.

*Printed or transcribed

#Microfilm copy available at the LDS Family History Library in Salt Lake City, Utah, and through the LDS Family History Centers.

‡Microfilm/microfiche copies available at above repository

Church of England (diocesan)
    Bishops' Transcripts (City of London)   17C–19C
    Marriage Licence Allegations   16C–20C
    Wills, Diocese of London‡‡#   14C–1858
Church of England (parish)
    Parish Registers (also#)   1538–
    Parish Register Transcripts*   16C–19C
Poor Law Records   17C–19C
    Apprenticeship Indentures
    Examinations
    Removal Orders
    Settlement Certificates
International Genealogical Index‡##
    (British Isles)
London Livery Companies
    Apprenticeship Records   16C–20C
Marriage Assessment
    City of London*   1695
    Bristol*   1696
Monumental Inscriptions*
Newspapers*   18C–20C
Nonconformist Registers   16C–20C
Obituaries*
School Records   16C–20C

---

‡‡Some wills for the City of London are at other repositories in London; see J.S.W. Gibson, *A Simplified Guide to Probate Jurisdictions* (3rd edn., 1986).

#Microfilm copy available at the LDS Family History Library in Salt Lake City, Utah, and through the LDS Family History Centers.

*Printed or transcribed

‡Microfilm/microfiche copies available at above repository

##Microfiche copy available at the LDS Family History Library in Salt Lake City, Utah, and through the LDS Family History Centers.

PUBLICATIONS†

Guide to Genealogical Sources in Guildhall Library
(2nd ed.) (OOP)

Guide to the archives of City Livery Companies and related organisations in Guildhall Library (2nd ed., 1983)

Handlist of Non-conformist, Roman Catholic, Jewish and Burial Ground Registers at Guildhall Library (1986)

Handlist of Parish Registers at Guildhall Library, Part I (5th ed., 1984)

Handlist of Parish Registers at Guildhall Library, Part II (5th ed., 1986)

The British Overseas: A Guide to Records of their Births, Baptisms, Marriages, Deaths and Burials (1984) (OOP)

---

†For additional information send 2 Postal Reply Coupons or 31 pence of English postage for reply to North America; 34 pence to Australia and New Zealand.

HOUSE OF LORDS RECORD OFFICE
London SW1A 0PW
Tel. (01) 219 3074

Hours: M-F 9:30-5

Admission free

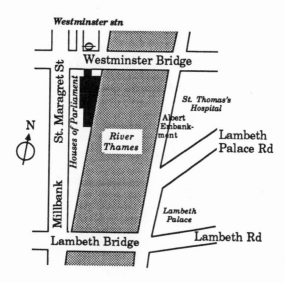

Westminster stn

Westminster Bridge

St. Thomas's Hospital

Albert Embank-ment

Lambeth Palace Rd

River Thames

Lambeth Palace

Houses of Parliament

St. Maragret St

Millbank

Lambeth Bridge   Lambeth Rd

N

HOLDINGS

Records of the House of Lords	1497–
Records of the House of Commons	1547–
including:	
Protestation Returns[#]	1642
Papist Returns	1680, 1706, 1767
Naturalisation Bills and Acts	1600–
Change of Name Bills and Acts	c. 1760–1907
Divorce Bills and Acts	1669–1922
Estate Bills and Acts	1512–

[#]Microfilm copy of the indexes available at the LDS Family History Library in Salt Lake City, Utah, and through the LDS Family History Centers.

Charges: 15p per A4 sheet of xerox (minimum charge £1)
            12p per frame of microfilm (minimum charge of £2
            for stock film and £5 where no master microfilm
            exists)
            Photographs and photocopies may be certified as a
            true copy of the original record at a fee of £2 per
            certificate.

RELATED PUBLICATION†

M.F. Bond, *Guide to the Records of Parliament* (1971)

---

†For additional information send 2 Postal Reply Coupons or 31 pence of English
postage for reply to North America; 34 pence to Australia and New Zealand.

HUGUENOT SOCIETY OF
GREAT BRITAIN AND IRELAND
University College, Gower Street
London WC1E 6BT
Tel. (01) 380 7094
Contact: Librarian

The Library is open only to Fellows[††] by prior appointment only. A Reader's Card must be obtained before the first visit.

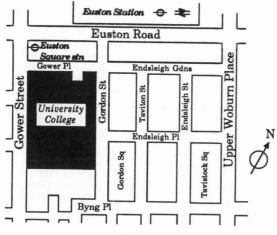

HOLDINGS

The Society's Library was merged in 1900 with that of the Corporation of the French Hospital, La Providence. This joint library forms the most complete and valuable body of Huguenot literature in England. It contains the archives of the Hospital and many other manuscripts, rare books, and a unique collection of pamphlets, mainly of the eighteenth century; the Wagner Collection and other collections of genealogy and pedigrees; and sets of periodicals of Huguenot Societies throughout the world.

[††]An application form to become a Fellow may be obtained from the Administrative Secretary at the above address. Entrance fee £5; Annual subscriptions: Fellows £12.50, Junior Fellows (to 18 years) £2.50, Libraries £10; First year subscription fees: Fellows £12.50, Junior Fellows £7.50, Libraries £15.

PUBLICATIONS[†]

The publications of the Society consist of the *Proceedings* and *Quarto Series*. Articles published in the annual *Proceedings* deal with various aspects of Huguenot history, such as the story of the French Protestant settlements in England and Ireland and events on the Continent which led to them; Huguenot settlements in other parts of the world, and records and pedigrees of Huguenot families. Other subjects treated have been the contributions made by Huguenots to art, craft, literature, science, commerce, and to the economic, social and military history of the country. The annual report, reviews and miscellaneous notes are also included. Thus many matters of general and particular interest are brought together and preserved in these illustrated and indexed volumes.

In the *Quarto Series*, 57 fully indexed volumes have been issued. The greater part of the series comprises carefully edited Huguenot church registers, often combined with the histories of the English and Irish communities, as well as the registers of some foreign churches; the records of the French Hospital, La Providence; extracts of Patents of Denization and Acts of Naturalisation as well as the naturalisation of French Protestants in the American colonies under Stat: 13 Geo. II; returns of aliens in London; calendars of numerous collections of manuscripts including those in the Huguenot Library and the French Protestant Church of London. The complete list of publications is included on the cover of all publications and can be separately supplied upon request.

It should be noted that the Society's publications are privately printed and are not available from bookshops. Copies in stock can be obtained by written order to the Hon. Secretary.

RELATED PUBLICATION[†]

Huguenot and Walloon Gazette

[†]For additional information send 2 Postal Reply Coupons or 31 pence of English postage for reply to North America; 34 pence to Australia and New Zealand.

LAMBETH PALACE LIBRARY
London SE1 7JU
Tel. (01) 928 6222

Hours: M-F 10-5; closed S;
Closed for 10 days at Christmas and at Easter

Admission: By letter of introduction
from someone of recognized status
The library does not undertake genealogical
searches on behalf of enquirers

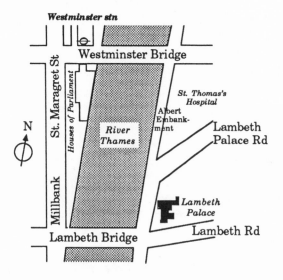

HOLDINGS

Church of England: records of the Vicar General of the Archbishop of Canterbury, the Faculty Office and the Court of Arches; papers of the Bishops of London relating to the American Colonies.

MARRIAGE RECORDS

Marriage Licences issued by the Archbishop of Canterbury, including licences for the province of Canterbury, and special licences throughout England.

Allegations – Faculty Office series from 1632; Vicar General series from 1660; Peculiars of Arches, Croydon and Shoreham, 1684–1859.

Bonds 1666–1823

Manuscript Indexes to the Marriage Licence applications are arranged in *chronological order.*#

For printed catalogues of the early series, see:

G.E. Cokayne and E.A. Fry, eds., *Calendar of Marriage Licences issued by the Faculty Office 1632–1714*, British Record Society, *Index Library* 33 (1905)

G.J. Armytage, ed., *Allegations for Marriage Licences issued by the Vicar-General of the Archbishop of Canterbury, 1660 to 1668,* Harleian Society 33 (1892)

G.J. Armytage, ed., *Allegations for Marriage Licences issued by the Vicar-General of the Archbishop of Canterbury, 1669 to 1679*, Harleian Society 34 (1892)

G.J. Armytage, ed., *Allegations for Marriage Licences issued by the Vicar-General of the Archbishop of Canterbury, July 1679 to June 1687*, Harleian Society, 30 (1890)

G.J. Armytage, ed., *Allegations for Marriage Licences issued by the Vicar-General of the Archbishop of Canterbury, July 1687 to June 1694*, Harleian Society, 31 (1890)

#Microfilm copy available at the LDS Family History Library in Salt Lake City, Utah, and through the LDS Family History Centers.

FULHAM PAPERS

Fulham Papers are papers of the Bishops of London concerning the clergy in the colonies (America and West Indies). These include ordinations and licences to officiate, late 17th–early 19th centuries.#

See: W.W. Manross, *The Fulham Papers in the Lambeth Palace Library, American Colonial Section. Calendar and Indexes* (1965)

VICAR GENERAL ACT BOOKS

Act Books of the Vicar General of the Archbishops of Canterbury, including records of ordinations and appointments of clergy, particularly in the Diocese of Canterbury.

See: E.H.W. Dunkin, ed. by C. Jenkins and E.A. Fry, *Index to the Act Books of the Archbishops of Canterbury, 1663–1859*, 1929, 1938. British Record Society, *Index Library* 55 (1929); 63 (1938)

TESTAMENTARY RECORDS

Wills, inventories and probate act books for the Archbishop's Peculiars of Arches, Croydon and Shoreham, 1614–1841.

See: Janet Foster, *Index to Testamentary Record of the Deanery of the Arches in Lambeth Palace Library, 1620–1845*, in British Record Society, *Index Library* 98 (1985), pp. 235–84

#Microfilm copy available at the LDS Family History Library in Salt Lake City, Utah, and through the LDS Family History Centers.

PARISH REGISTER TRANSCRIPTS

Parish Register Transcripts for the Peculiars of Arches, Croydon and Shoreham (i.e. Bishops' Transcripts). A very incomplete series.††

COURT OF ARCHES

Records of the Court of Arches, the court of appeal for the Province of Canterbury, including matrimonial and testamentary disputes.‡‡

See: J. Houston, ed., *Index of Cases in the Records of the Court of Arches at Lambeth Palace Library, 1660–1913*, British Record Society *Index Library* 85 (1972)

ARCHIEPISCOPAL REGISTERS

Archbishops' Registers, 1279–1645, include a small collection of wills mainly proved during the vacancy of a diocese within the Province of Canterbury, or during a visitation by the Archbishop.

See: J.C. Smith, *Index of Wills recorded in the Archiepiscopal Registers at Lambeth Palace* (1919) (Reprinted from *Genealogists N.S.* Vols. 34–35).

Calendar of Lambeth Administrations in *The Genealogist*, 7 (1883), 8 (1884).

---

††This class of original records pertains to Bishops' Transcripts sent from parish clergy in the peculiars of Arches, Croyden and Shoreham. They are not modern transcriptions of Parish Registers.

‡‡The Court of Arches process books are available on microfiche at the Center for Research Libraries, Chicago. Fiches of individual process books can be purchased from Chadwyck-Healey Limited, Cambridge Place, Cambridge CB2 1NR, England. Some of the other series of records, such as the act books, appeals, depositions, personal answers, muniment books and sentences, are also available on microfilm.#

#Microfilm copy available at the LDS Family History Library in Salt Lake City, Utah, and through the LDS Family History Centers.

LDS HYDE PARK FAMILY HISTORY CENTRE
64-68 Exhibition Road, London SW7 2PA
Tel. (01) 589 8561

Hours: M-F 9-9; S 9-3

Admission free
Does not undertake research for patrons

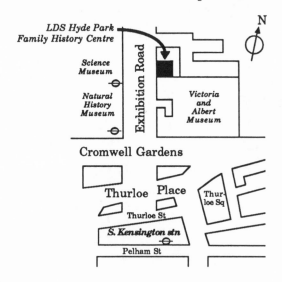

HOLDINGS

LDS Family History Library Catalog[‡##]
International Genealogical Index[‡##]

[‡]Microfilm/microfiche copies available at above repository
[##]Microfiche copy available at the LDS Family History Library in Salt Lake City, Utah, and through the LDS Family History Centers.

NATIONAL ARMY MUSEUM
Department of Records
Royal Hospital Road
London SW3 4HT
Tel. (01) 730 0717 ext. 222

Hours: T-S 10-4:30; closed M

Admission: By Reader's Ticket or means of identification
that gives name and address.

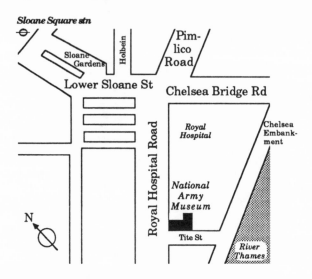

HOLDINGS

Printed resources relating to the history of the British Army
since 1485 and British colonial land forces to independence
dates. The Hodson Index contains biographical and career
information on Commissioned Officers of the Honourable East
India Company Army to 1861 and of the India Army 1861–1947.

The museum does not hold any official records, and can
provide only limited career information on Commissioned
Officers of the British Army from 1660. (Official Army records
will be found at the Public Record Office, Kew.)

NATIONAL MARITIME MUSEUM
Greenwich SE10 9NF
Tel. (01) 858 4422
Contact: Head, Enquiry Services Section

Hours: M-F 10-5; S 10-1, 2-5;
       (Closed 3rd week in February for stocktaking)

Admission by Readers' Ticket, obtained free of charge by application to Enquiry Services Section.

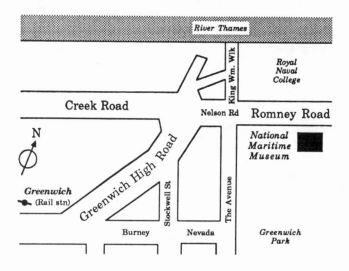

HOLDINGS

Vast collections of manuscripts, printed sources, pictures and plans pertaining to Merchant Shipping history and to Naval History.

Resources pertaining to Merchant Shipping history include general shipping histories, histories of major shipping companies, information on individual ships, officers and men.

Sources which pertain to Naval history include those on naval policy and operations, naval administration, information on individual ships, and some material about officers and men.

(The Public Record Office, Kew, holds a majority of official documents with genealogical information concerning officers and men of the Royal Navy and of Merchant Shipping. Lloyd's Captains' Registers are located at the Guildhall Library and the Society of Genealogists.)

MERCHANT SHIPPING RESOURCES

Crew Lists and Agreements[§]	1861–62,
(each decade)	1865–1935
Histories of Shipping[*]	
Lloyd's Lists	1741–1883
Masters[‡][#]	1836–1926
Lloyd's Registers (Masters)	1764–
Lloyd's Ship's Surveys	1830–1964
Index to Ships	1839–1914
Masters', Mates' Applications for Certificates[§]	1845–1890
Periodicals[*]	mid-19C–20C
Shipping Company Records	mid-19C–20C
Ship's Plans	early 19C–

NAVAL HISTORY RESOURCES

Lieutenants' Logs – Ships	1673–1809
Biographies[*]	
Navy List[*]	
Official Histories[*]	16C–20C
Periodicals[*]	
Personal Papers of Officers, men (re: Naval Policy and Operation)	
Ship's Plans	c. 1713–post-1945

[§]May provide vital data and/or proof of family relationships.
[*]Printed or transcribed
[‡]Microfilm/microfiche copies available at above repository
[#]Microfilm copy available at the LDS Family History Library in Salt Lake City, Utah, and through the LDS Family History Centers.

PUBLICATIONS[†]

R.J.B. Knight, ed., *Guide to Manuscripts in the National Maritime Museum,* I (1979), II (1980)

[†]For additional information send 2 Postal Reply Coupons or 31 pence of English postage for reply to North America; 34 pence to Australia and New Zealand.

PRINCIPAL REGISTRY OF THE FAMILY DIVISION
SOMERSET HOUSE
Strand, London WC2R 1LP

Tel. (01) 936 7000 – Probate Enquiries
      (01) 936 6995 – Decree Absolute (Divorce) Enquiries

Hours: M-F 10-4:30

Admission free

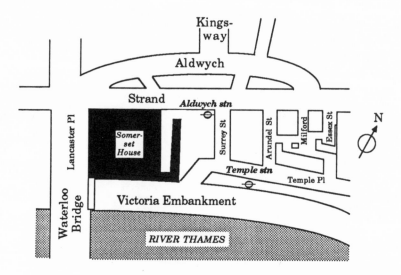

HOLDINGS

All Wills proven in England and Wales since 1858 and Indexes.# All Divorce Records and Indexes in England and Wales since 1858. The public can view only the Probate Indexes; Divorce Indexes are closed.

#Microfilm copy available at the LDS Family History Library in Salt Lake City, Utah, and through the LDS Family History Centers.

SEARCHES AND CHARGES

Postal application for a search in respect of a will and/or grant of representation, £2 per application (payable in advance).

Personal callers may search the Probate Index free of charge; there is a charge of 25 pence per page for any document obtained or charge of 25 pence for reading a document.

Postal or personal application for a copy Decree Absolute (Divorce) where a search has to be carried out £2 (payable in advance); where no search is required, there is only a copy charge of 25 pence per page.

A sealed and certified copy of a will and/or grant £3.

Cheques and/or postal orders to HM Paymaster General.

PUBLIC RECORD OFFICE, CHANCERY LANE
London WC2A 1LR
Tel. (01) 405 0741

Hours: M-F 9:30-5; closed S;
      Closed first 2 weeks in October for stocktaking

Admission: By Reader's Ticket, obtained through application at Chancery Lane or Kew; not necessary to obtain in advance; applicant should have positive means of identification.

Staff will search Census Returns for a fee and make limited searches for Trust Deeds and Probate Records.

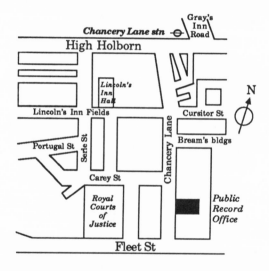

HOLDINGS

Legal records, state papers and other classes of records described the *Current Guide*, Part II: Class Descriptions.††

---

††The *Current Guide*, Part II: Class Descriptions is a microfiche guide to all records held at the PRO Chancery Lane, PRO Kew, and the PRO Portugal Street. It is arranged alphabetically by class and number. Part III of the guide is a subject index to the records on microfiche. Copies are available at the PRO Chancery Lane.

Included are records dating from the Norman conquest to approximately 1950.

SOURCES THAT IDENTIFY AN INDIVIDUAL
WITH A SPECIFIC LOCATION AFTER 1500

Class numbers, which must be used when ordering records, are listed to the left of each record group.

ASSI 1-73	Assize Court Records	16C–
E 115	Certificates of Residence	1547–1660
	Criminals	
PRIS 1	Fleet Prison Commitments	1685–1842
PRIS 10	King's (Queen's) Bench Prison and Fleet Prison	1628–1862
	Crown Employees	
LC 3	Registers of the Royal Household	1641–1902
LS 13	Establishment Books	1627–1812
LS 13	Warrants of Appointment§§	1627–1820
E 179	Hearth Tax Assessments‡#	1662–1689
HCA 25-26	High Court of Admiralty	1549–1814
E 179	Lay Subsidies	14C–1662
SC 6	Ministers' and Receivers' Accounts	13C–18C
E 36, E 101 SP 1-2, SP 10, SP 14, SP 16-17	Militia Muster Rolls	1522–1640
E 315, J 18, C 54	Name Change	16C–1957

---

§§Index to names located at the Royal Archives, Windsor Castle, Windsor, Berkshire SL4 1NJ

‡Microfilm/microfiche copies available at above repository

#Microfilm copy available at the LDS Family History Library in Salt Lake City, Utah, and through the LDS Family History Centers.

E 169, E 196,	Oath Rolls‡‡	1673–19C
KB 18, KB 24,	(Oaths of Allegiance,	
C 184, C 213-215	Test Oaths, Sacrament,	
	Naturalisation)‡‡	
SC 12	Rentals and Surveys	1216–1829

SOURCES THAT MAY ADDITIONALLY PROVIDE VITAL
DATA AND/OR PROVE FAMILY RELATIONSHIPS

B 3, B 9	Bankruptcy Files	18C–19C
HO 107	Census‡# (England,	1841, 1851
	Wales, Isle of Man	
	and Channel Islands	
C 1-3, C 5-16	Chancery Proceedings	14C–19C
	Calendars *# to 17C	
C 21-24	Depositions	1553–1852
E 331	Clergy	
	Institution Books	1544–1912
E 157	Emigration Records	17C
	(Licence to Pass	
	Beyond the Seas)*	
IR 26	Estate (Death) Duty Registers	1796–1903
IR 27	Index to IR 26	(1812–1857#)
C 132-142	Inquisitions Post Mortem*	13C–17C

---

‡‡Does not include Attorney's Oaths.
‡Microfilm/microfiche copies available at above repository
#Microfilm copy available at the LDS Family History Library in Salt Lake City, Utah, and through the LDS Family History Centers.
*Printed or transcribed

	Lawyers	
E 3-4, CHES 36, DURH 3, DURH 9, PL 23	Attorneys	17C–1875
CP 5, CP 8, CP 10-11, E 3-4, KB 104-107, J 8-9	Barristers	17C–1903
E 108, E 200	Solicitors	1772–1843
	Nonconformist Registers#	
RG 4	Baptist, Congregational, Huguenot, Methodist, Presbyterian, Roman Catholic (few), Unitarian, Dr. Williams's Library	17C–1837
RG 5	Dr. Williams's Library (cont.)	1742–1837
RG 6	Society of Friends	17C–1837
RG 7	Fleet Marriages, King's Bench Prison Marriages, Mint, and Mayfair Chapel Marriages	17C–1754
RG 8	Bunhill Fields Burials, British Lying-in Hospital Births, other Burial Grounds	17C–1837
E 174, KB 18	Papists' Forfeited Estates	16C–18C
	Probate Records	
C 21-24	Depositions	1558–1853
PROB 2-12, 18, 24-26, 28, 31-33, 36-37, 46-47, 51	Prerogative Court of Canterbury (Wills,*# Admon.,* Inven., Act Books#)	1383–1858
E 376-377	Recusant Rolls	17C

#Microfilm copy available at the LDS Family History Library in Salt Lake City, Utah, and through the LDS Family History Centers.
*Printed or transcribed

Title Deeds

E 40-43, E 326-329, DL 25, LR 14-15	Ancient*	prior to 17C
E 44, E 330, DL 26-27, LR 16, DURH 21, PL 29	Modern	17C–
C 54, CP 40, CP 43, CHES 2, DURH 13, PL 2, PL 15	Enrolments	13C–1837
J 18		1903–
C 60, C 66, E 159, E 168	Licences to Alienate	13C–1660
CP 25, CHES 31-32, DURH 12, PL 17	Feet of Fines	12C–1834
CP 40, CP 43, CHES 29, CHES 32, DURH 13, PL 15	Common Recoveries	15C–1834
SC 2 CHES 5, LR 3, LR 11, DL 30	Manorial Records	13C–1937

PUBLICATIONS†

Jane Cox and Timothy Padfield, *Tracing Your Ancestors in the Public Record Office* (3rd ed., 1985)

List of Nonparochial Registers and Records in England and Wales in Custody of the Registrar General of Births, Deaths and Marriages

---

*Printed or transcribed

†For additional information send 2 Postal Reply Coupons or 31 pence of English postage for reply to North America; 34 pence to Australia and New Zealand.

PUBLIC RECORD OFFICE, KEW
Ruskin Avenue, Kew
Richmond, Surrey TW9 4DU
Tel. (01) 876 3444

Hours: M-F 9:30-5; closed S
Closed first 2 weeks in October for stocktaking

Admission: By Reader's Ticket, obtained through application at the PRO Kew or PRO Chancery Lane; not necessary to apply in advance; applicant should have positive means of identification.

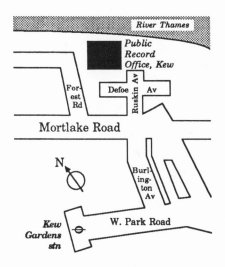

HOLDINGS

Records of the present and defunct government departments, public offices, etc., which are described in *Guide to the Contents of the Public Record Office*, Part II and Part III (on microfiche‡) and in unpublished supplements.

---

‡Available from the Public Record Office, Chancery Lane.

SOURCES THAT IDENTIFY AN INDIVIDUAL
WITH A SPECIFIC LOCATION AFTER 1800

AO 12,	**American Loyalists' Claims** (some#)	1776–1831
AO 13		1780–1835
	Army Records (War Office):	
	Commissioned Officers – Service	
WO 65	Army Lists* (some#)	1702–1823
WO 64	Army Lists§	1754–1879
WO 54	Ordnance Office Registers	1786–1850
	(Artillery, Engineers)	
	Commissioned Officers – Pension	
WO 24	Halfpay Pensions	1713–1824
	Other Ranks – Service	
	(*Must first determine Regiment*):	
WO 17	Monthly Returns	1759–1865
WO 73		1859–1949
WO 100	Campaign Medals	1791–1812
	(*When know Regiment*):	
WO 10	Muster Books: Artillery	1708–1878
WO 11	Muster Books: Engineers	1816–1878
WO 12	Muster Books: Cavalry, Guards,	1732–1878
	Infantry, Household Troops	
WO 16	Muster Books, New Series	1877–1898
	(continued from WO 10–WO 12)	
HO 129	**Ecclesiastical Census Returns**§	1851
	Emigration	
HO 11	Convict Transportation Registers#	1787–1870
	(New South Wales, Tasmania)	
T 53	Felons Transported	1719–1744
	(North American Colonies)	

#Microfilm copy available at the LDS Family History Library in Salt Lake City, Utah, and through the LDS Family History Centers.
*Printed or transcribed
§Manuscript copy

	Immigration	
HO 1,	Denizenations and	1789–1871
HO 4	Naturalisations	1804–1843
HO 2	Certificates of Aliens	1836–1852
HO 3	Lists of Immigrants	1836–1869
HO 5	Aliens' Applications for	1794–1921
	Denization# (Index to HO 1)	
HO 69,	Bouillon Papers§§	1789–1809
	Land Tax	
IR 8	Land Tax Redemption (gaps)	1863–1914
	Registers	
IR 23	Land Tax Quotas and	1798–1914
	Assessments	(gaps after 1832)
IR 22,	Land Tax Redemptions	1799–1953
IR 24		1799–1963
IR 58	Valuation Ofice: Field Books	1910
IR 91	Valuation Office:	1910
	Domesday Books	
	Enclosure	
MAF 1	Enclosure Awards	1847–1946
MAF 2	Enclosure Awards and Orders	1845–1963
	Merchant Shipping Records:	
	Masters, Mates, Engineers – Service	
BT 6	Shipping Returns††	1697–1850
ADM 7	Letters of Marque††	1777–1815
ADM 68	Receivers of Sixpence††	1696–1865
BT 107	Registers of Shipping††	1786–1854
		1814–1854‡‡
BT 98	Muster Rolls and Agreements#‡‡	1747–1835
	Other Ranks – Service‡‡	
BT 98	Muster Rolls and Agreements#	1747–1835

#Microfilm copy available at the LDS Family History Library in Salt Lake City, Utah, and through the LDS Family History Centers.
§§Written in French
††Masters only
‡‡Must know ship on which served to use records effectively

Militia

WO 13	Muster Rolls and Pay Lists	1780–1878
HO 51	Entry Books	1758–1855

Naval Records (Admiralty):
Commissioned Officers – Service

ADM 9	Returns of Officers' Services	1817–1848
ADM 10	Index to ADM 9	
ADM 6, ADM 11	Commission and Warrant Books	1695–1849
ADM 118	Seniority Lists	1717–1850

Warrant Officers – Service

ADM 6, ADM 11	Commission and Warrant Books	1695–1849
ADM 29	Warrant Officers' and Seamen's Services	1802–1919
ADM 104	Surgeons' Services	1742–1939
ADM 118	Seniority Lists	1717–1850

Ratings (Seamen) – Service[‡‡]

ADM 29	Warrant Officers' and Seamen's Services	1802–1919
ADM 31– ADM 35	Ships' Pay Lists	1691–1856
ADM 36– ADM 39	Ships' Musters Lists	1667–1878

Royal Marines:
Commissioned Officers – Service

ADM 192	Lists of Officers	1760–1886
ADM 118	Lists of Marine Officers (in Seniority Lists)	1757–1850
ADM 96	Pay Office Ledgers	1690–1832

Other Ranks – Service[§§]

ADM 96	Pay Office Ledgers	1688–1832
ADM 36– ADM 39	Ships' Musters	1690–1878
ADM 171	Campaign Medal Rolls	1793–1966

[‡‡]Must know ship on which served to use records effectively
[§§]Must know Division with which served to use records effectively

	Tithe Records	
IR 18	Tithe Files	c. 1836–1870
IR 29, IR 30	Tithe Apportionments	1837–1899
TITH 1	Boundary Awards	1839–1860
TITH 2	Awards and Agreements	1836–1866
TITH 3	Tithes and Tithe Rent-charge	1837–1937
MAF 8	City of London Tithe Rates	1879–1949

SOURCES THAT MAY ADDITIONALLY PROVIDE VITAL DATA AND/OR PROVE FAMILY RELATIONSHIPS

IR 1	Apprenticeship Records[#]	1710–1811
IR 17	Index to IR 1[#]	1710–1774
	Army Records (War Office)	
	Commissioned Officers – Service	
WO 76	Records of Officers' Services[#]	1764–1954
WO 25	Returns of Officers' Services	1660–1935
WO 31	Commander-in-Chief's Memoranda	1793–1870
	Commissioned Officers – Pensions, etc.	
WO 25	Casualty Returns	1797–1872
WO 25	Half-pay, Retired Pay Pensions	1684–1832
WO 24	Widows' Pensions	1713–1829
WO 24	Compassionate Fund Lists	1779–1812
WO 23	Royal Hospital Chelsea Registers	1824–1917
WO 22	Royal Hospital Chelsea Pensions	1842–1883
WO 42	Returns: Certificates of Birth,etc.[#]	1755–1908
	Other Ranks – Pensions, etc.[§§]	
WO 25	Casualty Returns	1797–1872
WO 25	Deaths and Effects	1810–1881
WO 23	Royal Hospital Chelsea Pensions	1702–1917
WO 116,	Royal Hospital Chelsea	1715–1913
WO 117	Admission Books	1823–1920

[#]Microfilm copy available at the LDS Family History Library in Salt Lake City, Utah, and through the LDS Family History Centers.
[§§]Must know regiment in order to use records effectively before 1883

WO 120	Royal Hospital Chelsea	c. 1715–1857
	Regimental Registers#	
WO 121	Royal Hospital Chelsea	1782–1887
	Discharge Documents (some#)	
WO 118	Royal Hospital Kil-	1704–1922
	mainham (Ire.)	
	Admission Books#	
WO 119	Royal Hospital Kilmainham	1783–1832
	Discharge Documents	

Other Ranks – Service§§

WO 97	Soldiers' Documents#	1760–1913
WO 69	Service Records – Artillery	1756–1911
WO 156	Registers of Baptism, Marriage	1808–1958
	Regimental Description Books	
WO 25	Infantry, Cavalry, Guards#	1756–1900
WO 54	Ordnance	1755–1863
WO 69	Artillery#	1756–1911
WO 67	Depot#	1768–1913

Criminals, Prisons††

HO 77	Newgate Calendar of Prisoners*	1782–1853
HO 26	Criminal Registers, Series I	1791–1849
HO 27	Criminal Registers, Series II	1808–1892
HO 9	Registers of Convicts on Hulks	1802–1849
ADM 6	Registers of Convict Ships and	1813–1852
	Prisoners	
HO 16	Old Bailey Sessions Returns	1815–1849
ADM 101	Medical Registers,	1817–1853
	Convict Ships	
HO 8	Convict Prison Lists	1824–1876
HO 23	Registers at County Prisons	1847–1866
HO 24	Prison Registers and Returns	1838–1875

#Microfilm copy available at the LDS Family History Library in Salt Lake City, Utah, and through the LDS Family History Centers.
§§Must know regiment in order to use records effectively before 1883
††Convicts transported overseas listed under Emigration
*Printed or transcribed

Emigration

T 47	Emigration Returns	1773–1776
BT 27	Convict Settlers	1789–1859
	(New South Wales, Tasmania)	
FO 610	Passport Registers	1795–1943
FO 611	Index of Names in FO 610	1851–1916
HO 7	Deaths of Convicts,	1823–1835
	New South Wales	
MH 12	Poor Law Union, Parish Assisted	1834–1900
	Transportation (North America)	
BT 158	Births, Deaths, Marriages	1854–1890
	of Passengers at Sea	
BT 159	Deaths at Sea of British Nationals	1875–1888
BT 160	Births at Sea of British Nationals	1875–1891
BT 27	Passenger Lists Outward	1890–1960

Enclosure

MAF 9	Deeds and Awards of	1841–1925
	Enfranchisement	
MAF 20	Manor Files	1840–1900

Immigration

BT 26	Passenger Lists Inward	1878–1960

Merchant Shipping:
Masters, Mates, Engineers – Service
Registers of Certificates of
Competency and Service

BT 122–	Foreign Trade: Masters, Mates	1845–1900
BT 124		
BT 125–	Home Trade: Masters, Mates	1854–1858
BT 126		
BT 127	Index to BT 122–126, BT 128	
BT 128	Colonial Trade: Masters, Mates	
BT 139,	Foreign Trade: Engineers	1861–1921
BT 140		
BT 141	Index to BT 139–140, BT 142	
BT 142	Colonial Trade: Engineers	1862–1921

BT 98,	Crew Lists and Agreements#	1835–1860
BT 99–100		1861–1954
	Other Ranks – Service	
	Registers of Seamen's Services	
BT 120	Series I	1835–1836
BT 112	Series II	1835–1844
BT 119	Index to BT 112	1835–1844
BT 151	Apprentices' Indentures§§	1845–1850
BT 150	Index to BT 151	1824–1853
BT 113	Register of Seamen's Tickets	1845–1854
BT 114	Index of Seamen in BT 113	
	Index of Masters in BT 113	
BT 116	Register of Seamen, Series III	1853–1857
BT 98,	Crew Lists and Agreements#	1835–1860
BT 99–100		1861–1954
	Militia	
WO 68	Militia Records#	1759–1925
WO 96	Militia Attestation Records	1806–1915
WO 116	Royal Hospital Chelsea, Pension Records	1715–1913
	Naval Records (Admiralty):	
	Commissioned Officers – Service	
ADM 6,	Navy Lists*	
ADM 13,	Lieutenants' Passing	1731–1820
ADM 107	Certificates	1851–1902
		1691–1832
ADM 196	Records of Officers' Services	1756–1954
ADM 13	Marriage Certificates	1806–1902

#Microfilm copy available at the LDS Family History Library in Salt Lake City, Utah, and through the LDS Family History Centers.

§§Only records for every fifth years preserved; one-tenth of those are located at PRO-Kew; one-tenth at the National Maritime Museum, Greenwich; rest at Memorial University of Newfoundland, St. John's, Newfoundland

*Printed or transcribed

Commissioned Officers — Pensions, etc.

ADM 45	Officers' Effects Papers (Wills)	1830–1860
ADM 106	Bounty to Next of Kin	1675–1822
ADM 23	Officers' and Widows' Pensions	1830–1934
ADM 6	Widows' Pensions	1732–1830

Warrant Officers – Service

ADM 196	Records of Officers' Services	1756–1954
ADM 22	Full Pay Ledgers	

Warrant Officers – Pensions, etc.

ADM 106	Bounty to Next of Kin	1675–1822
ADM 45	Officers' Effects Papers (Wills)	1830–1860
ADM 82	Chatham Chest Pensions	1617–1807
ADM 6	Widows' Pensions	1732–1830
ADM 23	Officers' and Widows' Pensions	1830–1934

Ratings – Service[tt]

ADM 139	Continuous Service	1853–1872
	Engagement Books[#]	
ADM 188	Seamen's Services	1873–1895
ADM 27	Allowance to Relatives	1795–1852

Ratings – Pensions, etc.[tt]

ADM 154	Ratings of Discharged Dead	1859–1878
ADM 44	Seamen's Effects Papers	1800–1860
ADM 141	Index to ADM 44	
ADM 48	Seamen's Wills	1786–1882
ADM 142	Index to ADM 48	
ADM 106	Bounty to Next of Kin	1689–1836
ADM 82	Chatham Chest Pensions	1617–1807
ADM 73,	Greenwich Hospital Pensions	1704–1881
ADM 166		1882–1949
ADM 22	Widows' Pension Paybooks,	1814–1846
	Naval Outpensions	

[tt]Must know ship on which served to use records effectively

[#]Microfilm copy available at the LDS Family History Library in Salt Lake City, Utah, and through the LDS Family History Centers.

Royal Marines:

Commissioned Officers – Service

ADM 196	Records of Officers' Services	1756–1954

Commissioned Officers – Pensions

ADM 165	Greenwich Hospital Pension Registers	1871–1961
ADM 23	Officers' and Widows' Pensions	1830–1934
ADM 6	Widows' Pensions	1732–1830

Warrant Officers – Service

ADM 196	Records of Officers' Services	1756–1954

Warrant Officers – Pensions

ADM 166	Greenwich Hospital Pensions	1882–1949
ADM 23	Officers' and Widows' Pensions	1830–1934
ADM 6	Widows' Pensions	1743–1830

Other Ranks – Service‡‡

ADM 183	Order Books – Chatham	1755–1961
ADM 184	Order Books – Plymouth	1760–1941
ADM 185	Order Books – Portsmouth	1783–1941
ADM 157	Attestation Forms#	1790–1901
ADM 158	Description Books	c. 1750–1940
ADM 159	Registers of Service	1842–1905
ADM 81	Order Books – Woolwich Division	1805–1869
NDO 1–2	Tontines and Annuities	1745–1888

PUBLICATION†

Jane Cox and Timothy Padfield, *Tracing Your Ancestors in the Public Record Office* (3rd ed., 1985)

---

‡‡Must know division in which served to use records effectively before 1884

#Microfilm copy available at the LDS Family History Library in Salt Lake City, Utah, and through the LDS Family History Centers.

†For additional information send 2 Postal Reply Coupons or 31 pence of English postage for reply to North America; 34 pence to Australia and New Zealand.

PUBLIC RECORD OFFICE, PORTUGAL STREET
(Land Registry Building)
London WC2A 1LR
Tel. (01) 405 3844 ext. 335

Hours: M-F 9:30-4:50; closed S

Admission free; (Reader's Ticket not required)

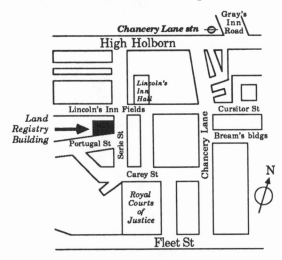

HOLDINGS

Microfilm copies of the census records for England, Wales. the Isle of Man, and Channel Islands taken in 1861, 1871, and 1881 listing all inhabitants of the two countries on a specific date in each dicennial year.

Microfilm copies of the 1841 and 1851 census for England, Wales, the Isle of Man, and Channel Islands are now located at the Public Record Office, Chancery Lane.

(All census records 1841–1881 are available on microfilm at the LDS Family History Library in Salt Lake City, Utah and through the LDS Family History Centers. Copies are also available at county and local record offices in England as specified, and at repositories with major genealogical collections worldwide.)

RELIGIOUS SOCIETY OF FRIENDS
Friends House, Euston Road
London NW1 2BJ
Tel. (01) 387 3601

Hours: T-F 10-5; closed M, S
(Closed for one week in August and for the
week preceding the Spring Bank Holiday)

Admission fee charged
Staff unable to answer postal enquiries

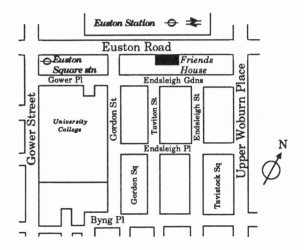

HOLDINGS

Digest Registers contain transcribed records of births,
marriages and burial information included in the original
registers for all of Great Britain to 1837, excepting for names of
witnesses to marriages and burials; records of London and
Middlesex General Meeting and its constituent monthly meetings; manuscripts, including diaries and family papers, of
Friends.

(Original registers of births, marriages and burials are
located at the Public Record Office, Chancery Lane. A micro-

film copy of the Original Registers is available at the LDS Family History Library in Salt Lake City, Utah and through the LDS Family History Centers; also at some county record offices and libraries in England as specified, and at a few libraries in other countries.)

HISTORICAL SOCIETY

FRIENDS HISTORICAL SOCIETY
c/o Friends House
Euston Road, London NW1 2BJ

PUBLICATION†

Journal of Friends Historical Society, 1–54 (1903–)

RELATED PUBLICATION†

Edward H. Milligan and Malcolm J. Thomas, *My Ancestors Were Quakers* (London: Society of Genealogists, 1983)

---

†For additional information send 2 Postal Reply Coupons or 31 pence of English postage for reply to North America; 34 pence to Australia and New Zealand.

ROYAL COMMISSION ON HISTORICAL MANUSCRIPTS
Quality House, Quality Court,
Chancery Lane, London WC2A 1HP
Tel. (01) 242 1198

Hours: M-F 9:30-5; closed S

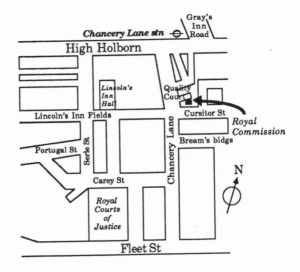

HOLDINGS

Acts as a central clearing house for information about the nature and location of all historical manuscripts and papers, excepting public records.

ACCESS

Public use of the National Register of Archives, Manorial Documents Register and Tithe Documents Register permitted without charge in the Search Room.

PUBLICATIONS[†§]

Accessions to Repositories and Reports added to the National Register of Archives (Annual)[#]

Guide to the Location of Collections described in the Reports and Calendars Series 1870–1980

Papers of British Churchmen 1780–1940

Record Repositories in Great Britain: A Geographical Directory (8th ed., 1987)

Sectional List 17, Publications of the Royal Commission on Historical Manuscripts (Annual)

[†]For additional information send 2 Postal Reply Coupons or 31 pence of English postage for reply to North America; 34 pence to Australia and New Zealand. Available at Her Majesty's Stationery Office, P.O. Box 276, London SE1 9NH.

[§]In Canada and the USA, copies available from Bernan-Unipub, 10033 M.L. King Highway, Lanham, MD 20706-4391, USA.

[#]Microfilm copy available at the LDS Family History Library in Salt Lake City, Utah, and through the LDS Family History Centers.

SOCIETY OF GENEALOGISTS
14 Charterhouse Buildings, Goswell Road
London EC1M 7BA
Tel. (01) 251 8799

Hours: T, F 10-6; W, Th 10-8; S 10-5; closed M
Prior appointment advised for microfilm
and microfiche readers
(Closed for stocktaking week of the first
Monday in February)

Admission to members free; fee charged for hours,
half-day, or day periods to non-members.§
Limited searches by staff for a fee†

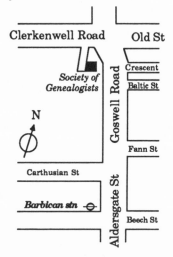

HOLDINGS

Published sources relating to all counties in England, as
well as some printed materials on Scotland, Ireland, Wales

---

§Membership subscriptions: Entrance fee £7.50 (U.S. $15.00); Annual – Town
Members £20, Country and Overseas Members £14 (U.S. $28). Includes
Genealogists' Magazine, published quarterly.
†For additional information send 2 Postal Reply Coupons or 31 pence of English
postage for reply to North America; 34 pence to Australia and New Zealand.

and areas of the Commonwealth. The library contains the largest collection of Modern Register Transcripts in England, has strong collections of family histories and genealogies, Poll Books and Directories, as well as British genealogical periodicals and books on heraldry.

Typescript and manuscript materials relating to individuals are primarily found in the Document Collection, the special Locality Collections for several counties, and through numerous indexes.

SOURCES THAT IDENTIFY AN INDIVIDUAL WITH A SPECIFIC LOCATION

Bernau's Index to Chancery Proceedings‡#	15C–18C
Boyd's Inhabitants of London#	16C–17C
County Histories*	
Directories*#	18C–20C
Lists of Officers in Army, Navy, Air Force*	17C–20C
Maps	19C–20C
Parish Histories*	
Poll Books*#	18C–19C

SOURCES THAT MAY ADDITIONALLY PROVIDE VITAL DATA AND/OR PROVE FAMILY RELATIONSHIPS

Apprentices of Great Britain Index‡#	1710–1774
Birth Briefs	late 18C–20C
Boyd's London Burials#	1538–1853
Boyd's Marriage Index#	1538–1837
Church of England (diocesan)	
Marriage Licence Indexes‡#	16C–1837
Will Indexes‡#	14C–1858

---

‡Microfilm/microfiche copies available at above repository

#Microfilm copy available at the LDS Family History Library in Salt Lake City, Utah, and through the LDS Family History Centers.

*Printed or transcribed

Church of England (parish)
  Parish Register Transcripts*   16C–19C
Document Collection
  Estate and Family Papers   11C–20C
  Manuscript Pedigrees   11C–20C
Genealogies and Family Histories*
Great Card Index   16C–19C
Heraldry   16C–17C
  Heralds' Visitations*
  Armorial Families*
International Genealogical Index‡##
  (British Isles)
Locality Collections   16C–20C
  Berkshire, Cheshire, Cornwall,
  London, Norfolk, Shropshire,
  Surrey, The North Country,
  Scotland, West Indies
Monumental Inscriptions*   16C–20C
Obituaries*   17C–20C
Periodicals*
School and University Registers   15C–19C
Trinity House Petitions#   mid-18C–19C

PUBLICATIONS†

Genealogists' Magazine 1925–

Lydia Collins, *Monumental Inscriptions in the Library of the Society of Genealogists*, Part I (1984)

---

*Printed or transcribed
‡Microfilm/microfiche copies available at above repository
##Microfiche copy available at the LDS Family History Library in Salt Lake City, Utah, and through the LDS Family History Centers.
#Microfilm copy available at the LDS Family History Library in Salt Lake City, Utah, and through the LDS Family History Centers.
†For additional information send 2 Postal Reply Coupons or 31 pence of English postage for reply to North America; 34 pence to Australia and New Zealand.

Lydia Collins and Mable Morton, eds., *Monumental Inscriptions in the Library of the Society of Genealogists*, Part II (1987)

L.W.L. Edwards, *Catalogue of Directories and Poll Books in the Possession of the Society of Genealogists* (1984)

P.S. Wolfston, *Greater London Cemeteries and Crematoria* (1986)

A List of Parishes in Boyd's Marriage Index (1987)

Computers in Genealogy 1982–

Parish Register Copies, Part One: Society of Genealogists Collection (1987)

Parish Register Copies, Part Two: Other than the Society of Genealogists Collection (1987)

Using the Library of the Society of Genealogists (1987)

Complete list of publications available upon request.[†]   (U.S. dollar cheques are accepted)

[†]For additional information send 2 Postal Reply Coupons or 31 pence of English postage for reply to North America; 34 pence to Australia and New Zealand.

UNITARIAN HISTORICAL SOCIETY
c/o Unitarian Information Department
Essex Hall, 1-6 Essex Street
Strand, London WC2R 3HY
Tel. (01) 240 2384
Contact: Information Officer

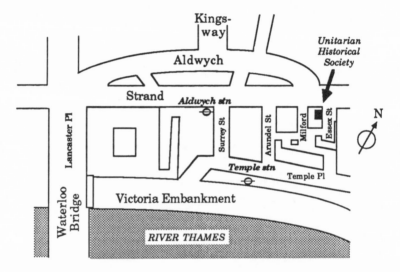

Accepts only queries relating to Unitarian ministers and/or Unitarian history. Unable to help with general genealogical queries.

Records of individual congregations prior to 1837 will normally be found at the Public Record Office, Chancery Lane. Later records of individual congregations may have been deposited at the appropriate county record office, Dr. Williams's Library, or still may be in possession of the local congregation.

UNITED REFORMED CHURCH HISTORY SOCIETY
86 Tavistock Place
London WC1H 9RT
Tel. (01) 837 7661

Hours: T, F 11-4; closed M, W, Th, S
(Prior appointment advised)

Admission free to members; donation
requested of non-members

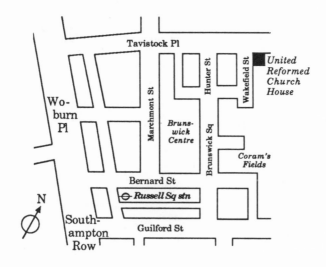

HOLDINGS

Presbyterian

Published material relating to Presbyterian churches in
England
Some 18C Presbyterian baptismal registers (Northumb-
erland)
Yearbooks of the Presbyterian Church with lists of min-
isters and obituaries of deceased ministers 1885–
Individual church histories

Congregational

Published materials relating to the Congregational (Independent) churches in England and Wales
Yearbooks of the Congregational Church with lists of ministers and obituaries of deceased ministers 1846–
Individual church histories

PUBLICATIONS[†]

Journal of the United Reformed Church History Society (1972–)

[†]For additional information send 2 Postal Reply Coupons or 31 pence of English postage for reply to North America; 34 pence to Australia and New Zealand.

ARCHIVES OF THE UNITED SYNAGOGUE

Office of the Chief Rabbi
Adler House, Tavistock Square
London WC1 9HN
Tel. (01) 387 1066

Hours: M-F 10:30-12:30; closed S

Enquiries: By letter only†

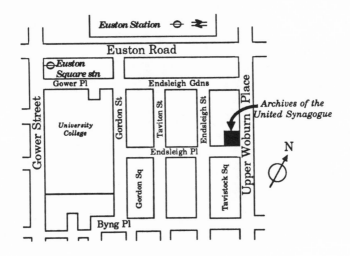

HOLDINGS

Records of the Great Synagogue, Hambro' Synagogue and New Synagogue in London.

Registers
  Great Synagogue
    Births   1771–1877
    Marriages   1791–1840
    Burials   1791–1872

---

†For additional information send 2 Postal Reply Coupons or 31 pence of English postage for reply to North America; 34 pence to Australia and New Zealand.

Hambro' Synagogue#	
Births	1770–1843
Marriages	1797–1837
Deaths and Burials	1797–1872
New Synagogue	
Births	1774–1896
Marriages	1790–1842
Burials	1801–1835

#Microfilm copy available at the LDS Family History Library in Salt Lake City, Utah, and through the LDS Family History Centers.

WESLEY HISTORICAL SOCIETY LIBRARY
c/o Southlands College of Education
Parkside, Wimbledon
London SW19 5NN

Hours: By prior appointment only

Contact Librarian: The Rev. K. Garlick, 50 Ashford Crescent,
    Ashford, Middlesex TW15 3ED, Tel. 07842 52559
    or the Bursar's Office at the College, Tel. (01) 946 2234
Correspondence: Mrs. J. Banks at the College

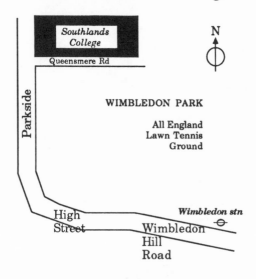

HOLDINGS

Records of Methodist ministers
Obituaries of some lay members
    (in denominational magazines)
Some individual church/chapel histories
Fairly large biographical section
(no baptismal or marriage registers)

(See also Methodist Archives and Research Center, John
    Rylands University Library, University of Manchester,
    listed under Greater Manchester County)

WESTMINSTER DIOCESAN ARCHIVES
16A Abingdon Road
London W8 6AF
Tel. (01) 834 1964
Archivist: Miss Elisabeth Poyser

Hours: By prior appointment only M-F 10-5; closed S

Admission free
Searches undertaken by staff for a fee

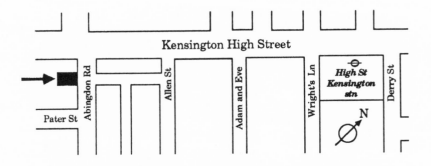

HOLDINGS

Baptismal and Marriage registers for five parishes in London and one in Hertfordshire dating from approximately 1790.[tt] Letters, correspondence, memoranda from the sixteenth to the twentieth centuries; some medieval deeds.

(Archivist will assist searchers in locating records for other parts of England.)

[tt]For specific list of registers see Donald J. Steel and Eagar R. Samuel, *Sources for Roman Catholic and Jewish Genealogy,* III in the series *National Index of Parish Registers* (1974) pp. 954–955.

DR. WILLIAMS'S LIBRARY
14 Gordon Square
London WC1H 0AG
Tel. (01) 387 3727

Hours: M, W, F 10-5; T, Th 10-6:30; closed S
Prior appointment suggested;
(Closed the week following Christmas, the first part of
August, from the Thursday before Good Friday to the
following Tuesday, Bank Holidays)

Admission free

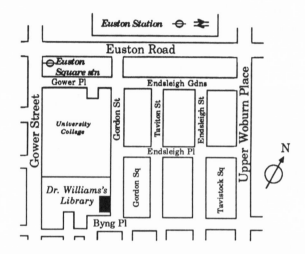

HOLDINGS

The foremost nonconformist library in England. Its special collections include histories of individual congregations,
histories of nonconformist denominations, transcribed registers, church books and minute books of congregations and
associations. Also included are Methodist yearbooks, Baptist
handbooks, proceedings of the Huguenot Society of Great Britain and Ireland, transactions of various historical societies

73

and the Charles Surman biographical index of Congregational ministers.

(The Register of Presbyterian, Independent and Baptist births in and around London 1742–1837, which was originally held at Dr. Williams's Library, is now located at the Public Record Office, Chancery Lane.#)

PUBLICATIONS

Nonconformist Congregations in Great Britain (1973)

#Microfilm copy available at the LDS Family History Library in Salt Lake City, Utah, and through the LDS Family History Centers; also at some county record offices and libraries in England for the respective areas.

PART II

COUNTY

REPOSITORIES

AVON

Post-1974 Counties of England

Avon county was created in 1974. It includes the cities of Bath and Bristol, as well as the areas formerly in the north-western quarter of Somerset county and the southern part of pre-1974 Gloucestershire, southward from Thornbury and the city of Bristol.

Administratively the city of Bristol was a County Corporate from the fourteenth century to 1889 and then a County Borough to 1974. The city of Bath was an incorporated Borough in Somerset county from the thirteenth century to 1889, and a County Borough between 1889 and 1974.

77

Except for Bristol, see the Record Offices of Gloucestershire and Somerset counties for pre-1974 source materials of their respective areas.

RECORD OFFICES

BATH CITY RECORD OFFICE
Guildhall, Bath BA1 5AW
Tel. 0225 61111 ext. 201

Hours: M-Th 9-1, 2-5; F 9-1, 2-4:30
          (Prior appointment advised)

Admission free

HOLDINGS

Official records for the city of Bath 1189–; some parish records, (but not Parish Registers) for the city of Bath; some local government records and other resources pertaining to the city.

(Diocesan records for the Diocese of Bath and Wells and Parish Registers over 100 years old are mostly located at the Somerset Record Office, Taunton.)

SOURCES THAT IDENTIFY AN INDIVIDUAL WITH A SPECIFIC LOCATION

Borough Records (Bath)	
Freemen's Lists	18C–20C
Rate Books	18C–20C
Church of England (diocesan)	
Tithe Maps§	1840's
Church of England (parish)	
Churchwardens' Accounts	18C–

---

§For Tithe Apportionments see Somerset Record Office.

Directories* (some#)		1833–1973
Postal		
Maps		
Poll Books* (some#)	(periodic)	1832–1857
Quarter Sessions		
Judicial Records		1862–1971
Lists of Jurors		18C–19C
Registers of Electors*		1832–

SOURCES THAT MAY ADDITIONALLY PROVIDE VITAL DATA AND/OR PROVE FAMILY RELATIONSHIPS

Borough Records (Bath)	
Court: Court of Record, Court of Requests,	
Quarter Sessions, Court Leet	
Guild: Company of Merchant Taylors	1666–1735
Freemen's Apprentices	
Enrolments, Admissions	1697–1776
Title Deeds	1218–20C
Church of England (parish)	
Parish Register Transcripts*	16C–19C
(Bath, Bathampton, Twerton, Weston)	
Monumental Inscriptions	
Nonconformist Registers	
Baptist	
Methodist	
Parish Poor Law Records	
Apprenticeship Indentures	18C–19C
Examinations	1758–1825
Removal Orders	19C
Settlement Papers	19C
Poor Law Union Records	1834–20C
School Records	1862–

---

*Printed or transcribed

#Microfilm copy available at the LDS Family History Library in Salt Lake City, Utah, and through the LDS Family History Centers.

BRISTOL RECORD OFFICE
The Council House, College Green
Bristol BS1 5TR
Tel. 0272 266031 ext. 442

Hours: M-Th 9:30-4:45; F 9:30-4:15
1st, 2nd S/mo. 9-12
(All visits by prior appointment only)
Closed last 2 weeks in January

Admission free
List of record searchers available upon request†

HOLDINGS

Church of England diocesan records (Diocese of Bristol); Church of England parish records including deposited Parish Registers for more than 100 churches in the Diocese of Bristol; local government records and other resources pertaining to the city of Bristol.

*SOURCES THAT IDENTIFY AN INDIVIDUAL
WITH A SPECIFIC LOCATION*

Borough Records (Bristol)	
Burgess Registers	1557–1599, 1607–
Parish Poor Rates	1696–
Registers of Electors*	1843–
Church of England (diocesan)	
Ecclesiastical Court Books	1545–1922
Ecclesiastical Visitations	1626–1951
Tithe Apportionments	1838–
Church of England (parish)	
Churchwardens' Accounts	1446–

---

†For additional information send 2 Postal Reply Coupons or 31 pence of English postage for reply to North America; 34 pence to Australia and New Zealand.
*Printed or transcribed

80

Directories* (some#)
Maps	17C–
Militia Lists	1782–1815
Parish Poor Law Records††	17C–1834
Parish Poor Rates	
Quarter Sessions	
Judicial Records	1595–1971
Hearth Tax Assessments*	1665–1673
Land Tax Assessments	1691–1849
Lists of Jurors	1718–
Shipping – Crew Lists	1861–1913

SOURCES THAT MAY ADDITIONALLY PROVIDE VITAL DATA AND/OR PROVE FAMILY RELATIONSHIPS

Borough Records (Bristol)	
Courts‡‡	1331–1971
Apprenticeship Registers	1532–1658, 1668–
Burgess Registers	1557–1599, 1607–
Title Deeds	14C–
Church of England (diocesan)	
Bishops' Transcripts#	1571–1906
Marriage Licence Bonds and Allegations	1633–1984
Wills, Admon., Inven.#	1546–1858
Church of England (parish)	
Parish Registers#	1538–
Estate and Family Papers	12C–
Manorial Records	14C–19C

---

*Printed or transcribed

#Microfilm copy available at the LDS Family History Library in Salt Lake City, Utah, and through the LDS Family History Centers.

††Parishes in Diocese of Bristol outside city boundaries only; those for city of Bristol located with Borough Records from 1696.

‡‡Includes Court of Orphans Register Copy Wills 1382–1674 (mostly in Latin).

Nonconformist Registers
Baptist (some#)	17C–20C
Congregational (some#)	18C–20C
Methodist (some#)	18C–20C
Presbyterian	1876–1972
Society of Friends (some#)	1667–
Unitarian (some#)	1690–
Parish Poor Law Records††	17C–1834
Apprenticeship Indentures	
Examinations	
Removal Orders	
Settlement Papers	
Poor Law Union	1834–
Workhouse Records	1847–
School Records	1854–
Title Deeds	12C–
Wills, Register Copies	1767–1941

PUBLICATIONS†

Guide to the Bristol Archives Office

Diocese of Bristol: A Catalogue of the Records of the Bishop and Archdeacons and of the Dean and Chapter

Information Leaflets:
No. 1: Sources for the Family Historian
No. 2: Sources for Ships, Seamen and Emigrants
No. 3: Sources for the History of Buildings
No. 4: Records Relating to Slavery
No. 5: Records of Poor Law Administration

#Microfilm copy available at the LDS Family History Library in Salt Lake City, Utah, and through the LDS Family History Centers.

††Parishes in Diocese of Bristol outside city boundaries only; those for city of Bristol located with Borough Records from 1696.

†For additional information send 2 Postal Reply Coupons or 31 pence of English postage for reply to North America; 34 pence to Australia and New Zealand.

Lists:
List of Parish Registers Deposited
List of Bishops' Transcripts Deposited
List of Nonconformist Registers Deposited

OTHER REPOSITORIES

The sources listed below include only those items reported on the Record Office Survey as located in the specified repositories. Each city and county library should have additional printed materials pertaining to its geographical area.

BATH REFERENCE LIBRARY†
18 Queens Square, Bath BA1 2HN
Tel. 0225 28144

Census‡# (Bath)	1841–1881
Church of England (parish)	
Parish Register Transcripts*	16C–19C
Directories* (some#)	
Postal	(gaps) 1783–1973
Poll Books* (some#)	(periodic) 1832–1857,
	1859, 1868
Registers of Electors*	1909–

---

†For additional information send 2 Postal Reply Coupons or 31 pence of English postage for reply to North America; 34 pence to Australia and New Zealand.
‡Microfilm/microfiche copies available at above repository
#Microfilm copy available at the LDS Family History Library in Salt Lake City, Utah, and through the LDS Family History Centers.
*Printed or transcribed

BRISTOL CENTRAL LIBRARY†
REFERENCE LIBRARY
College Green, Bristol BS1 5TR
Tel. 0272 276161

Census (Som, Glos)‡#   1841–1881
International Genealogical Index‡##
(Glos, Som, and adjacent counties)
Newspapers*

LDS FAMILY HISTORY CENTRE†
721 Wells Road, Bristol
Tel. 0272 833178

LDS Family History Library Catalog‡##
International Genealogical Index‡##

GENEALOGICAL AND FAMILY HISTORY SOCIETIES

The societies listed below may have recorded Monumental
(tombstone) Inscriptions, compiled an Index to Marriages
(from the Parish Registers), an Index to the 1851 Census, and
other special indexes, e.g., Strays, Members' Interests, for their

---

†For additional information send 2 Postal Reply Coupons or 31 pence of English
postage for reply to North America; 34 pence to Australia and New Zealand.
‡Microfilm/microfiche copies available at above repository
Microfilm copy available at the Family History Library in Salt Lake City,
Utah and through the LDS Branch Libraries
##Microfiche copy available at the LDS Family History Library in Salt Lake
City, Utah, and through the LDS Family History Centers.
*Printed or transcribed

geographical areas.** Each Society publishes a quarterly journal (listed in italics) which includes articles on family history, reports on the group's projects, and members' queries.

BRISTOL AND AVON FAMILY HISTORY SOCIETY†
Ms. V. Britton, Secretary
119 Holly Hill Road, Kingswood
Bristol BS15 4DL

Journal of the Bristol and Avon Family History Society

SOMERSET AND DORSET FAMILY HISTORY SOCIETY†
P.O. Box 170
Taunton, Somerset TA1 1HF

Greenwood Tree

WESTON-SUPER-MARE FAMILY HISTORY SOCIETY†
Mrs. P. Jeffery, Secretary
15 Clarence Grove Road
Weston-super-Mare, Avon BS23 4AG

Weston-super-Mare Family History Society Journal

**See *Current Publications by Member Societies* (annual), *List of Family History Project Coordinators*, 6th ed., and *Family History News and Digest* (biennial) — all published by the Federation of Family History Societies; available in the USA from the International Society for British Genealogy and Family History, P.O. Box 20425, Cleveland, OH 44120.

†For additional information send 2 Postal Reply Coupons or 31 pence of English postage for reply to North America; 34 pence to Australia and New Zealand.

BEDFORDSHIRE

Post-1974 Counties of England

There was no change in the geographical boundaries of Bedfordshire during the 1974 reorganization of local government.

Administratively Bedford was an incorporated Borough from the seventeenth century to 1974. Dunstable and Luton became Municipal Boroughs during the nineteenth century. Luton subsequently was a County Borough between 1889 and 1974.

RECORD OFFICE

BEDFORDSHIRE RECORD OFFICE

County Hall, Bedford MK42 9AP

Tel. 0234 63222 ext. 2833

Hours: M-F 9:15-1, 2-5

Admission free

List of record searchers available upon request†

HOLDINGS

Church of England records for the Archdeaconry of Bedford (Diocese of Lincoln to 1837, Diocese of Ely 1837–1914); Church of England parish records including deposited Parish Registers for approximately 140 churches within the county; local government and other resources for the county.

SOURCES THAT IDENTIFY AN INDIVIDUAL WITH A SPECIFIC LOCATION

Church of England (archidiaconal)
Ecclesiastical Court Books	1539–1850
Ecclesiastical Visitations	1642–1780
Tithe Apportionments	1840's

Church of England (parish)
Churchwardens' Accounts (some#)	17C–20C
Directories (some#)	19C–
Business/Trade, Postal	
Enclosure Awards and Maps*	18C–19C
Local Government Rates	19C

---

†For additional information send 2 Postal Reply Coupons or 31 pence of English postage for reply to North America; 34 pence to Australia and New Zealand.
#Microfilm copy available at the LDS Family History Library in Salt Lake City, Utah, and through the LDS Family History Centers.
*Printed or transcribed

Parish Poor Law Records (some#)   17C–1834
Parish Poor Rates
Poll Books* (some#)   (periodic) to 1832
Quarter Sessions‡#
  Judicial Records††   1650–1660,
                                                   1711–1971
Hearth Tax Assessments*   1671
Land Tax Assessments   1797-1832
Recusants Lists*
Registers of Electors*   1832–

*SOURCES THAT MAY ADDITIONALLY PROVIDE VITAL
DATA AND/OR PROVE FAMILY RELATIONSHIPS*

Cemetery Records
  (Bedford)   1855-1972
  (Luton)   1855–1965
  (Leighton Buzzard)   1884–1980
Census‡# (Beds)   1841–1881
Charity Records
Church of England (archidiaconal)
  Bishops' Transcripts‡# (also*)   1600-1850's
  Marriage Licence Bonds   1747-1885
    and Allegations‡# (also*)   (1812–1875#)
  Wills, Admon., Inven.# (also*)   1480-1856
Church of England (parish)
  Parish Registers‡   16C–20C
  Parish Register Transcripts*#   16C–19C
Estate and Family Papers   13C–20C

#Microfilm copy available at the LDS Family History Library in Salt Lake City,
Utah, and through the LDS Family History Centers.
*Printed or transcribed
‡Microfilm/microfiche copies available at above repository
††Modern records subject to embargo for 100 years

International Genealogical Index‡##
(Beds and adjacent counties, London)

Manorial Records	13C–20C
Newspapers‡#	18C–20C
Nonconformist Records	
Baptist (some#)	1724–1893
Congregational	19C–20C
Methodist (some*)	19C–20C
Moravian	1744–1871
Society of Friends (some#)	17C–20C
Parish Poor Law Records (some#)	17C–1834
Apprenticeship Indentures	
Examinations	
Removal Orders	
Settlement Papers	
Poor Law Union	1834–
Workhouse Records	
Probate Records	
Calendar of Grants of Probate*	1901–1935
Roman Catholic Records	19C
School Records	1870–
Title Deeds	13C–20C

PUBLICATIONS†

Guide to the Bedfordshire Record Office 1957# (OOP)
Supplement 1962# (OOP)

Publications for Sale at the Bedfordshire Record Office
(31 p)

---

‡Microfilm/microfiche copies available at above repository
##Microfiche copy available at the LDS Family History Library in Salt Lake City, Utah, and through the LDS Family History Centers.
#Microfilm copy available at the LDS Family History Library in Salt Lake City, Utah, and through the LDS Family History Centers.
*Printed or transcribed
†For additional information send 2 Postal Reply Coupons or 31 pence of English postage for reply to North America; 34 pence to Australia and New Zealand.

Leaflets:
*How to Trace the History of a Family Tree
in Bedfordshire*
*Parish Registers Deposited in the Bedfordshire
Record Office*

OTHER REPOSITORIES

The sources listed below include only those items reported on the Record Office Survey as located in the specified repositories. Each city and county library should have additional printed materials pertaining to its geographical area.

BEDFORD MUNIMENT ROOM†
Bedford Borough Archives
Town Hall, Bedford MK40 1SJ
Tel. 0234 67422

Bedford Borough Records

LDS FAMILY HISTORY CENTRE†
Cutenhoe Road and London Road
Luton, Bedfordshire
Tel: 0582 22242

LDS Family History Library Catalog‡##
International Genealogical Index‡##

---

†For additional information send 2 Postal Reply Coupons or 31 pence of English postage for reply to North America; 34 pence to Australia and New Zealand.
‡Microfilm/microfiche copies available at above repository
##Microfiche copy available at the LDS Family History Library in Salt Lake City, Utah, and through the LDS Family History Centers.

GENEALOGICAL AND FAMILY HISTORY SOCIETIES

The societies listed below may have recorded Monumental (tombstone) Inscriptions, compiled an Index to Marriages (from the Parish Registers), an Index to the 1851 Census, and other special indexes, e.g., Strays, Members' Interests, for their geographical areas.** Each Society publishes a quarterly journal (listed in italics) which includes articles on family history, reports on the group's projects, and members' queries.

BEDFORDSHIRE FAMILY HISTORY SOCIETY†
Mrs. P. Ormerod, Secretary
7 Braeside
Bedford MK41 9BL

Journal of the Bedfordshire Family History Society

**See *Current Publications by Member Societies* (annual), *List of Family History Project Coordinators*, 6th ed., and *Family History News and Digest* (biennial) — all published by the Federation of Family History Societies; available in the USA from the International Society for British Genealogy and Family History, P.O. Box 20425, Cleveland, OH 44120.

†For additional information send 2 Postal Reply Coupons or 31 pence of English postage for reply to North America; 34 pence to Australia and New Zealand.

BERKSHIRE

Post-1974 Counties of England

The pre-1974 geographical boundaries of Berkshire included the Vale of White Horse (Abingdon and Wantage), as
well as Wallingford, which are now in Oxfordshire. Present
boundaries additionally include the area of Slough, located in
Buckinghamshire before 1974.

Administratively Abingdon, Maidenhead, New Windsor,
and Newbury were all incorporated Boroughs from the seventeenth century to 1974. Reading was an incorporated Borough
from the seventeenth century to 1889 and a County Borough
between 1889 and 1974.

RECORD OFFICE

BERKSHIRE RECORD OFFICE
Shire Hall, Shinfield Park,
Reading RG2 9XD
Tel. 0734 875444 ext. 3182

Hours: M 2-5; T, W 9-5; Th 9-9; F 9-4:30; closed S
(Prior appointment usually essential)
Documents are produced at set intervals.
No documents are produced between 12:30 and 2.

Admission free
Fee paid record searcher available†

HOLDINGS

Church of England diocesan records for the Archdeaconry of Berkshire, Diocese of Sarum (Salisbury) to 1836, Diocese of Oxford 1836–; Wills only to 1836; Church of England parish records including deposited Parish Registers for approximately 170 churches within the pre-1974 boundaries of the county; local government records and other resources for the pre-1974 division of the county.

(Other Church of England diocesan records for Berkshire parishes are located at the Oxfordshire Record Office, Oxford, the Buckinghamshire Record Office, Aylesbury, and the Wiltshire Record Office, Trowbridge.)

---

†For additional information send 2 Postal Reply Coupons or 31 pence of English postage for reply to North America; 34 pence to Australia and New Zealand.

SOURCES THAT IDENTIFY AN INDIVIDUAL
WITH A SPECIFIC LOCATION

Borough Records (Abingdon)[††]	13C–20C
Freemen's Lists[#]	1696–1760
Rates	
Church of England (archidiaconal)	
Tithe Apportionments[§§]	1840's
Church of England (parish)	
Churchwardens' Accounts[‡#]	16C–20C
Directories* (some[#])	19C–20C
Business/Trade, Postal	
Enclosure Awards	19C
Maps	
Militia Lists[‡#]	1793–1796
Parish Poor Law Records (some[#])	17C–1834
Parish Poor Rates	
Periodicals* (some[#])	
Poll Books* (some[#])	(periodic) 18C–19C
Quarter Sessions	
Judicial Records (some[#])	18C–1888
Registers of Electors*	1839–

[††]Also a few Borough Records for Hungerford (parliamentary borough only), Maidenhead, Newbury, Reading, Wallingford, Wantage (parliamentary borough only), Windsor.

[#]Microfilm copy available at the LDS Family History Library in Salt Lake City, Utah, and through the LDS Family History Centers.

[§§]Parish copies only

[‡]Microfilm/microfiche copies available at above repository

*Printed or transcribed

SOURCES THAT MAY ADDITIONALLY PROVIDE VITAL DATA AND/OR PROVE FAMILY RELATIONSHIPS

Borough Records (Abingdon)‡‡,	
Court	17C–18C#
Guild: Apprenticeship Enrolment	1633–1793#
Admissions	
Title Deeds	13C–18C
Church of England (archidiaconal)§	
Wills‡#	16C–19C
Church of England (parish)	16C–19C
Parish Registers‡#	1538–
Parish Register Transcripts*	16C–19C
Estate and Family Papers	16C–20C
International Genealogical Index‡##	
(Berks and adjacent counties)	
Manorial Records#	14C–20C
Monumental Inscriptions	
Nonconformist Registers	17C–20C
Baptist‡#	1735–1819
Independent/Congregational (some‡#)	18C–20C
Methodist	
Society of Friends*‡#	1612–1837
Parish Poor Law Records	17C–1834
Apprenticeship Indentures	
Examinations	
Removal Orders	
Settlement Papers	

---

‡‡Also a few Borough Records for Maidenhead, New Windsor, Reading, and Wallingford.

#Microfilm copy available at the LDS Family History Library in Salt Lake City, Utah, and through the LDS Family History Centers.

§Extant Bishops' Transcripts, Marriage Licence Bonds and Allegations are located at the Oxfordshire Record Office, Oxford and the Wiltshire Record Office, Trowbridge.

‡Microfilm/microfiche copies available at above repository

*Printed or transcribed

##Microfiche copy available at the LDS Family History Library in Salt Lake City, Utah, and through the LDS Family History Centers.

Poor Law Union	1834–20C
Workhouse Records (some#)	
Roman Catholic Registers	19C–20C
School Records	19C–20C

PUBLICATIONS†

F. Hull, *Guide to the Berkshire Records Office* (1952) (OOP)
Leaflets/Lists:
    Finding Your Family: Sources for Genealogy in the
        Berkshire Record Office (1984)
    List of Parish Registers in the Berkshire Record Office

OTHER REPOSITORIES

The sources listed below include only those items reported on the Record Office Survey as located in the specified repositories. Each city and county library should have additional printed materials pertaining to its geographical area.

READING CENTRAL LIBRARY†
Reference Section
Blagrave Street, Reading RG2 9XD
Tel. 0734 55911

Census Returns‡# (England)	1841–1881
International Genealogical Index‡##	
(Berks, Bucks, Hants, Oxon, Wilts)	
Newspapers*	19C–20C

#Microfilm copy available at the LDS Family History Library in Salt Lake City, Utah, and through the LDS Family History Centers.
†For additional information send 2 Postal Reply Coupons or 31 pence of English postage for reply to North America; 34 pence to Australia and New Zealand.
‡Microfilm/microfiche copies available at above repository
##Microfiche copy available at the LDS Family History Library in Salt Lake City, Utah, and through the LDS Family History Centers.
*Printed or transcribed

LDS FAMILY HISTORY CENTRE†
280 The Meadway, Tilehurst
Reading, Berkshire
Tel. 0734 427524

LDS Family History Library Catalog‡##
International Genealogical Index‡##

GENEALOGICAL AND FAMILY HISTORY SOCIETIES

The societies listed below may have recorded Monumental (tombstone) Inscriptions, compiled an Index to Marriages (from the Parish Registers), an Index to the 1851 Census, and other special indexes, e.g., Strays, Members' Interests, for their geographical areas.** Each Society publishes a quarterly journal (listed in italics) which includes articles on family history, reports on the group's projects, and members' queries.

BERKSHIRE FAMILY HISTORY SOCIETY†
Mr. J. Gurnett, Secretary
Purley Lodge Cottage, Purley Lane
Purley on Thames, Berkshire R68 8AT

Berkshire Family History Society Journal

---

†For additional information send 2 Postal Reply Coupons or 31 pence of English postage for reply to North America; 34 pence to Australia and New Zealand.
‡Microfilm/microfiche copies available at above repository
##Microfiche copy available at the LDS Family History Library in Salt Lake City, Utah, and through the LDS Family History Centers.
**See *Current Publications by Member Societies* (annual), *List of Family History Project Coordinators*, 6th ed., and *Family History News and Digest* (biennial) — all published by the Federation of Family History Societies; available in the USA from the International Society for British Genealogy and Family History, P.O. Box 20425, Cleveland, OH 44120.

WINDSOR, SLOUGH AND DISTRICT
FAMILY HISTORY SOCIETY†
Mrs. S. Walton, Secretary
Flat 26, "In the Ray"
Ray Park Avenue
Maidenhead, Berkshire SL6 8DH

BUCKINGHAMSHIRE

Post-1974 Counties of England

The pre-1974 geographical boundaries of Buckinghamshire included the present county as well as the Slough area now in Berkshire.

Administratively, Buckingham and Wycombe (sometimes known as Chipping Wycombe and High Wycombe) were incorporated Boroughs between the sixteenth century and 1974.

99

RECORD OFFICE

BUCKINGHAMSHIRE RECORD OFFICE
County Offices,
Aylesbury, Buckinghamshire HP2O 1UA
Tel. 0296 382587

Hours: T-Th 9-5:15; F 9-4:45; closed M
By prior appointment: 1st Th/mo to 7:45
(Prior seat reservation for visit strongly advised)
Closed for stocktaking 2nd full week in February

Admission free; (Reader Ticket system to be introduced
in 1988. Write in advance for information.)
List of record searchers available upon request[†]

HOLDINGS

Church of England diocesan records for the Archdeaconry of Buckingham (Diocese of Lincoln to 1845, Diocese of Oxford 1845–); Church of England parish records including deposited Parish Registers for nearly 220 churches within the pre-1974 division of the county; local government records and other resources for the pre-1974 division of the county.

SOURCES THAT IDENTIFY AN INDIVIDUAL WITH A SPECIFIC LOCATION

Borough Records (Buckingham)	1533–1973
Freemen's Lists	1833–1915
Church of England (archidiaconal)	
Ecclesiastical Court Books	1521–1836
Ecclesiastical Visitations	1492–1833
Tithe Apportionments	1836–1850's
Church of England (parish)	
Churchwardens' Accounts	16C–20C

[†]For additional information send 2 Postal Reply Coupons or 31 pence of English postage for reply to North America; 34 pence to Australia and New Zealand.

Directories* (some#)
Business/Trade	1830–
Enclosure Awards*	18C–19C
Lay Subsidies*	1524
Maps	16C–20C
Militia Lists*‡#	1522, 1798
Parish Poor Law Records (some#)	17C–1834
Parish Poor Rates	
Protestation Returns‡#	1641
Poll Books* (some#)	(periodic) 1685–1868
Quarter Sessions	1718–1852‡#
Judicial Records	17C–1971
Land Tax Assessments#	1780–1832
Lists of Freeholders*	1723
Lists of Jurors	1769–1915
Registration of Papist Property*	1717–1748
Registers of Electors*	1832–
	(1832–1848#)

SOURCES THAT MAY ADDITIONALLY PROVIDE VITAL DATA AND/OR PROVE FAMILY RELATIONSHIPS

Borough Records (Buckingham)
Court	1534–1829
Church of England (archidiaconal)	
Bishops' Transcripts#	1600–1840
Marriage Licence Bonds	1633–1849
and Allegations (also*)	(1754–1852#)
Wills, Admon., Inven.#	1483–1858
Church of England (parish)	
Parish Registers#	1538–
Parish Register Transcripts*#	16C–19C

---

*Printed or transcribed
#Microfilm copy available at the LDS Family History Library in Salt Lake City, Utah, and through the LDS Family History Centers.
‡Microfilm/microfiche copies available at above repository

Estate and Family Papers	16C–20C
International Genealogical Index‡##	
(Bucks and adjacent counties)	
Manorial Records	14C–20C
Monumental Inscriptions*	18C–20C
Nonconformist Registers	
Baptist‡#	1773–1837
Independent (Congregational)‡#	1765–1837
Methodist‡#	1792–1837
Society of Friends‡#	17C–1837
Parish Poor Law Records	17C–1834
Apprenticeship Indentures	
Examinations	
Removal Orders	
Settlement Papers	
Poor Law Union	
Workhouse Records	1835–1948
(Winslow Union only)	
School Records	mainly 19C–20C
Title Deeds	13C–20C

PUBLICATIONS†

Leaflets/Lists:
List of Original Parish Registers Deposited
Notes for the Guidance of Genealogists (1987)

---

‡Microfilm/microfiche copies available at above repository

##Microfiche copy available at the LDS Family History Library in Salt Lake City, Utah, and through the LDS Family History Centers.

*Printed or transcribed

#Microfilm copy available at the LDS Family History Library in Salt Lake City, Utah, and through the LDS Family History Centers.

†For additional information send 2 Postal Reply Coupons or 31 pence of English postage for reply to North America; 34 pence to Australia and New Zealand.

OTHER REPOSITORIES

The sources listed below include only those items reported on the Record Office Survey as located in the specified repositories. Each city and county library should have additional printed materials pertaining to its geographical area.

BUCKINGHAMSHIRE COUNTY LIBRARY†
Reference Library
County Hall
Aylesbury, Buckinghamshire HP20 1VA
Tel. 0296 24671

Census‡#   1841–1881

GENEALOGICAL AND FAMILY HISTORY SOCIETIES

The societies listed below may have recorded Monumental (tombstone) Inscriptions, compiled an Index to Marriages (from the Parish Registers), an Index to the 1851 Census, and other special indexes, e.g., Strays, Members' Interests, for their geographical areas.** Each Society publishes a quarterly journal (listed in italics) which includes articles on family history, reports on the group's projects, and members' queries.

---

†For additional information send 2 Postal Reply Coupons or 31 pence of English postage for reply to North America; 34 pence to Australia and New Zealand.
‡Microfilm/microfiche copies available at above repository
#Microfilm copy available at the LDS Family History Library in Salt Lake City, Utah, and through the LDS Family History Centers.
**See *Current Publications by Member Societies* (annual), *List of Family History Project Coordinators*, 6th ed., and *Family History News and Digest* (biennial) — all published by the Federation of Family History Societies; available in the USA from the International Society for British Genealogy and Family History, P.O. Box 20425, Cleveland, OH 44120.

BUCKINGHAMSHIRE FAMILY HISTORY SOCIETY[†]
Mrs. E. McLaughlin, Secretary
18 Rudds Lane, Haddenhay
Aylesbury, Buckinghamshire HP17 8JP

 Origins

[†]For additional information send 2 Postal Reply Coupons or 31 pence of English postage for reply to North America; 34 pence to Australia and New Zealand.

CAMBRIDGESHIRE

Post-1974 Counties of England

Geographically the present Cambridgeshire contains the ancient county of Cambridgeshire (including the Isle of Ely), the ancient county of Huntingdonshire, and the Soke of Peterborough. The latter was originally part of the ancient county of Northamptonshire.

Administratively the Isle of Ely was virtually independent of the rest of the ancient county of Cambridgeshire from the tenth century until 1965, when it was united with Cambridgeshire to form the county of Cambridgeshire and Isle of Ely. The ancient county of Huntingdonshire was similarly united in 1965 with the Soke of Peterborough to form the administrative county of Huntingdon and Peterborough. In 1974 Huntingdon and Peterborough and Cambridgeshire and Isle of Ely were amalgamated to form the present county of Cambridgeshire.

Cambridge was called a borough in Domesday Book, 1086. Wisbech in the Isle of Ely was a borough from 1549. In Huntingdonshire, Huntingdon was also called a borough in Domesday, 1086, and Godmanchester was incorporated in 1604. The latter two were united to form a single borough in 1961. St. Ives became a borough in 1874. Peterborough was also a borough from 1874. All boroughs were abolished when local government was reformed in 1974.

RECORD OFFICES

COUNTY RECORD OFFICE, CAMBRIDGE
Shire Hall, Castle Hill, Cambridge CB3 0AP
Tel. 0223 317281 ext. 281

Hours: M-Th 9-12:45, 1:45-5:15; F 9-12:45, 1:45-4:15
      T 5:15-9 by prior appointment
      (Prior appointment advised for microfilm reader)

Admission free
List of record searchers available upon request[†]

HOLDINGS

Church of England parish records including deposited Parish Registers for approximately 180 churches in the pre-1974 division of Cambridgeshire and Isle of Ely; local government records and other resources for the pre-1974 division of the county.

(Church of England diocesan records for the Diocese of Ely are located in the Cambridge University Library. An area of the county around Newmarket was in the Diocese of Norwich

---

[†]For additional information send 2 Postal Reply Coupons or 31 pence of English postage for reply to North America; 34 pence to Australia and New Zealand.

until 1837. Bishops's Transcripts and most local probate records for this area are at the Suffolk Record Office, Bury St. Edwards; other diocesan records for the area are located at the Norfolk Record Office, Norwich.)

SOURCES THAT IDENTIFY AN INDIVIDUAL WITH A SPECIFIC LOCATION

Borough Records (Cambridge)	13C–20C
Freemen's Lists	1758–1848
Church of England (parish)	
Churchwardens' Accounts‡#	17C–20C
Vestry Minutes#	18C–19C
Directories* (some#)	
Business/Trade, Postal	
Enclosure Awards	1776–1889
Lay Subsidies‡#	1250–1611
Maps	
Parish Poor Law Records#	17C–1834
Parish Poor Rates	
Poll Books* (some#) (periodic)	1705–1868
Quarter Sessions (some#)	1660–1852
Judicial Records	
Cambridgeshire	1660–1971
Isle of Ely	1809–1971
Cambridge Borough	1733–1971
Hearth Tax Assessments‡#	1662–1678
Land Tax Assessments (some#)	1750–20C
Lists of Jurors	19C–20C
Registers of Electors*	1913–
Shipping – Crew Lists (Wisbech)	1863–1913

---

‡Microfilm/microfiche copies available at above repository
#Microfilm copy available at the LDS Family History Library in Salt Lake City, Utah, and through the LDS Family History Centers.
*Printed or transcribed

SOURCES THAT MAY ADDITIONALLY PROVIDE VITAL DATA AND/OR PROVE FAMILY RELATIONSHIPS

Borough Records (Cambridge)	13C–20C
Apprenticeship Registrations	
Boyd's Marriage Index[‡#]	1538–1625,
	1676–1837[††]
Census[‡#]	1841–1881
(ancient Cambs and Isle of Ely)[‡‡]	1871, 1881
Church of England (parish)	
Parish Registers[‡#]	1538–20C
Parish Register Transcripts[*#]	1538–20C
Estate and Family Papers	
International Genealogical Index[‡##]	
(Cambs and adjacent counties)	
Manorial Court Records[‡#]	14C–20C
Monumental Inscriptions[*]	
Nonconformist Registers	
Baptist[‡#]	1787–1837
Independent (Congregational)	1688–1837[‡#],
	1838–20C
Methodist [‡#]	1796–1837,
	1838–20C
Society of Friends	1648–1837[‡#],
	1839–20C
Parish Poor Law Records[‡#]	17C-1834
Apprenticeship Indentures	
Examinations	
Removal Orders	
Settlement Papers	

[‡]Microfilm/microfiche copies available at above repository
[#]Microfilm copy available at the LDS Family History Library in Salt Lake City, Utah, and through the LDS Family History Centers.
[††]With supplements
[‡‡]Indexed transcripts for 1851 for most parishes
[*]Printed or transcribed
[##]Microfiche copy available at the LDS Family History Library in Salt Lake City, Utah, and through the LDS Family History Centers.

Poor Law Union   1834–1930
    Workhouse Records
School Records   19C–20C
Title Deeds   13C–20C

PUBLICATIONS†

Michael Farrar, *Genealogical Sources in Cambridgeshire* (1979)

Guide to Education Records in the County Record Office, Cambridge

Summary Lists:
Parish Registers, Bishops' Transcripts, Registers on microfilm, Nonconformist Registers and Transcripts of Monumental Inscriptions.

Map of Parishes in Whole of new County

COUNTY RECORD OFFICE, HUNTINGDON

Grammar School Walk, Huntingdon PE18 6LF
Tel. 0480 425842

Hours: M-Th 9-12:45, 1:45-5:15; F 9-12:45, 1:45-4:15;
    By prior appointment only: 2nd S/mo 9-12

Admission free

List of record searchers available upon request†

HOLDINGS

Church of England diocesan records for the Archdeaconry of Huntingdon (Diocese of Lincoln to 1837, Diocese of Ely 1837–); Church of England parish records including deposited Parish Registers for more than 125 churches within the pre-1965 boundaries of Huntingdonshire; local government records and other resources of the pre-1974 division of the county. (Most Soke of Peterborough Records, however, are held by the Northamptonshire Record Office.)

---

†For additional information send 2 Postal Reply Coupons or 31 pence of English postage for reply to North America; 34 pence to Australia and New Zealand.

SOURCES THE IDENTIFY AN INDIVIDUAL
WITH A SPECIFIC LOCATION

Borough Records (Huntingdon,	1205–1974
Godmanchester, St. Ives)	
Freemen's Lists	1797–1896
Rates	1733–
Church of England (archidiaconal)	
Ecclesiastical Court Books	1559–1780
Ecclesiastical Visitations	1670–1876
Tithe Apportionments	1837–1936
Church of England (parish)	
Churchwardens' Accounts (some#)	1511–1973
Directories* (some#)	1784–1969
Postal	1847–1940
Enclosure Awards	1763–1884
Lay Subsidies‡#	1327–1664
Maps	1514–
Parish Poor Law Records	17C–mid-19C
Parish Poor Rates (some#)	
Poll Books* (some#) (periodic)	1768–1859
Protestation Returns*#	1641
Quarter Sessions	
Judicial Records	1734–20C
Hearth Tax Assessments‡#	1664–1674
Land Tax Assessments	1767,
	1798–1800,
	1804–1832
Lists of Freeholders	1767–1807
Registration of Papist Property	18C
Registers of Voters*	1835–1865

#Microfilm copy available at the LDS Family History Library in Salt Lake City, Utah, and through the LDS Family History Centers.
*Printed or transcribed
‡Microfilm/microfiche copies available at above repository

Registration of Electors*

1920, 1928–39,
1946–60, 1965,
1972–73,
1982–85

SOURCES THAT MAY ADDITIONALLY PROVIDE VITAL DATA AND/OR PROVE FAMILY RELATIONSHIPS

Borough Records (Huntingdon,	1205–1974
Godmanchester, St. Ives)	
Courts: H'don Q.S.	1765–1836
Ct. Pleas	1633–1782
God'r manor court books	1688–1878
Title Deeds	
Census‡#	1841–1881
(Hunts and Soke of Peterborough)	
Church of England (archidiaconal)	
Bishops' Transcripts#	1604–1858
Marriage Licence Bonds	1663–1883
and Allegations (some#)	
Wills, Admon., Inven.#	1479–1858
Church of England (parish)	
Parish Registers (some#)	1538–
Parish Register Transcripts* (some#)	16C–19C
Estate and Family Papers	c. 13C–20C
International Genealogical Index‡##	
(Hunts and adjacent counties)	
Manorial Records	1271–
Monumental Inscriptions	1377–1979

---

*Printed or transcribed

‡Microfilm/microfiche copies available at above repository

#Microfilm copy available at the LDS Family History Library in Salt Lake City, Utah, and through the LDS Family History Centers.

##Microfiche copy available at the LDS Family History Library in Salt Lake City, Utah, and through the LDS Family History Centers.

Nonconformist Registers
Baptist	1771-1837‡#, 1838-1963
Independent (Congregational)	1742-1807‡#, 1814-1835, 1893-1895
Methodist	1797-1837‡#, 1850-1970
Moravian	1823-1837‡#
Presbyterian	1820-1837‡#
Parish Poor Law Records (some#)	17C–mid-19C
Apprenticeship Indentures	
Churchwardens' Accounts	
Removal Orders	
Settlement Papers	
Poor Law Union	1834–
Workhouse Records	
School Records	19C
Title Deeds	14C–
Wills, Register Copies	1858–1932

PUBLICATIONS†

Michael Farrar, *Genealogical Sources in Cambridgeshire* (1979)

Guide to Education Records in the County Record Office, Cambridge (1972)

Map of Parishes in Whole of new County

---

‡Microfilm/microfiche copies available at above repository
#Microfilm copy available at the LDS Family History Library in Salt Lake City, Utah, and through the LDS Family History Centers.
†For additional information send 2 Postal Reply Coupons or 31 pence of English postage for reply to North America; 34 pence to Australia and New Zealand.

CAMBRIDGE UNIVERSITY LIBRARY
West Road, Cambridge CB3 9DR
Tel. 0223 337733 ext. 3143
Contact: Department of Manuscripts

Hours: By prior appointment only M-F 9:30-6:45; S 9:30-12:30
(No records produced 12:45-2, after 5)
Closed 1 week in September, Dec. 24-Jan.1, and
3 days at Easter
Seats not guaranteed 1 June-31 August

Admission free
List of record searchers available upon request[†]

HOLDINGS

Church of England diocesan records for the Diocese of Ely
(Cambridgeshire and the Isle of Ely, except for northeast Cambridgeshire).

SOURCES THAT IDENTIFY AN INDIVIDUAL
WITH A SPECIFIC LOCATION

Church of England (diocesan)
Ecclesiastical Court Books[††]   1374–1378;
                                        1552–1850
Ecclesiastical Visitations[††]   1549–1949
Tithe Apportionments   1838–1926
                             (mainly   1838–1845)

[†]For additional information send 2 Postal Reply Coupons or 31 pence of English
postage for reply to North America; 34 pence to Australia and New Zealand.
[††]Early records in Latin

113

*SOURCES THAT MAY ADDITIONALLY PROVIDE VITAL
DATA AND/OR PROVE FAMILY RELATIONSHIPS*

Church of England (diocesan)
Bishops' Transcripts#   1599–1875
Marriage Licence Bonds   1599–ca. 1850
and Allegations
Wills, Admon., Inven.#   1449–1858

PUBLICATIONS†

Dorothy M. Owen, *Ely Records* (1971)

OTHER REPOSITORIES

The sources listed below include only those items reported on the Record Office Survey as located in the specified repositories. Each city and county library should have additional printed materials pertaining to its geographical area.

LDS FAMILY HISTORY CENTRE†
670 Cherry Hinton Road
Cambridge
Tel. 0223 247010

LDS Family History Library Catalog‡##
International Genealogical Index‡##

#Microfilm copy available at the LDS Family History Library in Salt Lake City, Utah, and through the LDS Family History Centers.
†For additional information send 2 Postal Reply Coupons or 31 pence of English postage for reply to North America; 34 pence to Australia and New Zealand.
‡Microfilm/microfiche copies available at above repository
##Microfiche copy available at the LDS Family History Library in Salt Lake City, Utah, and through the LDS Family History Centers.

GENEALOGICAL AND FAMILY HISTORY SOCIETIES

The societies listed below may have recorded Monumental (tombstone) Inscriptions, compiled an Index to Marriages (from the Parish Registers), an Index to the 1851 Census, and other special indexes, e.g., Strays, Members' Interests, for their geographical areas.** Each Society publishes a quarterly journal (listed in italics) which includes articles on family history, reports on the group's projects, and members' queries.

CAMBRIDGESHIRE FAMILY HISTORY SOCIETY†
Mrs. J. Hulyer, Secretary
32 Lady Walk
Longstanton, Cambridgeshire CB4 5ED

Journal of the Cambridgeshire Family History Society

HUNTINGDONSHIRE FAMILY HISTORY SOCIETY†
Mrs. K.J. Wright, Secretary
16 Horseshoes Way
Brampton, Cambridgeshire PE18 8TN

PETERBOROUGH AND DISTRICT FAMILY HISTORY SOCIETY†
Mrs. D. Butler, Secretary
511 Fulbridge Road, Werrington
Peterborough, Cambridgeshire PE4 6SB

**See *Current Publications by Member Societies* (annual), *List of Family History Project Coordinators*, 6th ed., and *Family History News and Digest* (biennial) — all published by the Federation of Family History Societies; available in the USA from the International Society for British Genealogy and Family History, P.O. Box 20425, Cleveland, OH 44120.

†For additional information send 2 Postal Reply Coupons or 31 pence of English postage for reply to North America; 34 pence to Australia and New Zealand.

CHESHIRE

Post-1974 Counties of England

The pre-1974 geographical boundaries of Cheshire included the district of Wirral (Birkenhead and Wallasey) now in Merseyside County; the northern border area of Stockport, Trafford and Tameside districts now in Greater Manchester County; and the northeastern tip (Tintwistle) now in Derbyshire. Present boundaries include the remainder of the pre-1974 area, and additionally Hale, Warrington, and Widnes which previously formed the southern border of Lancashire.

Administratively the city of Chester was designated a County Corporate between 1506 and 1889, and a County Borough from 1889 to 1974. Other County Boroughs included Stockport and Birkenhead (1889–1974) and Wallasey (1913–1974). Incorporated Boroughs included Congleton (thirteenth century to 1974), Macclesfield (nineteenth century to 1974). Stockport and Birkenhead were also nineteenth-century Municipal Boroughs prior to 1889.

RECORD OFFICES

CHESHIRE RECORD OFFICE
Duke Street, Chester CH1 1RL
Tel. 0244 602574

Hours: M-F 9-4:30
     (Prior appointment necessary to
     view some records)

Admission free
List of record searchers available upon request†

HOLDINGS
Church of England diocesan record (Diocese of Chester); Church of England parish records including deposited Parish Registers for approximately 280 churches in the pre-1974 division of the county; civil records and other resources for the pre-1974 county area, excepting the city of Chester and the County Palatine of Chester.

SOURCES THAT IDENTIFY AN INDIVIDUAL
WITH A SPECIFIC LOCATION

Borough Records (Congleton, Crewe,	17C–20C
Hyde, Macclesfield, Warrington)	
Freemen's Lists	1770–1888
Rates	19C–20C

---

†For additional information send 2 Postal Reply Coupons or 31 pence of English postage for reply to North America; 34 pence to Australia and New Zealand.

Church of England (diocesan)

Ecclesiastical Court Books††	1502–1927
Ecclesiastical Visitations††	1578–1694
Tithe Apportionments	1838–1851

Church of England (parish)

Churchwardens' Accounts		1554–1781
Enclosure Awards		1767–1898
Maps‡‡		16C–
Militia Lists		1760–1815
Parish Poor Law Records		17C–19C
Parish Poor Rates		
Poll Books* (some#)	(periodic)	1714–1831
Quarter Sessions		
Judicial Records*		17C–1888
		(1559–1760#)
Hearth Tax Assessments‡#		1663, 1664,
		1665, 1674
Land Tax Assessments#		1780–1832
Lists of Jurors		16C–20C
Registration of Papist Property		1715–1759
Registers of Electors* (some#)		1832–
Shipping – Crew Lists		1861–1913

SOURCES THAT MAY ADDITIONALLY PROVIDE VITAL DATA AND/OR PROVE FAMILY RELATIONSHIPS

Borough Records (Congleton, Crewe,	17C–20C
Hyde, Macclesfield, Warrington)	
Court	
Title Deeds	
Census‡#	1841–1881

---

†† Early records in Latin
‡‡ Also for Lancashire and Yorkshire
* Printed or transcribed
# Microfilm copy available at the LDS Family History Library in Salt Lake City, Utah, and through the LDS Family History Centers.
‡ Microfilm/microfiche copies available at above repository

Church of England (diocesan)
  Bishops's Transcripts   16C–20C
  Marriage Licence Bonds
    and Allegations*‡#   1606–1965
  Wills, Admin., Inven.‡#   1492–1857
Church of England (parish)
  Parish Registers   1538–1979
  Parish Register Transcripts* (few#)   16C–19C
  Estate and Family Papers (some#)   12C–19C
  Manorial Records (some#)   15C–19C
  Monumental Inscriptions‡#*   17C–20C
  Nonconformist Registers
    Baptist‡#   1793–1838
    Independent/Congregational (some#)   1785–20C
    Methodist   1770–1837,‡#
        1838–20C
    Presbyterian‡#   1676–1837
    Society of Friends‡#   1648–1837
    Unitarian (some#)   1749–20C
  Parish Poor Law Records   17C–19C
    Apprenticeship Indentures
    Examinations
    Removal Orders
    Settlement Papers
  Poor Law Union
    Workhouse Records   1836–1929
  School Records   16C–20C
  Title Deeds   13C–20C
  Wills, Register Copies#   1858–1940

---

*Printed or transcribed
‡Microfilm/microfiche copies available at above repository
#Microfilm copy available at the LDS Family History Library in Salt Lake City, Utah, and through the LDS Family History Centers.

PUBLICATIONS†

Summary Guide to Cheshire Record Office

Source Sheets: (free on individual basis)
County Council Records, Private Collections, Diocesan Records, Society of Friends Cheshire Monthly Meetings, Methodist Records, Ecclesiastical Parish Records, Township and Civil Parish Records, Quarter Sessions, Militia Records, Public Records, Probate Records, School Records, Printed Maps, Congregational Records, Unitarian Records, Baptist Records, Family History, Clerical Records, Transportation Records, Nonconformist Records, Catholic Ancestors, and House History.

(Individual sheets are available upon request; the *Summary Guide* includes all Source Sheets.)

CHESTER CITY RECORD OFFICE

Town Hall, Chester CH1 2HJ
Tel. 0244 40144 ext. 2108

Hours: M 9-1, 2-9; T-F 9-1, 2-5;
       M after 5 by prior appointment

Admission free
Name of local record searcher available upon request†

HOLDINGS

Local government records (including Quarter Sessions) and other resources pertaining to the city of Chester.

---

†For additional information send 2 Postal Reply Coupons or 31 pence of English postage for reply to North America; 34 pence to Australia and New Zealand.

SOURCES THAT IDENTIFY AN INDIVIDUAL
WITH A SPECIFIC LOCATION

Borough Records‡ (Chester)	12C–20C
Accounts and Rentals	1436–1835
Freemen's Lists	1538–
Directories* (some#)	1781–1974
Electoral Records	
Burgess Rolls and Lists	1835–78
Parliamentary Voters Lists	1832–78,
	1832–1841#
Poll Books* (some#)	1733–1837
Registers of Electors*	1879–
Lay Subsidies	1601–1771
Maps	
Militia Lists	1804–1872
Quarter Sessions	
Judicial Records	1506–1971
Assessments	1641–1813
Lists of Jurors	1608–1817
Transportation Records	1731–75
City Gaol & House of	1802–72
Corrections Records	

SOURCES THAT MAY ADDITIONALLY PROVIDE VITAL
DATA AND/OR PROVE FAMILY RELATIONSHIPS

Borough Records‡ (Chester)	
Court	1295–
Guild: Apprenticeship Enrolments	15C–20C
Admissions	15C–20C
Title Deeds	c. 1347–1935
Census‡# (Chester)	1851, 1861,
	1881

---

‡Microfilm/microfiche copies available at above repository
*Printed or transcribed
#Microfilm copy available at the LDS Family History Library in Salt Lake City, Utah, and through the LDS Family History Centers.

Estate and Family Papers
Nonconformist Records
    Independent (Congregational)   1706–1975
    Methodist   1788–1982
    Presbyterian   1847–1982
    Unitarian   1641–1928
Nonconformist Registers
    Congregational   1848–1957
    Methodist   1839–1983
Poor Law Union Records   1850–1948
School Records   19C–20C

PUBLICATIONS[†]

Chester City Record Office: Sources for Genealogical Research (free)

Annette M. Kennett, *Archives and Records of the City of Chester* (1985)

OTHER REPOSITORIES

The sources listed below include only those items reported on the Record Office Survey as located in the specified repositories. Each city and county library should have additional printed materials pertaining to its geographical area.

LDS FAMILY HISTORY CENTRE[†]
30 Clifton Drive, Blacon, Chester
Tel. 0244 390796

LDS Family History Library Catalog[‡##]
International Genealogical Index[‡##]

[†]For additional information send 2 Postal Reply Coupons or 31 pence of English postage for reply to North America; 34 pence to Australia and New Zealand.
[‡]Microfilm/microfiche copies available at above repository
[##]Microfiche copy available at the LDS Family History Library in Salt Lake City, Utah, and through the LDS Family History Centers.

GENEALOGICAL AND FAMILY HISTORY SOCIETIES

The societies listed below may have recorded Monumental (tombstone) Inscriptions, compiled an Index to Marriages (from the Parish Registers), an Index to the 1851 Census, and other special indexes, e.g., Strays, Members' Interests, for their geographical areas.** Each Society publishes a quarterly journal (listed in italics) which includes articles on family history, reports on the group's projects, and members' queries.

FAMILY HISTORY SOCIETY OF CHESHIRE†
Mrs. D. Foxcroft, Research Advisor
5 Gordon Avenue, Bromborough
Wirral L62 6AL

Family History Society of Cheshire Journal

NORTH CHESHIRE FAMILY HISTORY SOCIETY†
Mrs. Rhoda Clarke, Secretary
2 Denham Drive
Bramhall
Stockport SK7 2AT

North Cheshire Family Historian

**See *Current Publications by Member Societies* (annual), *List of Family History Project Coordinators*, 6th ed., and *Family History News and Digest* (biennial) — all published by the Federation of Family History Societies; available in the USA from the International Society for British Genealogy and Family History, P.O. Box 20425, Cleveland, OH 44120.

†For additional information send 2 Postal Reply Coupons or 31 pence of English postage for reply to North America; 34 pence to Australia and New Zealand.

CLEVELAND

Post-1974 Counties of England

The county of Cleveland was created in 1974. Geographically it includes the areas of Stockton and Hartlepool which
previously formed the southeastern border of County Durham;
also the areas of Loftus and Guisborough formerly in the North
Riding of Yorkshire.

Administratively, Stockton-on-Tees and Hartlepool were
incorporated Boroughs in Durham from the seventeenth century
to 1968 and 1967, respectively. Middlesbrough and West Hartlepool were mid-nineteenth century Municipal Boroughs, and
then County Boroughs from 1889 and 1902 to 1968 and 1974,
respectively. Redcar and Thornaby-on-Tees were twentieth-

century Municipal Boroughs to 1968. That year the County Borough of Teeside was created, which included the former County Borough of Middlesbrough and Municipal Boroughs of Redcar, Stockton-on-Tees and Thornaby on Tees.

See the Record Offices in the counties of Durham and North Yorkshire for sources pertaining to localities in the respective pre-1974 counties.

RECORD OFFICE

CLEVELAND COUNTY ARCHIVES DEPARTMENT
Exchange House, 6 Martin Road
Middlesbrough, Cleveland TS1 1DB
Tel. 0642 248321

Hours: M-Th 9-1, 2-4:30; F 9-1, 2-4
        (Prior appointment needed to consult records)

Admission free

List of record searchers available upon request[†]

HOLDINGS

Church of England parish records including deposited Parish Registers for approximately 50 churches within the county; other resources pertaining to the present county area.

(Church of England diocesan records for the northern and western parts of the county are located at the University of Durham, Dept. of Palæography and Diplomatic, Durham; those for the southeastern part of the county are in the Borthwick Institute in York.)

[†]For additional information send 2 Postal Reply Coupons or 31 pence of English postage for reply to North America; 34 pence to Australia and New Zealand.

SOURCES THAT IDENTIFY AN INDIVIDUAL WITH A SPECIFIC LOCATION

Church of England (diocesan)	
Tithe Apportionments[§]	1768–1914
Church of England (parish)	
Churchwardens' Accounts	18C–19C
Enclosure Awards	1810–1864
Land Tax Assessments[‡#]	1781–1827
Parish Poor Law Records	
Parish Poor Rates	1780–20C
Poll Books* (some[#])	1841–1870
(Middlesbrough)	
Registers of Electors[‡#]	
(Yorkshire, N. Riding)	1832–1875
(Middlesbrough)	1853–1956

SOURCES THAT MAY ADDITIONALLY PROVIDE VITAL DATA AND/OR PROVE FAMILY RELATIONSHIPS

Boyd's Marriage Index[‡#]	1538–1837
(Durh and Yorks)	
Census[‡#] (for present county)	1841–1881
Church of England (parish)	
Parish Registers (also[‡#])	1539–20C
Monumental Inscriptions	1794–1968
Nonconformist Registers	
Congregational[‡#]	19C–20C
Methodist	19C–20C
Presbyterian	1843–20C

[§]Parish copies only; Church of England diocesan records are located at the University of Durham and the Borthwick Institute.

[‡]Microfilm/microfiche copies available at above repository

[#]Microfilm copy available at the LDS Family History Library in Salt Lake City, Utah, and through the LDS Family History Centers.

*Printed or transcribed

Parish Poor Law Records	17C–1888
Apprenticeship Indentures	1718–1830
Removal Orders	1780–1833
Settlement Papers	1699–1833
Poor Law Union	
Workhouse Records	1837–1930
Roman Catholic Registers‡#	1783–1840
School Records	19C–20C

PUBLICATIONS†

Leaflet: *Sources for Genealogical Study in the Cleveland County Archives Department* (free)

OTHER REPOSITORIES

The sources listed below include only those items reported on the Record Office Survey as located in the specified repositories. Each city and county library should have additional printed materials pertaining to its geographical area.

CLEVELAND CENTRAL LIBRARY†
Victoria Square, Middlesbrough
Cleveland TS1 2AY
Tel. 0642 248155 ext. 3357

International Genealogical Index‡##
(British Isles)

---

‡Microfilm/microfiche copies available at above repository
#Microfilm copy available at the LDS Family History Library in Salt Lake City, Utah, and through the LDS Family History Centers.
†For additional information send 2 Postal Reply Coupons or 31 pence of English postage for reply to North America; 34 pence to Australia and New Zealand.
##Microfiche copy available at the LDS Family History Library in Salt Lake City, Utah, and through the LDS Family History Centers.

LDS FAMILY HISTORY CENTRE†
The Linkway
Billingham, Cleveland TS23 3HJ
Tel. 0642 563162

LDS Family History Library Catalog‡##
International Genealogical Index‡##

GENEALOGICAL AND FAMILY HISTORY SOCIETIES

The societies listed below may have recorded Monumental (tombstone) Inscriptions, compiled an Index to Marriages (from the Parish Registers), an Index to the 1851 Census, and other special indexes, e.g., Strays, Members' Interests, for their geographical areas.** Each Society publishes a quarterly journal (listed in italics) which includes articles on family history, reports on the group's projects, and members' queries.

CLEVELAND FAMILY HISTORY SOCIETY†
Mr. A. Sampson, Secretary
1 Oxgang Close
Redcar, Cleveland TS10 4ND

Cleveland Family History Society Journal

---

†For additional information send 2 Postal Reply Coupons or 31 pence of English postage for reply to North America; 34 pence to Australia and New Zealand.
‡Microfilm/microfiche copies available at above repository
##Microfiche copy available at the LDS Family History Library in Salt Lake City, Utah, and through the LDS Family History Centers.
**See *Current Publications by Member Societies* (annual), *List of Family History Project Coordinators*, 6th ed., and *Family History News and Digest* (biennial) — all published by the Federation of Family History Societies; available in the USA from the International Society for British Genealogy and Family History, P.O. Box 20425, Cleveland, OH 44120.

CORNWALL

Post-1974 Counties of England

There was no change in the geographical boundaries of Cornwall during the 1974 reorganization of local government in England.

Administratively Bodmin, Falmouth, Helston, Launceston, Liskeard, Penzance, Penryn, Saltash, St. Ives and Truro were all incorporated Boroughs from the seventeenth century to 1974.

RECORD OFFICE

CORNWALL RECORD OFFICE

County Hall, Truro TR1 3AY

Tel. 0872 73698

Hours: T-Th 9:30-1, 2-5; F 9:30-1, 2-4:30;
S 9-12 (except before Bank Holidays)
Prior appointment needed to see records
(Closed for stocktaking 2 weeks in December)

Admission free

Genealogical search service available[†]

N.B.: The Cornwall Record Office is closed for remodeling until Spring 1988. However, research by correspondence is continuing.

HOLDINGS

Church of England diocesan records for the Archdeaconry of Cornwall (Diocese of Exeter to 1876; Church of England parish records including deposited Parish Registers for approximately 200 churches in the county; local government records and other resources for the county.

(Marriage Licence Bonds and Allegations and some Bishops' Transcripts are located at the Devon Record Office, Exeter.)

SOURCES THAT IDENTIFY AN INDIVIDUAL WITH A SPECIFIC LOCATION

Borough Records (Bodmin, Helston,   14C–20C
Liskeard, Penryn, St. Ives,
Truro, East Looe[§], West Looe[§],
Lostwithiel[§], Launceston, Penzance)
Freemen's Lists
Rates

[†]For additional information send 2 Postal Reply Coupons or 31 pence of English postage for reply to North America; 34 pence to Australia and New Zealand.
[§]Parliamentary Borough only

Church of England (archidiaconal)
Tithe Apportionments   1836–1846
Church of England (parish)
Churchwardens' Accounts   16C–19C
Directories* (some#)   late 18C–
Enclosure Awards (few)   1821–1882
Maps   17C–19C
Parish Poor Law Records
Parish Poor Rates   1601–1834
Quarter Sessions
Judicial Records   18C–20C

*SOURCES THAT MAY ADDITIONALLY PROVIDE VITAL
DATA AND/OR PROVE FAMILY RELATIONSHIPS*

Borough Records (Bodmin, Helston,   14C–20C
Liskeard, Penryn, St. Ives,
Truro, East Looe§, West Looe§,
Lostwithiel§, Launceston, Penzance)
Court
Title Deeds and Leases
Census‡#   1841–1871
Church of England (archidiaconal)
Bishops' Transcripts††   (gaps) 1677–1772
Wills#   1600–1857
Church of England (Parish)
Parish Registers#   1538–20C
Estate and Family Papers (some#)   17C–19C

---

*Printed or transcribed
#Microfilm copy available at the LDS Family History Library in Salt Lake City, Utah, and through the LDS Family History Centers.
§Parliamentary Borough only
‡Microfilm/microfiche copies available at above repository
††Some Bishops' Transcripts also at Devon Record Office, Exeter.

Nonconformist Registers
Baptist   18C–19C
Methodist   1837–20C
Society of Friends (some#)   17C–20C
Parish Poor Law Records   1601–1834
Apprenticeship Indentures
Examinations
Removal Orders
Settlement Papers
Poor Law Union
Workhouse Records   1834–
School Records   1863–
Title Deeds   13C–20C

PUBLICATIONS†

Cornwall Record Office: A Brief Guide to Sources (1985)
Leaflets/Lists:
  Guide to Cornish Family History Sources (1984)
  List of Methodist Registers
  List of Parish Registers
A complete list of publications is available upon request.†

#Microfilm copy available at the LDS Family History Library in Salt Lake City, Utah, and through the LDS Family History Centers.
†For additional information send 2 Postal Reply Coupons or 31 pence of English postage for reply to North America; 34 pence to Australia and New Zealand.

GENEALOGICAL AND FAMILY HISTORY SOCIETIES

The societies listed below may have recorded Monumental (tombstone) Inscriptions, compiled an Index to Marriages (from the Parish Registers), an Index to the 1851 Census, and other special indexes, e.g., Strays, Members' Interests, for their geographical areas.** Each Society publishes a quarterly journal (listed in italics) which includes articles on family history, reports on the group's projects, and members' queries.

CORNWALL FAMILY HISTORY SOCIETY†
Mr. M. Martyn, Secretary
Chimney Pots, Sunny Corner
Cusgarne, Truro, Cornwall TR4 8SE

Cornwall Family History Society Journal

**See *Current Publications by Member Societies* (annual), *List of Family History Project Coordinators*, 6th ed., and *Family History News and Digest* (biennial) — all published by the Federation of Family History Societies; available in the USA from the International Society for British Genealogy and Family History, P.O. Box 20425, Cleveland, OH 44120.

†For additional information send 2 Postal Reply Coupons or 31 pence of English postage for reply to North America; 34 pence to Australia and New Zealand.

CUMBERLAND

Pre-1974 Counties of England

The county of Cumberland was abolished in 1974. The area within its boundaries was united with the area of the former county of Westmorland, the Furness area formerly in Lancashire, and the Sedbergh district of the former West Riding of Yorkshire, to establish a new county called Cumbria.

Administratively Carlisle was an incorporated Borough in Cumberland from the seventeenth century to 1889 and a County Borough between 1889 and 1974. Whitehaven and Workington were Municipal Boroughs from 1894 and 1888, respectively, to 1974.

See Cumbria Record Office, Carlisle, for genealogical resources pertaining to the former county of Cumberland.

CUMBRIA

Post-1974 Counties of England

The county of Cumbria was created in 1974. Geographically it includes the former counties of Cumberland and West-morland, the Furness area formerly in Lancashire, and the Sedbergh district of the former West Riding of Yorkshire.

Administratively Carlisle, located in the former county of Cumberland, was an incorporated Borough from the seven-teenth century to 1889 and a County Borough between 1889 and 1974. Whitehaven and Workington, also located in that county before 1974, were Municipal Boroughs from 1894 and 1888, respectively, to 1974. Kendal, formerly in Westmorland County, was a Municipal Borough from 1575 to 1974. Barrow-in-

135

Furness was a Municipal Borough in Lancashire from 1867 to 1889, and then a County Borough to 1974.

RECORD OFFICES

CUMBRIA RECORD OFFICE
(Formerly Cumberland County Record Office)
The Castle, Carlisle CA3 8UR
Tel. 0228 23456 ext. 2416

Hours: M-F 9-5;
       Closed Bank Holidays;
       closed Easter Tuesday and
       Spring Bank Holiday Tuesday

Admission free
List of record searchers available upon request[†]

HOLDINGS

Church of England diocesan records (Wills, Marriage Licence Bonds and Allegations for the Diocese of Carlisle only); Bishops' Transcripts for the entire former county of Cumberland; Church of England parish records including deposited Parish Registers for approximately 180 churches located in the pre-1974 county of Cumberland; local government records and other resources for the former county.

(Church of England diocesan records — Wills, Marriage Licence Bonds and Allegations — for the Archdeaconry of Richmond (southwestern part of the former county of Cumberland) are located at the Lancashire Record Office, Preston.)

[†]For additional information send 2 Postal Reply Coupons or 31 pence of English postage for reply to North America; 34 pence to Australia and New Zealand.

SOURCES THAT IDENTIFY AN INDIVIDUAL
WITH A SPECIFIC LOCATION

Borough Records (Carlisle)
Freemen's Lists		1612–1835
Rates		1907–

Church of England (diocesan)
Ecclesiastical Court Books		1571–1910
Ecclesiastical Visitations		1606–1955
Tithe Apportionments		1837–1852

Church of England (parish)
Churchwardens' Accounts	mainly	18C–20C

Directories* (some#)
Business/Trade	mainly	1811–1938
Enclosure Awards		1699–late 19C
Lay Subsidies*		1333
Maps	mainly	18C–20C
Militia Lists#	(gaps)	1797–1830
Parish Poor Law Records		17C–1834
Parish Poor Rates	(gaps) mainly	18C–19C
Poll Books* (some#)	(periodic)	late 17C–1832
Protestation Returns*#		1641

Quarter Sessions
Judicial Records		1668–20C

Hearth Tax Assessments*#
Co. Cumberland		1664
Carlisle		1673
Land Tax Assessments	(gaps)	1760–1831
Lists of Freeholders		1714–1869
Lists of Jurors		1720–1822˙
Registration of Papist Property		18C
Registers of Electors*		1832–1974
Shipping – Crew Lists		1863–1912

---

*Printed or transcribed

#Microfilm copy available at the LDS Family History Library in Salt Lake City, Utah, and through the LDS Family History Centers.

*SOURCES THAT MAY ADDITIONALLY PROVIDE VITAL
DATA AND / OR PROVE FAMILY RELATIONSHIPS*

Borough Records (Carlisle)
Court of Common Council	1639–1836
Freeholders' Court	1636/7–1693
Quarter Sessions	1766–1885
Guild: Apprenticeship Enrolments	1675–1849
Admissions	1580–1950
Title Deeds	13C–20C
Cemetery Registers	1855–1939
Census‡# (Cumbld)	1841, 1851

Church of England (diocesan)
Bishops' Transcripts#		1660–late 19C
Marriage Licence Bonds	(gaps)	1668–1824
and Allegations		
Wills, Admon., Inven.#		1564–1858

Church of England (parish)
Parish Registers		1538–
Parish Register Transcripts*#		16C–19C
Estate and Family Papers	mainly	17C–
Manorial Records		15C–20C
Monumental Inscriptions*		
Nonconformist Registers		
Independent/Congregational (some#)		1651–
Methodist (some#)		1823–
Presbyterian (some#)		1712–
Society of Friends (some#)		1648–
Parish Poor Law Records		18C –1834
Apprenticeship Indentures		
Examinations		
Removal Orders	mainly	18C–19C
Settlement Papers	mainly	18C–19C

‡Microfilm/microfiche copies available at above repository
#Microfilm copy available at the LDS Family History Library in Salt Lake City,
Utah, and through the LDS Family History Centers.
*Printed or transcribed

138

Poor Law Union	1834–20C
Workhouse Records	
School Records	mainly 19C–20C
Title Deeds	mainly 17C–20C
Wills, Register Copies	1727–1941

PUBLICATIONS†

Leaflets:

Notes for Genealogical Searches in Cumberland and Westmorland (1987)

Sources for Family Historians (1987)

Cumbria Parish Map

CUMBRIA RECORD OFFICE

(formerly Westmorland County Record Office)
County Hall, Kendal LA9 4RQ
Tel. 0539 21000 ext. 329
Contact: County Archivist

Hours: M-F 9-5

Admission free
List of record searchers available upon request†

HOLDINGS

Church of England diocesan records: Bishops' Transcripts for the entire former county of Westmorland; Church of England parish records including deposited Parish Registers for approximately 100 churches located in the pre-1974 County of Westmorland as well as for Sedbergh, Garsdale, and Dent formerly in Yorkshire, and some parishes in eastern Furness

---

†For additional information send 2 Postal Reply Coupons or 31 pence of English postage for reply to North America; 34 pence to Australia and New Zealand.

formerly in Lancashire; local government records and other
resources pertaining to the former county of Westmorland.
(Other diocesan records, i.e., Wills, Marriage Licence
Bonds and Allegations, for the Diocese of Carlisle – northern
half of the former county of Westmorland – are at the Cumbria
Record Office, Carlisle. Those for the Archdeaconry of Richmond – southern half of the former county of Westmorland –
are located at the Lancashire Record Office, Preston.)

SOURCES THAT IDENTIFY AN INDIVIDUAL
WITH A SPECIFIC LOCATION

Borough Records (Kendal, Appleby)	17C–19C
Freemen's Lists	
Rates	
Census Returns	1787
(mainly Northern Westmorland)	
Church of England (diocesan)	
Tithe Apportionments§	1836–1850's
Church of England (parish)	
Churchwardens' Accounts	1588–20C
Directories* (some#)	
Business/Trade	1781–1938
Enclosure Awards	1760–1890
List of Inhabitants	1695
Maps	17C–20C
Parish Poor Law Records	17C–1834
Parish Poor Rates	
Poll Books* (some#)	(periodic) 18C–19C

---

§Also includes former County of Cumberland.
*Printed or transcribed
#Microfilm copy available at the LDS Family History Library in Salt Lake City,
Utah, and through the LDS Family History Centers.

Quarter Sessions
  Judicial Records   17C–1971
  Hearth Tax Assessments*#
    (Kendal)   1669
    (county except Kendal)   1674
  Land Tax Assessments#   1765–1832
  Lists of Jurors#   1775–20C
  Registration of Papist Property#   18C
  Transportation Bonds   18C
Registers of Electors*   1832–1983

*SOURCES THAT MAY ADDITIONALLY PROVIDE VITAL
DATA AND / OR PROVE FAMILY RELATIONSHIPS*

Borough Records (Kendal, Appleby)   17C–19C
  Court
  Guilds: Apprenticeship Enrolments
          Admissions
  Title Deeds
Cemetery Registers#   1855–1940
Church of England (diocesan)
  Bishops' Transcripts#   1644–1895
Church of England (parish)
  Parish Registers   1538–20C
  Parish Register Transcripts*#   16C–19C
Estate and Family Papers   13C–20C
International Genealogical Index‡##
  (Westmld and Cumbld)
Manorial Records   17C–20C
Monumental Inscriptions*   17C–20C
Newspapers*   19C–20C

---

*Printed or transcribed

#Microfilm copy available at the LDS Family History Library in Salt Lake City, Utah, and through the LDS Family History Centers.

‡Microfilm/microfiche copies available at above repository

##Microfiche copy available at the LDS Family History Library in Salt Lake City, Utah, and through the LDS Family History Centers.

Nonconformist Registers

Congregational	1775–1837#,
	1910–1938
Inghamite	1754–1837#,
	1832–1880
Methodist	1797–1837#,
	1837–1960
Presbyterian	1773–1858*
Society of Friends Digests	1635–1837
Unitarian (formerly Presbyterian)	1687–1840#
Parish Poor Law Records	17C–1834
Apprenticeship Indentures	
Examinations	
Removal Orders	
Settlement Papers	
Poor Law Union	1834–20C
Workhouse Records#	
Roman Catholic Records	18C–20C
School Records	16C–20C
Title Deeds	13C–20C

PUBLICATIONS†

Lists of Holdings of Parish Registers (1986)

H.W. Hodgson, comp., *A Bibliography of the History and Topography of Cumberland and Westmorland* (1968)

E.M. Wilson, comp., *Much Cry of Kendal Wool: An Anthology 1420–1720* (1980)

Maps:

Church of England Parishes in Cumbria, 1829

John Todd's Plan of Kendal, 1787

John Wood's Plan of Kendal, 1833

Henry Hogarth's Plan of Kendal, 1853

#Microfilm copy available at the LDS Family History Library in Salt Lake City, Utah, and through the LDS Family History Centers.

*Printed or transcribed

†For additional information send 2 Postal Reply Coupons or 31 pence of English postage for reply to North America; 34 pence to Australia and New Zealand.

CUMBRIA RECORD OFFICE, BARROW
140 Duke Street
Barrow-in-Furness LA14 1XW
Tel. 0229 31269
Hours: M-F 9-5
Admission free

HOLDINGS

Church of England parish records including deposited Parish Registers for churches in the Furness and South-West Cumberland areas; local government records and other resources pertaining to the areas.

(Some local government records and other resources are located at the Lancashire Record Office, Preston. Some Church of England diocesan records, for the Archdeaconry of Richmond, Western Deaneries, Diocese of Chester, i.e., Marriage Licence Bonds and Allegations, Wills, are also there.)

SOURCES THAT IDENTIFY AN INDIVIDUAL WITH A SPECIFIC LOCATION

Borough Records (Barrow-in-Furness)	1867–c. 1970
Rates[††]	
Church of England (archidiaconal)	
Tithe Apportionments[§]	1830's–1840's
Church of England (parish)	
Churchwardens' Accounts	18C–20C
Directories* (some[#])	
Business/Trade	1829–1963
Enclosure Awards (few)	c. 1800–1868
Maps	mostly 19C–20C

[††]Very limited for Barrow. Rather more complete for Dalton-in-Furness U.D.C., and Ulverston U.D.C., late 19C–20 C.

[§]Parish copies only

*Printed or transcribed

[#]Microfilm copy available at the LDS Family History Library in Salt Lake City, Utah, and through the LDS Family History Centers.

*SOURCES THAT MAY ADDITIONALLY PROVIDE VITAL
DATA AND/OR PROVE FAMILY RELATIONSHIPS*

Borough Records (Barrow-in-Furness)	1867–1970
Church of England (archidiaconal)	
Bishops' Transcripts#	(gaps) 1634–1914
(Furness)	
Church of England (parish)	
Parish Registers	1539–c. 1980
Parish Register Transcripts*	
Estate and Family Papers	1650–1970
Manorial Court Records	1740–1930
Nonconformist Registers	
Methodist	c. 1862–1980's
Presbyterian	1909–1957
Quaker (some#)	c. 1658–20C
Parish Poor Law Records (few)	18C–19C
Apprenticeship Indentures	
Examinations	
Removal Orders	
Settlement Papers	
Poor Law Union	
Workhouse Records	1835–1920
School Records	1870–1980's
Title Deeds	16C–20C
Wills, Register Copies	18C–20C

PUBLICATIONS†

*List of Parish Registers in the Cumbria Record Offices at
Carlisle, Kendal, and Barrow*
List of Parish Register Holdings at Barrow (free)
Map of Church of England parishes in Cumbria (rev. 1985)

#Microfilm copy available at the LDS Family History Library in Salt Lake City,
Utah, and through the LDS Family History Centers.
*Printed or transcribed
†For additional information send 2 Postal Reply Coupons or 31 pence of English
postage for reply to North America; 34 pence to Australia and New Zealand.

OTHER REPOSITORIES

The sources listed below include only those items reported on the Record Office Survey as located in the specified repositories. Each city and county library should have additional printed materials pertaining to its geographical area.

CUMBRIA COUNTY LIBRARY†
11 Globe Lane, Carlisle CA3 8NX
Tel. 0228 24166

Census‡# (Cumbld)	1841–1881
International Genealogical Index‡##	
(British Isles)	

KENDAL LIBRARY†
Strick Landgate, Kendal
Tel. 0539 20254

Census‡# (Westmld)	1841–1881
International Genealogical Index‡##	
(Westmld and adjacent pre-1974 counties)	

BARROW-IN-FURNESS LIBRARY†
Ramsden Square, Barrow-in-Furness
Tel. 0229 20650

Census‡#	1841–1881
International Genealogical Index‡##	
(Cumbld, Lancs, Westmld, Yorks)	

---

†For additional information send 2 Postal Reply Coupons or 31 pence of English postage for reply to North America; 34 pence to Australia and New Zealand.

‡Microfilm/microfiche copies available at above repository

#Microfilm copy available at the LDS Family History Library in Salt Lake City, Utah, and through the LDS Family History Centers.

##Microfiche copy available at the LDS Family History Library in Salt Lake City, Utah, and through the LDS Family History Centers.

GENEALOGICAL AND FAMILY HISTORY SOCIETIES

The societies listed below may have recorded Monumental (tombstone) Inscriptions, compiled an Index to Marriages (from the Parish Registers), an Index to the 1851 Census, and other special indexes, e.g., Strays, Members' Interests, for their geographical areas.** Each Society publishes a quarterly journal (listed in italics) which includes articles on family history, reports on the group's projects, and members' queries.

CUMBRIA FAMILY HISTORY SOCIETY†
Mrs. M. Russell, Secretary
32 Granada Road, Denton
Manchester M34 2LJ

Journal of the Cumbria Family History Society

**See *Current Publications by Member Societies* (annual), *List of Family History Project Coordinators*, 6th ed., and *Family History News and Digest* (biennial) — all published by the Federation of Family History Societies; available in the USA from the International Society for British Genealogy and Family History, P.O. Box 20425, Cleveland, OH 44120.

†For additional information send 2 Postal Reply Coupons or 31 pence of English postage for reply to North America; 34 pence to Australia and New Zealand.

DERBYSHIRE

Post-1974 Counties of England

The present geographical boundaries of Derbyshire include the pre-1974 county, and in addition Tintwistle, formerly the northeastern tip of Cheshire.

Administratively the City of Derby was an incorporated Borough from the seventeenth century to 1889 and a County Borough between 1889 and 1974. Chesterfield was an incorporated Borough from the sixteenth century to 1974.

147

RECORD OFFICE

DERBYSHIRE RECORD OFFICE
County Offices, Matlock
Derbyshire DE4 3AG
Tel. 0629 580000 ext. 7347

Hours: M-F 9:30-1, 2-4:45

Admission free
List of record searchers available upon request†

HOLDINGS

Church of England parish records including Parish Registers for approximately 140 churches in the pre-1974 county area; local government records and other resources for the county.

(Church of England diocesan records are primarily located at the Lichfield Joint Record Office, Lichfield, Staffs.)

SOURCES THAT IDENTIFY AN INDIVIDUAL WITH A SPECIFIC LOCATION

Church of England (diocesan)	
Tithe Apportionments§	1836–
Church of England (parish)	
Churchwardens' Accounts (some#)	17C–20C
Directories* (some#)	19C–20C
Postal, Business/Trade, Professional	
Enclosure Awards	18C–19C
Lay Subsidies	16C
Maps	16C–20C

---

†For additional information send 2 Postal Reply Coupons or 31 pence of English postage for reply to North America; 34 pence to Australia and New Zealand.
§Parish copies only
#Microfilm copy available at the LDS Family History Library in Salt Lake City, Utah, and through the LDS Family History Centers.
*Printed or transcribed

Militia Lists	19C
Parish Poor Law Records (some#)	1662–1929
Parish Poor Rates	
Quarter Sessions	
Judicial Records	17C–19C
Land Tax Assessments#	1780–1832
Lists of Jurors#	1776–1876
Registration of Papist Property	1716–1778
Registers of Electors*	1832–

SOURCES THAT MAY ADDITIONALLY PROVIDE VITAL DATA AND/OR PROVE FAMILY RELATIONSHIPS

Church of England (parish)	
Parish Registers#	1538–20C
Estate and Family Papers	ca.1300–20C
Manorial Court Records	14C–20C
Monumental Inscriptions	
Nonconformist Registers	
Congregational#	18C–1840
Methodist#	18C–1840
Independent#	18C–1840
Society of Friends#	1641–1837
Unitarian#	18C–1840
Parish Poor Law Records (some#)	1662–1834
Apprenticeship Indentures	
Examinations	
Removal Orders	
Settlement Papers	
Roman Catholic Records	18C–19C
School Records	19C–20C
Title Deeds	ca. 1200–20C
Wills, Registers Copies	1858–
	(1858–1880#)

#Microfilm copy available at the LDS Family History Library in Salt Lake City, Utah, and through the LDS Family History Centers.
*Printed or transcribed

PUBLICATIONS†

J.M. Bestall and D.V. Fowkes, eds., *Chesterfield Wills and Inventories, 1521–1603* (1977)

OTHER REPOSITORIES

The sources listed below include only those items reported on the Record Office Survey as located in the specified repositories. Each city and county library should have additional printed materials pertaining to its geographical area.

DERBYSHIRE LIBRARY SERVICE:

DERBYSHIRE COUNTY LIBRARY†
Local Studies Department
County Offices, Matlock DE4 3AG
Tel. 0629 580000 ext. 6840

Census‡# (Derbys)	1841–1881
International Genealogical Index‡## (Derbys)	
Newspapers*	19C–20C

DERBY LOCAL STUDIES DEPARTMENT†
25b Irongate, Derby DE1 3GL
Tel. 0332 31111 ext. 2184

Borough Records (Derby)
    Freemen's Lists
    Rates
    Court
    Title Deeds

---

†For additional information send 2 Postal Reply Coupons or 31 pence of English postage for reply to North America; 34 pence to Australia and New Zealand.
‡Microfilm/microfiche copies available at above repository
#Microfilm copy available at the LDS Family History Library in Salt Lake City, Utah, and through the LDS Family History Centers.
##Microfiche copy available at the LDS Family History Library in Salt Lake City, Utah, and through the LDS Family History Centers.
*Printed or transcribed

Census‡# (Derbys)	1841–1881
Directories* (some#)	
International Genealogical Index‡##	
Newspapers*	1732–20C
Registers of Electors* (Derby)	19C–20C
School Records	19C–20C

GENEALOGICAL AND FAMILY HISTORY SOCIETIES

The societies listed below may have recorded Monumental (tombstone) Inscriptions, compiled an Index to Marriages (from the Parish Registers), an Index to the 1851 Census, and other special indexes, e.g., Strays, Members' Interests, for their geographical areas.** Each Society publishes a quarterly journal (listed in italics) which includes articles on family history, reports on the group's projects, and members' queries.

DERBYSHIRE FAMILY HISTORY SOCIETY†
Mrs. P. Marples, Secretary
15 Elmhurst Road, Forest Town
Mansfield, Notts NG19 0EU

Derbyshire Family History Society Journal

---

‡Microfilm/microfiche copies available at above repository

#Microfilm copy available at the LDS Family History Library in Salt Lake City, Utah, and through the LDS Family History Centers.

*Printed or transcribed

##Microfiche copy available at the LDS Family History Library in Salt Lake City, Utah, and through the LDS Family History Centers.

**See *Current Publications by Member Societies* (annual), *List of Family History Project Coordinators*, 6th ed., and *Family History News and Digest* (biennial) — all published by the Federation of Family History Societies; available in the USA from the International Society for British Genealogy and Family History, P.O. Box 20425, Cleveland, OH 44120.

†For additional information send 2 Postal Reply Coupons or 31 pence of English postage for reply to North America; 34 pence to Australia and New Zealand.

DEVON(SHIRE)

Post-1974 Counties of England

There was no change in the geographical boundaries of Devon(shire) during the 1974 reorganization of local government in England.

Administratively the city of Exeter was an incorporated Borough from the twelfth century, a County Corporate from the sixteenth century to 1889, and a County Borough from 1889 to 1974. Plymouth and Devonport were incorporated Boroughs from the fifteenth and nineteenth centuries, respectively, and then County Boroughs to 1974.

Barnstaple, Bideford, Dartmouth, Plympton Earle, South Molton, Tavistock, Tiverton, Torrington and Totnes were all

152

incorporated Boroughs from the sixteenth century to 1974. Honiton was a Municipal Borough from the mid-nineteenth century to 1974.

RECORD OFFICES

DEVON RECORD OFFICE
Castle Street, Exeter EX4 3PU
Tel. 0392 273509

Hours: M-Th 9:30-5; F 9:30-4:30;
   1st, 3rd S/mo. 9:30-12; closed 1 week at Christmas.
   Some documents available only with 24 hours notice

Admission charge
Operates own genealogical research service;
   details of fees on request[†]

HOLDINGS

Most Church of England diocesan records for the Diocese of Exeter; (Wills for Devon were destroyed during World War II. Estate Duty copies of probate records and duplicates of earlier wills used as a substitute.); Church of England parish records including deposited Parish Registers for over 400 churches within the county; local government records and other resources for Devon.

(Some records for Plymouth are located at the West Devon Record Office, Plymouth.)

[†]For additional information send 2 Postal Reply Coupons or 31 pence of English postage for reply to North America; 34 pence to Australia and New Zealand.

*SOURCES THAT IDENTIFY AN INDIVIDUAL
WITH A SPECIFIC LOCATION*

Borough Records (Exeter)	11C–20C
Freemen's Lists	13C–20C
Rates	
Business Records	18C–20C
Church of England (diocesan)	
Ecclesiastical Court Books	1614–1820
Ecclesiastical Visitations	1622–1910
Tithe Apportionments	1836–1844
Church of England (parish)	
Churchwardens' Accounts	14C–20C
Directories* (some#)	
Postal	19C
Enclosure Awards	1804–1874
Maps	16C–
Militia Lists	1808–1873
Parish Poor Law Records	16C–1834
Parish Poor Rates	
Poll Books* (some#)	(periodic) 1816–1830
Quarter Sessions	
Judicial Records	16C–20C
Hearth Tax Assessments	(few) 1662–1688
Land Tax Assessments	1780–1832
Lists of Jurors	1728–1915
Registration of Papist Property	1717–1776
Registers of Electors*	1832–
Shipping – Crew Lists and Shipping Registers (all Devon ports)	19C–1913

---

*Printed or transcribed
#Microfilm copy available at the LDS Family History Library in Salt Lake City, Utah, and through the LDS Family History Centers.

SOURCES THAT MAY ADDITIONALLY PROVIDE VITAL DATA AND/OR PROVE FAMILY RELATIONSHIPS

Borough Records (Exeter)	
Court	1264–20C
Title Deeds	1100–20C
Cemetery Registers	1834–1970
Church of England (diocesan)	
Bishops' Transcripts* (also#)	1598–mid 19C
Marriage Licence Bonds (some#)	1664–1842
and Allegations	
Wills, Admon.§ (some*,#)	1812–1857
Church of England (parish)	
Parish Registers	
Estate and Family Papers	12C–
Manorial Records	14C–20C
Nonconformist Registers	
Baptist (some#)	1794–1970
Independent (some#)	1763–1948
Methodist (some#)	1813–20C
Society of Friends (some#)	1765–1961
Unitarian	1832–1961
Parish Poor Law Records	16C–1834
Apprenticeship Indentures	
Examinations	
Removal Orders	
Settlement Papers	
Poor Law Union	1836–
Workhouse Records	
Roman Catholic Registers	
School Records	19C–
Title Deeds – Enrolled (also*)	1536–

---

*Printed or transcribed

#Microfilm copy available at the LDS Family History Library in Salt Lake City, Utah, and through the LDS Family History Centers.

§Estate Duty Office copy of probate records for this period. Indexes and duplicates of a number of wills prior to 1812.

PUBLICATIONS†

Devon Record Office, Brief Guide: Part I, Official and Ecclesiastical (out of print)
Devon Record Office Report 1985–86
Parish, Non-Parochial and Civil Registers in the Devon Record Office
Leaflets:
Family History, Transport History, Farming History, Mining History, Maritime History, Crime and Punishment, Tithe Records, Electoral Registration Records, and Land Tax Records.

WEST DEVON RECORD OFFICE
Unit 3, Clare Place
Coxside, Plymouth PL4 0JW
Tel. 0752 264685

Hours: M-Th 9:30-5; F 9:30-4:30;
    first Wednesday of each month 5-7 pm
    (Prior appointment advised)
Admission charge

HOLDINGS

Church of England parish records including deposited Parish Registers pertaining to the southwest region of Devon; local government records and other resources pertaining to Plymouth and the southwest region of Devon.

(Church of England Diocesan records for the Diocese of Exeter are located at the Devon Record Office, Exeter.)

---

†For additional information send 2 Postal Reply Coupons or 31 pence of English postage for reply to North America; 34 pence to Australia and New Zealand.

156

SOURCES THAT IDENTIFY AN INDIVIDUAL
WITH A SPECIFIC LOCATION

Borough Records (Plymouth, Devonport)	16C–
Freemen's Lists	17C–19C
Rates	
Business Records	18C–
Church of England (diocesan)	
Tithe Apportionments§	1840's
Church of England (Parish)	
Churchwardens' Accounts	16C–20C
Hospital Records	1798–
Maps	17C–

SOURCES THAT MAY ADDITIONALLY PROVIDE VITAL
DATA AND/OR PROVE FAMILY RELATIONSHIPS

Borough Records (Plymouth, Devonport)	16C–
Court	
Title Deeds	
Church of England (diocesan)	
Bishops' Transcripts*#	1597–1812
Church of England (parish)	
Parish Registers	1538–1980's
(Plymouth and SW Devon)	
Estate and Family Papers	14C–
Manorial Records	16C–
Nonconformist Registers	
Methodist	19C–20C
Parish Poor Law Records	17C–1834
Apprenticeship Indentures	
Examinations	
Removal Orders	
Settlement Papers	

§Parish copy only; main series at Devon Record Office, Exeter.
*Printed or transcribed
#Microfilm copy available at the LDS Family History Library in Salt Lake City, Utah, and through the LDS Family History Centers.

School Records	late 19C–20C
Title Deeds	14C–

PUBLICATIONS†

E. Welch, *A Guide to the Archives Department of Plymouth City Libraries, Part I* (1962)

NORTH DEVON RECORD OFFICE (to open 11 April 1988)
North Devon Library
Tuly Street, Barnstaple, N. Devon
Admission charge

HOLDINGS

Plans to hold materials pertaining to North Devon:

Church of England parish records for	
Archdeaconry of Barnstaple	16C–20C
Nonconformist Records – Methodist	19C–20C
Shipping Records for North Devon ports	1786–20C
Solicitors's Collections (Estate Papers)	
North Devon and Torridge District Councils	
(and their predecessor authorities)	
Rates	

OTHER REPOSITORIES

The sources listed below include only those items reported on the Record Office Survey as located in the specified repositories. Each city and county library should have additional printed materials pertaining to its geographical area.

---

†For additional information send 2 Postal Reply Coupons or 31 pence of English postage for reply to North America; 34 pence to Australia and New Zealand.

EXETER CENTRAL LIBRARY†
(West Country Studies Library)
Castle Street, Exeter EX4 3PU
Tel. 0392 273422

Census‡# (Devon)   1841–1881
International Genealogical Index‡##
(Devon and adjacent counties)

PLYMOUTH CENTRAL LIBRARY†
Local Studies Section
Tavistock Road, Plymouth PL4 8AL
Tel. 0752 21312

Census#   1841–1881
(Plymouth and Southwest Devon)
International Genealogical Index##
(Devon and Cornw)

LDS FAMILY HISTORY CENTRE†
Hartley Chapel, Mannamead Road
Plymouth, Devon
Tel. 0752 668998

LDS Family History Library Catalog‡##
International Genealogical Index‡##

---

†For additional information send 2 Postal Reply Coupons or 31 pence of English
postage for reply to North America; 34 pence to Australia and New Zealand.
‡Microfilm/microfiche copies available at above repository
#Microfilm copy available at the LDS Family History Library in Salt Lake City,
Utah, and through the LDS Family History Centers.
##Microfiche copy available at the LDS Family History Library in Salt Lake
City, Utah, and through the LDS Family History Centers.

GENEALOGICAL AND FAMILY HISTORY SOCIETIES

The societies listed below may have recorded Monumental (tombstone) Inscriptions, compiled an Index to Marriages (from the Parish Registers), an Index to the 1851 Census, and other special indexes, e.g., Strays, Members' Interests, for their geographical areas.** Each Society publishes a quarterly journal (listed in italics) which includes articles on family history, reports on the group's projects, and members' queries.

DEVON FAMILY HISTORY SOCIETY†

Miss V. Bluett, Secretary
63 Old Laira Road, Laira
Plymouth, Devon PL3 5BL

The Devon Family Historian

** See *Current Publications by Member Societies* (annual), *List of Family History Project Coordinators*, 6th ed., and *Family History News and Digest* (biennial) — all published by the Federation of Family History Societies; available in the USA from the International Society for British Genealogy and Family History, P.O. Box 20425, Cleveland, OH 44120.

† For additional information send 2 Postal Reply Coupons or 31 pence of English postage for reply to North America; 34 pence to Australia and New Zealand.

DORSET

Post-1974 Counties of England

The present geographical boundaries of Dorset include the pre-1974 county area, and in addition, the Bournemouth area previously located in Hampshire.

Administratively Bournemouth was a Municipal Borough from 1889 to 1900, a County Borough between 1900 and 1974, and a part of Hampshire prior to 1889. Blandford Forum, Bridport, Dorchester, Lyme Regis, and Shaftesbury were all incorporated Boroughs from early in the seventeenth century to 1974. Poole was a County Corporate from the mid-sixteenth century to 1889 and a Municipal Borough between 1889 and 1974.

161

Weymouth and Melcombe Regis became an incorporated Borough in 1572. Wareham, an ancient parliamentary borough, became a Municipal Borough in 1886. Both were abolished in 1974. Christchurch, in Hampshire until 1974, was a Municipal Borough from 1835 until it was transferred.

RECORD OFFICE

DORSET COUNTY RECORD OFFICE
County Hall, Dorchester DT1 1XJ
Tel. 0305 251000 ext. 4411; (UK) (3035) 20-4411
Contact: County Archivist

Hours: M-F 9-1, 2-5
      (Prior appointment advised)

Admission free
Genealogical search service available[†]

HOLDINGS
Church of England deposited parish records, including Parish Registers, for all the ancient parishes of Dorset (some 300 churches) in the ancient county of Dorset and the Diocese of Bristol 1541–1836 and the Diocese of Sarum (Salisbury) 1836–; for Christchurch, Bournemouth and Holdenhurst (Diocese of Winchester) see Hampshire Record Office for original records; microfilm copies of Parish Registers for Christchurch, Holdenhurst and Bournemouth St. Peter are located in this repository.

(Church of England diocesan records except probate for the Archdeaconry of Dorset, Diocese of Bristol to 1836 are mostly located at the Wiltshire Record Office, Trowbridge.)

[†]For additional information send 2 Postal Reply Coupons or 31 pence of English postage for reply to North America; 34 pence to Australia and New Zealand.

SOURCES THAT IDENTIFY AN INDIVIDUAL
WITH A SPECIFIC LOCATION

Borough Records†† (Blandford Forum, Bridport, Dorchester, Lyme Regis, Shaftesbury, Wareham)		11C–19C
Freemen's Admissions		
Rates		
Church of England (diocesan)		
Tithe Apportionments§		1830's–1850's
Church of England (parish)		
Churchwardens' Accounts		15C–20C
Directories* (some#)		
Business/Trade, Postal	(periodic)	1783–1939
Enclosure Awards		18C–19C
Lay Subsidies*		1327, 1332
Maps		17C–20C
Militia Lists		1759–1799
Parish Poor Law Records		17C–20C
Parish Poor Rates		
Protestation Returns*#		1642
Poll Books* (some#)	(periodic)	1727–1831
Quarter Sessions		
Judicial Records§§		1625–20C
Hearth Tax Assessments*#		1662–1664
Lists of Jurors		1719–1791, 1825–1922
Registers of Electors* (some#)		1833–
Shipping – Crew Lists		1863–1913

---

††Varying time periods for different records in various Boroughs.

§Parish copies only, main series at the Wiltshire Record Office, Trowbridge.

*Printed or transcribed

#Microfilm copy available at the LDS Family History Library in Salt Lake City, Utah, and through the LDS Family History Centers.

§§Modern records are subject to embargo.

*SOURCES THAT MAY ADDITIONALLY PROVIDE VITAL
DATA AND/OR PROVE FAMILY RELATIONSHIPS*

Borough Records†† (Blandford Forum,
    Bridport, Dorchester, Lyme Regis,
    Shaftesbury, Wareham)

Court	12C–20C
Title Deeds	13C–20C
Church of England (diocesan)	
Bishops' Transcripts#§	17C–19C
Wills#§	16C–19C
Church of England (parish)	
Parish Registers	1538–1970's
Parish Register Transcripts*#	1538–1931
Estate and Family Records	mainly 17C–20C
Manorial Records	13C–20C
Nonconformist Registers	
Independent	1740–1847*; 1838–1918
Methodist	1796–1837*; 1816–1970's
Society of Friends#	1648–1838
Unitarian#	1704–1838
Parish Poor Law Records	16C–19C
Apprenticeship Indentures	
Examinations	
Removal Orders	
Settlement Papers	
Roman Catholic Registers*	1755–1856
School Records	19C–20C
Title Deeds	10C–20C
Wills, etc. (Originals)	1557–1857
Wills, Register Copies	1858–1941

---

††Varying time periods for different records in the various Boroughs.
#Microfilm copy available at the LDS Family History Library in Salt Lake City, Utah, and through the LDS Family History Centers.
§Microfilm copies will be available at above repository in 1988.
*Printed or transcribed

PUBLICATIONS†

Leaflets/Lists:
A.C. Cox, *Index to the Dorset County Records*
   (1938)(OOP)
Outside Dates of Nonconformist Registers and
   Copy Registers
Guide to the Location of the Parish Registers of Dorset
Map of Dorset Parishes

OTHER REPOSITORIES

The sources listed below include only those items reported on the Record Office Survey as located in the specified repositories. Each city and county library should have additional printed materials pertaining to its geographical area.

DORCHESTER REFERENCE LIBRARY†
(Dorset County Library)
Colliton Park, Dorchester DT1 1XJ
Tel. 0305 63131

Census# (Dorset)	1841–1881
International Genealogical Index##	
(Dorset)	
Newspapers*	

---

†For additional information send 2 Postal Reply Coupons or 31 pence of English postage for reply to North America; 34 pence to Australia and New Zealand.
#Microfilm copy available at the LDS Family History Library in Salt Lake City, Utah, and through the LDS Family History Centers.
##Microfiche copy available at the LDS Family History Library in Salt Lake City, Utah, and through the LDS Family History Centers.
*Printed or transcribed

LDS FAMILY HISTORY CENTRE[†]
8 Mount Road, Parkstone
Poole, Dorset
Tel. 0202 730646

LDS Family History Library Catalog[‡##]
International Genealogical Index[‡##]

GENEALOGICAL AND FAMILY HISTORY SOCIETIES

The societies listed below may have recorded Monumental (tombstone) Inscriptions, compiled an Index to Marriages (from the Parish Registers), an Index to the 1851 Census, and other special indexes, e.g., Strays, Members' Interests, for their geographical areas.** Each Society publishes a quarterly journal (listed in italics) which includes articles on family history, reports on the group's projects, and members' queries.

SOMERSET AND DORSET FAMILY HISTORY SOCIETY[†]
P.O. Box 170
Taunton, Somerset TA1 1HF

Greenwood Tree

[†]For additional information send 2 Postal Reply Coupons or 31 pence of English postage for reply to North America; 34 pence to Australia and New Zealand.

[‡]Microfilm/microfiche copies available at above repository

[##]Microfiche copy available at the LDS Family History Library in Salt Lake City, Utah, and through the LDS Family History Centers.

**See *Current Publications by Member Societies* (annual), *List of Family History Project Coordinators*, 6th ed., and *Family History News and Digest* (biennial) — all published by the Federation of Family History Societies; available in the USA from the International Society for British Genealogy and Family History, P.O. Box 20425, Cleveland, OH 44120.

DURHAM

Post-1974 Counties of England

The pre-1974 geographical and administrative boundaries of County Durham included the Stockton area, Hartlepool and West Hartlepool, now in the county of Cleveland.

Administratively West Hartlepool became a Municipal Borough in 1867 and a County Borough in 1902. Hartlepool, a Municipal Borough from the late nineteenth century to 1967, was united with West Hartlepool in 1967 to become the County Borough of Hartlepool until 1974. County Durham also included the County Boroughs of Gateshead, South Shields, and Sunderland, now in the county of Tyne and Wear.

167

Present county boundaries additionally include the north-western tip of the former North Riding of Yorkshire. Administratively, Darlington was a Municipal Borough from 1867 to 1915, and then a County Borough to 1974.

During the eleventh century County Durham, together with parts of Northumberland and Yorkshire, were elevated by the King to be a County Palatine and granted to the Bishop of Durham. The County Palatine had its own courts (chancery, common pleas, criminal) which were exempt from those of the Crown. The Bishop of Durham, known as the Prince Palatine, appointed the officers — sheriff, justices of the peace, administrative officers, coroner. Fiscal affairs were also exempt from those of the crown. In 1836 the Palatine status of Durham was abolished, although the Court of Common Pleas continued until 1873, and the Chancery Court until 1971.

Administrative and court records of the County Palatine of Durham are located in the Public Record Office, Chancery Lane. Fiscal records for the County Palatine, however, are now located at the University of Durham, Department of Palæography and Diplomatic, The Prior's Kitchen, Durham.

RECORD OFFICES

DURHAM COUNTY RECORD OFFICE
County Hall, Durham DH1 5UL
Tel. (091) 386 4411 ext. 2474/2253
Contact: County Archivist

Hours: M, T, Th 8:45-4:45; F 8:45-4:15; closed S
    W 8:45am-8:30pm (appointment preceding day)
    Prior appointment necessary to consult
    documents or microfilm at other times

Admission free
List of record searchers available upon request[†]

[†]For additional information send 2 Postal Reply Coupons or 31 pence of English postage for reply to North America; 34 pence to Australia and New Zealand.

HOLDINGS

Church of England parish records including deposited parish registers for nearly 200 churches in the pre-1974 county areas; civil records and other resources pertaining to the pre-1974 division of the county.

(Church of England diocesan records for the Diocese of Durham are located at the University of Durham, Department of Palæography and Diplomatic.)

SOURCES THAT IDENTIFY AN INDIVIDUAL WITH A SPECIFIC LOCATION

Borough Records (Durham)		
Freemen's Lists		1728–
Rates	(periodic)	1790–
Church of England (diocesan)		
Tithe Apportionments§		1836–
Church of England (parish)		16C–20C
Churchwardens' Accounts		
Directories* (some#)		
Business		19C–20C
Enclosure Awards		19C
Maps		18C–
Militia Records#		1807–1811
Parish Poor Law Records		17C–1834
Parish Poor Rates		
Poll Books* (some#)	(periodic)	1675–1869
Protestation Returns*#		1641

---

§Parish copies only; main series at the University of Durham Department of Palæography and Diplomatic.
*Printed or transcribed
#Microfilm copy available at the LDS Family History Library in Salt Lake City, Utah, and through the LDS Family History Centers.

Quarter Sessions
Judicial Records (some#)   17C–1834
Hearth Tax Assessments‡#   (few) 17C
Land Tax Assessments#   1759, 1831
Lists of Jurors   1766, 1796,
                                            1838–1848#
Registration of Papist Property   1717–1778
Registers of Electors* (some#)   1832–

*SOURCES THAT MAY ADDITIONALLY PROVIDE VITAL
DATA AND/OR PROVE FAMILY RELATIONSHIPS*

Borough Records (Durham)
Court   1752–1868
Title Deeds   16C–
Census‡# (County)   1841–1871
Church of England (parish)
Parish Registers#   1538–1900's
Estate and Family Papers
International Genealogical Index‡##
(Co. Durh, Nthbld, Cumbld, Westmld, Yorks)
Monumental Inscriptions#   19C–
Newspapers*   19C–20C
Nonconformist Registers
Baptist   19C–20C
Independent/Congregational (some#)   18C–20C
Methodist   19C–20C
Unitarian   19C–20C
Obituary Notices*   19C
Parish Poor Law Records   17C–1834
Settlement Papers
Title Deeds   16C–

#Microfilm copy available at the LDS Family History Library in Salt Lake City, Utah, and through the LDS Family History Centers.
‡Microfilm/microfiche copies available at above repository
*Printed or transcribed
##Microfiche copy available at the LDS Family History Library in Salt Lake City, Utah, and through the LDS Family History Centers.

PUBLICATIONS†

The Londonderry Papers: Catalogue of Documents... (1969)

North-Eastern Ancestors (1986)

Map of Parish and Chapelry Boundaries c. 1800 (1983)

Handlists: (free)†
    Non-conformist Church Registers held in the
        Durham Record Office
    Parish Registers held in the Durham Record Office
    Modern Transcripts and Indexes (Church of England)
    Quarter Sessions Records held in the
        Durham Record Office
    Census Indexes
    Modern Transcripts and Indexes (Non-conformist)
    Modern Transcripts and Indexes
        (New County Durham)

Subject Guides: (free)†
    Records relating to Inclosure held in the
        Durham Record Office
    Sources for the Study of Local History
    Guide to the Darlington Branch
    Records relating to Tithe held in the
        Durham Record Office

Parish Registers / Civil Registration – General Information

Archives in Durham City

Streatland and Gibside, *The Bowes and Strathmore*
    Families in County Durham (1984)

---

†For additional information send 2 Postal Reply Coupons or 31 pence of English
postage for reply to North America; 34 pence to Australia and New Zealand.

DURHAM COUNTY RECORD OFFICE, DARLINGTON BRANCH

Durham County Library, Darlington Branch
Crown Street, Darlington DL1 1ND
Tel. 0325 462034/469858

Hours: M-F 9-1, 2:15-7; S 9-1, 2:15-5
    Prior appointment necessary M-F after 5 and S

HOLDINGS

Resources pertaining to the Darlington area.

SOURCES THAT IDENTIFY AN INDIVIDUAL WITH A SPECIFIC LOCATION

Borough Records (Darlington)	19C–20C
Rates	
Business Records	19C–20C
Church of England (diocesan)	
Tithe Apportionments§	mid-19C
Directories* (some#)	19C–20C
Local Histories*	19C–20C
Maps	19C–20C
Periodicals*	
Poor Law Union	
Rates	1840–1910
Registers of Electors*	1974–

---

§Parish copies only
*Printed or transcribed
#Microfilm copy available at the LDS Family History Library in Salt Lake City, Utah, and through the LDS Family History Centers.

SOURCES THAT MAY ADDITIONALLY PROVIDE VITAL DATA AND/OR PROVE FAMILY RELATIONSHIPS

Bishop's Borough Records	
Court Books	1612–1639,
	1710–1769
Burial Board	
Minute Book	1855–1865
Census‡#	1841–1881
Charity Records	19C–20C
Church of England (parish)	
Parish Registers‡#	16C–
Estate and Family Papers	12C–20C
International Genealogical Index‡##	
(Co. Durh, Nthbld)	
Nonconformist Registers	
Congregational	1806–1972
Presbyterian	1862–1974
Poor Law Union	
Workhouse Records	20C
School Records	19C–20C
Society Records	19C–20C
Title Deeds	12C–20C

PUBLICATIONS†

Leaflet: *Subject Guide 3: Guide to the Darlington Branch*

---

‡Microfilm/microfiche copies available at above repository

#Microfilm copy available at the LDS Family History Library in Salt Lake City, Utah, and through the LDS Family History Centers.

##Microfiche copy available at the LDS Family History Library in Salt Lake City, Utah, and through the LDS Family History Centers.

†For additional information send 2 Postal Reply Coupons or 31 pence of English postage for reply to North America; 34 pence to Australia and New Zealand.

UNIVERSITY OF DURHAM
DEPARTMENT OF PALÆOGRAPHY AND DIPLOMATIC
5 The College, Durham DH1 3EQ
Tel. (091) 374 3610

Hours: M-F 10-1, 2-5;
In addition, the search-room remains open until 8pm on Tuesday evenings during University terms only; closed for three weeks during August, a week at Christmas and Easter; (prior appointment advised)

Admission free
List of record searchers available upon request†
(Staff members do not undertake research)

HOLDINGS

Church of England diocesan records (Diocese of Durham); Durham city guild records; manuscript collections of estate and family papers, maps;   Durham Bishopric Halmote Court records.

SOURCES THAT IDENTIFY AN INDIVIDUAL
WITH A SPECIFIC LOCATION

Church of England (diocesan)	
Ecclesiastical Court Books and Papers	16C–20C
(most not indexed)	
Ecclesiastical Visitations	
Tithe Apportionments and Plans	1830's, 1840's
Enclosure Awards	16C–19C
Plans	18C–19C
Maps	

---

†For additional information send 2 Postal Reply Coupons or 31 pence of English postage for reply to North America; 34 pence to Australia and New Zealand.

*SOURCES THAT MAY ADDITIONALLY PROVIDE VITAL
DATA AND/OR PROVE FAMILY RELATIONSHIPS*

Guild Records (Durham city)
   Apprentices, Freemen‡‡ and Guild members
Church of England (diocesan)
   Bishops' Transcripts   (gaps) c. 1760–1840
   Marriage Licence Bonds   1664–
     and Allegations*
   Probate Records# (Wills, Admon.,   1540–1857
    Inven.)   17C–18C
   Durham Halmote Court Records   16C–20C
   (copyhold tenants of the Bishop of Durham)
   Obituary Notices# (Durham city Directories) 1858–1916

PUBLICATIONS†

A copy of the leaflet *Published Lists of Records* is available
without charge. Payment and postage for any specific publication ordered should not be sent until an invoice is received.
Payment of invoices must be made in sterling or by
international money order.

OTHER REPOSITORIES

The sources listed below include only those items reported
on the Record Office Survey as located in the specified repositories. Each city and county library should have additional
printed materials pertaining to its geographical area.

---

‡‡Other information about Freemen will be found in the Durham City Records
deposited in the Durham County Record Office.
*Printed or transcribed
#Microfilm copy available at the LDS Family History Library in Salt Lake City,
Utah, and through the LDS Family History Centers.
†For additional information send 2 Postal Reply Coupons or 31 pence of English
postage for reply to North America; 34 pence to Australia and New Zealand.

DURHAM COUNTY LIBRARY†
Reference Library
South Street, Durham DH1 5UL
Tel. 0385 64411

Census‡#   1841–1881
International Genealogical Index‡##
(Co. Durh)

GENEALOGICAL AND FAMILY HISTORY SOCIETIES

The societies listed below may have recorded Monumental (tombstone) Inscriptions, compiled an Index to Marriages (from the Parish Registers), an Index to the 1851 Census, and other special indexes, e.g., Strays, Members' Interests, for their geographical areas.** Each Society publishes a quarterly journal (listed in italics) which includes articles on family history, reports on the group's projects, and members' queries.

**NORTHUMBERLAND AND DURHAM
FAMILY HISTORY SOCIETY†**
Mr. J.K. Brown, Secretary
33 South Bend, Brunton Park
Newcastle upon Tyne NE3 5TR
   *Journal of the Northumberland and Durham
   Family History Society*

---

†For additional information send 2 Postal Reply Coupons or 31 pence of English postage for reply to North America; 34 pence to Australia and New Zealand.
‡Microfilm/microfiche copies available at above repository
#Microfilm copy available at the LDS Family History Library in Salt Lake City, Utah, and through the LDS Family History Centers.
##Microfiche copy available at the LDS Family History Library in Salt Lake City, Utah, and through the LDS Family History Centers.
**See *Current Publications by Member Societies* (annual), *List of Family History Project Coordinators*, 6th ed., and *Family History News and Digest* (biennial) — all published by the Federation of Family History Societies; available in the USA from the International Society for British Genealogy and Family History, P.O. Box 20425, Cleveland, OH 44120.

ESSEX

Post-1974 Counties of England

The pre-1965 geographical boundaries of Essex included the present county, and in addition, the areas of Barking, Chingford, Dagenham, Hornchurch, Ilford, Leyton, Romford, Walthamstow, and Wanstead and Woodford which were transferred to the newly created area of Greater London that year. There were no additional boundary changes in 1974.

Administratively all localities transferred in 1965, excepting Hornchurch, were twentieth-century Municipal Boroughs. Colchester, Harwich, Maldon, and Sudbury (partly in Suffolk) all were incorporated Boroughs in Essex from the seventeenth century to 1974. Saffron Walden was a Municipal Borough

177

from the mid-nineteenth century through 1974, and the Liberty of Havering atte Bower was exempt from most county jurisdiction during the same period. Southend-on-Sea was a County Borough from 1914 to 1974, and before that was a Municipal Borough from 1892.

RECORD OFFICES

ESSEX RECORD OFFICE
County Hall, Chelmsford CM1 1LX
Tel. 0245 492211

Hours: M 10-8:45; T, W, Th 9:15-5:15; F 9:15-4:15
Prior appointment necessary for
original documents or microfilms

Admission free
List of record searchers available upon request[†]

HOLDINGS

Church of England diocesan records (Diocese of London, Archdeaconry of Essex to 1846, Diocese of Rochester 1846–1877); Church of England parish records including deposited Parish Registers for approximately 390 ancient and modern parishes. For Branch holdings see below; microfilms of Branch parish register holdings are available at Chelmsford. Local government records and other resources pertaining to the pre-1965 County area.

(Parish records, including Parish Registers, for Walthamstow, Leyton and Chingford are held on behalf of the Essex Record Office at Vestry House Museum and Archives, Vestry Road, Walthamstow E17 9NH.)

[†]For additional information send 2 Postal Reply Coupons or 31 pence of English postage for reply to North America; 34 pence to Australia and New Zealand.

SOURCES THAT IDENTIFY AN INDIVIDUAL WITH A SPECIFIC LOCATION

Borough Records (Maldon)	14C–19C
Church of England (archidiaconal)	
Ecclesiastical Court Records§	1540–
Ecclesiastical Visitations§	1565–
Tithe Apportionments	1839–1859
Church of England (parish)	
Churchwardens' Accounts	1439–
Directories* (some#)	
Postal	1793–1937
Enclosure Awards	1770–1895
Lay Subsidies	1319, 1327,*
	1380–81,
	1524–25
Maps	16C–20C
Militia Lists#	1804–1827
Parish Poor Law Records	1662–1834
Parish Poor Rates	
Poll Books* (some#)	1679–1868
Quarter Sessions	
Judicial Records (some#)	16C–20C
Hearth Tax Assessments#	1662–1672
Land Tax Assessments	1782–1832
Lists of Freeholders*# (periodic)	1734–1774
Lists of Jurors#	1838–1848
Registration of Papist Property	18C
Registers of Electors*	1832–
Shipping – Crew Lists	1863–1913
(Colchester, Harwich, Maldon)	

§Early records mostly in Latin
*Printed or transcribed
#Microfilm copy available at the LDS Family History Library in Salt Lake City, Utah, and through the LDS Family History Centers.

SOURCES THAT MAY ADDITIONALLY PROVIDE VITAL
DATA AND/OR PROVE FAMILY RELATIONSHIPS

Borough Records (Maldon)
Court   1384–
Title Deeds   1343–1893
Boyd's Marriage Index# (Essex)   1538–1837
Census‡# (Essex)   1841–1881
Church of England (diocesan)
  Bishops' Transcripts   1800–1878
  Marriage Licence Bonds   1665–1851
    and Allegations*
  Wills, Admon., Inven. (some#)   1400–1858
Church of England (parish)
  Parish Registers   1538–20C
  Parish Register Transcripts* (some#)   16C–19C
Estate and Family Papers   13C–20C
International Genealogical Index‡##
  (British Isles)
Manorial Court Records   12C–20C
Monumental Inscriptions   19C
Newspapers*   1764–20C
Nonconformist Registers
  Methodist (some#)   18C–20C
  Society of Friends Digests*#   17C–1837
Parish Poor Law Records
  Apprenticeship Indentures   17C–19C
  Examinations   17C–19C
  Removal Orders#   1671–1874
  Settlement Papers#   1574–1865
Poor Law Union
  Workhouse Records   1834–

#Microfilm copy available at the LDS Family History Library in Salt Lake City, Utah, and through the LDS Family History Centers.
‡Microfilm/microfiche copies available at above repository
*Printed or transcribed
##Microfiche copy available at the LDS Family History Library in Salt Lake City, Utah, and through the LDS Family History Centers.

Roman Catholic Registers	18C–19C
School Records	19C–20C
Title Deeds (some#)	12C–20C

PUBLICATIONS†

Guide to the Essex Record Office (1967)
D.H. Allen, Essex Quarter Sessions Order Book 1652–1661 (1974)
F.G. Emmison, Catalogue of Essex Parish Records 1240–1894 (1966)
F.G. Emmison, Wills at Chelmsford 1400–1858 (1959–1969)
F.G. Emmison, Catalogue of Maps in the Essex Record Office (1947)
    First Supplement (1952)
    Second Supplement (1964)
    Third Supplement (1968)
Leaflets/Lists:
    Handlist of Parish and Nonconformist Registers Deposited (1982–3)
    List of Special Indexes

**ESSEX RECORD OFFICE,
COLCHESTER AND NORTHEAST ESSEX BRANCH**
Stanwell House, Stanwell Street
Colchester CO2 7DL
Tel. 0206 572099

Hours: M-Th 9:15-5:15; F 9:15-4:15

Admission Free

#Microfilm copy available at the LDS Family History Library in Salt Lake City, Utah, and through the LDS Family History Centers.
†For additional information send 2 Postal Reply Coupons or 31 pence of English postage for reply to North America; 34 pence to Australia and New Zealand.

HOLDINGS

Church of England parish records including deposited Parish Registers for approximately 80 ancient and modern parishes; local government records and other resources pertaining to the area of the present Colchester Borough and Tendring District Councils.

SOURCES THAT IDENTIFY AN INDIVIDUAL WITH A SPECIFIC LOCATION

Borough Records (Colchester)	14C–
Church of England (parish)	
Churchwardens's Accounts	1550–
Poor Law Records	1576–1834
Maps	16C–20C

SOURCES THAT ADDITIONALLY PROVIDE VITAL DATA AND/OR PROVE FAMILY RELATIONSHIPS

Borough Records (Colchester)	14C–
Court of Quarter Sessions	16C–19C
Enrolled Wills	14C–17C
Enrolled Title Deeds	14C–20C
Enrolled Apprenticeship Indentures	16C–18C
Freeburgess Admissions	14C–
Church of England (parish)	
Parish Registers	1538–
Poor Law Union (Colchester, Tendring,	
Lexden and Winstree)	
Workhouse Records	1834–

(See under main Essex Record Office entry: Estate and Family Papers, Manorial Court Records, Nonconformist Registers, School Records, Title Deeds.)

**ESSEX RECORD OFFICE,
SOUTHEND BRANCH**
Central Library, Victoria Avenue
Southend-on-Sea SS2 6EX
Tel. 0702 612621 ext. 215

Hours: M, W, Th 9:15-5:15; T 9:45-5:15;
F 9:15-4:15; closed S
Admission free

HOLDINGS

Church of England parish records, including deposited
Parish Registers for approximately 30 ancient and modern
parishes; local government records and other resources pertaining to Southend-on-Sea.

Borough Records (Southend-on-Sea)
Rates	1906–1954
Title Deeds§	1739–1912
Estate and Family Papers§	16C–20C
Poor Law Union	
Workhouse Records§	1834–1929
School Records§	late 18C–20C
Title Deeds§	15C–20C

OTHER REPOSITORIES

The sources listed below include only those items reported
on the Record Office Survey as located in the specified repositories. Each city and county library should have additional
printed materials pertaining to its geographical area.

---

§May provide vital data and/or proof of family relationships.

LDS FAMILY HISTORY CENTRE†
64 Butts Green Road
Hornchurch, Essex RM11 2JJ
Tel. 0424 58412

LDS Family History Library Catalog‡##
International Genealogical Index‡##

GENEALOGICAL AND FAMILY HISTORY SOCIETIES

The societies listed below may have recorded Monumental (tombstone) Inscriptions, compiled an Index to Marriages (from the Parish Registers), an Index to the 1851 Census, and other special indexes, e.g., Strays, Members' Interests, for their geographical areas.** Each Society publishes a quarterly journal (listed in italics) which includes articles on family history, reports on the group's projects, and members' queries.

ESSEX SOCIETY FOR FAMILY HISTORY†
Mr. C. Lewis, Secretary
48 Walton Road
Frinton-on-Sea, Essex CO13 0AG

   Essex Journal

---

†For additional information send 2 Postal Reply Coupons or 31 pence of English postage for reply to North America; 34 pence to Australia and New Zealand.
‡Microfilm/microfiche copies available at above repository
##Microfiche copy available at the LDS Family History Library in Salt Lake City, Utah, and through the LDS Family History Centers.
**See *Current Publications by Member Societies* (annual), *List of Family History Project Coordinators*, 6th ed., and *Family History News and Digest* (biennial) — all published by the Federation of Family History Societies; available in the USA from the International Society for British Genealogy and Family History, P.O. Box 20425, Cleveland, OH 44120.

GLOUCESTERSHIRE

Post-1974 Counties of England

The pre-1974 geographical boundaries of Gloucestershire
included the present county, and in addition, the area of Thornbury and part of the city of Bristol now in Avon County.
Administratively, the city of Bristol (partly in Somerset
County) and the city of Gloucester were designated as County
Corporates from the fourteenth and sixteenth centuries, respectively, to 1889. Both were County Boroughs from 1889 to 1974.
Tewkesbury was an incorporated Borough from 1698 to 1974, as
was Chipping Campden from 1605 to 1885.

185

RECORD OFFICE

GLOUCESTERSHIRE RECORD OFFICE
Clarence Row, Alvin Street
Gloucester GL1 3DW
Tel. 0452 425295

Hours: M, T, W, F 9-1, 2-5; Th 9-1, 2-8

Admission details available on request[†]

Genealogical research undertaken for a fee[†]

HOLDINGS

Church of England diocesan records (Diocese of Gloucester); Church of England parish records, including deposited Parish Registers for approximately 300 churches in the pre-1974 area of the county; local government records and other resources for the pre-1974 division of the county.

SOURCES THAT IDENTIFY AN INDIVIDUAL WITH A SPECIFIC LOCATION

Borough Records (Gloucester, Tewkesbury)   15C–
   Freemen's Lists
   Rates
Church of England (diocesan)
   Ecclesiastical Court Books[#]   1541–
   Ecclesiastical Visitations   1541–
   Tithe Apportionments   mid-19C
Church of England (parish)
   Churchwardens' Accounts

[†]For additional information send 2 Postal Reply Coupons or 31 pence of English postage for reply to North America; 34 pence to Australia and New Zealand.
[#]Microfilm copy available at the LDS Family History Library in Salt Lake City, Utah, and through the LDS Family History Centers.

Directories* (some#) (gaps) 18C–
   Business, Postal
Enclosure Awards (also*) 19C
Lay Subsidies (also#) 17C
Maps 16C–
Militia Lists (also*)
Parish Poor Law Records 1662–1834
Parish Poor Rates
Poll Books* (some#) (periodic) 1776–
Quarter Sessions#
   Judicial Records 17C–20C
   Hearth Tax Assessments#
   Land Tax Assessments 1775–1832
   Lists of Freeholders
   Lists of Jurors 1728–1878
   Registration of Papist Property 18C
Registers of Electors* 1832–1886
                          (1843–1886#)
Shipping – Crew Lists#

*SOURCES THAT MAY ADDITIONALLY PROVIDE VITAL
DATA AND/OR PROVE FAMILY RELATIONSHIPS*

Borough Records (Gloucester) 15C–
   Court
   Title Deeds
Cemetery Registers (some#)
Church of England (diocesan)
   Bishops' Transcripts# 1569–1860
   Marriage Licence Bonds
      and Allegations#
   Wills, Admon., Inven.# 1541–1858

---

*Printed or transcribed
#Microfilm copy available at the LDS Family History Library in Salt Lake City,
Utah, and through the LDS Family History Centers.

Church of England (parish)
   Parish Registers#   1538–20C
   Parish Register Transcripts*
Estate and Family Papers#   12C–
Manorial Records
Monumental Inscriptions
Nonconformist Registers
   Baptist   18C–20C
   Independent (Congregational)   18C–20C
   Methodist#   19C–20C
   Society of Friends#   17C–20C
   Unitarian   18C–19C
Parish Poor Law Records   1662–1834
   Apprenticeship Indentures
   Examinations
   Removal Orders
   Settlement Papers
Poor Law Union   1834–
   Workhouse Records
School Records   19C–20C
Title Deeds   12C–
Wills, Register Copies   1858–1931

PUBLICATIONS†

M.E. Richards, *Gloucestershire Family History*

Leaflets/Lists:
   Guide to Parish Registers of Bristol and Gloucester
   Wills Proven in Peculiar Courts

#Microfilm copy available at the LDS Family History Library in Salt Lake City, Utah, and through the LDS Family History Centers.
*Printed or transcribed
†For additional information send 2 Postal Reply Coupons or 31 pence of English postage for reply to North America; 34 pence to Australia and New Zealand.

OTHER REPOSITORIES

The sources listed below include only those items reported on the Record Office Survey as located in the specified repositories. Each city and county library should have additional printed materials pertaining to its geographical area.

GLOUCESTER CITY LIBRARY†
Reference Library
Brunswick Road, Gloucester GL1 1HT
Tel. 0452 20020

Census‡#	1841–1881
International Genealogical Index‡##	
(Glos and adjacent counties)	
Newspapers (some‡#)	18C

LDS FAMILY HISTORY CENTRE†
Thirlestaine Road
Cheltenham, Gloucestershire GL52 3PR
Tel. 0242 523433

LDS Family History Library Catalog‡##
International Genealogical Index‡##

---

†For additional information send 2 Postal Reply Coupons or 31 pence of English postage for reply to North America; 34 pence to Australia and New Zealand.
‡Microfilm/microfiche copies available at above repository
#Microfilm copy available at the LDS Family History Library in Salt Lake City, Utah, and through the LDS Family History Centers.
##Microfiche copy available at the LDS Family History Library in Salt Lake City, Utah, and through the LDS Family History Centers.

GENEALOGICAL AND FAMILY HISTORY SOCIETIES

The societies listed below may have recorded Monumental (tombstone) Inscriptions, compiled an Index to Marriages (from the Parish Registers), an Index to the 1851 Census, and other special indexes, e.g., Strays, Members' Interests, for their geographical areas.** Each Society publishes a quarterly journal (listed in italics) which includes articles on family history, reports on the group's projects, and members' queries.

GLOUCESTERSHIRE FAMILY HISTORY SOCIETY†
Mrs. P. Jackson, Secretary
"Hollington House," 74 Woodfield Road, Cam
Dursley, Glos GL11 6HF

Gloucestershire Family History Society Journal

**See *Current Publications by Member Societies* (annual), *List of Family History Project Coordinators,* 6th ed., and *Family History News and Digest* (biennial) — all published by the Federation of Family History Societies; available in the USA from the International Society for British Genealogy and Family History, P.O. Box 20425, Cleveland, OH 44120.

†For additional information send 2 Postal Reply Coupons or 31 pence of English postage for reply to North America; 34 pence to Australia and New Zealand.

HAMPSHIRE

Post-1974 Counties of England

The pre-1974 geographical boundaries of Hampshire included the Bournemouth region now in Dorset. The Isle of Wight, now a separate county, was also part of Hampshire prior to 1891.

Administratively Southampton was a County Corporate from the twelfth century to 1889 and a County Borough between 1889 and 1974. Portsmouth was an incorporated Borough from the seventeenth century to 1889 and then a County Borough to 1974. Bournemouth was a Municipal Borough from 1889 to 1900 and a County Borough from 1900 to 1974. Andover, Basingstoke, Lymington, Petersfield, Romsey and Winchester were all incorporated Boroughs from the seventeenth century to 1974.

191

RECORD OFFICES

HAMPSHIRE RECORD OFFICE
20 Southgate Street, Winchester S023 9EF
Tel. 0962 63153

Hours: M-Th 9-4:45; F 9-4:15;
        Oct-Mar: S 9-12;
        Apr-Sep: 2nd/4th S/mo 9-12
        (Prior appointment advised)

Admission free
List of record searchers available upon request[†]

HOLDINGS

Church of England diocesan records for the Diocese of Winchester; Church of England parish records including deposited Parish Registers for churches in the present county (cities of Southampton and Portsmouth on microfiche); local government records and other resources for the pre-1974 division of the county, except for Southampton and Portsmouth.

SOURCES THAT IDENTIFY AN INDIVIDUAL WITH A SPECIFIC LOCATION

Borough Records (Basingstoke,	16C–20C
Winchester, Lymington)	
Freemen's Lists	
Rates	
Church of England (diocesan)	
Ecclesiastical Court Books	16C–20C
Ecclesiastical Visitations	16C–20C
Tithe Apportionments	1840's
Church of England (parish)	
Churchwardens' Accounts	16C–20C

[†]For additional information send 2 Postal Reply Coupons or 31 pence of English postage for reply to North America; 34 pence to Australia and New Zealand.

Directories* (some#)	(gaps) 1784–
Business/Trade, Postal	18C–19C
Enclosure Awards	19C
Maps	17C–
Militia Lists	late 16C–17C
Parish Poor Law Records	1600's–1834
Parish Poor Rates	
Poll Books* (some#)	(periodic) 18C–1832
Quarter Sessions	
Judicial Records	17C–20C
Hearth Tax Assessments#	(gaps) 1664–1674
Land Tax Assessments	1800–1834
Lists of Freeholders	
Lists of Jurors	
Registration of Papist Property	18C
Registers of Electors*	1832–

SOURCES THAT MAY ADDITIONALLY PROVIDE VITAL DATA AND/OR PROVE FAMILY RELATIONSHIPS

Borough Records (Basingstoke,	17C–19C
Winchester, Lymington, Andover)	
Court	
Guilds: (Winchester only)	
Admissions	
Apprenticeship Enrolments	
Title Deeds	
Cemetery Registers	1859–1949
Census‡# (Hants and Isle of Wight)	1841–1881
Church of England (diocesan)	
Bishops' Transcripts	1780–1858
Marriage Licence Bonds	1607–1942
and Allegations	(‡# to 1837)
Wills, Admon., Inven.#	c. 1500–1858

*Printed or transcribed

#Microfilm copy available at the LDS Family History Library in Salt Lake City, Utah, and through the LDS Family History Centers.

‡Microfilm/microfiche copies available at above repository

Church of England (parish)
  Parish Registers (some#)   1538–1980's
  Parish Register Transcripts* (some#)   16C–19C
  International Genealogical Index‡##
    (Hants)
  Manorial Records   13C–20C
  Monumental Inscriptions*   16C–20C
  Newspapers*   18C–20C
  Nonconformist Registers (also#)
    Baptist   1730–1858
    Independent   1691–1983
    Methodist   1798–1984
    Society of Friends (some#)   1638–1910
  Obituary Notices*   19C
  Parish Poor Law Records   17C–1834
    Apprenticeship Indentures
    Examinations
    Removal Orders
    Settlement Papers
  Poor Law Union
    Workhouse Records   1835–1948
  Roman Catholic Registers‡#   18C–20C
    (Winchester St. Peter)
  School Records   19C–20C
  Title Deeds   13C–
  Wills, Register Copies#   1858–1941

#Microfilm copy available at the LDS Family History Library in Salt Lake City, Utah, and through the LDS Family History Centers.
*Printed or transcribed
‡Microfilm/microfiche copies available at above repository
##Microfiche copy available at the LDS Family History Library in Salt Lake City, Utah, and through the LDS Family History Centers.

PUBLICATIONS†

Leaflets/Lists:

Hampshire Record Office: Transcripts of
  Parish Registers
Hampshire Record Office: Sources for Genealogy
List of Parishes for which Registers are Held

PORTSMOUTH CITY RECORDS OFFICE

3 Museum Road, Portsmouth PO1 2LE

Tel. 0705 829765

Hours: M, T, W 9:30-12:30, 2-5;
  Th 9:30-12:30, 2-7;
  F 9:30-12:30, 2-4

Admission free

List of record searchers available upon request†

HOLDINGS

Church of England parish records including deposited Parish Registers for approximately 60 churches in part of the Diocese of Portsmouth; local government and other resources pertaining exclusively to the city.

SOURCES THAT IDENTIFY AN INDIVIDUAL WITH A SPECIFIC LOCATION

Borough Records (Portsmouth) (some*#)	1313–
Burgesses and Freemen	1445–
Rates	1705–

---

†For additional information send 2 Postal Reply Coupons or 31 pence of English postage for reply to North America; 34 pence to Australia and New Zealand.
*Printed or transcribed
#Microfilm copy available at the LDS Family History Library in Salt Lake City, Utah, and through the LDS Family History Centers.

Church of England (diocesan)
Tithe Apportionments§   1838
Church of England (parish)
Churchwardens' Accounts   1632–
Directories* (some#)   mid-19C
Postal
Enclosure Awards   1785–1822
Maps   16C–20C
Militia Lists
Poll Books* (some#)   18C–19C
Quarter Sessions
Judicial Records   17C–19C
Lists of Jurors   17C–19C
Parish Poor Law Records   17C–19C
Parish Poor Rates   1705–
Registers of Electors*   1835–
Shipping–Crew Lists   1863–1913

*SOURCES THAT MAY ADDITIONALLY PROVIDE VITAL
DATA AND/OR PROVE FAMILY RELATIONSHIPS*

Borough Records (Portsmouth) (some*#)   1313–
Court   1531–1834
Title Deeds   16C–
Cemetery Registers   1831–1955
Church of England (parish)
Parish Registers (SE Hants)   1538–
Estate and Family Papers   16C–20C
Manorial Records   16C–20C
Monumental Inscriptions

§Parish copies only; main series at Hampshire Record Office, Winchester.
*Printed or transcribed
#Microfilm copy available at the LDS Family History Library in Salt Lake City,
Utah, and through the LDS Family History Centers.

Nonconformist Registers

Independent/Congregational (some#)	1785–
Methodist (some#)	1798–
Presbyterian	1856–
Unitarian	1837–

Parish Poor Law Records

Apprenticeship Indentures	1654–1776
Examinations	1826–1836
Removal Orders	1698–1832
Settlement Papers	1681–1836

Poor Law Union

Workhouse Records	1834–c. 1950
Roman Catholic Records	1794–
School Records	18C–20C
Title Deeds	16C–

PUBLICATIONS†

Leaflet: *Portsmouth City Records Office*

SOUTHAMPTON CITY RECORD OFFICE
Civic Centre, Southampton SO9 4XR
Tel. 0703 832251

Hours: M-F 9-1, 1:30-5;
Other times by appointment

Admission free
List of record searchers available upon request†

#Microfilm copy available at the LDS Family History Library in Salt Lake City, Utah, and through the LDS Family History Centers.

†For additional information send 2 Postal Reply Coupons or 31 pence of English postage for reply to North America; 34 pence to Australia and New Zealand.

HOLDINGS

Southampton Borough Records 12C–20C; Church of England parish records for most city parishes; other records relating to the area of the present city of Southampton.

SOURCES

Borough Administration
Rates and Tax Lists#§	1552–
Burgess and Freemen Registers#	1496–1726
Nomination Rolls (Town Officers)	1617–1836
(partial index)	
Title Deeds	mid-13C–
Borough Remembrance and Minute Books††	13C–
Registers of Enrolled Documents	1392–1689††
Militia Lists	1544–1589, 1788–1831
Poll Books*#	1727–1837
Registers of Electors*	1835–1918, 1930–
Stewards' (Treasurers') Accounts††	1428–1705
Port or Petty Customs Accounts††	1426–1601, 1723–1773
Brokage (Landgate Dues) Accounts††	1430–1566
Smallpox Innoculation Committee Minutes and Lists‡‡	1774–1783
Survey of all Properties in Southampton*	1454
Survey of Council Properties on Lease	1617
School Attendance Registers	1863–

#Microfilm copy available at the LDS Family History Library in Salt Lake City, Utah, and through the LDS Family History Centers.
§Borough and/or parish-poor, scavage, water rates; land, hearth, window and various other parlimentary taxes.
††Partly printed
*Printed or transcribed
‡‡Indexed

Borough Courts
    Court Leet (proceedings, stall and art lists)   1549–
                                                      (* to 1624)
    Quarter Sessions (Court rolls, order   1609–1842
        books, indictments and papers)
    Court Examination Books‡‡   1575–1698
    Town and Piepowder Courts (difficult to use)   1474–1785
    Admiralty Court   1488–1827
                                                      (1566–1585*)
Church of England (parish)
    Parish Registers§§ (some#,##)   16C–20C
        (Southampton)
    Churchwardens' Accounts   16C–
    Church Rates#

Nonconformist Churches and
        Civil Registrar's Registers
    Congregational/Independent (some#)   1674–1868
    Methodist   1837–1969
    Presbyterian (Communicants Rolls)   1851–1960
    Unitarian   1883–1940
    Civil Registrar's Marriage Notice Books   1871–1936

Poor Law Records (borough and parish)
    Rates (see under Borough Administration)
    Apprenticeship Registers*   1609–1740
    Registers of Examination for Settlement   1711–1901
    Registers of Examinations as to Bastardy   1811-1839
    Removal Orders (St. Mary Parish)

---

*Printed or transcribed
‡‡Indexed
§§Indexed to 1850
#Microfilm copy available at the LDS Family History Library in Salt Lake City, Utah, and through the LDS Family History Centers.
##Microfiche copy available at the LDS Family History Library in Salt Lake City, Utah, and through the LDS Family History Centers.

Other Records and Sources

Title Deeds	14C–
Crew Lists	1863–1913
Funeral Firms' Order Books	1866–1962
Notes on Quakers Living	1650–1699
Maps	17C–
Street Directories* (some#)	1803–
Street Directory* (compiled from records)	1620

PUBLICATIONS†

Southampton's History (list of publications for sale)

OTHER REPOSITORIES

The sources listed below include only those items reported on the Record Office Survey as located in the specified repositories. Each city and county library should have additional printed materials pertaining to its geographical area.

HAMPSHIRE COUNTY LIBRARY†
Central Reference Library
81 North Walls
Winchester SO23 8BY
Tel. 0926 60644

International Genealogical Index‡##
(British Isles)

---

*Printed or transcribed

#Microfilm copy available at the LDS Family History Library in Salt Lake City, Utah, and through the LDS Family History Centers.

†For additional information send 2 Postal Reply Coupons or 31 pence of English postage for reply to North America; 34 pence to Australia and New Zealand.

‡Microfilm/microfiche copies available at above repository

##Microfiche copy available at the LDS Family History Library in Salt Lake City, Utah, and through the LDS Family History Centers.

PORTSMOUTH CENTRAL LIBRARY†
Reference Library
Guildhall Square, Portsmouth, PO1 2DX
Tel. 0705 819311

Census‡# (Portsmouth)   1841–1881
International Genealogical Index‡##
(Hants and Sussex)

SOUTHAMPTON CENTRAL LIBRARY†
Reference Library
Civic Centre, Southampton S09 4XP
Tel. 0703 23855

Census‡# (Southampton)   1841–1881
International Genealogical Index‡##   1978
(Hants, Dorset, Sussex, Wilts)

LDS FAMILY HISTORY CENTRE†
Chetwynd Road
Bassett, Southampton
Tel. 0703 767476

LDS Family History Library Catalog‡##
International Genealogical Index‡##

---

†For additional information send 2 Postal Reply Coupons or 31 pence of English
postage for reply to North America; 34 pence to Australia and New Zealand.
‡Microfilm/microfiche copies available at above repository
#Microfilm copy available at the LDS Family History Library in Salt Lake City,
Utah, and through the LDS Family History Centers.
##Microfiche copy available at the LDS Family History Library in Salt Lake
City, Utah, and through the LDS Family History Centers.

GENEALOGICAL AND FAMILY HISTORY SOCIETIES

The societies listed below may have recorded Monumental (tombstone) Inscriptions, compiled an Index to Marriages (from the Parish Registers), an Index to the 1851 Census, and other special indexes, e.g., Strays, Members' Interests, for their geographical areas.** Each Society publishes a quarterly journal (listed in italics) which includes articles on family history, reports on the group's projects, and members' queries.

HAMPSHIRE GENEALOGICAL SOCIETY†
Mr. N.W. Thompson, Secretary
37 Russell Road
Lee-on-the-Solent, Hampshire PO13 9HR

The Hampshire Family Historian

**See *Current Publications by Member Societies* (annual), *List of Family History Project Coordinators*, 6th ed., and *Family History News and Digest* (biennial) — all published by the Federation of Family History Societies; available in the USA from the International Society for British Genealogy and Family History, P.O. Box 20425, Cleveland, OH 44120.

†For additional information send 2 Postal Reply Coupons or 31 pence of English postage for reply to North America; 34 pence to Australia and New Zealand.

HEREFORD AND WORCESTER

Post-1974 Counties of England

The County of Hereford and Worcester was created in 1974. Geographically it includes the area formerly in Herefordshire and most of the former county of Worcestershire. The northern tip of the latter (Stourbridge, Halesowen and Dudley areas) àre now in the West Midlands Metropolitan County.

Administratively the former county of Herefordshire contained the incorporated Boroughs of Hereford (fourteenth century to 1974) and Leominster (sixteenth century to 1974).

The former county of Worcestershire included the city of Worcester which was a County Corporate from the seventeenth century to 1889 and a County Borough between 1889 and 1974.

203

Bewdley, Droitwich, Evesham and Kidderminster were all incorporated Boroughs from the seventeenth century to 1974.

RECORD OFFICES

HEREFORD AND WORCESTER RECORD OFFICE (HEREFORD SECTION)

(Formerly Herefordshire Record Office)
Old Barracks, Harold Street
Hereford HR1 2QX
Tel. 0432 265441

Hours: M 10-1, 2-4:45;
      T, W, Th 9:15-1, 2-4:45;
      F 9:15-1, 2-4
      Closed first two full weeks in October

Admission free
Names of panel record searchers available upon request[†]

HOLDINGS

Most Church of England diocesan records for the Diocese of Hereford; Church of England parish records including deposited Parish Registers for approximately 150 churches formerly in Herefordshire; local government records and other resources pertaining to the pre-1974 area of Herefordshire.

(Some records for Herefordshire have been deposited in the National Library of Wales, Aberystwyth, Dyfed, Wales, and may have been microfilmed by the Genealogical Society of Utah.)

[†]For additional information send 2 Postal Reply Coupons or 31 pence of English postage for reply to North America; 34 pence to Australia and New Zealand.

SOURCES THAT IDENTIFY AN INDIVIDUAL WITH A SPECIFIC LOCATION

Borough Records (Hereford)	c. 1400–20C
Freemen's Lists	
Rates	
Church of England (diocesan)	
Ecclesiastical Court Books	1445–1831
Ecclesiastical Visitations	16C–19C
Tithe Apportionments	19C
Church of England (parish)	
Churchwardens' Accounts	17C–
Directories* (some#)	19C–
Business/Trade	
Enclosure Awards	19C
Maps	17C–20C
Parish Poor Law Records	17C–1834
Parish Poor Rates	
Poll Books* (some#) (periodic)	18C
Quarter Sessions (some#)	
Judicial Records	17C–20C
Land Tax Assessments (some#)	1780–1832
Registration of Papist Property (some#)	18C
Registers of Electors*	1832–

SOURCES THAT MAY ADDITIONALLY PROVIDE VITAL DATA AND/OR PROVE FAMILY RELATIONSHIPS

Borough Records (Hereford)	c. 1400–20C
Court	
Title Deeds	
Census‡# (Most of Hereford)	1841–1881

---

*Printed or transcribed

#Microfilm copy available at the LDS Family History Library in Salt Lake City, Utah, and through the LDS Family History Centers.

‡Microfilm/microfiche copies available at above repository

Church of England (diocesan)

Bishops' Transcripts[#]	1660–1850
Marriage Licence Bonds	1662–
and Allegations[#]	
Wills, Admon., Inven.[§#]	1540–1858

Church of England (parish)

Parish Registers	1538–
Parish Register Transcripts[*]	
Estate and Family Papers	17C
International Genealogical Index[‡##]	
(British Isles)	
Manorial Records	13C–19C
Newspapers[*]	1770–1911
Nonconformist Registers	
Baptist	17C–1837[#], 19C–20C
Independent (Congregational)	17C–1837[#], 19C–20C
Methodist	19C–20C
Presbyterian	
Society of Friends	17C–1837[#], 19C–20C
Parish Poor Law Records	17C–1834
Apprenticeship Indentures	
Examinations	
Removal Orders	
Settlement Papers	
Poor Law Union	1834–
Workhouse Records	

[#]Microfilm copy available at the LDS Family History Library in Salt Lake City, Utah, and through the LDS Family History Centers.
[§]Abstracts of wills microfilmed.
[*]Printed or transcribed
[‡]Microfilm/microfiche copies available at above repository
[##]Microfiche copy available at the LDS Family History Library in Salt Lake City, Utah, and through the LDS Family History Centers.

Roman Catholic Registers	19C–20C
School Records	19C
Title Deeds	11C–

PUBLICATIONS†

The Parish Registers of Herefordshire

COUNTY OF HEREFORD AND WORCESTER RECORD OFFICE
WORCESTER HEADQUARTERS
County Hall, Spetchley Road
Worcester WR5 2NP
Tel. 0905 353366 ext. 3612††

Hours: M 10-4:45;
       T, W, Th 9:15-4:45;
       F 9:15-4
       Closed first two full weeks in October

Admission free
List of record searchers available upon request†

HOLDINGS

Local government records pertaining to pre-1974 Worcestershire. Original and microfilm copies of some Church of England diocesan and parish records, and other resources.

SOURCES THAT IDENTIFY AN INDIVIDUAL WITH A SPECIFIC LOCATION

Borough Records (Bewdley, Droitwich, Evesham)
    Freemen's Lists
    Rates

---

†For additional information send 2 Postal Reply Coupons or 31 pence of English postage for reply to North America; 34 pence to Australia and New Zealand.
††Change of telephone number proposed for early 1988; to be 0905 763763 ext. 3612

Directories* (some#)	late 18C–
Enclosure Awards	19C
Photographs	
Quarter Sessions	
Judicial Records (some#)	17C–20C
Hearth Tax Assessments#	1665
Land Tax Assessments (some#)	1781–1832
Lists of Freeholders (some#)	
Lists of Jurors (some#)	
Registers of Electors*	1832–
	(1843–1888#)

SOURCES THAT MAY ADDITIONALLY PROVIDE VITAL DATA AND/OR PROVE FAMILY RELATIONSHIPS

Borough Records (Bewdley, Droitwich, Evesham)	
Court	
Title Deeds	
Census‡# (Worcs)	1841–1881
Church of England (diocesan)	
Bishops' Transcripts (some#)	17C–19C
Marriage Licence Bonds	1604–
and Allegations (some#)	
Probate Records#	16C–1858
(Wills, Admon., Inven.)	
Church of England (parish)	
Parish Registers#	1538–
Parish Register Transcripts*#	16C–19C
Civil Registration Indexes‡‡	1837–1912
(births, marriages and deaths)	
Hospital Records§§	

---

*Printed or transcribed

#Microfilm copy available at the LDS Family History Library in Salt Lake City, Utah, and through the LDS Family History Centers.

‡Microfilm/microfiche copies available at above repository

‡‡Microfilm copy filmed by the General Register Office, London

§§Subject to 100 years' embargo

International Genealogical Index[‡##]
Newspapers[#]   18C–20C
Nonconformist Registers
  Methodist   19C–
  Society of Friends (some[#])   1686–1837
Poor Law Union   1834–1929
  Workhouse Records
School Records   19C–
Wills, Register Copies[#]   1858–1928

PUBLICATIONS[†]

Genealogical Resources in Worcestershire
Herefordshire Parish Registers

HEREFORD AND WORCESTER RECORD OFFICE
(WORCESTER BRANCH)
(formerly part of Worcestershire Record Office)
St. Helen's, Fish Street
Worcester WR1 2HN
Tel. 0905 353366 ext. 3616[††]

Hours: M 10-4:45;
        T, W, Th 9:15-4:45;
        F 9:15-4
        Closed first two full weeks in October

Admission free
List of record searchers available upon request[†]

[‡]Microfilm/microfiche copies available at above repository
[##]Microfiche copy available at the LDS Family History Library in Salt Lake City, Utah, and through the LDS Family History Centers.
[#]Microfilm copy available at the LDS Family History Library in Salt Lake City, Utah, and through the LDS Family History Centers.
[†]For additional information send 2 Postal Reply Coupons or 31 pence of English postage for reply to North America; 34 pence to Australia and New Zealand.
[††]Change of telephone number proposed for early 1988: to be 0905 763763 ext. 3616

HOLDINGS

Church of England diocesan records (Diocese of Worcester) excluding Bishops's Transcripts and Marriage Allegations and Bonds. Church of England parish records, excluding original Parish Registers; other non-official Worcestershire resources pertaining to the pre-1974 county.

SOURCES THAT IDENTIFY AN INDIVIDUAL WITH A SPECIFIC LOCATION

Borough Records (city of Worcester)   16C–20C
   Freemen's Lists
   Apprenticeship Records
   Rates
Church of England (diocesan)
   Ecclesiastical Court Books   16C–20C
   Ecclesiastical Visitations   16C–20C
   Tithe Apportionments   mid-19C
Church of England (parish)
   Churchwardens's Accounts   17C–
Directories* (some#)
   Business, Postal
Maps   12C–
Parish Poor Law Records   17C–1834
   Parish Poor Rates

SOURCES THAT MAY ADDITIONALLY PROVIDE VITAL DATA AND / OR PROVE FAMILY RELATIONSHIPS

Borough Records (city of Worcester)   16C–20C
   Court
   Title Deeds
Estate and Family Papers   12C–
Manorial Records   12C–

---

*Printed or transcribed
#Microfilm copy available at the LDS Family History Library in Salt Lake City, Utah, and through the LDS Family History Centers.

Parish Poor Law Records	17C–1834
Apprenticeship Indentures	
Examinations	
Removal Orders	
Settlement Papers	
Title Deeds	12C–

OTHER REPOSITORIES

The sources listed below include only those items reported on the Record Office Survey as located in the specified repositories. Each city and county library should have additional printed materials pertaining to its geographical area.

HEREFORD PUBLIC LIBRARY†
Broad Street, Hereford HR4 9AU
Tel.

Census‡# (Herefordshire)	1841–1881
International Genealogical Index‡##	
(Herefordshire)	

---

†For additional information send 2 Postal Reply Coupons or 31 pence of English postage for reply to North America; 34 pence to Australia and New Zealand.
‡Microfilm/microfiche copies available at above repository
#Microfilm copy available at the LDS Family History Library in Salt Lake City, Utah, and through the LDS Family History Centers.
##Microfiche copy available at the LDS Family History Library in Salt Lake City, Utah, and through the LDS Family History Centers.

GENEALOGICAL AND FAMILY HISTORY SOCIETIES

The societies listed below may have recorded Monumental (tombstone) Inscriptions, compiled an Index to Marriages (from the Parish Registers), an Index to the 1851 Census, and other special indexes, e.g., Strays, Members' Interests, for their geographical areas.** Each Society publishes a quarterly journal (listed in italics) which includes articles on family history, reports on the group's projects, and members' queries.

HEREFORDSHIRE FAMILY HISTORY SOCIETY†
Miss V.J. Robinson, Secretary
4 Burmarsh
Sutton St. Nicholas
Hereford HR1 3BW

Herefordshire Family History Society Journal

BIRMINGHAM AND MIDLAND SOCIETY FOR GENEALOGY AND HERALDRY†
Mrs. J. Watkins, Secretary
92 Dimmingsdale Bank
Birmingham, W. Midlands B32 1ST

Midland Ancestor

**See *Current Publications by Member Societies* (annual), *List of Family History Project Coordinators*, 6th ed., and *Family History News and Digest* (biennial) — all published by the Federation of Family History Societies; available in the USA from the International Society for British Genealogy and Family History, P.O. Box 20425, Cleveland, OH 44120.

†For additional information send 2 Postal Reply Coupons or 31 pence of English postage for reply to North America; 34 pence to Australia and New Zealand.

HEREFORDSHIRE

Pre-1974 Counties of England

The county of Herefordshire was abolished in 1974. The area within its boundaries was united with most of the former county of Worcestershire to establish the county of Hereford and Worcester.

Administratively Hereford and Leominster were incorporated Boroughs in Herefordshire from the fourteenth and sixteenth centuries, respectively, to 1974.

See the Hereford and Worcester Record Office (Hereford Section) for genealogical sources pertaining to the former county of Herefordshire.

HERTFORDSHIRE

Post-1974 Counties of England

The pre-1965 geographical boundaries of Hertfordshire included the present county, and in addition, the area of Barnet now in the area of Greater London. That year the parish of South Mimms was transferred from Middlesex County to Hertfordshire. There were no additional boundary changes in 1974.

Administratively Hertford was an incorporated Borough from the mid-sixteenth century to 1974, and the Liberty of St. Albans was exempt from most county jurisdiction during the same period.

214

RECORD OFFICE

HERTFORDSHIRE RECORD OFFICE
County Hall, Hertford SG13 8DE
Tel. 0992 555105

Hours: M-Th 9:15-5:15; F 9:15-4:30
(Prior appointment advised)

Admission free

List of record searchers available upon request†

HOLDINGS

Church of England archidiaconal records for the Archdeaconry of St. Albans (Diocese of London), and the Archdeaconry of Huntingdon (Hitchin Division, Diocese of Lincoln to 1845, Diocese of Rochester 1845–1877, Diocese of St. Albans 1877–); Church of England parish records including deposited Parish Registers for approximately 140 churches in these archdeaconries; local government records and other resources for the county.

SOURCES THAT IDENTIFY AN INDIVIDUAL WITH A SPECIFIC LOCATION

Borough Records (Hertford)	late 16C–20C
Freemen's Lists	
Rates	
Church of England (archidiaconal)	
Ecclesiastical Court Books	16C–18C
Ecclesiastical Visitations	17C–19C
Tithe Apportionments	1836–20C
Church of England (parish)	
Churchwardens' Accounts	15C–20C

---

†For additional information send 2 Postal Reply Coupons or 31 pence of English postage for reply to North America; 34 pence to Australia and New Zealand.

Directories* (some#)	19C–20C
Business/Trade, Postal	
Enclosure Awards	late 18C, 19C
Maps	16C–20C
Militia Lists#	1758–1801
Parish Poor Law Records	17C–1834
Parish Poor Rates	
Poll Books* (some#)	(periodic) 1697–1832
Quarter Sessions	
Judicial Records	
County	1588–
Borough of Hertford	1573–
Liberty of St. Albans	1758–
Hearth Tax Assessments#	(gaps) 1662–1623
Land Tax Assessments (some#)	1690,
	1715–1830's
Lists of Jurors	1728–1920
Registration of Papist Property	1717–1765
Registers of Electors*	1832–

SOURCES THAT MAY ADDITIONALLY PROVIDE VITAL DATA AND/OR PROVE FAMILY RELATIONSHIPS

Borough Records (Hertford)	late 16C–
Court	
Title Deeds	
Church of England (archidiaconal)	
Bishops' Transcripts	1561–1883
Marriage Licence Bonds	17C–19C
and Allegations#	
Wills, Admon., Inven.#	15C–1858
Church of England (parish)	
Parish Registers#	1538–1900's
Parish Register Transcripts*#	16C–19C

---

*Printed or transcribed

#Microfilm copy available at the LDS Family History Library in Salt Lake City, Utah, and through the LDS Family History Centers.

Estate and Family Papers	12C–20C
International Genealogical Index‡##	
(Herts)	
Manorial Records	13C–20C
Nonconformist Registers	
Baptist‡#	1717–1837
Independent (Congregational)‡#	1748–1855
Methodist‡#	1825–1837
Presbyterian‡#	1729–1799
Society of Friends*#	1643–1838
Newspapers*	1816–1972
Parish Poor Law Records	17C–1834
Apprenticeship Indentures	
Examinations	
Removal Orders	
Settlement Papers	
Poor Law Union	1834–1929
Workhouse Records	
School Records	18C–20C
Title Deeds	11C–20C

PUBLICATIONS†

A Brief Guide to the Hertfordshire Record Office Genealogical Sources (rev. 1987)

---

‡Microfilm/microfiche copies available at above repository

##Microfiche copy available at the LDS Family History Library in Salt Lake City, Utah, and through the LDS Family History Centers.

#Microfilm copy available at the LDS Family History Library in Salt Lake City, Utah, and through the LDS Family History Centers.

†For additional information send 2 Postal Reply Coupons or 31 pence of English postage for reply to North America; 34 pence to Australia and New Zealand.

OTHER REPOSITORIES

The sources listed below include only those items reported on the Record Office Survey as located in the specified repositories. Each city and county library should have additional printed materials pertaining to its geographical area.

HERTFORDSHIRE COUNTY LIBRARY†
(Local Studies)
County Hall, Hertford SG13 8EJ
Tel. 0992 54242

Census‡# (Herts)   1841–1881

GENEALOGICAL AND FAMILY HISTORY SOCIETIES

The societies listed below may have recorded Monumental (tombstone) Inscriptions, compiled an Index to Marriages (from the Parish Registers), an Index to the 1851 Census, and other special indexes, e.g., Strays, Members' Interests, for their geographical areas.** Each Society publishes a quarterly journal (listed in italics) which includes articles on family history, reports on the group's projects, and members' queries.

---

†For additional information send 2 Postal Reply Coupons or 31 pence of English postage for reply to North America; 34 pence to Australia and New Zealand.
‡Microfilm/microfiche copies available at above repository
#Microfilm copy available at the LDS Family History Library in Salt Lake City, Utah, and through the LDS Family History Centers.
**See *Current Publications by Member Societies* (annual), *List of Family History Project Coordinators*, 6th ed., and *Family History News and Digest* (biennial) — all published by the Federation of Family History Societies; available in the USA from the International Society for British Genealogy and Family History, P.O. Box 20425, Cleveland, OH 44120.

**HERTFORDSHIRE FAMILY HISTORY
AND POPULATION SOCIETY**[†]
Mrs. P. Betty, Secretary
6 The Crest
Ware, Hertfordshire SG12 0RR
  Journal of the Hertfordshire Family History Society

[†]For additional information send 2 Postal Reply Coupons or 31 pence of English
postage for reply to North America; 34 pence to Australia and New Zealand.

HUMBERSIDE

Post-1974 Counties of England

The county of Humberside was created in 1974. It contains most of the former East Riding of Yorkshire, including the areas of Beverley, Bridlington and Hedon. Hedon was an incorporated Borough from the seventeenth century; Beverly and Bridlington were nineteenth-century Municipal Boroughs until 1974. Kingston upon Hull was a County Corporate from the fourteenth century to 1889 and then a County Borough to 1974. (Great) Grimsby, an incorporated Borough in Lincolnshire from the thirteenth century to 1889 and then a County Borough to 1974, was also transferred to Humberside that year.

(See also the South Humberside Area Record Office in Grimsby, the Kingston upon Hull Record Office, and the Lincolnshire Archives Office for genealogical resources pertaining to the respective pre-1974 areas.)

RECORD OFFICES

HUMBERSIDE COUNTY RECORD OFFICE
County Hall, Beverley HU17 9BA
Tel. 0482 867131 ext. 3393/4

Hours: By prior appointment only:
M, W, Th 9-4:45; T 9-8; F 9-4; closed S

Admission free
Professional genealogical searching service:
details available upon request[†]

HOLDINGS
Church of England parish records including deposited Parish Registers for more than 160 churches in the Archdeaconry of the East Riding (mainly in the pre-1974 East Riding of Yorkshire, but also some within the pre-1974 North Riding of Yorkshire and the present county of North Yorkshire); local government records and other resources for the pre-1974 East Riding of Yorkshire.

(Church of England diocesan records and some parish records including deposited Parish Registers for 785 churches are located in the Borthwick Institute in York.)

[†]For additional information send 2 Postal Reply Coupons or 31 pence of English postage for reply to North America; 34 pence to Australia and New Zealand.

SOURCES THAT IDENTIFY AN INDIVIDUAL WITH A SPECIFIC LOCATION

Borough Records (Beverley,*# Hedon)	13C–20C
Freemen's Lists	
Quarter Sessions (Beverley)	1706–20C
Rates	
Business Records	16C–20C
Church of England (diocesan)	
Tithe Apportionments§	1838–20C
Church of England (parish)	16C–20C
Churchwardens' Accounts	
Enclosure Awards	18C–1904
Militia Lists	1763–1848
Parish Poor Law Records	17C–1834
Parish Poor Rates	
Poll Books* (some#)	18C–19C
Quarter Sessions	
Judicial Records	17C–20C
Hearth Tax Assessments‡#	17C
Land Tax Assessments	1782–1832
Lists of Freeholders	1757–1789
Lists of Jurors	1757–1789
Registration of Papist Property	18C
Registers of Electors*	1832–

SOURCES THAT MAY ADDITIONALLY PROVIDE VITAL DATA AND/OR PROVE FAMILY RELATIONSHIPS

Borough Records (Beverley,*# Hedon)	13C–20C
Court	
Title Deeds	
Cemetery Registers	19C–20C

---

*Printed or transcribed

#Microfilm copy available at the LDS Family History Library in Salt Lake City, Utah, and through the LDS Family History Centers.

§Parish copies mainly; principal series at the Borthwick Institute, York.

‡Microfilm/microfiche copies available at above repository

Census‡# (Yorkshire, East Riding)	1841–1881
Church of England (parish)	
Parish Registers	1538–
Estate and Family Papers	12C–20C
Manorial Records	14C–20C
Nonconformist Registers	
Baptist	1698–1837‡#;
	1838–
Independent	1691–1837‡#;
	1838–
Methodist	1797–1837‡#;
	1838–
Society of Friends	1655–1792‡#
Unitarian	1705–1835‡#
Parish Poor Law Records	17C–1834
Apprenticeship Indentures	
Examinations	
Removal Orders	
Settlement Papers	
Poor Law Union	1836–1930
Workhouse Records	
Roman Catholic Registers	1744–1810‡#
School Records	19C–20C
Title Deeds	12C–
Yorkshire, East Riding Register	1708–1976
of Deeds	

---

‡Microfilm/microfiche copies available at above repository
#Microfilm copy available at the LDS Family History Library in Salt Lake City, Utah, and through the LDS Family History Centers.

PUBLICATIONS†

Leaflets/Lists:
East Riding Register of Deeds: Guide for Users
List of Parish Registers on Deposit
List of Nonanglican Church Records on Deposit
Summary List of Quarter Sessions Records (free)
Summary List of Education Records (free)
An Introduction to the Sources for Genealogy

KINGSTON UPON HULL RECORD OFFICE
79 Lowgate
Kingston upon Hull HU1 2AA
Tel. 0482 222015/6

Hours: M-Th 8:30-5; F 8:30-4:30;
By prior appointment alternate W 5-8
(Prior appointment advised)

Admission free
List of researchers available upon request†

HOLDINGS

Local government records and other resources for the city
and the former County of Kingston upon Hull.

(Church of England diocesan records are located at the
Borthwick Institute of Historical Research in York. Original
parish records are located at the Humberside Record Office,
Beverley.)

---

†For additional information send 2 Postal Reply Coupons or 31 pence of English
postage for reply to North America; 34 pence to Australia and New Zealand.

SOURCES THAT IDENTIFY AN INDIVIDUAL WITH A SPECIFIC LOCATION

Borough Records		14C–19C
Rates		
Local Histories*		
Maps		18C–20C
Militia Lists	(few)	16C–19C
Parish Poor Law Records	(few)	17C–1747
Rates and Tax Lists		17C–20C
Quarter Sessions		
Judicial Records		17C–20C
Registers of Electors*		1832–

SOURCES THAT MAY ADDITIONALLY PROVIDE VITAL DATA AND/OR PROVE FAMILY RELATIONSHIPS

Borough Records	
Apprentices	1651–1886
Freemen's Lists	14C–
Index	1545–1835
Freemen's Admission Documents	1797–1818
Burial Ground Records	19C–20C
Manorial Records	14C–20C
Nonconformist Records	
Congregational	19C–20C
Methodist	19C–20C
Quarter Sessions	
Coroners' Inquests	1837–1899
Marriage Tax Assessments	1695,1697
School Registers	19C–20C
Title Deeds*	14C–20C

---

*Printed or transcribed

PUBLICATIONS†

Leaflet: *An Introduction to Sources of Genealogy, Biography and Family History ... in Kingston upon Hull* (1985)

SOUTH HUMBERSIDE AREA RECORD OFFICE
Town Hall Square
Grimsby, South Humberside DN31 1HX
Tel. 0472 353481

Hours: M-Th 9:30-12, 1-5; F 9:30-12, 1-4; closed S
   By prior appointment T evening

HOLDINGS

Resources pertaining to the South Humberside area.
(Church of England diocese and parish records are located at the Lincolnshire Archives Office.)

SOURCES THAT IDENTIFY AN INDIVIDUAL
WITH A SPECIFIC LOCATION

Borough Records (Great Grimsby)
   Rate Books   1871–
Rate Books   1889–1974
Shipping – Crew Lists   1864–1914
Fishing Apprentice Registers   1880–1937
   (Grimsby port)

---

†For additional information send 2 Postal Reply Coupons or 31 pence of English postage for reply to North America; 34 pence to Australia and New Zealand.

SOURCES THAT MAY ADDITIONALLY PROVIDE VITAL DATA AND/OR PROVE FAMILY RELATIONSHIPS

Cemetery Records	1855–1943
Estate and Family Papers	16C–20C
Hospital Records	1890–1948
Nonconformist Records	
Methodist	1769–1823
Poor Law Union	
Workhouse Records	1890–1930
Registers of Births	1895–1953
Registers of Deaths	1894–1956
Creed Registers	1910–1951
School Records††	1863–1974
Title Deeds	16C–1974

OTHER REPOSITORIES

The sources listed below include only those items reported on the Record Office Survey as located in the specified repositories. Each city and county library should have additional printed materials pertaining to its geographical area.

BEVERLEY LIBRARY†
Local History Library
Champney Road, Beverley
Tel. 0482 867108

Census‡# (Yorkshire, East Riding)   1841–1881

††Closed schools in Grimsby Borough
†For additional information send 2 Postal Reply Coupons or 31 pence of English postage for reply to North America; 34 pence to Australia and New Zealand.
‡Microfilm/microfiche copies available at above repository
#Microfilm copy available at the LDS Family History Library in Salt Lake City, Utah, and through the LDS Family History Centers.

KINGSTON UPON HULL CENTRAL LIBRARY†
Local Studies Library
Albion Street, Hull HU1 3TF
Tel. 0482 224040

Census‡#	1841–1881
Directories* (some#)	1790–
Poll Books*	18C–19C

GRIMSBY CENTRAL LIBRARY†
Town Hall Square
Grimsby, South Humberside DN31 1HG
Tel. 0472 240410

Census‡#	1841–1881
Directories* (some#)	
Ecclesiastical Census‡#	1851
Monumental Inscriptions	
Newspapers*	19C–20C
Obituary Notices*	
Poll Books* (some#)	

LDS FAMILY HISTORY CENTRE†
Springfield Way,
Anlaby near Hull, North Humberside
Tel. 0482 572623

LDS Family History Library Catalog‡##
International Genealogical Index‡##

---

†For additional information send 2 Postal Reply Coupons or 31 pence of English postage for reply to North America; 34 pence to Australia and New Zealand.
‡Microfilm/microfiche copies available at above repository
#Microfilm copy available at the LDS Family History Library in Salt Lake City, Utah, and through the LDS Family History Centers.
*Printed or transcribed
##Microfiche copy available at the LDS Family History Library in Salt Lake City, Utah, and through the LDS Family History Centers.

GENEALOGICAL AND FAMILY HISTORY SOCIETIES

The societies listed below may have recorded Monumental (tombstone) Inscriptions, compiled an Index to Marriages (from the Parish Registers), an Index to the 1851 Census, and other special indexes, e.g., Strays, Members' Interests, for their geographical areas.** Each Society publishes a quarterly journal (listed in italics) which includes articles on family history, reports on the group's projects, and members' queries.

EAST YORKSHIRE FAMILY HISTORY SOCIETY†
Mr. R.E. Walgate, Secretary
9 Stepney Grove
Scarborough, N. Yorkshire YO12 5DF

The Banyan Tree

SOCIETY FOR LINCOLNSHIRE
HISTORY AND ARCHÆOLOGY†
(FAMILY HISTORY SUBCOMMITTEE / SECTION)
Mrs. E. Robson, Secretary
135 Baldertongate
Newark, Nottinghamshire NG24 1RY

Lincolnshire Family Historian

**See *Current Publications by Member Societies* (annual), *List of Family History Project Coordinators*, 6th ed., and *Family History News and Digest* (biennial) — all published by the Federation of Family History Societies; available in the USA from the International Society for British Genealogy and Family History, P.O. Box 20425, Cleveland, OH 44120.

†For additional information send 2 Postal Reply Coupons or 31 pence of English postage for reply to North America; 34 pence to Australia and New Zealand.

HUNTINGDONSHIRE

Pre-1974 Counties of England

In 1965 the former county of Huntingdonshire was united with the Soke of Peterborough (geographically in Northampton-shire) to form the county of Huntingdon and Peterborough. In 1974 the county of Huntingdon and Peterborough was united with the county of Cambridgeshire and Isle of Ely to form the present county of Cambridgeshire.

Administratively Huntingdon and Godmanchester were incorporated Boroughs in Huntingdonshire from the seven-teenth century to 1961. That year they were united to form the Municipal Borough of Huntingdon and Godmanchester, which extended to 1974.

See the county of Cambridgeshire for genealogical sources pertaining to the former county of Huntingdonshire and the former county of Huntingdon and Peterborough.

KENT

Post-1974 Counties of England

The pre-1889 geographical boundaries of Kent included the present county, the area which became part of the area of Greater London in 1965, and the areas of Deptford (partly in Surrey), Greenwich, Lewisham and Woolwich which became part of the newly formed County of London in 1889. When the County of London was abolished in 1965, the area within its boundaries was transferred to the newly created area of Greater London. In addition Beckenham, Bexley, Bromley and Erith, all twentieth-century Municipal Boroughs in Kent, were transferred to the area of Greater London that year. There was no change in the geographical boundaries of Kent in 1974.

Administratively the city of Canterbury was a County Corporate from the mid-fifteenth century to 1889 and a County Borough between 1889 and 1974. Dover, Faversham, Folkestone, Gravesend, Hythe, Maidstone, Rochester, (New) Romney, Sandwich, Deal and Tenterden were all incorporated Boroughs in Kent from the end of the seventeenth century to 1974.

The Cinque Ports, a confederation of port towns in Sussex and Kent formed during the eleventh century, originally provided ships and men for the King's service. Dover, Hastings, Hythe, Romney and Sandwich were the original head ports, with the ancient towns of Rye and Winchelsea added later. Thirty other towns in the two counties were attached to one of the head ports, either as a corporate member (by royal charter) or as a noncorporate member (by private agreement). Corporate members were as follows: Seaford and Pevensey attached to Hastings (Sussex), Tenterden (Kent) attached to Rye (Sussex), Faversham and Folkestone attached to Dover (Kent), and Deal attached to Sandwich (Kent). All of the head ports and corporate members had become incorporated Boroughs by the end of the seventeenth century.

RECORD OFFICES

CATHEDRAL ARCHIVES AND LIBRARY, AND CITY AND DIOCESAN RECORD OFFICE, CANTERBURY
The Precincts, Canterbury CT1 2DG
Tel. 0227 463510
Contact: Archivist

Hours: By prior appointment only M-F 9:30-12:45, 2-4:30
        Letter of Introduction necessary for first visit
        (Reserve at least two weeks in advance during
        summer months)
        Closed 3rd week in January, July, and October; a week
        in April, depending on the date of Easter.
Daily fee charged
List of record searchers available upon request[†]

HOLDINGS

Church of England diocesan records excepting wills
(Diocese of Canterbury – East Kent); Church of England Parish
Registers and records for over 100 churches in the Arch-
deaconry of Canterbury; Archives of the city of Canterbury;
Archives of the Dean and Chapter of Canterbury.

(Wills proven in the Diocese of Canterbury before 1858 are
located at the Kent Archives Office, Maidstone.)

SOURCES THAT IDENTIFY AN INDIVIDUAL
WITH A SPECIFIC LOCATION

Borough Records (Canterbury)
Freemen's Lists   c. 1400–1887
Accounts   1393–1830
Census for part of city   c. 1565
Directories* (some#)
Business/Trade   1784, 1826,
                                             1828, 1846

[†]For additional information send 2 Postal Reply Coupons or 31 pence of English
postage for reply to North America; 34 pence to Australia and New Zealand.
*Printed or transcribed
#Microfilm copy available at the LDS Family History Library in Salt Lake City,
Utah, and through the LDS Family History Centers.

Church of England (diocesan)
    Ecclesiastical Court Books††   1399–1728
    Ecclesiastical Call Books††   1598–1794
    Tithe Apportionments   1836–1852
Church of England (parish)
    Catalogues available in Search room;
    (Registers and Records are listed together)
Land Tax Assessments   18C
Lay Subsidies   1542–1607
Parish Poor Law Records
    Dover Workhouse   1773–1836
Plague Tax   1605
Poll Books* (some#)   1792,
                                  1898–1904
Registers of Electors*   1960–1978
Window Tax Assessments   1721–1788

SOURCES THAT MAY ADDITIONALLY PROVIDE VITAL DATA AND/OR PROVE FAMILY RELATIONSHIPS

Borough Records (Canterbury)
    Borough Court of Pleas   1300–1624
    Borough Court of Quarter Sessions   1437–1970
        Order Books##   17C–1970
    Title Deeds: Lease Books
Church of England (diocesan)
    Bishops' Transcripts   c. 1561–1639,
                                    1661–c. 1880
    Marriage Licence Bonds
        and Allegations   1700–1860
    Wills proved *Sede Vancante*   1278–1603
    Wills (all classes)   1570–1639

---

††Early records in Latin
*Printed or transcribed
#Microfilm copy available at the LDS Family History Library in Salt Lake City, Utah, and through the LDS Family History Centers.
##Microfiche copy available at the LDS Family History Library in Salt Lake City, Utah, and through the LDS Family History Centers.

Church of England (parish)
 Parish Registers   1538–20C
 Parish Register Transcripts*   1538–19C
 Manorial Records
  Chapter manors throughout Kent‡‡   13C–18C
 Poor Law Union (Canterbury)
  Minutes only   1728–1929

KENT ARCHIVES OFFICE
County Hall, Maidstone ME14 1XQ
Tel. 0622 671411 ext. 4363
Hours: T-F 9-4:30; closed M, S
Admission free
List of record searchers available upon request†

HOLDINGS

Church of England diocesan records (Diocese of Rochester –
western Kent); Church of England parish records including
deposited Parish Registers for approximately 215 churches
(mainly in the Diocese of Rochester); local government records
and other resources pertaining to the pre-1965 division of
County; pre-1858 Wills for the Diocese of Canterbury.

(Other Church of England diocesan and parish records for
the Diocese of Canterbury are located at the Canterbury
Cathedral Archives.)

---

*Printed or transcribed
‡‡Records of various types, but very difficult to use
†For additional information send 2 Postal Reply Coupons or 31 pence of English
postage for reply to North America; 34 pence to Australia and New Zealand.

SOURCES THAT IDENTIFY AN INDIVIDUAL
WITH A SPECIFIC LOCATION

Borough Records (Maidstone)	14C–20C
Rates	
Church of England (diocesan)	
Ecclesiastical Court Books	15C–17C
Tithe Apportionments	1840's
Church of England (parish)	
Churchwardens' Accounts	16C–
Vestry Minutes	16C–
Directories* (some#)	(gaps) 1839–1938
Postal	
Enclosure Awards	18C–
	early 19C
Maps	1590–
Parish Poor Law Records	17C–1834
Parish Poor Rates	
Poll Books* (some#)	(periodic) 1713–1867
Quarter Sessions	
Judicial Records	17C–20C
Hearth Tax Assessments#	1664
Land Tax Assessments	1780–1832
Lists of Freeholders	1696–1907
Lists of Jurors	1696–1907
Registers of Electors*	1832–
Shipping – Crew Lists	19C

---

*Printed or transcribed

#Microfilm copy available at the LDS Family History Library in Salt Lake City, Utah, and through the LDS Family History Centers.

SOURCES THAT MAY ADDITIONALLY PROVIDE VITAL DATA AND/OR PROVE FAMILY RELATIONSHIPS

Borough Records (Maidstone)
Court   16C–20C
Church of England (diocesan)
Bishops' Transcripts (some#)   18C–20C
Marriage Licence Bonds   (gaps) 1637–1909
and Allegations
Wills, Admon., Inven.#   14C–1858
Church of England (parish)
Parish Registers (some‡#)   1538–20C
Parish Register Transcripts* (some#)   16C–19C
Estate and Family Papers   12C–
Monumental Inscriptions
Nonconformist Registers
Baptist   (few) 17C–1837‡#
1838–
Congregational   (few) 17C–1837‡#
1838–
Methodist‡#   18C
Society of Friends   17C–20C
Parish Poor Law Records   17C–1834
Apprenticeship Indentures
Examinations
Removal Orders
Settlement Papers
Poor Law Union   1834–1929
Workhouse Records
School Records   19C
Title Deeds   12C–

#Microfilm copy available at the LDS Family History Library in Salt Lake City, Utah, and through the LDS Family History Centers.
‡Microfilm/microfiche copies available at above repository
*Printed or transcribed

238

PUBLICATIONS†

Guide to the Kent County Archives Office##(1958)
First Supplement (1971); *Second Supplement* (1983)
Leaflets/Lists:
A Guide to Sources for Family History
List of Parish Registers Deposited

**KENT COUNTY ARCHIVES OFFICE,
SOUTHEAST KENT BRANCH**
Folkestone Central Library
Grace Hill, Folkestone CT20 1HP
Tel. 0303 850123
Hours: M, Th 9-6; W 9-1; T, F 9-7; S 9-5
Prior appointment necessary
Admission free

HOLDINGS

Local government records and other resources pertaining primarily to the Folkestone area.

SOURCES THAT IDENTIFY AN INDIVIDUAL WITH A SPECIFIC LOCATION

Borough Records (Folkestone)	1515–1974
Freement's Lists	1739–1835
Rates	1776–1950
Maps/Plans	1851–1945
Parish Poor Law Records	17C–1888
Parish Poor Rates	1668–1835

†For additional information send 2 Postal Reply Coupons or 31 pence of English postage for reply to North America; 34 pence to Australia and New Zealand.
##Microfiche copy available at the LDS Family History Library in Salt Lake City, Utah, and through the LDS Family History Centers.

Poll Books* (some#)	1754–1865
Quarter Sessions	
Judicial Records (case papers)	1767–1828
Land Tax Assessments	1777–1784
Lists of Jurors	1774–1828

SOURCES THAT MAY ADDITIONALLY PROVIDE VITAL DATA AND/OR PROVE FAMILY RELATIONSHIPS

Borough Records (Folkestone)	1515–1974
Court	1640–1920
Title Deeds	1650–1930
Estate and Family Papers	c. 1650–1920
Nonconformist Records	
Methodist	19C–20C
Parish Poor Law Records	
Apprenticeship Indentures and Papers	1676–1805
Examinations	1698–1832
Removal Orders	1698–1832
Settlement Papers	1698–1932
School Records (Church)	
Log Books	1863–1941

PUBLICATIONS†

Elizabeth Melling, ed., *Kent Archives Office: Second Supplement to Guide* (1983)

---

*Printed or transcribed

#Microfilm copy available at the LDS Family History Library in Salt Lake City, Utah, and through the LDS Family History Centers.

†For additional information send 2 Postal Reply Coupons or 31 pence of English postage for reply to North America; 34 pence to Australia and New Zealand.

OTHER REPOSITORIES

The sources listed below include only those items reported on the Record Office Survey as located in the specified repositories. Each city and county library should have additional printed materials pertaining to its geographical area.

INSTITUTE OF HERALDIC AND GENEALOGICAL STUDIES
79-82 Northgate
Canterbury, Kent CT1 1BA
Tel. 0227 68664

ADMISSION AND ACCESS

The Institute is open from 9am to 5pm daily Monday to Friday. Graduate and associate members of the Institute have limited access to most of the facilities and collections. The library is in constant use by students and accommodation is restricted.

Members of the general public may be admitted by appointment only on Monday, Wednesday and Friday 10am to 4:30pm on payment of a daily fee. Special arrangements can be made for open days usually on a Saturday for parties of not more than 35 people. A lecture and instruction programme, access to the library and a guided tour of the Cathedral are included, if required, along with buffet lunch and refreshments. Arrangements for such open days must be made not less than six months in advance.

HOLDINGS

The Institute does not collect original genealogical documents or make extensive collections of modern parish register transcriptions. It has a comprehensive working genealogist's library covering all principal reference and record sources and published indexes. It has an extensive social history section, large and unique indexes and collections of materials for London and Middlesex, including the Pallot Marriage Index

1780–1837, Kent, Sussex and Hampshire. It also contains one of the most comprehensive heraldic libraries which includes most European armorials. There is also an archive containing results from genealogical research on over twenty thousand families. Many collections and indexes are now available on microform, including the International Genealogical Index, from which printouts can often be obtained.

SEARCHES

Postal applications for searches in the indexes housed at the Institute are welcomed. A leaflet about the library and the cost of such searches can be obtained on receipt of a self-addressed envelope or reply mail coupons.

BOOKSHOP

The Institute holds stocks of most of the standard source and textbooks essential for the researcher in the British Isles. It also publishes the unique series of county parish maps for England, Wales and Scotland. A booklist and mail order deliveries are available. U.S. dollar cheques or credit card payments are accepted.

RELEVANT PUBLICATIONS[†]

Journal: *Family History* (1962–)

Cecil R. Humphery-Smith, *Introducing Family History* (1987)

Cecil R. Humphery-Smith, ed., *The Phillimore Atlas and Index of Parish Registers* (1984). This volume was entirely produced by the Institute based upon its famous series of parish maps of the counties of England and Wales.

A Guide to the Library and Collections of the Institute of Heraldic and Genealogical Studies

---

[†]For additional information send 2 Postal Reply Coupons or 31 pence of English postage for reply to North America; 34 pence to Australia and New Zealand.

Family History Diary available annually September to December listing details of genealogical events throughout British Isles and courses run by the Institute.

The Institute also produces detailed syllabuses for teachers of family history and runs residential, evening, Saturday and correspondence courses.†

KENT COUNTY LIBRARY†
Local Studies Library
Springfield, Maidstone ME1 3HU
Tel. 0622 671411 ext. 3240

    Census‡# (Kent)   1841–1881
    International Genealogical Index‡##
    (Kent and adjacent counties)

LDS FAMILY HISTORY CENTRE†
London Road
Maidstone, Kent
Tel. 0622 57811

    LDS Family History Library Catalog‡##
    International Genealogical Index‡##

---

†For additional information send 2 Postal Reply Coupons or 31 pence of English postage for reply to North America; 34 pence to Australia and New Zealand.
‡Microfilm/microfiche copies available at above repository
#Microfilm copy available at the LDS Family History Library in Salt Lake City, Utah, and through the LDS Family History Centers.
##Microfiche copy available at the LDS Family History Library in Salt Lake City, Utah, and through the LDS Family History Centers.

GENEALOGICAL AND FAMILY HISTORY SOCIETIES

The societies listed below may have recorded Monumental (tombstone) Inscriptions, compiled an Index to Marriages (from the Parish Registers), an Index to the 1851 Census, and other special indexes, e.g., Strays, Members' Interests, for their geographical areas.** Each Society publishes a quarterly journal (listed in italics) which includes articles on family history, reports on the group's projects, and members' queries.

FOLKESTONE AND DISTRICT FAMILY HISTORY SOCIETY†
Mrs. P. Wire, Secretary
100 Orchard Valley
Hythe, Kent CT21 4EB
Folkestone and District Family History Society Journal

KENT FAMILY HISTORY SOCIETY†
Mrs. H. Lewis, Secretary
17 Abbots Place
Canterbury, Kent CT1 2AH
Kent Family History Society Journal

NORTH WEST KENT FAMILY HISTORY SOCIETY†
Mrs. H.F. Norris, Secretary
190 Beckenham Road
Beckenham, Kent BR3 4RJ
North West Kent Family History

**See *Current Publications by Member Societies* (annual), *List of Family History Project Coordinators*, 6th ed., and *Family History News and Digest* (biennial) — all published by the Federation of Family History Societies; available in the USA from the International Society for British Genealogy and Family History, P.O. Box 20425, Cleveland, OH 44120.

†For additional information send 2 Postal Reply Coupons or 31 pence of English postage for reply to North America; 34 pence to Australia and New Zealand.

LANCASHIRE

Post-1974 Counties of England

The pre-1974 geographical boundaries of Lancashire included the areas of Bootle, Liverpool, Prescot, St. Helens, and Southport, (southwestern part) now in Merseyside County; Bolton, Bury, Denton, Leigh, Manchester, Mossley, Oldham, Rochdale, Salford, and Wigan (southeastern part) now in Greater Manchester County; the Barrow-in-Furness area now in Cumbria; and the southern border (Warrington and Widnes) now in Cheshire. Blackburn, Blackpool, Burnley, and Preston, all administratively County Boroughs between 1889 and 1974, have otherwise been a part of Lancashire. Prior to 1889 Preston was an incorporated Borough from the twelfth

century, and Blackburn, Blackpool and Burnley were all nineteenth-century Municipal Boroughs.

The county of Lancashire was originally called the county
of Lancaster. In 1351 this area was elevated by the King to be a
County Palatine, and granted to the Duke of Lancaster. The
County Palatine of Lancaster had its own courts (Chancery,
Common Pleas, Criminal) which were exempt from those of the
Crown. The Duke of Lancaster appointed the officers – sheriff,
justices of the peace, administrative officers, coroner. Fiscal
affairs were also exempt from those of the Crown. In 1873
common law and criminal jurisdiction was transferred from
the Duchy to the newly established Supreme Court of Judicature.

Administrative, fiscal and court records of the County
Palatine of Lancaster are located in the Public Record Office,
Chancery Lane.

RECORD OFFICE

LANCASHIRE RECORD OFFICE
Bow Lane, Preston PR1 2RE
Tel. 0772 54868 ext. 3039

Hours: T 10-8:30; W-F 10-5; closed M, S
Reader's tickets required; must be obtained
in advance of visit; write for application[†]

Admission free
List of record searchers available upon request[†]

HOLDINGS

Church of England diocesan records (excepting Bishops'
Transcripts for the Furness area, and Marriage Licence Bonds
and Allegations for the Diocese of Chester south of the River
Ribble); Church of England parish records including deposited

[†]For additional information send 2 Postal Reply Coupons or 31 pence of English
postage for reply to North America; 34 pence to Australia and New Zealand.

Parish Registers for approximately 200 churches in the pre-1974 division of the county (excepting the Furness area); civil records and other resources for the pre-1974 area of Lancashire. (Diocesan and parish records for the Furness area are now located at the Cumbria Record Office, Barrow-in-Furness. Marriage Licence Bonds and Allegations for the Diocese of Chester south of the River Ribble are located in the Cheshire Record Office, Chester.)

SOURCES THAT IDENTIFY AN INDIVIDUAL WITH A SPECIFIC LOCATION

Borough Records	16C–20C
Freemen's Lists	17C–20C
Rates	18C–20C
Church of England (diocesan)	
Ecclesiastical Court Books††	17C–20C
Ecclesiastical Visitations††	17C–20C
Tithe Apportionments§	19C
Directories* (some#)	18C–20C
Business/Trade, Postal	
Lay Subsidies	1216–1307, 1322*
Maps*	16C–20C
Militia Lists*	1487–1620; 1759–1870
Parish Poor Law Records	17C–1834
Parish Poor Rates	17C–20C
Poll Books* (some#)	1688–1744

††Mostly in Latin
§Parish copies only
*Printed or transcribed
#Microfilm copy available at the LDS Family History Library in Salt Lake City, Utah, and through the LDS Family History Centers.

Quarter Sessions
Judicial Records[#]   16C–1971
Hearth Tax Assessments[‡#]   (gaps) 1663–1673
Land Tax Assessments[#]   1780–1832
Lists of Jurors[#]   (periodic) 1696–1832
Registration of Papist Estates[#]   1717–1788
Shipping – Crew Lists   19C–20C

*SOURCES THAT MAY ADDITIONALLY PROVIDE VITAL
DATA AND/OR PROVE FAMILY RELATIONSHIPS*

Borough Records
Court   16C–20C
Title Deeds   17C–20C
Cemetery Registers   19C–20C
Church of England (diocesan)
Bishops' Transcripts   16C–19C
Marriage Licence Bonds   17C–19C,
and Allegations   (1746–1799[#])
Wills, Admin., Inven.[*#]   1545–1858
Church of England (parish)
Parish Registers[#]   16C–20C
Estate and Family Papers (some[#])   14C–20C
International Genealogical Index[‡##]   (1981 edn.)
(Great Britain)
Manorial Records   12C–16C
Monumental Inscriptions[*]
Newspapers[*]   19C–20C

[#]Microfilm copy available at the LDS Family History Library in Salt Lake City, Utah, and through the LDS Family History Centers.
[‡]Microfilm/microfiche copies available at above repository
[*]Printed or transcribed
[##]Microfiche copy available at the LDS Family History Library in Salt Lake City, Utah, and through the LDS Family History Centers.

Nonconformist Registers
  Baptist   18C–20C
  Methodist#   19C–20C
  Presbyterian (some#)   19C–20C
  Society of Friends   17C–20C
  Unitarian   18C–20C
Parish Poor Law Records   17C–1834
  Apprenticeship Indentures
  Examinations
  Removal Orders
  Settlement Papers
Poor Law Union   1834–20C
  Workhouse Records   18C–20C
Roman Catholic Records   18C–20C
School Records   16C–20C
Title Deeds   12C–20C
Wills, Register Copies   1858–1940
  (Indexes)*   1858–1935
  (Lancaster, Liverpool only)

PUBLICATIONS†

Guide to the Lancashire Record Office# (1985)
Handlist of Genealogical Sources (1986)

OTHER REPOSITORIES

The sources listed below include only those items reported on the Record Office Survey as located in the specified repositories. Each city and county library should have additional printed materials pertaining to its geographical area.

#Microfilm copy available at the LDS Family History Library in Salt Lake City, Utah, and through the LDS Family History Centers.
*Printed or transcribed
†For additional information send 2 Postal Reply Coupons or 31 pence of English postage for reply to North America; 34 pence to Australia and New Zealand.

LDS FAMILY HISTORY CENTRE[†]
Tweedale Street
Rochdale, Lancashire OL11 3TZ
Tel. 0706 526292

> LDS Family History Library Catalog[‡##]
> International Genealogical Index[‡##]

LDS FAMILY HISTORY CENTRE[†]
Haslington Road
Rawtenstall, Lancashire
Tel. 0706 213466

> LDS Family History Library Catalog[‡##]
> International Genealogical Index[‡##]

GENEALOGICAL AND FAMILY HISTORY SOCIETIES

The societies listed below may have recorded Monumental (tombstone) Inscriptions, compiled an Index to Marriages (from the Parish Registers), an Index to the 1851 Census, and other special indexes, e.g., Strays, Members' Interests, for their geographical areas.[**] Each Society publishes a quarterly journal (listed in italics) which includes articles on family history, reports on the group's projects, and members' queries.

[†]For additional information send 2 Postal Reply Coupons or 31 pence of English postage for reply to North America; 34 pence to Australia and New Zealand.

[‡]Microfilm/microfiche copies available at above repository

[##]Microfiche copy available at the LDS Family History Library in Salt Lake City, Utah, and through the LDS Family History Centers.

[**]See *Current Publications by Member Societies* (annual), *List of Family History Project Coordinators*, 6th ed., and *Family History News and Digest* (biennial) — all published by the Federation of Family History Societies; available in the USA from the International Society for British Genealogy and Family History, P.O. Box 20425, Cleveland, OH 44120.

LANCASHIRE FAMILY HISTORY AND HERALDRY SOCIETY[†]
Mr. R. Hampson, Secretary
7 Margaret Street, Shaw
Oldham, Lancashire OL2 8RP

Lancashire

MANCHESTER AND LANCASHIRE FAMILY HISTORY SOCIETY[†]
Mr. A.M. Berrell, Secretary
5th floor, Clayton House, 39 Piccadilly
Manchester M1 2AQ

The Manchester Genealogist

[†]For additional information send 2 Postal Reply Coupons or 31 pence of English postage for reply to North America; 34 pence to Australia and New Zealand.

LEICESTERSHIRE

Post-1974 Counties of England

The present county includes the pre-1974 geographical area of Leicestershire, and in addition, the former county of Rutland.

Administratively the city of Leicester was an incorporated Borough from 1589 to 1889 and a County Borough between 1889 and 1974.

RECORD OFFICE

LEICESTERSHIRE RECORD OFFICE
57 New Walk, Leicester LE1 7JB
Tel. 0533 544566

Hours: M-Th 9:15-5; F 9:15-4:45; S 9:15-12:15

Admission free: Reader's ticket required;
apply to record office well in advance of visit
List of record searchers available upon request[†]

HOLDINGS

Church of England diocesan records (Archdeaconry of Leicester, Diocese of Lincoln); Church of England parish records including deposited Parish Registers for approximately 215 churches within the pre-1974 county boundaries and 25 for the former county of Rutland; local government and other resources pertaining to the pre-1974 division of the county.

SOURCES THAT IDENTIFY AN INDIVIDUAL WITH A SPECIFIC LOCATION

Borough Records[#] (Leicester)	1196–1930
Freemen's Lists*	
Apprenticeship Records*	
Rates	
Church of England (archidiaconal)	
Ecclesiastical Court Books	16C–19C
Ecclesiastical Visitations	16C–19C
Tithe Apportionments	19C
Church of England (parish)	
Churchwardens' Accounts	1546–1923

[†]For additional information send 2 Postal Reply Coupons or 31 pence of English postage for reply to North America; 34 pence to Australia and New Zealand.
[#]Microfilm copy available at the LDS Family History Library in Salt Lake City, Utah, and through the LDS Family History Centers.
*Printed or transcribed

Directories* (some#)		19C–20C
Business/Trade, Postal		
Enclosure Awards		19C
Lay Subsidies#		1327, 1603–4
Maps		
Militia Lists#	(periodic)	late 18C
Parish Poor Law Records		17C–1834
Parish Poor Rates		
Poll Books*#	(periodic)	18C–19C
Quarter Sessions		1607–1795#
Judicial Records#		17C–20C
Hearth Tax Assessments*‡#	(gaps)	1664–1673
Land Tax Assessments#		1773–1832
Lists of Freeholders		18C–19C
Registration of Papist Property		18C
Registers of Electors*		1832–

SOURCES THAT MAY ADDITIONALLY PROVIDE VITAL DATA AND/OR PROVE FAMILY RELATIONSHIPS

Borough Records (Leicester)	1103–1835
Court	1607–1795#
Guild: Apprenticeship Enrolments	1196–1568
Admissions	
Census# (Leics)	1841–1881
Church of England (archidiaconal)	
Bishops' Transcripts#	1561–c. 1876
Marriage Licence Bonds	1570–1891
and Allegations*#	
Wills, Admon., Inven.*#	1496–1941
Church of England (parish)	
Parish Registers#	1538–20C
Parish Register Transcripts*	16C–19C

---

*Printed or transcribed

#Microfilm copy available at the LDS Family History Library in Salt Lake City, Utah, and through the LDS Family History Centers.

‡Microfilm/microfiche copies available at above repository

Estate and Family Papers
International Genealogical Index##
   (Leics, Rutl.)
Jewish Records††   1903–1968
Monumental Inscriptions* (some also#)
Nonconformist Registers   1667–1982
   Baptist
   Independent (Congregational)
   Methodist
   Society of Friends‡ (some#)   1667–1961
   Unitarians
Parish Poor Law Records   17C–1834
   Apprenticeship Indentures
   Examinations
   Removal Orders
   Settlement Papers
Poor Law Union   1834–
   Workhouse Records
School Records   19C
Title Deeds   13C–
Wills, Register Copies   1858–

PUBLICATIONS†

Leaflets/Lists:
  *Family Forbears: A Guide to Tracing Your Family
    Tree in the Leicestershire Record Office*
  Nevill Holt, *The Study of a Leicestershire Estate*
  List of Deposited Parish Registers

##Microfiche copy available at the LDS Family History Library in Salt Lake City, Utah, and through the LDS Family History Centers.
††Must have special permission to view.
*Printed or transcribed
#Microfilm copy available at the LDS Family History Library in Salt Lake City, Utah, and through the LDS Family History Centers.
‡Microfilm/microfiche copies available at above repository
†For additional information send 2 Postal Reply Coupons or 31 pence of English postage for reply to North America; 34 pence to Australia and New Zealand.

Handlist of Leicestershire Parish
Register Transcripts (BT's)
Handlist of Records of Leicester Archdeaconry
The Records of the Corporation of Leicester
Family and Estate Records in the
Leicestershire Record Office
Quarter Sessions Records in the
Leicestershire Record Office

OTHER REPOSITORIES

The sources listed below include only those items reported on the Record Office Survey as located in the specified repositories. Each city and county library should have additional printed materials pertaining to its geographical area.

LEICESTER CENTRAL LIBRARY[†]
(Information Centre)
Bishop Street, Leicester LE1 6AA
Tel. 0533 556699

Census[‡#]
   Leicester   1841, 1861
   England   1851
International Genealogical Index[‡##]
   (British Isles)

[†]For additional information send 2 Postal Reply Coupons or 31 pence of English postage for reply to North America; 34 pence to Australia and New Zealand.
[‡]Microfilm/microfiche copies available at above repository
[#]Microfilm copy available at the LDS Family History Library in Salt Lake City, Utah, and through the LDS Family History Centers.
[##]Microfiche copy available at the LDS Family History Library in Salt Lake City, Utah, and through the LDS Family History Centers.

LDS FAMILY HISTORY CENTRE[†]
Thorp Hill, Allan Moss Road
Loughborough, Leicestershire
Tel. 0509 214991

LDS Family History Library Catalog[‡##]
International Genealogical Index[‡##]

GENEALOGICAL AND FAMILY HISTORY SOCIETIES

The societies listed below may have recorded Monumental (tombstone) Inscriptions, compiled an Index to Marriages (from the Parish Registers), an Index to the 1851 Census, and other special indexes, e.g., Strays, Members' Interests, for their geographical areas.[**] Each Society publishes a quarterly journal (listed in italics) which includes articles on family history, reports on the group's projects, and members' queries.

LEICESTERSHIRE FAMILY HISTORY SOCIETY[†]
Miss S. Brown, Secretary
25 Homecroft Drive
Packington, Ashby de la Zouch, Leicestershire LE6 5WG

Leicestershire Family History Society Journal

[†]For additional information send 2 Postal Reply Coupons or 31 pence of English postage for reply to North America; 34 pence to Australia and New Zealand.
[‡]Microfilm/microfiche copies available at above repository
[##]Microfiche copy available at the LDS Family History Library in Salt Lake City, Utah, and through the LDS Family History Centers.
[**]See *Current Publications by Member Societies* (annual), *List of Family History Project Coordinators*, 6th ed., and *Family History News and Digest* (biennial) — all published by the Federation of Family History Societies; available in the USA from the International Society for British Genealogy and Family History, P.O. Box 20425, Cleveland, OH 44120.

LINCOLNSHIRE

Post-1974 Counties of England

The pre-1974 geographical boundaries of Lincolnshire included the present county, and in addition, the northern border area of Brigg, Barton-upon-Humber and (Great) Grimsby now in the county of Humberside.

Administratively the city of Lincoln was a County Corporate between the fifteenth century and 1889, and then a County Borough from 1889 to 1974. (Great) Grimsby was also a County Borough (1889–1974) and before that period an incorporated Borough from the thirteenth century. Boston, Grantham, Louth and Stamford were all incorporated Boroughs from the sixteenth century (or earlier) to 1974.

258

Before 1974 the county was divided into three areas for administrative purposes, called Parts of Holland, Parts of Kesteven and Parts of Lindsey. Holland, located in the southeastern corner of Lincolnshire, contained about one-seventh of the total geographical area of the county. Border parishes of Holland included Crowland, Deeping St. Nicholas, Pinchbeck, Dowsby, Quadring, Donington, Bicker, Swineshead, Amber Hill, Holland Fen, Brothertoft, Boston, Skirbeck, Fishtoft, Frieston, Benington, Leake and Wrangle.

Kesteven was located in the southwestern quadrant of the county. Its border parishes included Deeping St. James, Market Deeping, Langtoft, Baston, Bourne, Morton, Hacconby, Dunsby, Rippingale, Aslackby, Sempringham, Billingborough, Swaton, Helpringham, Great Hale, Heckington, South Kyme, North Kyme, Billinghay, Walcot, Timberland, Martin, Blankney, Metheringham, Dunston, Nocton, Branston, Washingborough, Potterhanworth, Canwick, Bracebridge, North Hyckham, Boultham, Doddington, Skellingthorpe.

The northern area, Lindsey, covered more than half of the county. Its border parishes included Friskney, Eastville, Midville, Stickney, Sibsey, Langriville, Wildmore, Coningsby, Tattershall, Kirkstead, Woodhall, Southrey, Bardney, Bucknall, Stainfield, Fiskerton, Cherry Willingham, Greetwell, Nettleham, Burton, Saxelby.

With the exception of the Lord Lieutenant (Militia Records) and the Sheriff, the three Parts of Lincolnshire each had jurisdiction equal to a separate county.

RECORD OFFICE

LINCOLNSHIRE ARCHIVES OFFICE
The Castle, Lincoln LN1 3AB
Tel. 0522 25158

Hours: M-F 9:15-4:45
          Prior appointment necessary
Admission free
List of record searchers available upon request[†]

HOLDINGS

Church of England diocesan records (Archdeaconry of Lincoln, Diocese of Lincoln); Church of England parish records, including deposited Parish Registers for approximately 565 churches within the pre-1974 county boundaries; local government records and other resources pertaining to the pre-1974 division of the county.

SOURCES THAT IDENTIFY AN INDIVIDUAL WITH A SPECIFIC LOCATION

Borough Records	16C–20C
(Lincoln, Louth, Grantham)	
Freemen's Lists	
Rates	
Church of England (diocesan)	
Ecclesiastical Court Books[††]	15C–19C
Ecclesiastical Visitations[††]	15C–19C
Tithe Apportionments	1830–1850
Church of England (parish)	
Churchwardens' Accounts	17C–19C
Directories* (some[#])	
Business/Trade, Postal, Professional	1826–1937
Enclosure Awards (some[#])	18C–19C

[†]For additional information send 2 Postal Reply Coupons or 31 pence of English postage for reply to North America; 34 pence to Australia and New Zealand.
[††]Partly in Latin
*Printed or transcribed
[#]Microfilm copy available at the LDS Family History Library in Salt Lake City, Utah, and through the LDS Family History Centers.

Maps   17C–
Militia Lists   1760–1820
Parish Poor Law Records   17C–mid-19C
Parish Poor Rates
Poll Books* (some#)   (periodic) 17C–19C
Quarter Sessions (Holland, Kesteven, Lindsey)
   Judicial Records   17C–1888
   Land Tax Assessments   1760–1832
   Lists of Freeholders   (periodic) 18C, 1826–
   Lists of Jurors   1720–1866
   Registration of Papist Property   1717
Registers of Electors*   1832–
Shipping – Crew Lists   19C

SOURCES THAT MAY ADDITIONALLY PROVIDE VITAL
DATA AND/OR PROVE FAMILY RELATIONSHIPS

Borough Records (Lincoln,   16C–20C
   Louth, Grantham)
   Court
   Title Deeds
Cemetery Registers (Louth only)   (few) 19C
Census‡# (Lincs)   1841–1881
Church of England (diocesan)
   Bishops' Transcripts#   1562–1840's
   Marriage Licence Bonds   1574–1846
     and Allegations#
   Wills, Admon., Inven.#   1320–1858
Church of England (parish)
   Parish Registers#   1538–1900's
Estate and Family Papers   16C–

---

*Printed or transcribed
#Microfilm copy available at the LDS Family History Library in Salt Lake City, Utah, and through the LDS Family History Centers.
‡Microfilm/microfiche copies available at above repository

International Genealogical Index‡## (for most counties)	1978
Manorial Records	14C–20C
Monumental Inscriptions	18C–
Nonconformist Registers	
Baptist	19C–20C
Independent (Congregational)	19C–20C
Methodist	1800–
	(1800–1837#)
Society of Friends*#	late 17C–1837
Parish Poor Law Records	mid-17C–1835
Apprenticeship Indentures	
Examinations	
Removal Orders	
Settlement Papers	
Poor Law Union	1834–20C
Workhouse Records	
School Records	19C–20C
Title Deeds	12C–20C
Wills, Register Copies	1858–1874
Probate Calendars*	1858–1935

PUBLICATIONS†

Leaflets/Lists:
Your Family History in Lincolnshire's Archives
Deposited Parish Registers
Deposited Non-Parochial Registers
Handlist of Lincoln Diocesan Records
(includes list of Bishops' Transcripts)

---

‡Microfilm/microfiche copies available at above repository
##Microfiche copy available at the LDS Family History Library in Salt Lake City, Utah, and through the LDS Family History Centers.
*Printed or transcribed
#Microfilm copy available at the LDS Family History Library in Salt Lake City, Utah, and through the LDS Family History Centers.
†For additional information send 2 Postal Reply Coupons or 31 pence of English postage for reply to North America; 34 pence to Australia and New Zealand.

OTHER REPOSITORIES

The sources listed below include only those items reported on the Record Office Survey as located in the specified repositories. Each city and county library should have additional printed materials pertaining to its geographical area.

LINCOLN CENTRAL LIBRARY†
(Local Studies)
Free School Lane, Lincoln LN2 1EZ
Tel. 0522 33541

Census‡# (Lincs)	1841–1881
International Genealogical Index‡##	
(British Isles)	
Newspapers*	

---

†For additional information send 2 Postal Reply Coupons or 31 pence of English postage for reply to North America; 34 pence to Australia and New Zealand.
‡Microfilm/microfiche copies available at above repository
#Microfilm copy available at the LDS Family History Library in Salt Lake City, Utah, and through the LDS Family History Centers.
##Microfiche copy available at the LDS Family History Library in Salt Lake City, Utah, and through the LDS Family History Centers.
*Printed or transcribed

GENEALOGICAL AND FAMILY HISTORY SOCIETIES

The societies listed below may have recorded Monumental (tombstone) Inscriptions, compiled an Index to Marriages (from the Parish Registers), an Index to the 1851 Census, and other special indexes, e.g., Strays, Members' Interests, for their geographical areas.** Each Society publishes a quarterly journal (listed in italics) which includes articles on family history, reports on the group's projects, and members' queries.

SOCIETY FOR LINCOLNSHIRE
HISTORY AND ARCHÆOLOGY†
(FAMILY HISTORY SUBCOMMITTEE / SECTION)
Ms. E. Robson, Secretary
135 Baldertongate
Newark, Nottinghamshire NG24 1RY

Lincolnshire Family Historian

SPALDING GENTLEMEN'S SOCIETY†
Mr. N. Simson, Hon. Secretary
The Museum
Broad Street
Spalding, Lincolnshire PE11 1TB

**See *Current Publications by Member Societies* (annual), *List of Family History Project Coordinators*, 6th ed., and *Family History News and Digest* (biennial) — all published by the Federation of Family History Societies; available in the USA from the International Society for British Genealogy and Family History, P.O. Box 20425, Cleveland, OH 44120.

†For additional information send 2 Postal Reply Coupons or 31 pence of English postage for reply to North America; 34 pence to Australia and New Zealand.

LONDON

Pre-1965 County of London

The County of London was formed in 1889 from parts of Kent, Middlesex and Surrey counties. It did not include the (ancient) City of London.

The following areas were transferred to the County of London in 1889. From Kent: Deptford (part), Greenwich, Lewisham (including Lee), and Woolwich; from Middlesex: Bethnal Green, Chelsea, Finsbury, Fulham, Hackney, Hammersmith, Hampstead, Holborn, Islington, Kensington, Paddington, Poplar, St. Marylebone, St. Pancras, Shoreditch, Stepney, Stoke Newington, and the City of Westminster; from Surrey: Battersea, Bermondsey, Camberwell, Deptford (part),

265

Lambeth, Southwark, and Wandsworth. All were made Metropolitan Boroughs of London from 1900 to 1965. However, they did not have the same functions as the Municipal Boroughs established under the Act of 1835. The Metropolitan Boroughs of London were under jurisdiction of the county.

Administratively, the London County Council took over the records and functions of the Metropolitan Board of Works. The latter agency, formed in 1855, was responsible for the regulation and supervision of sewer drainage, building code, toll bridge companies, and other services for areas contiguous to, but not including the (ancient) City of London.

Quarter Sessions began in the County of London in 1889. Prior to that year, Sessions records for the areas which became part of the new county were under jurisdiction of the respective counties in which they were previously located: Kent, Middlesex, and Surrey. After 1889 the County of London was also responsible for the enrolment, registration, and deposit of records pertaining to individuals, institutions, agencies, traders and companies within its jurisdiction.

The County of London was abolished in 1965 at the same time the metropolitan area of Greater London was established (see Part III).

Records of the former County of London are located in the Greater London Record Office. Those pertaining to the former Metropolitan Boroughs of London will be found in the respective borough repositories.

GREATER MANCHESTER

Post-1974 Counties of England

Greater Manchester is one of the metropolitan counties created in 1974. Its geographical boundaries include the area formerly comprising the southeast quadrant of Lancashire (Manchester and Salford Cities, and the Metropolitan Districts or Boroughs of Bolton, Bury, Oldham, Rochdale, Stockport, Tameside District, and Wigan), as well as the northeast border area of Cheshire (parts of the modern Stockport and Tameside and Trafford), the parish of Saddleworth, formerly in the West Riding of Yorkshire, and a small area of north Derbyshire.

It must be remembered that the following explanation of the responsibility for each area is very simplistic, as townships

267

were moved between parishes, poor law unions, urban districts and the other administrative areas created in an attempt to meet the rapid changes in this growing urban area. The major reorganisations were in 1889, 1935 and 1974.

Administratively Wigan was an incorporated Borough in Lancashire from the thirteenth century to 1889. Bolton, Bury, Manchester, Oldham, Rochdale and Salford were nineteenth-century Municipal Boroughs in that county. All became County Boroughs in 1889 and Metropolitan Districts in 1974.

Salford Metropolitan District includes Eccles, which was a nineteenth-century Municipal Borough, Swinton and Pendlebury, an Urban District which became a Municipal Borough in 1934, and Salford, which became a County Borough in 1889. Farnworth was a twentieth-century Municipal Borough which became part of Bolton Metropolitan Borough in 1974. The Municipal Borough of Heywood was established in 1881, Prestwich in 1939, and Radcliffe in 1935, and all became part of Bury Metropolitan Borough in 1974. Rochdale Metropolitan Borough includes Middleton Municipal Borough (1886). Stockport was a medieval borough becoming in the nineteenth century a Municipal, and later County Borough in Cheshire. The post-1974 Metropolitan Borough includes the former District of Sale, which became a Municipal Borough in 1935. Stalybridge, partly in Lancashire and partly in Cheshire, was established as a Municipal Borough in 1857. In 1889 the whole borough was included in Cheshire. Dukinfield was a Municipal Borough in Cheshire prior to 1974. Stalybridge and Dukinfield became part of Tameside Metropolitan District in 1974, along with Hyde (1881), Ashton-under-Lyme (1947), and Mossley (1885). The Metropolitan Borough of Trafford includes the former Municipal Boroughs of Altrincham (1937), and Sale (1935), which were in north Cheshire, and Stretford in Lancashire, which became a Municipal Borough in 1933.

In 1986 the Greater Manchester County Council was abolished, although the county itself remains as a geographical area with a Lord Lieutenant and High Sheriff. Certain county-wide functions also remain, including the County Record Office. In addition, the ten metropolitan district councils and four joint boards have archive powers.

RECORD OFFICES

GREATER MANCHESTER RECORD OFFICE
56 Marshall Street, New Cross
Manchester M4 5FU
Tel. (061) 832 5284
Contact: County Archivist
Hours: M-F 9-5; 2nd, 4th S/mo 9-12
   Prior appointment necessary to use microfilm readers
   for Civil Registration Indexes 9-12, 12-2, 2-5. (May
   reserve two time periods per day, but not consecutively.)
Admission free
Reader's Ticket now required. Write in advance
   for information.
List of record searchers available upon request†

HOLDINGS

The Greater Manchester Record Office, established in 1976, is the repository for archives and records relating, generally, to more than one metropolitan district in the county, including material of regional or national importance. Local authority and Public Records are held on behalf of some districts.

Volumes of the Lancashire and Cheshire Parish Record Society and other published resources relating to the county are also available.

(Manchester City Archives Department, Central Library, Manchester is the repository for Church of England diocesan and parish records, including Parish Registers, for the Diocese of Manchester, established in 1847.)

Church of England records for the Archdeaconry of Chester prior to 1847 are deposited in the Cheshire Record Office, Duke Street, Chester.

(Administrative records and other archives are in the custody of the appropriate district or county record office.)

---

†For additional information send 2 Postal Reply Coupons or 31 pence of English postage for reply to North America; 34 pence to Australia and New Zealand.

SOURCES THAT IDENTIFY AN INDIVIDUAL
WITH A SPECIFIC LOCATION

Business Records	18C–
Directories* (some#)	19C–20C
Local Histories*	
Maps (mainly O.S.)	
Periodicals*	19C–20C
Trade Union Records	19C–20C

SOURCES THAT MAY ADDITIONALLY PROVIDE VITAL
DATA AND/OR PROVE FAMILY RELATIONSHIPS

Civil Registration Indexes‡§	1837–1912
Church of England	
Parish Register Transcripts*	16C–19C
Estate and Family Papers	13C–
Nonconformist Records	
Methodist	19C–20C
Society and Charity Records	19C–20C
Title Deeds	17C–20C
Will Indexes (Manchester)	1856–1936

PUBLICATIONS†

K. Howarth, *Dark Days: Memories of the Lancashire Coal-Mining Industry* (2nd edn., 1985)

C. A. Wright, *Summary of Collection* (1985) (OOP)

---

*Printed or transcribed

#Microfilm copy available at the LDS Family History Library in Salt Lake City, Utah, and through the LDS Family History Centers.

‡Microfilm/microfiche copies available at above repository

§Microfilm copies filmed by the General Register Office, London.

†For additional information send 2 Postal Reply Coupons or 31 pence of English postage for reply to North America; 34 pence to Australia and New Zealand.

Leaflets:
A Guide to Civil Registration, England and Wales
Greater Manchester Archives: A Guide to
  Local Repositories
Greater Manchester Record Office: Information
Probate Records for Greater Manchester County

METROPOLITAN DISTRICT ARCHIVES AND LOCAL HISTORY LIBRARIES

Genealogical resources for metropolitan districts within the county of Greater Manchester may also be found in the respective repositories in the cities and boroughs listed below.

The sources may vary considerably from one district to another. Those most likely to be found in the Archives Department of a library or record office include Borough Records, Church of England parish records including deposited Parish Registers, Estate and Family Papers, Manorial Records and Title Deeds.

Sources most likely to be in the Local History/Studies Department of a library include transcribed or microfilm copies of Church of England Parish Registers, microfilm copies of Census Records 1841–1881, Postal and Trade Directories, International Genealogical Index, and microfilm copies of Nonconformist Registers for groups within the specific areas.

BOLTON METROPOLITAN DISTRICT

(Bolton, Farnworth, Blackrod, Horwich, Kearsley,
Little Lever, West Houghton, pt. Turton)

BOLTON ARCHIVE SERVICE
Central Library and Museaum
Le Mans Crescent
Bolton BL1 1SE
Tel. 0204 22311 ext. 2179
Contact: Archivist
Hours: By prior appointment only: M 9:30-4:30, T 9:30-12:30,
Th 1:30-7, F 9:30-4:30; closed W, S
Admission free

HOLDINGS

Resources pertaining to the areas now in Bolton Metropolitan District and to their administrative predecessors.

SOURCES THAT IDENTIFY AN INDIVIDUAL
WITH A SPECIFIC LOCATION

Borough Records (Bolton)	1838–
Rates	
Business Records	1790's
Maps	16C–
Trade Unions	1870–20C

SOURCES THAT MAY ADDITIONALLY PROVIDE VITAL
DATA AND/OR PROVE FAMILY RELATIONSHIPS

Borough Records (Bolton)	
Magistrate's Court	1901–
Quarter Sessions	1839–1971
Census (Great Bolton)	1811–1831
Estate and Family Papers	16C–

Newspapers*	1825–
Nonconformist Registers	
Methodist	1838–
Parish Poor Law Records	17C–1834
Apprenticeship Indentures	
Settlement Papers	
Removal Orders	
Poor Law Union	
Workhouse Records	19C–1929
Society and Charity Records	19C–20C
Title Deeds	1550–

PUBLICATIONS†

Leaflet: *Tracing Your Ancestors in Bolton* (free)

BURY METROPOLITAN DISTRICT

(Bury, Prestwich, Radcliffe, Tottington,
Whitefield, pt. Ramsbottom)

BURY LIBRARY SERVICE:

CENTRAL LIBRARY
Manchester Road, Bury BL9 0DR
Tel. (061) 705 5871
Contact: Reference Librarian
Hours: M, T 9-5:30; W-F 9-7:30; S 9-4:30
Admission free

---

*Printed or transcribed

†For additional information send 2 Postal Reply Coupons or 31 pence of English
postage for reply to North America; 34 pence to Australia and New Zealand.

ARCHIVES
22a Union Arcade
Bury BL9 0QF
Tel. (061) 797 6697
Hours: T 10-1, 2-5;
    Other weekdays by prior appointment only
Admission free
List of record searchers available upon request†

HOLDINGS

Some resources that pertain to the areas now in Bury Metropolitan District, and their administrative predecessors. (Some local government records for Bury are also located at the Greater Manchester Record Office.)

Library:

Census‡#§	1841–1881
Directories* (some#)	1818–
International Genealogical Index‡##††	
(Lancs)	
Local Histories*	
Maps	
Periodicals*	c. 1780–

---

†For additional information send 2 Postal Reply Coupons or 31 pence of English postage for reply to North America; 34 pence to Australia and New Zealand.
‡Microfilm/microfiche copies available at above repository
#Microfilm copy available at the LDS Family History Library in Salt Lake City, Utah, and through the LDS Family History Centers.
§May provide vital data and/or proof of family relationships.
*Printed or transcribed
##Microfiche copy available at the LDS Family History Library in Salt Lake City, Utah, and through the LDS Family History Centers.
††No postal correspondence

Archives:

Business Records	late 18C–
Estate and Family Papers	19C–20C
Local Government Records	1845–
Rates	
Nonconformist Registers	1795–
Society Records	late 18C–

PUBLICATIONS†

Leaflet:

Routes – A Guide to Family History in the Bury Area

MANCHESTER METROPOLITAN DISTRICT

(Manchester, pt. Bucklow)

MANCHESTER CENTRAL LIBRARY
ARCHIVES DEPARTMENT
St. Peter's Square
Manchester M2 5PD
Tel. (061) 236 9422 ext. 269
Contact: Archivist

Hours: M 9-9 (orders must be placed before 4);
T-F 9-12, 1-5; closed S
(Prior appointment advised)

Admission free
List of record searchers available upon request†

---

†For additional information send 2 Postal Reply Coupons or 31 pence of English postage for reply to North America; 34 pence to Australia and New Zealand.

HOLDINGS§§

Church of England diocesan and parish records (Diocese of Manchester 1847–); Manchester and Stockport Methodist District Records (excluding Stockport circuits).

Church of England (parish)
   Parish Registers
Jewish Records
Nonconformist Registers
   Methodist

(See also Manchester Central Library, Local History Department under Other Repositories, below.)

OLDHAM METROPOLITAN DISTRICT

(Oldham, Chadderton, Crompton, Failsworth,
Leeds, Royton, Saddleworth)

OLDHAM LIBRARY SERVICE
Local Studies Library
84 Union Street, Oldham OL1 1DN
Tel. (061) 678 4654
Contact: Local Studies Officer
Hours: M, W, Th, F 10-7; T 10-1; S 10-4
Admission free

HOLDINGS

Resources pertaining to the areas now in Oldham Metropolitan District, and to their administrative predecessors.

---

§§At the request of the Archivist, this listing is limited to the above named resources. See *Greater Manchester Archives: A Guide to Local Repositories* (available at the Greater Manchester Record Office) for more complete information.

Borough Records (Oldham)	19C–20C
Rates	19C–20C
Business Records	19C–20C
Census‡#§	1841–1881
Directories* (some#)	1817–
Estate and Family Papers§	17C
Local Histories*	
Maps	
Newspapers*§	19C–
Periodicals*	19C
Registers of Electors*	19C–
Trade Union Records	19C

ROCHDALE METROPOLITAN DISTRICT

(Rochdale, Heywood, Middleton,
Littleborough, Milnrow, Wardle)

ROCHDALE LIBRARY SERVICE
Central Library, The Esplanade
Rochdale OL16 1AQ
Tel. 0706 47474 ext. 4915
Contact: Local Studies Librarian

Hours: M, T, Th 9:30-7:30; W 9:30-5;
　　　　F 9:30-5:30; S 9:30-4

Admission free

---

‡Microfilm/microfiche copies available at above repository
#Microfilm copy available at the LDS Family History Library in Salt Lake City, Utah, and through the LDS Family History Centers.
§May provide vital data and/or proof of family relationships.
*Printed or transcribed

HOLDINGS

Resources pertaining to the areas now in Rochdale Metropolitan District, and to their administrative predecessors.

SOURCES THAT IDENTIFY AN INDIVIDUAL WITH A SPECIFIC LOCATION

Borough Records	1856–
Rates	
Business Records	19C–1940
Directories* (some#)	1796–1964
Local Histories*	
Maps	mid-19C–
Periodicals*	
Registers of Electors*	1832–

SOURCES THAT MAY ADDITIONALLY PROVIDE VITAL DATA AND/OR PROVE FAMILY RELATIONSHIPS

Census‡#	1841–1881
Estate and Family Papers	18C–19C
Newspapers*	mid-19C–
Nonconformist Registers	
Methodist	1786–20C
	(# to 1837)
Poor Law Union	mid-19C–1929

---

*Printed or transcribed

#Microfilm copy available at the LDS Family History Library in Salt Lake City, Utah, and through the LDS Family History Centers.

‡Microfilm/microfiche copies available at above repository

SALFORD METROPOLITAN DISTRICT

(Salford, Eccles, Swinton and
Pendlebury, Irlam, Worsley)

SALFORD CITY ARCHIVE SERVICE
Archives Centre
658/662 Liverpool Road, Irlam
Manchester M30 5AD
Tel. (061) 775 5643
Contact: Salford City Archivist
Hours: M-F 9-4:30; closed S
          (Appointment advised)
Admission free

HOLDINGS

Resources pertaining to the areas now in Salford Metropolitan District, and to their adminstrative predecessors.

Borough Records	
Rates	19C–20C
Quarter Sessions§	1870–1974
Coroners' Records§††	1912–25;
	1937–74
Estate and Family Papers	
Hospital Records§††	1875–1981
Maps	19C–20C
Nonconformist Records§	
Independent/Congregational	19C–20C
	(# to 1837)
Poor Law Union Records§	1838–1930
Society and Charity Records§	19C–20C
Trade Union Records	19C–20C

§May provide vital data and/or proof of family relationships.
††Subject to embargo for 100 years
#Microfilm copy available at the LDS Family History Library in Salt Lake City, Utah, and through the LDS Family History Centers.

PUBLICATIONS†

Leaflets:
Genealogical Sources for the City of Salford (free)
The History of Houses (free)

STOCKPORT METROPOLITAN DISTRICT

(Stockport, Bredbury and Romiley, Cheadle and
Gatley, Hazel Grove and Bramhall, Marple)

STOCKPORT ARCHIVE SERVICE
Central Library
Wellington Road South
Stockport SK1 3RS
Tel. (061) 480 7297 ext. 4534
Hours: M-F 9-8; S 9-12
       Prior appointment necessary after 5 and on S
Admission free

HOLDINGS

Resources pertaining to the areas now in Stockport Metropolitan District, and to their administrative predecessors.‡‡

SOURCES THAT IDENTIFY AN INDIVIDUAL
WITH A SPECIFIC LOCATION

Borough Records	
Rates	1731–1781, 1837–1940
Business Records	mainly 18C–20C

---

†For additional information send 2 Postal Reply Coupons or 31 pence of English postage for reply to North America; 34 pence to Australia and New Zealand.
‡‡See Stockport Central Library, Reference Library and Local Studies Library (under Other Repositories, below) for printed materials and microfilms.

Church of England (diocesan)
Tithe Apportionments[§§]   1840–1850
Maps   18C–20C

SOURCES THAT MAY ADDITIONALLY PROVIDE VITAL DATA AND/OR PROVE FAMILY RELATIONSHIPS

Borough Records
Magistrates' Court   late 19C–20C
Title Deeds   19C
Church of England (parish)
Parish Registers   16C–20C
Coroners' Records[††]
Estate and Family Papers   13C–20C
Hospital Records[††]   19C–20C
Monumental Inscriptions   19C
Nonconformist Registers
Methodist   18C–20C
Unitarian   18C–19C
School Records   19C–20C

PUBLICATIONS[†]

Brief Introduction to the Archive Service (1981) (free)
Genealogy in Stockport (1984)
Guide to Archive Calendars, 1–14 (1982)
Local History and Reference Material on Microfilm (1980)

[§§]Parish copies only
[††]Subject to embargo for 100 years
[†]For additional information send 2 Postal Reply Coupons or 31 pence of English postage for reply to North America; 34 pence to Australia and New Zealand.

TAMESIDE METROPOLITAN DISTRICT

(Dukinfield, Hyde, Stalybridge,
Longdendale, Ashton-under-Lyme,
Mossley, Audenshaw, Denton, Droylsden)

TAMESIDE ARCHIVE SERVICE
Tameside Local Studies Library
Stalybridge Library, Trinity Street
Stalybridge SK15 2BN
Tel. (061) 338 2708
Contact: Archivist
Hours: M, T, W, F 9-7:30; S 9-4; closed Th
Admission free

HOLDINGS

Resources pertaining to the areas now in Tameside Metropolitan District, and to their administrative predecessors.

SOURCES THAT IDENTIFY AN INDIVIDUAL WITH A SPECIFIC LOCATION

Borough Records	1745–1974
Business Records	1831–1981
Directories* (some#)	1772–
Local Histories*	19C–20C
Maps (O.S.)	1843–1970's
Trade Union Records	1862–1976

---

*Printed or transcribed

#Microfilm copy available at the LDS Family History Library in Salt Lake City, Utah, and through the LDS Family History Centers.

SOURCES THAT MAY ADDITIONALLY PROVIDE VITAL DATA AND/OR PROVE FAMILY RELATIONSHIPS

Census‡#	1841–1881
Church of England (parish)	
Parish Register Transcripts‡	
Hospital Records††	1858–1967
Newspapers*	19C–
Nonconformist Registers	1676–1981
School Records	1859–1974

PUBLICATIONS†

Leaflets:
Guide to the Archive Collection (1982)
Tracing Your Family Tree (1987)(free)

TRAFFORD METROPOLITAN DISTRICT

(Altrincham, Sale, Bowdon, Hale,
Stretford, Urmston, pt. Bucklow)

TRAFFORD LIBRARY SERVICE:

SALE LIBRARY
Tatton Road
Sale, Greater Manchester M33 1YH
Tel. (061) 973 3142 ext. 3458
Contact: Reference Librarian

---

‡Microfilm/microfiche copies available at above repository
#Microfilm copy available at the LDS Family History Library in Salt Lake City, Utah, and through the LDS Family History Centers.
††Subject to embargo for 100 years
*Printed or transcribed
†For additional information send 2 Postal Reply Coupons or 31 pence of English postage for reply to North America; 34 pence to Australia and New Zealand.

Hours: M, T, Th, F 10-7:30; W 10-1; S 10-4
(Prior appointment advised for microfilm reader)

HOLDINGS

Resources pertaining to the former Municipal Borough of Sale and its administrative predecessors.

Census‡#§	1841–1881
Church of England (diocesan)	
Tithe Apportionments‡‡	1845
(Sale, Ashton upon Mersey)	
Directories* (some#)	
Postal, Trade	(gaps) 1788–
Enclosure Awards (Sale)	1806
Local Histories*	
Maps (O.S.)	late 19C–20C
Newspapers‡#§	1926–
Periodicals*	
Rate Books	1830–1849,
	1856–1968
Registers of Electors*	1937–1940,
	1945

URMSTON LIBRARY
Crofts Bank Road
Urmston, Greater Manchester
Tel. (061) 748 0774
Hours: M, T, Th, F 10-7:30; W 10-1; S 10-4

---

‡Microfilm/microfiche copies available at above repository
#Microfilm copy available at the LDS Family History Library in Salt Lake City, Utah, and through the LDS Family History Centers.
§May provide vital data and/or proof of family relationships.
‡‡Parish copies only
*Printed or transcribed

HOLDINGS

Resources pertaining to the former urban district of Urmston and its administrative predecessors.

Church of England (diocesan)		
Tithe Apportionments‡‡		1840's
Church of England (parish)		
Parish Registers‡#§		16C–20C
Directories* (some#)	(gaps)	1788–
Postal, Trade		
Family Histories*		
International Genealogical Index‡##§		
(Lancs, Ches)		
Local Histories*		1848–
Maps (O.S.)		
Newspapers*§	(gaps)	1895–
Nonconformist Registers		
Methodist‡#§		1799–1837
Rate Books		
Registers of Electors*		1974–

ALTRINCHAM LIBRARY
20 Stamford New Road
Altrincham, Greater Manchester
Tel. (061) 928 0317

Hours: M, T, Th, F 10-7:30; W 10-1; S 10-4

---

‡‡Parish copies only

‡Microfilm/microfiche copies available at above repository

#Microfilm copy available at the LDS Family History Library in Salt Lake City, Utah, and through the LDS Family History Centers.

§May provide vital data and/or proof of family relationships.

*Printed or transcribed

##Microfiche copy available at the LDS Family History Library in Salt Lake City, Utah, and through the LDS Family History Centers.

HOLDINGS

Resources pertaining to the former Municipal Borough of Altrincham and its administrative predecessors.

STRETFORD LIBRARY
Kingsway
Stretford, Greater Manchester
Tel. (061) 865 2218
Hours: M, T, Th, F 10-7:30; W 10-1; S 10-4

HOLDINGS

Resources pertaining to the former Municipal Borough of Stretford and its administrative predecessors.

WIGAN METROPOLITAN DISTRICT

(Wigan, Leigh, Abram, Aspull, Atherton, Hindley, Ince-in-Makerfield, Orrell, Standish-with-Langtree, Tyldesley, pt. Ashton-in-Makerfield, pt. Golborne, pt. Billinge-and-Winstanley)

WIGAN RECORD OFFICE
Town Hall
Leigh, Wigan WN7 2DY
Tel. 0942 672421 ext. 266
Contact: Archivist
Hours: M-F 10-4; closed S
        (Appointment advised)
Admission free

HOLDINGS

Resources pertaining to the areas now in Wigan Metropolitan District, and to their administrative predecessors. Church of England parish records, including deposited parish registers for more than 30 churches in the former Metropolitan Borough of Wigan.

SOURCES THAT IDENTIFY AN INDIVIDUAL WITH A SPECIFIC LOCATION

Borough Records (Wigan)	
Rates	c. 1800–20C
Business Records	19C–20C
Directories* (some#)	1787–1931
Hearth Tax Assessments‡# (Lancs)	1662–1672
Local Histories*	
Maps	19C–
Periodicals*	
Poll Books* (Wigan) (some#)	1768–1841
Registers of Electors*	1694–1866
Trade Union Records	19C–20C

SOURCES THAT MAY ADDITIONALLY PROVIDE VITAL DATA AND/OR PROVE FAMILY RELATIONSHIPS

Borough Records (Wigan)	
Court – Borough Sessions	1733–1971
Court – Leet	1626–1834
Cemetery Records‡#	1856–1980
Census‡#	1841
Church of England (parish)	
Parish Registers	16C–20C
Parish Register Transcripts*	16C–19C

---

*Printed or transcribed

#Microfilm copy available at the LDS Family History Library in Salt Lake City, Utah, and through the LDS Family History Centers.

‡Microfilm/microfiche copies available at above repository

Estate and Family Papers	13C–20C
International Genealogical Index‡##††	
(Lancs)	
Manorial Records	(few) 17C–19C
Monumental Inscriptions	
Nonconformist Records (some#)	
Congregational	late 18C–20C
Methodist	late 18C–20C
Presbyterian/Unitarian	17C–20C
Roman Catholic Records	18C–20C
School Records	17C–20C
Society and Charity Records	17C–20C

PUBLICATIONS†

Guide to Genealogical Sources, with supplements to 1984
Leaflets:
  Civil Registration
  Coal Mining
  Tracing the History of Your Home
  Records of Local Government
  Administration of Wigan
  Maps and Plans
Those Dark Satanic Mills (1981)

---

‡Microfilm/microfiche copies available at above repository

##Microfiche copy available at the LDS Family History Library in Salt Lake City, Utah, and through the LDS Family History Centers.

††No postal correspondence

#Microfilm copy available at the LDS Family History Library in Salt Lake City, Utah, and through the LDS Family History Centers.

†For additional information send 2 Postal Reply Coupons or 31 pence of English postage for reply to North America; 34 pence to Australia and New Zealand.

OTHER REPOSITORIES

The sources listed below include only those items reported on the Record Office Survey as located in the specified repositories. Each city and county library should have additional printed materials pertaining to its geographical area.

METHODIST ARCHIVES AND RESEARCH CENTRE†
c/o John Rylands University Library
Deansgate, Manchester M3 3EH
Tel. (061) 834 5343
Contact: Methodist Church Archivist

Hours: M-F 10-5:30; restricted service S mornings

HOLDINGS

Methodist Archives and Research Centre consists of a collection of books and manuscripts relating to the religious history of the denomination, and the doctrinal, theological controversies relating thereto. No baptismal, marriage or burial certificates are here, nor is there a professional genealogical researcher. Holdings relevant to family history are mostly published materials pertaining to ministers and lay leaders of various branches of the Methodist Church.

Local Histories*	19C–
Methodist Magazines*	18C–
Newspapers*	19C–
Minutes of Conference	18C–

(Information folder available from the Archivist)

---

†For additional information send 2 Postal Reply Coupons or 31 pence of English postage for reply to North America; 34 pence to Australia and New Zealand.
*Printed or transcribed

BOLTON CENTRAL LIBRARY†
Reference Library
Civic Centre, Le Mans Crescent
Bolton BL1 1SE
Tel. 0204 22311

Census‡#§	1841–1881
Directories* (some#)	1825–
International Genealogical Index‡##	
(England, Ireland, Wales)	
Local Histories*	
Maps	1850–
Newspapers*	18C–

MANCHESTER CENTRAL LIBRARY
Local History Department†
St. Peter's Square
Manchester M2 5PD
Tel. (061) 236 9422

Hours: M-F 9-9; S 9-5

Census‡#	1841–1881
Church of England (parish)	
Parish Registers#	16C–1837
Directories* (some#)	1772–1969
International Genealogical Index‡##	
(Lancs, Ches)	
Nonconformist Registers#	to 1837
Registers of Electors*	1832–

---

†For additional information send 2 Postal Reply Coupons or 31 pence of English postage for reply to North America; 34 pence to Australia and New Zealand.
‡Microfilm/microfiche copies available at above repository
#Microfilm copy available at the LDS Family History Library in Salt Lake City, Utah, and through the LDS Family History Centers.
§May provide vital data and/or proof of family relationships.
*Printed or transcribed
##Microfiche copy available at the LDS Family History Library in Salt Lake City, Utah, and through the LDS Family History Centers.

SALFORD CITY LIBRARY†
Salford Local History Library
Peel Park, Salford M5 4WU
Tel. (061) 736 3353

Census‡# (Salford City)	1841–1881
International Genealogical Index‡##	

STOCKPORT CENTRAL LIBRARY†
Reference Library and Local Studies Library
Wellington Road South
Stockport SK1 3RS
Tel. (061) 480 7297

Census‡#	1841–1881
Church of England (parish)	
Parish Registers‡#	16C–20C
Parish Register Transcripts*	16C–19C
Coroners' Records‡# (Stockport)	1851–1856
Directories* (some#)	18C–20C
International Genealogical Index‡##	
Local Histories* (some#)	
Maps#	19C–20C
Newspapers#	18C–20C
Periodicals*	19C–20C
Registers of Electors*	1834–1978
Roman Catholic Records‡#	1886–1896
School Records (some#)	late 19C–20C

---

†For additional information send 2 Postal Reply Coupons or 31 pence of English postage for reply to North America; 34 pence to Australia and New Zealand.
‡Microfilm/microfiche copies available at above repository
#Microfilm copy available at the LDS Family History Library in Salt Lake City, Utah, and through the LDS Family History Centers.
##Microfiche copy available at the LDS Family History Library in Salt Lake City, Utah, and through the LDS Family History Centers.
*Printed or transcribed

LDS FAMILY HISTORY CENTRE[†]
Altrincham Road
Wythenshawe, Manchester M22 4BJ
Tel. (061) 902 9279
    LDS Family History Library Catalog[‡##]
    International Genealogical Index[‡##]

LDS FAMILY HISTORY CENTRE[†]
Tweedale Street
Rochdale, OL1 3TZ
Tel. 0706 526292
    LDS Family History Library Catalog[‡##]
    International Genealogical Index[‡##]

GENEALOGICAL AND FAMILY HISTORY SOCIETIES

The societies listed below may have recorded Monumental (tombstone) Inscriptions, compiled an Index to Marriages (from the Parish Registers), an Index to the 1851 Census, and other special indexes, e.g., Strays, Members' Interests, for their geographical areas.** Each Society publishes a quarterly

---

[†]For additional information send 2 Postal Reply Coupons or 31 pence of English postage for reply to North America; 34 pence to Australia and New Zealand.
[‡]Microfilm/microfiche copies available at above repository
[##]Microfiche copy available at the LDS Family History Library in Salt Lake City, Utah, and through the LDS Family History Centers.
**See *Current Publications by Member Societies* (annual), *List of Family History Project Coordinators*, 6th ed., and *Family History News and Digest* (biennial) — all published by the Federation of Family History Societies; available in the USA from the International Society for British Genealogy and Family History, P.O. Box 20425, Cleveland, OH 44120.

journal (listed in italics) which includes articles on family history, reports on the group's projects, and members' queries.

MANCHESTER AND LANCASHIRE FAMILY HISTORY SOCIETY[†]
Mr. A.M. Berrell, Secretary
5th floor, Clayton House
39 Piccadilly
Manchester M1 2AQ

The Manchester Genealogist

[†]For additional information send 2 Postal Reply Coupons or 31 pence of English postage for reply to North America; 34 pence to Australia and New Zealand.

MERSEYSIDE

Post-1974 Counties of England

The Merseyside Metropolitan County was established in 1974. Its geographical boundaries included the areas of Birkenhead, Hoylake and Wallasey formerly in Cheshire, as well as Liverpool, Bootle, Southport, and St. Helens previously in Lancashire.

Administratively Birkenhead (1889–1974) and Wallasey (1913–1974) were County Boroughs. Birkenhead was a nineteenth-century Municipal Borough in Cheshire. Liverpool was a thirteenth-century incorporated Borough to 1889 and a County Borough between 1889 and 1974. Bootle, Southport and St. Helens

294

were all Municipal Boroughs in Lancashire from the mid-nineteenth century to 1974.

Except for Liverpool, see the Record Offices in Cheshire and Lancashire for sources pertaining to localities in the respective pre-1974 counties.

The Merseyside Metropolitan County Council was abolished by Act of Parliament 1 April 1986. At that time the name of the county was changed to Merseyside County. Councils of the five metropolitan districts within the county (Liverpool, Knowsley, St. Helens, Sefton, and Wirral) now administer the archives and library services for local resources within their respective areas.

DISTRICT ARCHIVES AND LIBRARIES

Genealogical resources for metropolitan districts within the county of Merseyside may be found in the respective repositories in the cities and boroughs listed below.

The sources may vary considerably from one district to another. Those most likely to be found in the Archives Department of a library or record office include Borough Records, Church of England parish records including deposited Parish Registers, Estate and Family Papers, Manorial Records and Title Deeds.

Sources most likely to be in the Local History/Studies Department of a library include transcribed or microfilm copies of Church of England Parish Registers, microfilm copies of Census Records 1841–1881, Postal and Trade Directories, International Genealogical Index, and microfilm copies of Nonconformist Registers for groups within the specific areas.

LIVERPOOL METROPOLITAN DISTRICT
(Liverpool)

LIVERPOOL RECORD OFFICE
City Libraries, William Brown Street
Liverpool L3 8EW
Tel. (051) 207 2147 ext. 34

Hours: M-F 9-9; S 9-5

Admission free
List of record searchers available upon request[†]

HOLDINGS

Church of England parish records including deposited Parish Registers for more than 90 churches in Liverpool; local government records and other resources pertaining to Liverpool.

(Church of England diocesan records for the Archdeaconry of Richmond, Western Deaneries, Diocese of Chester, are primarily located in the Lancashire Record Office.)

SOURCES THAT IDENTIFY AN INDIVIDUAL WITH A SPECIFIC LOCATION

Borough Records (Liverpool)

Freemen's Lists		1692–1939
Rates		18C only
Directories* (some#)		1766–1970
Maps (Liverpool)		1725–
Poll Books* (some#)	(periodic)	1734–1832
Registers of Electors*		1832–

[†]For additional information send 2 Postal Reply Coupons or 31 pence of English postage for reply to North America; 34 pence to Australia and New Zealand.
*Printed or transcribed
#Microfilm copy available at the LDS Family History Library in Salt Lake City, Utah, and through the LDS Family History Centers.

SOURCES THAT MAY ADDITIONALLY PROVIDE VITAL DATA AND/OR PROVE FAMILY RELATIONSHIPS

Borough Records (Liverpool)	1550–1835
Court	
Title Deeds	
Cemetery Records	1825–
Census‡# (Liverpool)	1841–1881
Church of England (diocesan)	
Marriage Licence Allegations	1908–
Church of England (parish)	
Parish Registers	1654–
Estate and Family Papers	13C–
International Genealogical Index‡##	
(British Isles)	
Jewish Registers††	1804–
Manorial Records	15C–
Monumental Inscriptions	c. 1800–
Newspapers*	1756–
Nonconformist Registers	
Methodist	1837–
Baptist	mainly 19C
Congregational	mainly 19C
Presbyterian	mainly 19C
Unitarian	mainly 19C
Poor Law Union	
Workhouse Records	1834–
Roman Catholic Registers	pre-1900
School Records	19C
Wills, Principal Probate Registry	
Indexes‡‡	1858–

‡Microfilm/microfiche copies available at above repository

#Microfilm copy available at the LDS Family History Library in Salt Lake City, Utah, and through the LDS Family History Centers.

##Microfiche copy available at the LDS Family History Library in Salt Lake City, Utah, and through the LDS Family History Centers.

††Written permission required to consult records.

*Printed or transcribed

‡‡At least fifty years old

PUBLICATIONS†

Leaflets/Lists (free):
A Brief Guide for Genealogists
Tracing Your Ancestry: A General Guide
Parish Records: Church of England (1987)
Records of Roman Catholic Churches (1987)

Archival Guides:
1. *Methodist Records*
2. *Parish Registers*
3. *Census Enumeration Returns*
4. *Probate Records*
5. *Title Deeds*
6. *Congregational, Presbyterian, Baptist and Unitarian Records*

KNOWSLEY METROPOLITAN DISTRICT

(Huyton-with Roby, Kirkby, Prescot,
pt. West Lancashire, pt. Whiston)

KNOWSLEY LIBRARIES
Reference and Information Services
Derby Road
Huyton, Merseyside L36 9UJ
Tel. (051) 443 3738
Contact: Local Studies Librarian
Hours: M, T, W, F 10-7; S 10-1, 2-5; closed Th
Admission free

HOLDINGS

Resources pertaining to the areas now in the Knowsley Metropolitan District, and to their administrative predecessors.

---

†For additional information send 2 Postal Reply Coupons or 31 pence of English postage for reply to North America; 34 pence to Australia and New Zealand.

SOURCES THAT IDENTIFY AN INDIVIDUAL
WITH A SPECIFIC LOCATION

Church of England (parish)	18C–19C
Directories* (some#)	18C–20C
Hearth Tax Assessments* (Lancs)	1662, 1664, 1673
Local Histories*	
Maps	1850–
Periodicals*	
Registers of Electors*	1959–
Trade Union Records	20C

SOURCES THAT MAY ADDITIONALLY PROVIDE VITAL
DATA AND/OR PROVE FAMILY RELATIONSHIPS

Census‡#	1841–1881
Church of England (diocesan)	
Bishops' Transcripts#	17C–19C
Church of England (parish)	
Parish Registers (some#, ##)	16C–
Parish Register Transcripts*	16C–
Estate and Family Papers	18C–19C
International Genealogical Index‡##	
(British Isles)	
Manorial Records‡#	13C– early 19C
Monumental Inscriptions	18C–19C
Newspapers‡#	(few gaps) 1859–

---

*Printed or transcribed

#Microfilm copy available at the LDS Family History Library in Salt Lake City, Utah, and through the LDS Family History Centers.

‡Microfilm/microfiche copies available at above repository

##Microfiche copy available at the LDS Family History Library in Salt Lake City, Utah, and through the LDS Family History Centers.

Nonconformist Registers
  Methodist‡#   1806–1836
  Presbyterian‡#   1776–1839
  Unitarian (some*)   1724–1969
Poor Law Union Records   1834–1900
School Registers   17C–20C
Society and Charity Records   18C–20C

PUBLICATIONS†

Leaflets/Lists:
  Local Government Material (printed) (1985)
  *Parish Registers and Bishops' Transcripts (Printed
    and Microfilm) in Stock at Huyton Central Library
    (including Non-conformist Records)* (1985)
  Borough Records (1987)
  *Cronton Parish Archives Deposited at Huyton
    Library* (1985)
  Census (microfilm) (1985)
  Items from Roby Church (1985)
  Huyton Parish Registers (microfilm)
  Ogle Roll c. 1602 (microfilm)
  Societies and Charities

---

‡Microfilm/microfiche copies available at above repository
#Microfilm copy available at the LDS Family History Library in Salt Lake City,
Utah, and through the LDS Family History Centers.
*Printed or transcribed
†For additional information send 2 Postal Reply Coupons or 31 pence of English
postage for reply to North America; 34 pence to Australia and New Zealand.

ST. HELENS METROPOLITAN DISTRICT

(St. Helens, Haydock, Newton-le-Willows, Rainford,
Rainhill, pt. Bold, pt. Billinge-and-Winstanley,
pt. Ashton-in-Makerfield, pt. Whiston)

ST. HELENS CENTRAL LIBRARY
Local History and Archives
Gamble Institute, Victoria Square
St. Helens WA10 1DY
Tel. (051) 0744 24061 ext. 2952

Hours: M, W 9:30-8; T, Th, F, S 9:30-5

HOLDINGS

Resources pertaining to the areas now in St. Helens Metropolitan District, and to their administrative predecessors.

SOURCES THAT IDENTIFY AN INDIVIDUAL
WITH A SPECIFIC LOCATION

Church of England (diocesan)
Tithe Apportionments[§]   1840's
Directories* (some[#])   (gaps) 1766–
Hearth Tax Assessments[‡][#] (Lancs)   1662–1664,
                                             1671
Land Tax Assessments (Lancs)   1782–1794
Oath Rolls* (Lancs)   1696
Papists Estates   1717–1718
Poll Books* (some[#])   (few) 1855–1863
Rate Books   19C
Registers of Electors* (St. Helens)   1871–

[§]Parish copies only
*Printed or transcribed
[#]Microfilm copy available at the LDS Family History Library in Salt Lake City, Utah, and through the LDS Family History Centers.
[‡]Microfilm/microfiche copies available at above repository

SOURCES THAT MAY ADDITIONALLY PROVIDE VITAL DATA AND/OR PROVE FAMILY RELATIONSHIPS

Census‡#	1841–1881
Civil Registration Indexes‡‡	1837–1912
Church of England (parish)	
Parish Registers*	16C–
Funeral Certificates* (Ches, Lancs)	1600–1678
International Genealogical Index‡##	
(British Isles)	
Newspapers* (some‡#)	19C–
Nonconformist Registers	
Congregational*	18C–19C
	(# to 1837)
Methodist	18C–
	(# to 1837)
Society of Friends‡#	17C–19C
Unitarian*	18C–19C
Probate Records	
Wills, Admin., Inven.*	15C–19C
Roman Catholic Records#	18C–19C
School Records	19C–20C

PUBLICATIONS†

List: *Genealogical Holdings*
(2nd edn. to be published in 1988)

---

‡Microfilm/microfiche copies available at above repository
#Microfilm copy available at the LDS Family History Library in Salt Lake City, Utah, and through the LDS Family History Centers.
‡‡Microfilm copies filmed by the General Register Office, London.
*Printed or transcribed
##Microfiche copy available at the LDS Family History Library in Salt Lake City, Utah, and through the LDS Family History Centers.
†For additional information send 2 Postal Reply Coupons or 31 pence of English postage for reply to North America; 34 pence to Australia and New Zealand.

SEFTON METROPOLITAN DISTRICT

(Bootle, Southport, Crosby, Formby,
Litherland, pt. West Lancashire))

BOOTLE LIBRARY
Sefton Libraries and Arts Services
Local History Library
220 Stanley Road, Bootle
Liverpool L20 3EN
Tel. (051) 933 4508

Hours: M, T 10-5; W, F 10-8; Th, S 10-1

Admission free

HOLDINGS

Resources pertaining to the areas now in Sefton Metropolitan District, and to their administrative predecessors.

Census‡#§	1841–1881
Directories (some#)	18C–
International Genealogical Index‡##§	
(Lancs)	
Local Histories*	
Maps	19C–
Newspapers#§	19C–
Registers of Electors*	20C

PUBLICATIONS†

Leaflet: *This is Your Library* (free)

---

‡Microfilm/microfiche copies available at above repository

#Microfilm copy available at the LDS Family History Library in Salt Lake City,
Utah, and through the LDS Family History Centers.

§May provide vital data and/or proof of family relationships.

##Microfiche copy available at the LDS Family History Library in Salt Lake
City, Utah, and through the LDS Family History Centers.

*Printed or transcribed

†For additional information send 2 Postal Reply Coupons or 31 pence of English
postage for reply to North America; 34 pence to Australia and New Zealand.

WIRRAL METROPOLITAN DISTRICT
(Birkenhead, Wallasey, Bebington,
Hoylake, Wirral)

WIRRAL ARCHIVES SERVICE
Birkenhead Reference Library
Borough Road, Birkenhead L41 2XB
Tel. (051) 652 6106/7/8
Contact: Archivist

Hours: M, T, Th, F 10-8; S 10-1, 2-5; closed W

HOLDINGS

Resources pertaining to the areas now in Wirral Metropolitan District, and to their administrative predecessors.

SOURCES THAT IDENTIFY AN INDIVIDUAL WITH A SPECIFIC LOCATION

Borough Records (Birkenhead)
Rates   (gaps) 1851–1970's
Business Records   19C–20C
Church of England (diocesan)
Tithe Apportionments§§   1840's
Directories* (some#)   (gaps) 1766–1972
Local Histories*   18C–20C
Maps   18C–20C
Periodicals*   19C–20C
Poll Books* (some#)   19C
Rate Books   1784–1970's
Registers of Electors*   1863–

---

§§Parish copies only
*Printed or transcribed
#Microfilm copy available at the LDS Family History Library in Salt Lake City, Utah, and through the LDS Family History Centers.

SOURCES THAT MAY ADDITIONALLY PROVIDE VITAL DATA AND/OR PROVE FAMILY RELATIONSHIPS

Borough Records (Birkenhead)	
Court	1832–1971
Census‡#	1841–1881
Church of England (diocesan)	
Wills* (Ches)	1545–1837
Marriage Licences* (Ches)	1606–1719
Church of England (parish)	
Parish Registers‡#	16C–20C
Parish Register Transcripts* (Lancs)	16C–19C
Estate and Family Papers	18C–19C
Funeral Certificates*	1600–1678
International Genealogical Index‡##	
(England, Scotland, Wales)	
Monumental Inscriptions*	
Newspapers‡#	19C–20C
School Records	19C–20C
Society and Charity Records	19C–20C
Title Deeds	18C–20C

PUBLICATIONS†

Leaflets/Lists:
  Local Records (1987)
  Wirral Archives (1985)

(also various lists covering Directories, Census Returns, Parish Registers, etc.)

---

‡Microfilm/microfiche copies available at above repository

#Microfilm copy available at the LDS Family History Library in Salt Lake City, Utah, and through the LDS Family History Centers.

*Printed or transcribed

##Microfiche copy available at the LDS Family History Library in Salt Lake City, Utah, and through the LDS Family History Centers.

†For additional information send 2 Postal Reply Coupons or 31 pence of English postage for reply to North America; 34 pence to Australia and New Zealand.

OTHER REPOSITORIES

The sources listed below include only those items reported on the Record Office Survey as located in the specified repositories. Each city and county library should have additional printed materials pertaining to its geographical area.

MERSEYSIDE MARITIME MUSEUM†
NATIONAL MUSEUMS AND
GALLERIES ON MERSEYSIDE
The Archives Department, Securicor Building
64-66 Islington, Liverpool L3 8LG
Tel. (051) 207 3697

After 1 May 1988:
   P.O. Box 33
   127 Dale Street
   Liverpool L69 3LA
   Tel. (051) 236 2696

Hours: By prior appointment: M-F 9:30-4:30; closed S
       Documents not issued 1-2, and after 4

Admission free; one-day Reader's Ticket
       available at reception desk

HOLDINGS

The museum contains primarily history of Maritime commerce and industry. Specific collections include the Bryson Collection of Business Archives and Ephemera, the Danson family archive, archives of many businesses such as the British Insulated Callendar's Cables (BICC DLC) and the Cammell Laird Shipbuilders, of social organizations such as the Liverpool Seaman's Orphan Institution. Shipping registers and records of the Pilotage Service and of the Port Authority are also housed at this museum.

---

†For additional information send 2 Postal Reply Coupons or 31 pence of English postage for reply to North America; 34 pence to Australia and New Zealand.

PUBLICATIONS†

Leaflets/Lists:
Gordon Read, *Survey of Records of Migration to North America from Europe via the Port of Liverpool* (1987)
Gordon Read and Kristina Grant, *Tracing Your Emigrant Ancestors*§ (1982)
Archives of the Port of Liverpool I, II
The National Museums and Galleries on Merseyside Archives Department (1987) (free)

LDS FAMILY HISTORY CENTRE†
4 Mill Bank
Liverpool L13 0BW
Tel. (051) 228 0433

LDS Family History Library Catalog‡##
International Genealogical Index‡##

---

†For additional information send 2 Postal Reply Coupons or 31 pence of English postage for reply to North America; 34 pence to Australia and New Zealand.
§The guide is now obsolete; remaining copies available for £1.
‡Microfilm/microfiche copies available at above repository
##Microfiche copy available at the LDS Family History Library in Salt Lake City, Utah, and through the LDS Family History Centers.

GENEALOGICAL AND FAMILY HISTORY SOCIETIES

The societies listed below may have recorded Monumental (tombstone) Inscriptions, compiled an Index to Marriages (from the Parish Registers), an Index to the 1851 Census, and other special indexes, e.g., Strays, Members' Interests, for their geographical areas.** Each Society publishes a quarterly journal (listed in italics) which includes articles on family history, reports on the group's projects, and members' queries.

LIVERPOOL AND DISTRICT
FAMILY HISTORY SOCIETY†
Mr. H. Culling, Secretary
11 Lisburn Lane, Tuebrook
Liverpool L13 9AD

The Liverpool Family Historian

**See *Current Publications by Member Societies* (annual), *List of Family History Project Coordinators*, 6th ed., and *Family History News and Digest* (biennial) — all published by the Federation of Family History Societies; available in the USA from the International Society for British Genealogy and Family History, P.O. Box 20425, Cleveland, OH 44120.

†For additional information send 2 Postal Reply Coupons or 31 pence of English postage for reply to North America; 34 pence to Australia and New Zealand.

MIDDLESEX

Pre-1974 Counties of England

Prior to 1889 the geographical boundaries of Middlesex County included the river Thames on the south, the river Lea on the east, and the river Colne on the west. Its northern boundary was contiguous with the county of Hertfordshire.

That year the following areas were transferred to the newly created County of London, and were subsequently made Metropolitan Boroughs: Bethnal Green, Chelsea, Finsbury, Fulham, Hackney, Hammersmith, Hampstead, Holborn, Islington, Kensington, Paddington, Poplar, St. Marylebone, St. Pancras, Shoreditch, Stepney, Stoke Newington, and the City of

Westminster. At the same time the area of Monken Hadley was transferred to Hertfordshire.

In 1965 Middlesex County was abolished. Most of the areas formerly within its boundaries were transferred to the newly established area of Greater London (which also included the Metropolitan Boroughs previously in the County of London). The following Middlesex areas were included: Acton, Brentford and Chiswick, Ealing, Edmonton, Enfield, Finchley, Harrow, Hendon, Heston and Isleworth, Hornsey, Southall, Southgate, Tottenham, Twickenham, Uxbridge, Wembley, Willesden, and Wood Green, all of which had become Municipal Boroughs during the twentieth century.

The parishes of Ashford, Laleham, Littleton, Shepperton, Staines, Stanwell and Sunbury, formerly in Middlesex County, were transferred to Surrey County in 1965, and South Mimms became part of Hertfordshire that year.

Administrative records for the former Middlesex County are located at the Greater London Record Office. Church of England diocesan and parish records for areas formerly in the county are located partly at the Guildhall Library, Lambeth Palace Library, and the Greater London Record Office.

WEST MIDLANDS

Post-1974 Counties of England

The West Midlands Metropolitan County was created in 1974. Its geographical boundaries include the region which was formerly the northwestern part of Warwickshire (including Birmingham, Coventry, Sutton Coldfield and Solihull); the areas of Halesowen, Dudley and Stourbridge previously in Worcestershire; and the areas of Warley, Walsall, West Bromwich and Wolverhampton formerly in Staffordshire.

Administratively Coventry, Sutton Coldfield and Birmingham were incorporated Boroughs in Warwickshire from the mid-fifteenth, sixteenth, and nineteenth centuries, respectively, to 1889 and then County Boroughs to 1974. Dudley was a

311

Municipal Borough in the former county of Worcestershire during the nineteenth century and later a County Borough. Walsall became an incorporated Borough in Staffordshire in the seventeenth century, while West Bromwich and Wolverhampton were Municipal Boroughs from the nineteenth century to 1974. Warley, a County Borough from 1965 to 1974 included the former County Borough of Smethwick and the twentieth-century Municipal Boroughs of Oldbury and Rowley Regis.

The Metropolitan County Council of West Midlands was abolished by Act of Parliament 1 April 1986. At the same time the county name was changed to West Midland County. Councils of the metropolitan districts within the county (Birmingham, Coventry, Dudley, Sandwell, Solihull, Walsall and Wolverhampton) now administer the archives services for their respective areas.

See the Record Offices in Staffordshire, Warwickshire, and Hereford and Worcester (Worcester Branch) for sources pertaining to localities in the respective pre-1974 counties.

(Church of England diocesan and some parish records for that part of the county in the Diocese of Lichfield – Warwickshire and Staffordshire areas – are located in the Lichfield Joint Record Office, Lichfield, Staffs; Church of England diocesan records for that part of the new county located in the Diocese of Worcester – Worcestershire area – are located in the Hereford and Worcester Record Office, Worcester Branch.)

DISTRICT ARCHIVES AND LIBRARIES

Genealogical resources for metropolitan districts within the county of West Midlands may be found in the respective repositories in the cities and boroughs listed below.

The sources may vary considerably from one district to another. Those most likely to be found in the Archives Department of a library or record office include Borough Records, Church of England parish records including deposited Parish

Registers, Estate and Family Papers, Manorial Records and Title Deeds.

Sources most likely to be in the Local History/Studies Department of a library include transcribed or microfilm copies of Church of England Parish Registers, microfilm copies of Census Records 1841–1881, Postal and Trade Directories, International Genealogical Index, and microfilm copies of Nonconformist Registers for groups within the specific areas.

BIRMINGHAM METROPOLITAN DISTRICT

(Birmingham, Sutton Coldfield)

BIRMINGHAM REFERENCE LIBRARY
Chamberlain Square, Birmingham B3 3HQ
Tel. (021) 235 4217

Hours: Archives Department: M-F 9-6; S 9-5;
             Reference Library: M-F 9-8; S 9-5
Admission free
List of record searchers available upon request†

HOLDINGS

Church of England parish records including deposited Parish Registers for approximately 90 churches in the Birmingham area; local government records and other resources mainly pertaining to the city.

---

†For additional information send 2 Postal Reply Coupons or 31 pence of English postage for reply to North America; 34 pence to Australia and New Zealand.

SOURCES THAT IDENTIFY AN INDIVIDUAL WITH A SPECIFIC LOCATION

Borough Records (Birmingham, Sutton Coldfield)	18C–
Rates	
Business Records	mid-18C
Church of England (diocesan)	
Tithe Apportionments§	1840's
Directories* (some#)	1767–
Local Histories*	
Maps	
Periodicals*	
Poll Books* (some#)	17C–18C
Quarter Sessions	
Judicial Records	1839–
Registers of Electors*	1838–

SOURCES THAT MAY ADDITIONALLY PROVIDE VITAL DATA AND/OR PROVE FAMILY RELATIONSHIPS

Borough Records (Birmingham, Sutton Coldfield)	19C–
Court	
Title Deeds	
Census‡# (Birmingham and environs)	1841–1881
Church of England (parish)	
Parish Registers‡#	1539–
Parish Register Copies*	16C–19C
Civil Registration Indexes‡§§	1866–1912
Estate and Family Papers	

---

§Parish copies only
*Printed or transcribed
#Microfilm copy available at the LDS Family History Library in Salt Lake City, Utah, and through the LDS Family History Centers.
‡Microfilm/microfiche copies available at above repository
§§Microfilm copy filmed by the General Register Office, London

International Genealogical Index‡##
(British Isles)
Manorial Records 14C–
Monumental Inscriptions*
Newspapers* 18C–
Nonconformist Registers
Congregational 1785–1937
Methodist 19C–20C
Unitarian 18C–20C
Obituaries (Index) 1741–1863
Pedigrees
Roman Catholic Registers‡#* 17C–18C
Wills, Register Copies 1858–1941
Index* 1858–

PUBLICATIONS†

List of Parish Registers (free)

‡Microfilm/microfiche copies available at above repository
##Microfiche copy available at the LDS Family History Library in Salt Lake City, Utah, and through the LDS Family History Centers.
*Printed or transcribed
#Microfilm copy available at the LDS Family History Library in Salt Lake City, Utah, and through the LDS Family History Centers.
†For additional information send 2 Postal Reply Coupons or 31 pence of English postage for reply to North America; 34 pence to Australia and New Zealand.

COVENTRY METROPOLITAN DISTRICT

(Coventry, pt. Meridan)

COVENTRY CITY RECORD OFFICE
Mandela House, Bayley Lane
Coventry CV1 5RG
Tel. 0203 832418

Hours: M-Th 8:45-4:45; F 8:45-4:15

Admission free
List of record searchers available upon request[†]

HOLDINGS

Local government records and other resources pertaining exclusively to the city of Coventry.

SOURCES THAT IDENTIFY AN INDIVIDUAL WITH A SPECIFIC LOCATION

Borough Records (Coventry)	
Corporation Ecclesiastical Records	
Tithe Books (Church of England)[§]	early 19C
Court Leet	1420–1555,[*]
	1751–1834
Freemen's Court Index	1715–1935
Quarter Sessions	17C–1832
Judicial Records	
Jury Lists	
Land Tax Assessments	
Sacramental Certificates	1682–1828
Business Records	18C–20C

[†]For additional information send 2 Postal Reply Coupons or 31 pence of English postage for reply to North America; 34 pence to Australia and New Zealand.
[§]Parish copies only
[*]Printed or transcribed

Local Histories*
Maps
Poll Books* (some#)   1777–1868
Registers of Electors*   1833–
Trade Union Records   20C

*SOURCES THAT MAY ADDITIONALLY PROVIDE VITAL
DATA AND/OR PROVE FAMILY RELATIONSHIPS*

Borough Records
    Apprentices' Enrolment Registers   1780–
    Freemen's Admission Registers   1780–
Cemetery Records (London Road)   1847–1896
    Index   1847–1906
Estate and Family Papers   late 18C–20C
Midwives' Register of Cases   1904–1911
    (Foles Hill)
Nonconformist Registers
    Baptist   18C–20C
    Methodist   19C–20C
    United Reformed   1899–1953
School Records   late 19C–20C
Society and Charity Records   20C
Title Deeds   19C–20C

PUBLICATIONS†

Leaflets/Lists:
  How to Trace Your Family Tree
  Notes for Genealogists

---

*Printed or transcribed
#Microfilm copy available at the LDS Family History Library in Salt Lake City,
Utah, and through the LDS Family History Centers.
†For additional information send 2 Postal Reply Coupons or 31 pence of English
postage for reply to North America; 34 pence to Australia and New Zealand.

DUDLEY METROPOLITAN DISTRICT

(Dudley, Halesowen, Stourbridge)

ARCHIVES AND LOCAL HISTORY DEPARTMENT
DUDLEY LIBRARY

St. James Road
Dudley, West Midlands DY1 1HR
Tel. 0384 55433 ext. 5526
Contact: Archivist

Hours: M, W, F 9-1, 2-5; T, Th 2-7;
(Appointment advised)
By prior appointment: 1st, 3rd S/mo 9:30-12:30

Admission free

HOLDINGS

Resources pertaining to the areas now in Dudley Metropolitan District, and to their administrative predecessors

SOURCES THAT IDENTIFY AN INDIVIDUAL WITH A SPECIFIC LOCATION

Business Records	19C–20C
Directories* (some#)	18C–
(Trade)	
Local Histories*	
Rate Books (Dudley)	17C–20C
Registers of Electors*	late 19C–

---

*Printed or transcribed
#Microfilm copy available at the LDS Family History Library in Salt Lake City, Utah, and through the LDS Family History Centers.

318

SOURCES THAT MAY ADDITIONALLY PROVIDE VITAL DATA AND/OR PROVE FAMILY RELATIONSHIPS

Census‡# (Dudley)	1841–1881
Church of England (parish)	
Parish Registers‡#	16C–
Parish Register Transcripts*	16C–19C
Estate and Family Papers	12C–20C
International Genealogical Index‡##	
(Staffs, Worcs)	
Manorial Records	14C–20C
Newspapers‡#	19C–
Nonconformist Registers	
Baptists (some also‡#*)	17C–20C
Congregational (some also‡#*)	late 18C–20C
Methodist (some also‡#*)	19C–20C
Society of Friends*	17C–19C
Unitarian‡#	18C–20C
Pedigrees	
Roman Catholic Registers*	1795–1851
Wills*	15C–19C

PUBLICATIONS†

Leaflets/Lists:
   Archives and Local History Section (free)
   Brief Checklist of Sources Available for
      Genealogical Enquirers
   List of Parish Registers
   List of Nonconformist Registers

---

‡Microfilm/microfiche copies available at above repository

#Microfilm copy available at the LDS Family History Library in Salt Lake City, Utah, and through the LDS Family History Centers.

*Printed or transcribed

##Microfiche copy available at the LDS Family History Library in Salt Lake City, Utah, and through the LDS Family History Centers.

†For additional information send 2 Postal Reply Coupons or 31 pence of English postage for reply to North America; 34 pence to Australia and New Zealand.

SANDWELL METROPOLITAN DISTRICT
(Warley, West Bromwich)

SANDWELL CENTRAL LIBRARY
High Street
West Bromwich B70 8DZ
Tel. (021) 569 2478
Hours: M, F 9-7; T, W 9-6; Th, S 9-1
Admission free

HOLDINGS

Resources pertaining to the areas now in Sandwell Metropolitan District, and to their administrative predecessors.

SOURCES THAT IDENTIFY AN INDIVIDUAL WITH A SPECIFIC LOCATION

Borough Records (West Bromwich)	
Rates	19C–20C
Business Records	19C–20C
Directories* (some#)	19C–
Local Histories*	
Maps	19C–
Periodicals*	19C–
Registers of Electors*	19C–

SOURCES THAT MAY ADDITIONALLY PROVIDE VITAL DATA AND/OR PROVE FAMILY RELATIONSHIPS

Borough Records (West Bromwich)	
Court	19C–20C
Title Deeds	17C–

---

*Printed or transcribed
#Microfilm copy available at the LDS Family History Library in Salt Lake City, Utah, and through the LDS Family History Centers.

Census‡#	1841–1881
Church of England (parish)	
Parish Registers (some‡#)	16C–
Parish Register Transcripts*	16C–19C
Estate and Family Papers	17C–20C
International Genealogical Index‡##	
(Shrops, Staffs, Warws, Worcs)	
Monumental Inscriptions*	18C–20C
Newspapers*	19C–
Nonconformist Registers	
Methodist	19C–20C
School Records	19C–20C
Wills	17C–20C

SOLIHULL METROPOLITAN DISTRICT

(Solihull, pt. Stratford upon Avon, pt. Meridan)

SOLIHULL LIBRARIES AND ARTS DEPARTMENT
SOLIHULL CENTRAL LIBRARY
Homer Road
Solihull, West Midlands B91 3RG
Tel. (021) 704 6977
Contact: Local History Librarian

Hours: M, T 9:30-5:30; Th, F 9:30-8;
      S 9:30-5; closed W
      Appointment needed to see records

Admission free

---

‡Microfilm/microfiche copies available at above repository
#Microfilm copy available at the LDS Family History Library in Salt Lake City, Utah, and through the LDS Family History Centers.
*Printed or transcribed
##Microfiche copy available at the LDS Family History Library in Salt Lake City, Utah, and through the LDS Family History Centers.

HOLDINGS

Resources pertaining to the areas now in Solihull Metropolitan District, except for Stratford upon Avon, and to their
administrative predecessors.

SOURCES THAT IDENTIFY AN INDIVIDUAL
WITH A SPECIFIC LOCATION

Business Records		20C
Church of England (diocesan)		
Tithe Apportionments[§]		1840
Coroners' Records[††]		19C–20C
Directories* (some[#])	(some)	19C–20C
(Warws)		
Enclosure Awards		1843
Hospital Records[††]		19C–20C
Local Histories*		
Magistrates' Court[††]		19C–20C
Maps		19C–20C
Periodicals*		20C
Quarter Sessions		19C–20C

SOURCES THAT MAY ADDITIONALLY PROVIDE VITAL
DATA AND/OR PROVE FAMILY RELATIONSHIPS

Census[‡#]	1841–1881
International Genealogical Index[‡##]	
Newspapers[‡#]	19C–20C

[§]Parish copies only; Church of England diocesan copies are located at the Warwickshire County Record Office.

[††]Subject to embargo for 100 years

*Printed or transcribed

[#]Microfilm copy available at the LDS Family History Library in Salt Lake City, Utah, and through the LDS Family History Centers.

[‡]Microfilm/microfiche copies available at above repository

[##]Microfiche copy available at the LDS Family History Library in Salt Lake City, Utah, and through the LDS Family History Centers.

PUBLICATIONS†

Leaflet: *Local History Collection Reader's Guide* (1985)
(free)

WALSALL METROPOLITAN DISTRICT

(Walsall, Aldridge-Brownhills)

WALSALL LOCAL HISTORY CENTRE
Essex Street, Walsall WS2 7AS
Tel. 0922 721305 / 721306

Hours: T, Th 9:30-5:30; W 9:30-7;
F 9:30-5; S 9:30-1; closed M

HOLDINGS

Resources pertaining to the areas now in Walsall Metropolitan District, and to their administrative predecessors.

Borough Records (Walsall)	16C–20C
Burgess Lists	late 14C–19C
Business Records	19C–20C
Census§	1801–1831,
	1841–1881‡#
Charity Records	17C–
Church of England (parish)	
Parish Registers‡§	16C–20C
(St. Mathew's Walsall)	

---

†For additional information send 2 Postal Reply Coupons or 31 pence of English postage for reply to North America; 34 pence to Australia and New Zealand.
§May provide vital data and/or proof of family relationships.
‡Microfilm/microfiche copies available at above repository
#Microfilm copy available at the LDS Family History Library in Salt Lake City, Utah, and through the LDS Family History Centers.

Directories* (some#)	19C–20C
Guild Records§	15C–
Local Histories*	
Maps	
Nonconformist Registers	
Methodist§	19C–20C
Periodicals*§	19C–20C
Society Records§	1920

PUBLICATIONS†

Leaflet: *Walsall Local History News* (free)

WOLVERHAMPTON METROPOLITAN DISTRICT

(Wolverhampton)

WOLVERHAMPTON CENTRAL LIBRARY
Snow Hill, Wolverhampton
West Midlands WV1 3AX
Tel. 0902 773824
Contact: Archivist

Hours: M-S 10-1, 2-5

HOLDINGS

Printed and microfilm copies of resources pertaining to the Metropolitan District of Wolverhampton. Original records for the borough of Wolverhampton, and some Nonconformist records.

---

*Printed or transcribed
#Microfilm copy available at the LDS Family History Library in Salt Lake City, Utah, and through the LDS Family History Centers.
§May provide vital data and/or proof of family relationships.
†For additional information send 2 Postal Reply Coupons or 31 pence of English postage for reply to North America; 34 pence to Australia and New Zealand.

SOURCES THAT IDENTIFY AN INDIVIDUAL
WITH A SPECIFIC LOCATION

Borough Records (Wolverhampton)	19C–
Directories* (some#)	1770–1976
Hearth Tax Assessments*	1665
Land Tax Assessments (Staffs)	1798, 1800
Lists of Freeholders*	1653
Local Histories*	
Maps	18C–
Oath Books (Wolverhampton)	1696
Periodicals*	
Rate Books	1777–1829,
	1913–1917
Roman Catholic Lists	1767
Registers of Electors*	1852–

SOURCES THAT MAY ADDITIONALLY PROVIDE VITAL
DATA AND/OR PROVE FAMILY RELATIONSHIPS

Apprenticeship Registers*	1710–1763
Census‡#	1841–1881
Church of England (parish)	
Parish Register Transcripts*	16C–19C
Manorial Records	17C–20C
Nonconformist Registers	
Congregational (some‡#)	1771–1865
Methodist (some‡#)	18C–20C
Unitarian‡#	1830–1838
Newspapers‡#	18C–
School Records	19C–20C
Wills* (few original)	17C–20C

---

*Printed or transcribed

#Microfilm copy available at the LDS Family History Library in Salt Lake City, Utah, and through the LDS Family History Centers.

‡Microfilm/microfiche copies available at above repository

PUBLICATIONS†

Leaflets:
No. 11: *A Selection of Books and Documents in the Library Collections for Study of Demography and Genealogy Handlist of Nonconformist Registers in Wolverhampton Borough Archives*

OTHER REPOSITORIES

The sources listed below include only those items reported on the Record Office Survey as located in the specified repositories. Each city and county library should have additional printed materials pertaining to its geographical area.

COVENTRY CENTRAL LIBRARY†
Local Studies Library
Smithfield Way
Coventry CV1 1FY
Tel. 0203 25555 ext. 2215

Census‡#	1841–1881
Church of England (parish) Parish Register Transcripts*	16C–19C

---

†For additional information send 2 Postal Reply Coupons or 31 pence of English postage for reply to North America; 34 pence to Australia and New Zealand.
‡Microfilm/microfiche copies available at above repository
#Microfilm copy available at the LDS Family History Library in Salt Lake City, Utah, and through the LDS Family History Centers.
*Printed or transcribed

LDS FAMILY HISTORY CENTRE[†]
185 Penns Lane
Sutton Coldfield
Birmingham
Tel. (021) 384 2028

LDS Family History Library Catalog[‡##]
International Genealogical Index[‡##]

GENEALOGICAL AND FAMILY
HISTORY SOCIETIES

The societies listed below may have recorded Monumental (tombstone) Inscriptions, compiled an Index to Marriages (from the Parish Registers), an Index to the 1851 Census, and other special indexes, e.g., Strays, Members' Interests, for their geographical areas.[**] Each Society publishes a quarterly journal (listed in italics) which includes articles on family history, reports on the group's projects, and members' queries.

BIRMINGHAM AND MIDLAND SOCIETY
FOR GENEALOGY AND HERALDRY[†]
Mrs. J. Watkins, Secretary
92 Dimmingsdale Bank
Birmingham, West Midlands B32 1ST
Midland Ancestor

[†]For additional information send 2 Postal Reply Coupons or 31 pence of English postage for reply to North America; 34 pence to Australia and New Zealand.
[‡]Microfilm/microfiche copies available at above repository
[##]Microfiche copy available at the LDS Family History Library in Salt Lake City, Utah, and through the LDS Family History Centers.
[**]See *Current Publications by Member Societies* (annual), *List of Family History Project Coordinators*, 6th ed., and *Family History News and Digest* (biennial) — all published by the Federation of Family History Societies; available in the USA from the International Society for British Genealogy and Family History, P.O. Box 20425, Cleveland, OH 44120.

NORFOLK

Post-1974 Counties of England

The present geographical boundaries of Norfolk include the entire pre-1974 area of the county, and additionally, a small section south of Great Yarmouth which was in Suffolk prior to that year.

The city of Norwich, an ancient borough, was a county of a city from the early fifteenth century until 1974. Great Yarmouth, an ancient borough, was incorporated in the seventeenth century, designated a Municipal Borough in 1835 and a County Borough from 1889–1974. King's Lynn and Thetford, also ancient boroughs, were incorporated in the sixteenth century and designated Municipal Boroughs from 1835 to 1974.

328

RECORD OFFICE

NORFOLK RECORD OFFICE
Central Library, Bethel Street
Norwich NR2 1NJ
Tel. 0603 611277 ext. 51
Hours: M-F 9-5; S 9-12
          (Seat reservation advisable 3 weeks in advance)
Admission free
List of record searchers available upon request[†]

HOLDINGS

Church of England diocesan records (Diocese of Norwich: Archdeaconry of Norfolk, Archdeaconry of Norwich); Church of England parish records including deposited Parish Registers for more than 550 churches within the Diocese of Norwich (including part of northeast Suffolk); local government records and other resources pertaining to the pre-1974 division of the county. (The borough records of King's Lynn are stored in that city and prior arrangements to consult them must be made with the record office.)

SOURCES THAT IDENTIFY AN INDIVIDUAL WITH A SPECIFIC LOCATION

Borough Records (city of Norwich, borough of Great Yarmouth, borough of King's Lynn)	
Freemen's Lists	14C–19C
	(1548–1713[#])
Rates	18C–20C

[†]For additional information send 2 Postal Reply Coupons or 31 pence of English postage for reply to North America; 34 pence to Australia and New Zealand.

[#]Microfilm copy available at the LDS Family History Library in Salt Lake City, Utah, and through the LDS Family History Centers.

Church of England (diocesan)
  Ecclesiastical Court Books   16C–20C
  Ecclesiastical Visitations   16C–20C
  Tithe Apportionments   c. 1840
Church of England (parish)
  Churchwardens' Accounts   15C–19C
  Overseers' Accounts   17C–19C
Enclosure Awards   late 18C–19C
Maps   15C–20C
Parish Poor Law Records
  Parish Poor Rates   17C–19C
Quarter Sessions
  Judicial Records   16C–20C
  Land Tax Assessments   1767–1832
  Oath Books, Rolls   1673–19C
  Registration of Papist Property   1716–1717
Registers of Electors*   (gaps) 1832–

*SOURCES THAT MAY ADDITIONALLY PROVIDE VITAL
DATA AND/OR PROVE FAMILY RELATIONSHIPS*

Borough Records (city of Norwich,
        borough of Great Yarmouth,
        borough of King's Lynn)
  Court   13C–20C
  Guild: Admissions   15C–17C
  Title Deeds   13C–19C
Church of England (diocesan)
  Bishops'/Archdeacons' Transcripts#   1600–1838
  Marriage Licence Bonds   1557–1969
    and Allegations
  Wills, Admon., Inven.#   1370–1858

---

*Printed or transcribed

#Microfilm copy available at the LDS Family History Library in Salt Lake City,
Utah, and through the LDS Family History Centers.

Church of England (parish)
  Parish Registers   1538–1900's
  Parish Register Transcripts*#
  Estate and Family Papers   15C–20C
  Manorial Records#   16C–18C
  Nonconformist Registers
    Baptist (some#)   (few) 18C–20C
    Independent (some#)   (few) 17C–20C
    Methodist (some#)   (few) 18C–20C
    Society of Friends* (some#)   1613–1837
    Unitarian (some#)   (few) 18C–20C
  Parish Poor Law Records   16C–19C
    Apprenticeship Indentures
    Examinations
    Removal Orders
    Settlement Papers
  Title Deeds   12C–20C
  Wills, Register Copies   1858–

PUBLICATIONS†

Guide to Genealogical Sources (1985)

Guide to the Great Yarmouth Borough Records (1972)

Leaflets/Lists:
  Parish Registers Deposited Including Dates
  Microfilm and Other Copies of Parish Registers
  Not Held by the Norfolk Record Office

Norfolk Parish Map (1984)

---

*Printed or transcribed

#Microfilm copy available at the LDS Family History Library in Salt Lake City, Utah, and through the LDS Family History Centers.

†For additional information send 2 Postal Reply Coupons or 31 pence of English postage for reply to North America; 34 pence to Australia and New Zealand.

OTHER REPOSITORIES

The sources listed below include only those items reported on the Record Office Survey as located in the specified repositories. Each city and county library should have additional printed materials pertaining to its geographical area.

NORWICH CENTRAL LIBRARY†
(Local Studies)
Bethel Street, Norwich NR2 1NJ
Tel. 0603 611277

Directories* (some#)	
(Trade, Postal)	
Norfolk	1836–1927
Norwich	1778–20C
Poll Books* (some#)	(periodic) 1702–1871

Boyd's Marriage Index‡# (Norf)
Census‡# 1841–1881
International Genealogical Index‡##
    (British Isles)
Newspapers*

LDS FAMILY HISTORY CENTRE†
19 Greenways, Easton
Norwich, Norfolk
Tel. 0603 52440

LDS Family History Library Catalog‡##
International Genealogical Index‡##

---

†For additional information send 2 Postal Reply Coupons or 31 pence of English postage for reply to North America; 34 pence to Australia and New Zealand.
*Printed or transcribed
#Microfilm copy available at the LDS Family History Library in Salt Lake City, Utah, and through the LDS Family History Centers.
‡Microfilm/microfiche copies available at above repository
##Microfiche copy available at the LDS Family History Library in Salt Lake City, Utah, and through the LDS Family History Centers.

GENEALOGICAL AND FAMILY HISTORY SOCIETIES

The societies listed below may have recorded Monumental (tombstone) Inscriptions, compiled an Index to Marriages (from the Parish Registers), an Index to the 1851 Census, and other special indexes, e.g., Strays, Members' Interests, for their geographical areas.** Each Society publishes a quarterly journal (listed in italics) which includes articles on family history, reports on the group's projects, and members' queries.

NORFOLK AND NORWICH GENEALOGICAL SOCIETY†
Miss A. Doggett, Secretary
22 Chestnut Hill
Norwich NR4 6NL

The Norfolk Ancestor

**See *Current Publications by Member Societies* (annual), *List of Family History Project Coordinators*, 6th ed., and *Family History News and Digest* (biennial) — all published by the Federation of Family History Societies; available in the USA from the International Society for British Genealogy and Family History, P.O. Box 20425, Cleveland, OH 44120.

†For additional information send 2 Postal Reply Coupons or 31 pence of English postage for reply to North America; 34 pence to Australia and New Zealand.

NORTHAMPTONSHIRE

Post-1974 Counties of England

The pre-1889 geographical boundaries of Northamptonshire included the present county, and in addition much of the Soke of Peterborough, which, after being for local government purposes a county from 1889 to 1965, was united in 1965 with the former county of Huntingdonshire to form the administrative county of Huntingdon and Peterborough.

Peterborough was administered by the Abbots of St. Peter until the dissolution. When the See of Peterborough was created in 1541 the Abbey estates were divided and the Bishop acquired Boroughbury and the Soke while the Dean and Chapter became lords of Peterborough and Longthorpe, i.e., the city of Peter-

334

borough. Until the Peterborough Paving and Improvement Act in 1970 three bodies shared the administration of the city: the Dean and Chapter as Lords of the Manor, the magistrates and the churchwardens. The City of Peterborough became a Municipal Borough in 1874.

Northampton was granted a Borough charter in 1189 and was declared a County Borough under legislation of 1888.

Higham Ferrers, Brackley and Daventry were ancient Boroughs, returning members to Parliament from the sixteenth century. All three became Municipal Boroughs in the nineteenth century. Municipal and County Boroughs were discontinued in 1974.

RECORD OFFICE

NORTHAMPTONSHIRE RECORD OFFICE
Delapre Abbey, Northampton NN4 9AW
Tel. 0604 762129

Hours: M, T, W 9-4:45; Th 9-7:45;
        F 9-4:30; S 9-12:15 (twice a month)
        (Open M-F 12-2, but no production of
        documents during these hours)
        Documents required on Th evenings, S mornings,
        or M-F 12-2 should be ordered in advance

Admission free
List of record searchers available upon request[†]

HOLDINGS

Church of England diocesan records (Diocese of Peterborough, covering Northamptonshire, the Soke of Peterborough and Rutland); probate records of the same area; Church of England parish records including deposited Parish

---

[†]For additional information send 2 Postal Reply Coupons or 31 pence of English postage for reply to North America; 34 pence to Australia and New Zealand.

Registers for approximately 300 churches within the present county boundaries and the Soke of Peterborough; nonconformist church records including registers; charity records; official, judicial and administrative records of the county and other local government bodies.

SOURCES THAT IDENTIFY AN INDIVIDUAL WITH A SPECIFIC LOCATION

Borough Records (Northampton)	16C–19C
Freemen's Lists#	1606–1727
Rates	1836–1924
Church of England (diocesan)	
Ecclesiastical Court Books	1550–1841
Ecclesiastical Visitations	1561–1931
Tithe Apportionments	1836–1856
Church of England (parish)	
Churchwardens' Accounts	c. 1600–
Directories* (some#)	
Business/Trade, Postal	1784–1940
Enclosure Awards	18C–19C
Lay Subsidies#	1523–1546
Maps	1572–
Militia Lists#	mainly 1762,1771, 1774,1777, 1781,1786, 1800
Parish Poor Law Records	c. 1600–1834
Parish Poor Rates	
Poll Books* (some#)	(periodic) 1695–1868

#Microfilm copy available at the LDS Family History Library in Salt Lake City, Utah, and through the LDS Family History Centers.
*Printed or transcribed

Quarter Sessions
Judicial Records   1630,
                                                    1657–1971
Hearth Tax Assessments#   1662, 1670,
                                                    1674
Land Tax Assessments   1746–;
                                        (mainly   1780–1832)
Lists of Freeholders   1699–1826
Lists of Jurors   1823–1923
Registration of Papist Property   1717–1720,
                                                    1745–1778
Registers of Electors*   1833–

*SOURCES THAT MAY ADDITIONALLY PROVIDE VITAL
DATA AND/OR PROVE FAMILY RELATIONSHIPS*

Borough Records (Northampton)
Apprenticeship Registers‡#   1559–1817
    (Daventry)   c. 1590–1802
Court
Title Deeds
Census‡#
    (Northants and Soke of Peterborough)   1841–1881
Church of England (diocesan)
Bishops' Transcripts   1706–1860
Marriage Licence Registers or Bonds   1598–
    (Allegations from 1823)
Wills, Admon., Inven.#   1467–1858;
                                                    1858–1942ˑ

    2 series: Northampton#
              Peterborough#

#Microfilm copy available at the LDS Family History Library in Salt Lake City,
Utah, and through the LDS Family History Centers.
*Printed or transcribed
‡Microfilm/microfiche copies available at above repository

Church of England (parish)
Parish Registers   1538–
Parish Register Transcripts*   16C–19C
Estate and Family Papers   12C–
International Genealogical Index‡##
(Northants and adjacent counties)
Manorial Records
Monumental Inscriptions
Newspapers (early‡#)   1720–
Nonconformist Registers
Baptist‡#   1755–1977
Independent (Congregational)‡#   1714–1963
Methodist‡#   1803–1977
Moravian‡#   1796–1840
Society of Friends‡#   1647–1837
Parish Poor Law Records   c. 1600–1834
Apprenticeship Indentures   mainly 1700–1830
Examinations
Removal Orders
Settlement Papers
Pedigrees*
Poor Law Union   1834–1940
Workhouse Records
Roman Catholic Register   1793–1855
School Records
Title Deeds   12C–
Wills, Register Copies   1858–1930

---

*Printed or transcribed
‡Microfilm/microfiche copies available at above repository
##Microfiche copy available at the LDS Family History Library in Salt Lake City, Utah, and through the LDS Family History Centers.
#Microfilm copy available at the LDS Family History Library in Salt Lake City, Utah, and through the LDS Family History Centers.

PUBLICATIONS†

Leaflet:
Parish and Nonconformist Registers in the Northamptonshire Record Office (1987)

OTHER REPOSITORIES

The sources listed below include only those items reported on the Record Office Survey as located in the specified repositories. Each city and county library should have additional printed materials pertaining to its geographical area.

NORTHAMPTON CENTRAL LIBRARY†
Abington Street, Northampton NN1 2BA
Tel. 0604 34823

Census‡# (Northants)   1861
International Genealogical Index‡##
(Northants and adjacent counties)

LDS FAMILY HISTORY CENTRE†
137 Harlestone Road
Northampton
Tel. 0604 51348

LDS Family History Library Catalog‡##
International Genealogical Index‡##

---

†For additional information send 2 Postal Reply Coupons or 31 pence of English postage for reply to North America; 34 pence to Australia and New Zealand.
‡Microfilm/microfiche copies available at above repository
#Microfilm copy available at the LDS Family History Library in Salt Lake City, Utah, and through the LDS Family History Centers.
##Microfiche copy available at the LDS Family History Library in Salt Lake City, Utah, and through the LDS Family History Centers.

GENEALOGICAL AND FAMILY HISTORY SOCIETIES

The societies listed below may have recorded Monumental (tombstone) Inscriptions, compiled an Index to Marriages (from the Parish Registers), an Index to the 1851 Census, and other special indexes, e.g., Strays, Members' Interests, for their geographical areas.** Each Society publishes a quarterly journal (listed in italics) which includes articles on family history, reports on the group's projects, and members' queries.

NORTHAMPTONSHIRE FAMILY HISTORY SOCIETY†
Miss L. Wesley, Secretary
83 Southampton Road
Far Cotton, Northampton NN4 9DZ

Footprints

**See *Current Publications by Member Societies* (annual), *List of Family History Project Coordinators*, 6th ed., and *Family History News and Digest* (biennial) — all published by the Federation of Family History Societies; available in the USA from the International Society for British Genealogy and Family History, P.O. Box 20425, Cleveland, OH 44120.

†For additional information send 2 Postal Reply Coupons or 31 pence of English postage for reply to North America; 34 pence to Australia and New Zealand.

NORTHUMBERLAND

Post-1974 Counties of England

The pre-1974 geographical boundaries of Northumberland included the present county, and in addition the districts of Newcastle upon Tyne and North Tyneside now in the county of Tyne and Wear.

Administratively the city of Newcastle upon Tyne was a County Corporate from 1400 to 1889 and a County Borough from 1889 to 1974. Berwick upon Tweed and Morpeth were both incorporated Boroughs from the mid-seventeenth century to 1974. Tynemouth was a Municipal Borough from the mid-nineteenth century to 1904, and then a County Borough between 1904 and 1974.

RECORD OFFICES

NORTHUMBERLAND RECORD OFFICE
Melton Park, North Gosforth
Newcastle upon Tyne NE3 5QX
Tel. (091) 236 2680

Hours: M 9-9; T-Th 9-5; F 9-4:30; closed S
Restricted service M-F 1-2 (No original
documents produced)

Admission free
List of record searchers available upon request[†]

HOLDINGS

Church of England diocesan records (Diocese of Newcastle) and a majority of records for parishes in the Diocese of Durham that were transferred in 1882 to the Diocese of Newcastle; Church of England parish records including deposited Parish Registers for approximately 180 churches within the present county; local government and other resources for the pre-1974 division of the county.

(Some pre-1882 Church of England diocesan records for the Diocese of Durham remain at the University of Durham, Department of Palæography and Diplomatic, Durham. Original County Corporate and Borough Records for Newcastle upon Tyne are located at the Tyne and Wear Record Office.)

[†]For additional information send 2 Postal Reply Coupons or 31 pence of English postage for reply to North America; 34 pence to Australia and New Zealand.

SOURCES THAT IDENTIFY AN INDIVIDUAL
WITH A SPECIFIC LOCATION

Borough Records	12C–19C
Freemen's Lists*#	1645–1710
(Newcastle upon Tyne)	
Church of England (diocesan)	
Tithe Apportionments§	1836–1840's
Church of England (parish)	
Churchwardens' Accounts	16C–20C
Directories* (some#)	19C–20C
Postal	
Enclosure Awards	19C
Maps	17C–20C
Militia Lists*	1762
Parish Poor Law Records	17C–1834
Rate Books (some#)	
Poll Books* (some#)	1710–1826
Quarter Sessions	
Judicial Records#	17C–20C
Land Tax Assessments*#	1664,
	1748–1831
Lists of Jurors#	1763–1824
Registration of Papist Property#	1715–1745
Registers of Electors* (some#)	1832–

SOURCES THAT MAY ADDITIONALLY PROVIDE VITAL
DATA AND / OR PROVE FAMILY RELATIONSHIPS

Boyd's Marriage Index*#	1538–1824
Cemetery Registers	19C–20C

---

*Printed or transcribed

#Microfilm copy available at the LDS Family History Library in Salt Lake City, Utah, and through the LDS Family History Centers.

§Parish copies only; main series located at the University of Durham.

343

Census‡#
(pre-1974 County except Newcastle)   1841, 1851,
                                          1871
(pre-1974 County)   1861
(post-1974 County)   1881
Church of England (diocesan)
Marriage Licence Bonds   1590–1815
and Allegations#
(Nthbld, Durh)
Church of England (parish)
Parish Registers#   1538–1900's
Estate and Family Papers   12C–20C
International Genealogical Index‡##
(England and Scotland)
Manorial Records#   16C–19C
Monumental Inscriptions*#   17C–20C
Nonconformist Registers
Independent‡#   18C–19C
Methodist (some#)   19C–20C
Presbyterian‡#   18C–19C
Poor Law Union   1834–
Workhouse Records
Roman Catholic Registers   18C–19C
School Records   19C–20C
Title Deeds††   13C–
Wills, Register Copies   1858–

PUBLICATIONS†

Northumberland Record Office 1958–1974
Guides to Records: Coalmining, Education,
   Quarter Sessions, Transport
Leaflets/Lists:
   Genealogical Source List
   List of Deposited Parish Records
Annual Reports, 1974–

BERWICK UPON TWEED RECORD OFFICE
Council Offices, Wallace Green
Berwick upon Tweed
Hours: Th 10-1, 2-5
Enquiries to Northumberland Record Office (above)
Admission free

HOLDINGS

Resources pertaining mainly to the Berwick upon Tweed
area.

Borough Records	16C–20C
Freemen's Lists and Admittances#	16C–20C
Apprenticeship Records#	16C–early 20C
Census Returns‡#	1841–1881
(Berwick, North Nthbld)	
Church of England (parish)	
Parish Registers‡#	1574–1963
Manorial Records	
(Tweedmouth)	17C–20C
(Berwick)	18C–19C
Nonconformist Registers‡#	18C–c. 1840

---

†For additional information send 2 Postal Reply Coupons or 31 pence of English
postage for reply to North America; 34 pence to Australia and New Zealand.
#Microfilm copy available at the LDS Family History Library in Salt Lake City,
Utah, and through the LDS Family History Centers.
‡Microfilm/microfiche copies available at above repository

GENEALOGICAL AND FAMILY
HISTORY SOCIETIES

The societies listed below may have recorded Monumental (tombstone) Inscriptions, compiled an Index to Marriages (from the Parish Registers), an Index to the 1851 Census, and other special indexes, e.g., Strays, Members' Interests, for their geographical areas.** Each Society publishes a quarterly journal (listed in italics) which includes articles on family history, reports on the group's projects, and members' queries.

NORTHUMBERLAND AND DURHAM
FAMILY HISTORY SOCIETY†
Mr. J.K. Brown, Secretary
33 South Bend, Brunton Park
Newcastle upon Tyne NE3 5TR

Journal of the Northumberland and Durham Family History Society

---

**See *Current Publications by Member Societies* (annual), *List of Family History Project Coordinators*, 6th ed., and *Family History News and Digest* (biennial) — all published by the Federation of Family History Societies; available in the USA from the International Society for British Genealogy and Family History, P.O. Box 20425, Cleveland, OH 44120.

†For additional information send 2 Postal Reply Coupons or 31 pence of English postage for reply to North America; 34 pence to Australia and New Zealand.

NOTTINGHAMSHIRE

Post-1974 Counties of England

There was no change in the geographical boundaries of Nottinghamshire during the 1974 reorganization of local government.

Administratively the city of Nottingham was a County Corporate (except the Castle) from the fifteenth century to 1836, and a County Borough between 1836 and 1974. Newark and East Retford were incorporated Boroughs from the sixteenth century to 1974.

RECORD OFFICES

NOTTINGHAMSHIRE ARCHIVES OFFICE
County House, High Pavement
Nottingham NG1 1HR
Tel. 0602 504524

Hours: M, W, Th, F 9-4:45; T 9-7:15; S 9-12:15

Admission free

List of record searchers available upon request†

HOLDINGS

Church of England diocesan records (Diocese of Southwell): microfilm copies of Bishops' Transcripts; Church of England parish records including microfilmed copies of Parish Registers to 1900 for all churches in the pre-1974 division of the county; local government and other resources for the county and for the city of Nottingham.

(Church of England diocesan records for the Archdeaconry of Nottingham are primarily located at the University of Nottingham Manuscript Department of the University Library, and at the Borthwick Institute in York. All diocesan records for the Peculiar of Southwell, however, and all original Bishops' Transcripts have been deposited at the Southwell Minster Library, Southwell. A registered copy of all wills should be found at the Borthwick Institute, York.)

SOURCES THAT IDENTIFY AN INDIVIDUAL WITH A SPECIFIC LOCATION

Borough Records	(Nottingham)	12C–20C
	(Newark)	17C–20C
	(E. Retford)	18C–20C
Freemen's Lists		
Rates		

---

†For additional information send 2 Postal Reply Coupons or 31 pence of English postage for reply to North America; 34 pence to Australia and New Zealand.

Church of England (archidiaconal)	19C–20C
Tithe Apportionments	1836–
Church of England (parish)	
Churchwardens' Accounts	16C–20C
Directories* (some#)	18C–20C
Business/Trade	
Enclosure Awards	18C–19C
Lay Subsidies	16C–17C
Maps	16C–20C
Militia Lists	18C
Parish Poor Law Records	
Parish Poor Rates	18C–19C
Protestation Returns#	1641
Poll Books* (some#)	1698–1831
Quarter Sessions	
Judicial Records#	17C–1888
Hearth Tax Assessments‡#	(gaps) 1664–1674
Land Tax Assessments#	1780–1832
Lists of Freeholders#	1734–1781,
	1804–1824
Lists of Jurors#	1760–1804
Registration of Papist Property#	18C
Registers of Electors*	1832–

*SOURCES THAT MAY ADDITIONALLY PROVIDE VITAL
DATA AND/OR PROVE FAMILY RELATIONSHIPS*

Borough Records	(Nottingham)	12C–20C
	(Newark)	17C–20C
	(E. Retford)	18C–20C
Court		
Title Deeds		
Cemetery Registers		19C–20C

---

*Printed or transcribed

#Microfilm copy available at the LDS Family History Library in Salt Lake City, Utah, and through the LDS Family History Centers.

‡Microfilm/microfiche copies available at above repository

Census‡# (Notts)	1851
Church of England (archidiaconal)	
Bishops' Transcripts‡#	17C–19C
Marriage Licence Bonds	1577–1854
and Allegations#*	
Wills, Admon., Inven.#	
Church of England (parish)	
Parish Registers#	1538–20C
Parish Register Transcripts#*	1538–20C
Estate and Family Papers	12C–20C
International Genealogical Index‡##	
(Notts and adjacent counties)	
Manorial Records‡#	14C–19C
Monumental Inscriptions*	
Nonconformist Registers	
Baptist (some#)	18C–20C
Independent (Congregational)	19C–20C
Methodist (some#)	18C–20C
Society of Friends (some#)	17C–19C
Parish Poor Law Records	17C–19C
Apprenticeship Indentures	
Examinations	
Removal Orders	
Settlement Papers	
Poor Law Unions	19C
Workhouse Records	
School Records	18C
Title Deeds	13C–20C
Wills, Register Copies	1858–

---

‡Microfilm/microfiche copies available at above repository

#Microfilm copy available at the LDS Family History Library in Salt Lake City, Utah, and through the LDS Family History Centers.

*Printed or transcribed

##Microfiche copy available at the LDS Family History Library in Salt Lake City, Utah, and through the LDS Family History Centers.

PUBLICATIONS†

User's Guide to the Nottinghamshire Record Office (1980)
Nottinghamshire Parish Registers on Microfilm, 1538–1900
(1984)

UNIVERSITY OF NOTTINGHAM
MANUSCRIPTS DEPARTMENT OF
THE UNIVERSITY LIBRARY
University Park, Nottingham NG7 2RD
Tel. 0602 506101 ext. 3440
    (change in telephone number pending)
Hours: M-F 9-5

Admission free

List of record searchers available upon request†

HOLDINGS

Church of England diocesan records (Archdeaconry of Nottingham, Diocese of York); Marriage Licence Bonds and Allegations; some published and microfilm copies of records pertaining to the county; deposited private records.

SOURCES THAT IDENTIFY AN INDIVIDUAL
WITH A SPECIFIC LOCATION

Church of England (archidiaconal)§
   Ecclesiastical Court Records   16C–20C
   Ecclesiastical Visitations   16C–19C
   Tithe Apportionments   1830–1850

---

†For additional information send 2 Postal Reply Coupons or 31 pence of English postage for reply to North America; 34 pence to Australia and New Zealand.
§Other Church of England diocesan records are located at the Nottinghamshire Record Office and at the Southwell Minster, Southwell.

Directories*# (Postal)
    Notts, Derbys, Leics, Lincs   19C
Enclosure Awards   1760–1860
Lists of Freeholders*   16C–
Maps   16C–20C
Poll Books* (some#)   17C–19C

SOURCES THAT MAY ADDITIONALLY PROVIDE VITAL DATA AND/OR PROVE FAMILY RELATIONSHIPS

Census‡# (Notts)   1841–1881
Church of England (archidiaconal)§
    Marriage Licence Bonds   1594–1884
        and Allegations
Estate and Family Papers   12C–20C
Manorial Records   13C–20C
Newspapers*   18C–20C
Nonconformist Registers
    Baptist#   1775–1925
    Independent/Congregational (some#)   1738–1974
    Presbyterian   1865–1957
    Unitarian (some#)   1691–1960

PUBLICATIONS†

Information Leaflet No. 13 (1984)

---

*Printed or transcribed

#Microfilm copy available at the LDS Family History Library in Salt Lake City, Utah, and through the LDS Family History Centers.

‡Microfilm/microfiche copies available at above repository

§Other Church of England diocesan records are located at the Nottinghamshire Record Office and at the Southwell Minster, Southwell.

†For additional information send 2 Postal Reply Coupons or 31 pence of English postage for reply to North America; 34 pence to Australia and New Zealand.

OTHER REPOSITORIES

The sources listed below include only those items reported on the Record Office Survey as located in the specified repositories. Each city and county library should have additional printed materials pertaining to its geographical area.

NOTTINGHAM CENTRAL LIBRARY†
Angel Row, Nottingham NG1 6HP
Tel. 0602 412121

Census‡# (Notts)	1841–1881
International Genealogical Index‡##	
(British Isles)	

LDS FAMILY HISTORY CENTRE†
Hempshill Lane, Bulwell
Nottingham NG6 8PA
Tel. 0602 274194

LDS Family History Library Catalog‡##
International Genealogical Index‡##

---

†For additional information send 2 Postal Reply Coupons or 31 pence of English postage for reply to North America; 34 pence to Australia and New Zealand.
‡Microfilm/microfiche copies available at above repository
#Microfilm copy available at the LDS Family History Library in Salt Lake City, Utah, and through the LDS Family History Centers.
##Microfiche copy available at the LDS Family History Library in Salt Lake City, Utah, and through the LDS Family History Centers.

GENEALOGICAL AND FAMILY HISTORY SOCIETIES

The societies listed below may have recorded Monumental (tombstone) Inscriptions, compiled an Index to Marriages (from the Parish Registers), an Index to the 1851 Census, and other special indexes, e.g., Strays, Members' Interests, for their geographical areas.** Each Society publishes a quarterly journal (listed in italics) which includes articles on family history, reports on the group's projects, and members' queries.

**NOTTINGHAMSHIRE
FAMILY HISTORY SOCIETY†**
Miss S.M. Leeds, Secretary
35 Kingswood Road
West Bridgford, Nottingham NG2 7HT

Nottinghamshire Family History Society Journal

**MANSFIELD AND DISTRICT
FAMILY HISTORY SOCIETY†**
Miss H. Hargate, Secretary
2 Millersdale Avenue
Mansfield, Nottinghamshire NG18 5HS

**See *Current Publications by Member Societies* (annual), *List of Family History Project Coordinators*, 6th ed., and *Family History News and Digest* (biennial) — all published by the Federation of Family History Societies; available in the USA from the International Society for British Genealogy and Family History, P.O. Box 20425, Cleveland, OH 44120.

†For additional information send 2 Postal Reply Coupons or 31 pence of English postage for reply to North America; 34 pence to Australia and New Zealand.

OXFORDSHIRE

Post-1974 Counties of England

The present geographical boundaries of Oxfordshire include the pre-1974 county area, and in addition, the Vale of White Horse district (Abingdon and Wantage) and part of the South Oxfordshire district (Wallingford), located in Berkshire prior to 1974.

Administratively the city of Oxford was an incorporated Borough from the seventeenth century to 1889, and then a County Borough to 1974. Banbury, Chipping Norton, Henley on Thames, and New Woodstock were all incorporated Boroughs from the seventeenth century to 1974.

355

RECORD OFFICE

OXFORDSHIRE COUNTY RECORD OFFICE
County Hall, New Road, Oxford OX1 1ND
Tel. 0865 815203
Hours: M-Th 9-5; F 9-4
Admission free
List of Record searchers available upon request[†]

HOLDINGS

Church of England diocesan records (Diocese of Oxford and Archdeaconry of Oxford); Church of England parish records including deposited Parish Registers for more than 220 churches within the county; local government records and other resources pertaining to the pre-1974 division of the county.

(Borough Records for the city of Oxford are located at the Oxford Central Library – see Other Repositories, below.)

SOURCES THAT IDENTIFY AN INDIVIDUAL
WITH A SPECIFIC LOCATION

Borough Records (Banbury,	18C–20C
Chipping Norton,	
Henley-on-Thames)	
Freemen's Lists	
Rates	
Church of England (diocesan)	
Ecclesiastical Court Books	1567–1871
Ecclesiastical Visitations	1630–1878
Tithe Apportionments	mid-19C

[†]For additional information send 2 Postal Reply Coupons or 31 pence of English postage for reply to North America; 34 pence to Australia and New Zealand.

Directories* (some#)
Postal   19C–20C
Ecclesiastical Census‡* (also#)   1851
Enclosure Awards   18C–19C
Maps   17C–20C
Parish Poor Law Records   17C–1834
Parish Poor Rates
Protestation Returns*#   1641
Poll Books* (some#)   1754–1862
Quarter Sessions
  Judicial Records (some#)   17C–20C
  Hearth Tax Assessments* (some#)   1665
  Land Tax Assessments (some#)   1785–1832
  Lists of Jurors (some#)   1687–1970
  Registration of Papist Property (some#)   18C
Registers of Electors*   1832–
(excluding the city of Oxford)

*SOURCES THAT MAY ADDITIONALLY PROVIDE VITAL
DATA AND/OR PROVE FAMILY RELATIONSHIPS*

Borough Records (Banbury,   18C–20C
    Chipping Norton,
    Henley-on-Thames)
  Court
  Title Deeds
Church of England (diocesan)
  Bishops's Transcripts (some#)
    Archdeaconry of Oxford   c. 17C–1875
    Archdeaconry of Berkshire   c. 1836–1875
    Archdeaconry of Buckinghamshire   c. 1845–1875
  Marriage Licence Bonds   1623–1954
    and Allegations (some*#)

Wills, Admon., Inven.	1516–1857
Consistory and Archdeaconry Courts of Oxford#	
Peculiars in Diocese#	
Church of England (parish: Archdeaconry of Oxford)	
Parish Registers (some#)	1538–
Parish Register Transcripts*	16C–20C
Estate and Family Papers	c. 1150–20C
International Genealogical Index‡# (Great Britain)	
Manorial Records	13C–20C
Nonconformist Registers	
Baptist	1699–1869
Methodist (early years*)	1801–20C
Society of Friends#	18C–19C
(Banbury M.M. Digests)	
Parish Poor Law Records	17C–1834
Apprenticeship Indentures	
Examinations	
Removal Orders	
Settlement Papers	
Poor Law Union	1834–1900
School Records	1604–20C
Title Deeds	c. 1150–20C

PUBLICATIONS†

D.M. Barratt and D.G. Vaisey, ed., *Oxfordshire: A Handbook for Students of Local History*, (1973) pp. 72–77 (OOP)

C.G. Harris, *Oxfordshire Parish Registers and Bishops' Transcripts* (1984)

#Microfilm copy available at the LDS Family History Library in Salt Lake City, Utah, and through the LDS Family History Centers.
*Printed or transcribed
‡Microfilm/microfiche copies available at above repository
†For additional information send 2 Postal Reply Coupons or 31 pence of English postage for reply to North America; 34 pence to Australia and New Zealand.

*An Index to Oxford Consistory and Archdeaconry Court
Probate Records: 1512–1732.* Part I, A–K (British
Record Society, *Index Library* 93, 1981); Part II, K–Z
(British Record Society, *Index Library*, 1982)

*Summary Catalogue of the Privately-Deposited Records in
the Oxfordshire County Record Office* (OOP)

Leaflets/Lists:
   *A Handlist of Enclosure Acts and Awards Relating to
   the County of Oxford*
   *A Handlist of Plans, Sections and Books of Reference
   for the Proposed Railways in Oxfordshire* (1983)

OTHER REPOSITORIES

The sources listed below include only those items reported
on the Record Office Survey as located in the specified repositories. Each city and county library should have additional
printed materials pertaining to its geographical area.

BODLEIAN LIBRARY
DEPARTMENT OF WESTERN MANUSCRIPTS
Oxford OX1 3BG
Tel. 0865 277000

Hours: M-F 9 am–10 pm; S 9-1 (term);
       M-F 9-7; S 9-1 (holiday)
       Closed last week in August and last week in December

Admission: Reader's Ticket necessary, obtained through
       application upon the recommendation of someone of
       recognized status; fee payable.
(The staff does not undertake searches for mail queries)

HOLDINGS

Vast collections of manuscripts and printed volumes relating largely to ancient, medieval and modern history, theology and literature. Family historians and genealogists will find the areas of British topography and heraldry most useful.

British Topography: County collections (for all counties) include many sources for advanced research in family history: charters, chartularies, county histories, deeds, estate and family papers, family histories, manorial records, maps.

Heraldry: The third largest heraldry collection in England is located at the Bodleian Library. It includes register books of Heralds' Visitations 1530–1666; pedigrees of nobility and gentry (abstracts of deeds, charters and family settlements, coats of arms and inquisitions post mortem); monumental inscriptions, and lists of coats of arms.

OXFORD CENTRAL LIBRARY†
Local Studies Section
Westgate, Oxford OX1 1OJ
Tel. 0865 815749

Borough Records
City of Oxford
Census‡# (Oxon)   1841–1881

---

†For additional information send 2 Postal Reply Coupons or 31 pence of English postage for reply to North America; 34 pence to Australia and New Zealand.
‡Microfilm/microfiche copies available at above repository
#Microfilm copy available at the LDS Family History Library in Salt Lake City, Utah, and through the LDS Family History Centers.

GENEALOGICAL AND FAMILY HISTORY SOCIETIES

The societies listed below may have recorded Monumental (tombstone) Inscriptions, compiled an Index to Marriages (from the Parish Registers), an Index to the 1851 Census, and other special indexes, e.g., Strays, Members' Interests, for their geographical areas.** Each Society publishes a quarterly journal (listed in italics) which includes articles on family history, reports on the group's projects, and members' queries.

OXFORDSHIRE FAMILY HISTORY SOCIETY†
Mrs. J. Muir, Secretary
10 Bellamy Close, Southmoor
Abingdon, Oxon OX13 4AB

The Oxfordshire Family Historian

**See *Current Publications by Member Societies* (annual), *List of Family History Project Coordinators*, 6th ed., and *Family History News and Digest* (biennial) — all published by the Federation of Family History Societies; available in the USA from the International Society for British Genealogy and Family History, P.O. Box 20425, Cleveland, OH 44120.

†For additional information send 2 Postal Reply Coupons or 31 pence of English postage for reply to North America; 34 pence to Australia and New Zealand.

RUTLAND

Pre-1974 Counties of England

The county of Rutland was abolished in 1974, and the area within its boundaries was transferred to the county of Leicestershire.

Church of England diocesan records (Diocese of Peterborough) for the former county are located at the Northamptonshire Record Office.

Church of England parish records, including deposited Parish Registers, are mostly located at the Leicestershire Record Office (see also the Northamptonshire Record Office). Local government and other resources pertaining to the former county are located at the Leicestershire Record Office.

362

SHROPSHIRE

Post-1974 Counties of England

The geographical boundaries of Shropshire did not change during the 1974 reorganization of local government in England.

Administratively the county was called Salop prior to 1980. In that year the title of the administrative county was changed to Shropshire.

Bridgnorth, Ludlow, Oswestry, Shrewsbury and Wenlock were all incorporated Boroughs from the seventeenth century to 1974.

RECORD OFFICE

SHROPSHIRE RECORD OFFICE
The Shirehall, Abbey Foregate
Shrewsbury SY2 6ND
Tel. 0743 252851 / 252853

Hours: M, T, Th 9:30-12:40, 1:20-5;
       F 9:30-12:40, 1:20-4; closed W, S
       (Prior appointment necessary for visit)
       Closed for Stocktaking usually the last week in
       November and first week of December each year. Also
       closed Tuesdays following Spring Bank Holiday and
       August Bank Holiday.

Admission free
List of record searchers available upon request[†]

HOLDINGS

Church of England parish records including deposited Parish Registers for approximately 190 churches within the county; local government records and other resources for the county.

(Church of England diocesan records for the southern half of the County – Diocese of Hereford – are located at the Hereford and Worcester Record Office, Hereford Section; those for the northeastern part of the county – Diocese of Lichfield – and those for the Diocese of St. Asaph's in the northwestern corner of the county are located at the Lichfield Joint Record Office, Lichfield, Staffs. Parish Registers for some Shropshire parishes have been deposited in the Shrewsbury Local Studies Library.)

[†]For additional information send 2 Postal Reply Coupons or 31 pence of English postage for reply to North America; 34 pence to Australia and New Zealand.

SOURCES THAT IDENTIFY AN INDIVIDUAL
WITH A SPECIFIC LOCATION

Borough Records (Bridgnorth, Ludlow, Oswestry, Shrewsbury††)	18C–19C
Freemen's Lists	
Rates	
Church of England (diocesan)	
Tithe Apportionments§	1836
Church of England (parish)	
Churchwardens' Accounts	mid-16C–20C
Directories* (some#)	19C
Postal	
Enclosure Awards‡#	1773–1891
Lay Subsidies (Shrewsbury)	1297–1677
Maps	17C–20C
Parish Poor Law Records	17C–1834
Parish Poor Rates	
Poll Books* (some#)	1713–1714, 1832–
Quarter Sessions	
Judicial Records	1722–1841
Hearth Tax Assessments*#	1672
Lists of Freeholders	1808
Lists of Jurors	17C–
Registration of Papist Property	1717–1790
Registers of Electors*	1832–

††A few borough records are still held by the Borough Office at Shrewsbury Guildhall.
§Parish copies only; main series at the respective diocesan repositories.
*Printed or transcribed
#Microfilm copy available at the LDS Family History Library in Salt Lake City, Utah, and through the LDS Family History Centers.
‡Microfilm/microfiche copies available at above repository

SOURCES THAT MAY ADDITIONALLY PROVIDE VITAL DATA AND/OR PROVE FAMILY RELATIONSHIPS

Borough Records (Bridgnorth, Ludlow, Oswestry, Shrewsbury††)	
Court	12C–19C
Title Deeds	
Church of England (parish)	
Parish Registers#	1538–20C
Estate and Family Papers	12C–16C
International Genealogical Index‡##	
(Shrops and adjacent counties)	
Manorial Records	13C–20C
Nonconformist Registers	
Baptist (some#)	1718–1877
Independent (Congregational)	1848–1898
Methodist (some#)	1818–1969
Parish Poor Law Records	17C–1888
Apprenticeship Indentures	
Examinations	
Removal Orders	
Settlement Papers	
Poor Law Union	1834–
Workhouse Papers	
School Records	(mainly) 19C–20C
Title Deeds	12C–
Wills, Register Copies	1858–1940

---

††A few borough records are still held by the Borough Office at Shrewsbury Guildhall.
#Microfilm copy available at the LDS Family History Library in Salt Lake City, Utah, and through the LDS Family History Centers.
‡Microfilm/microfiche copies available at above repository
##Microfiche copy available at the LDS Family History Library in Salt Lake City, Utah, and through the LDS Family History Centers.

PUBLICATIONS†

Shropshire County Record Office (1952)
List of Parish Registers Deposited

OTHER REPOSITORIES

The sources listed below include only those items reported on the Record Office Survey as located in the specified repositories. Each city and county library should have additional printed materials pertaining to its geographical area.

SHROPSHIRE LIBRARIES†
(Local Studies)
Castle Gates, Shrewsbury SY1 2AS
Tel. 0743 61058

Census‡# (Shrops)   1841–1881
International Genealogical Index‡##
   (Shrops and adjacent counties)

---

†For additional information send 2 Postal Reply Coupons or 31 pence of English postage for reply to North America; 34 pence to Australia and New Zealand.
‡Microfilm/microfiche copies available at above repository
#Microfilm copy available at the LDS Family History Library in Salt Lake City, Utah, and through the LDS Family History Centers.
##Microfiche copy available at the LDS Family History Library in Salt Lake City, Utah, and through the LDS Family History Centers.

GENEALOGICAL AND FAMILY HISTORY SOCIETIES

The societies listed below may have recorded Monumental (tombstone) Inscriptions, compiled an Index to Marriages (from the Parish Registers), an Index to the 1851 Census, and other special indexes, e.g., Strays, Members' Interests, for their geographical areas.** Each Society publishes a quarterly journal (listed in italics) which includes articles on family history, reports on the group's projects, and members' queries.

SHROPSHIRE FAMILY HISTORY SOCIETY†
Mrs. G. Lewis, Secretary
15 Wesley Drive, Oakengates
Telford, Shropshire TF2 0DZ

Shropshire Family History Society Journal

**See *Current Publications by Member Societies* (annual), *List of Family History Project Coordinators*, 6th ed., and *Family History News and Digest* (biennial) — all published by the Federation of Family History Societies; available in the USA from the International Society for British Genealogy and Family History, P.O. Box 20425, Cleveland, OH 44120.

†For additional information send 2 Postal Reply Coupons or 31 pence of English postage for reply to North America; 34 pence to Australia and New Zealand.

SOMERSET

Post-1974 Counties of England

The pre-1974 geographical boundaries of Somerset included the present county, and in addition, the northwestern quarter (including Clevedon and Weston-super-Mare) plus the city of Bath which were transferred to Avon County that year.

Administratively the city of Bath was a County Borough from 1889 to 1974 and an incorporated Borough prior to that year. Bridgwater, Glastonbury and Wells were incorporated Boroughs from the thirtenth, eighteenth and sixteenth centuries respectively, to 1974. Langport was an incorporated Borough from the seventeenth century to 1883. Taunton was also an incorporated Borough from the seventeenth century (with gaps) to 1974.

369

RECORD OFFICE

SOMERSET RECORD OFFICE

Obridge Road, Taunton TA2 7PU

Tel. 0823 337600 (Search Room appointments);
0823 288871 (Staff)

Contact: County Archivist

Hours: By prior appointment: M-Th 9-4:50;
F 9-4:20; S 9:15-12:15
Secondary search room closed 12:45-1:45 weekdays

Admission free

List of record searchers available upon request†

HOLDINGS

Church of England diocesan records for the Diocese of Bath and Wells; Church of England parish records including deposited Parish Registers for all parishes (except 8); local government records and other resources pertaining to the pre-1974 division of the county.

SOURCES THAT IDENTIFY AN INDIVIDUAL
WITH A SPECIFIC LOCATION

Borough Records	
Taunton	18C-20C
Bridgwater	13C-20C
Chard and Langport	17C-20C
Freemen's Lists (Bridgwater only)	1700-1724
Rates	
Church of England (diocesan)	
Ecclesiastical Court Books	1458-1917
Ecclesiastical Visitations	1526-1907
Tithe Apportionments	1836-c. 1846

---

†For additional information send 2 Postal Reply Coupons or 31 pence of English postage for reply to North America; 34 pence to Australia and New Zealand.

Church of England (parish)
Churchwardens' Accounts   late 17C–
Directories* (some#)   1784–1939
Business/Trade, Postal, Professional
Enclosure Awards   1720–1913
Gaol Registers and   1809–
  Description Books   mid-19C
Lay Subsidies#   (periodic)   1581–1666
Maps   mid-18C–
Parish Poor Law Records   17C–1834
Parish Poor Rates
Poll Books* (some#)   1807–1837
Quarter Sessions
  Judicial Records (some#)   17C–20C
  Hearth Tax Assessments* (some#)   1664–1665
  Land Tax Assessments‡#   1766–1767,
                                          1780–1832
  Lists of Jurors (some#)   1608–1865
  Registration of Papist Property (some#) 1717–1788
Registers of Electors*#   1832–1986
Shipping – Crew Lists   1863–1913

*SOURCES THAT MAY ADDITIONALLY PROVIDE VITAL
DATA AND/OR PROVE FAMILY RELATIONSHIPS*

Borough Records
  Taunton   18C–20C
  Bridgwater   13C–20C
  Chard and Langport   17C–20C
  Court
  Title Deeds
Census‡# (Soms)   1841–1881

---

*Printed or transcribed

#Microfilm copy available at the LDS Family History Library in Salt Lake City,
Utah, and through the LDS Family History Centers.

‡Microfilm/microfiche copies available at above repository

Church of England (diocesan)	
Bishops' Transcripts (some#)	1597–1837
Marriage Licence Bonds	1579–1899
and Allegations#	
Wills††	
Register Copies	15C–20C
Estate Duty#	1805–1857
Church of England (parish)	
Parish Registers (some#)	1538–
Parish Register Transcripts*#	16C–19C
Estate and Family Papers	18C–
Manorial Records	13C–
Monumental Inscriptions* (also#)	18C–
Newspapers*	1740–1969
Nonconformist Registers	
Baptist‡#	1759–1979
Independent (Congregational)‡#	1691–1980
Methodist	18C–19C
	(‡# to 1837)
Presbyterian	1691–1980
	(‡# to 1837)
Society of Friends (also#)	17C
Unitarian	1694–1980
	(‡# to 1837)
Parish Poor Law Records	17C–1834
Apprenticeship Indentures	
Bastardy Papers	
Examinations	
Removal Orders	
Settlement Papers	

#Microfilm copy available at the LDS Family History Library in Salt Lake City, Utah, and through the LDS Family History Centers.

††A majority of original wills were destroyed during World War II.

*Printed or transcribed

‡Microfilm/microfiche copies available at above repository

Poor Law Union‡#   1834–
   Workhouse Records
School Records   1863–
Title Deeds   12C–

PUBLICATIONS†

*Primary Genealogical Sources in the
Somerset Record Office*
(1983 with updating to 1987)

OTHER REPOSITORIES

The sources listed below include only those items reported
on the Record Office Survey as located in the specified repositories. Each city and county library should have additional
printed materials pertaining to its geographical area.

TAUNTON CENTRAL LIBRARY†
Local History Library
The Castle, Castle Green
Taunton, Somerset
Tel. 0823 88871

   International Genealogical Index‡##   1978
   (Soms)

---

‡Microfilm/microfiche copies available at above repository
#Microfilm copy available at the LDS Family History Library in Salt Lake City,
Utah, and through the LDS Family History Centers.
†For additional information send 2 Postal Reply Coupons or 31 pence of English
postage for reply to North America; 34 pence to Australia and New Zealand.
##Microfiche copy available at the LDS Family History Library in Salt Lake
City, Utah, and through the LDS Family History Centers.

GENEALOGICAL AND FAMILY HISTORY SOCIETIES

The societies listed below may have recorded Monumental (tombstone) Inscriptions, compiled an Index to Marriages (from the Parish Registers), an Index to the 1851 Census, and other special indexes, e.g., Strays, Members' Interests, for their geographical areas.** Each Society publishes a quarterly journal (listed in italics) which includes articles on family history, reports on the group's projects, and members' queries.

SOMERSET AND DORSET FAMILY HISTORY SOCIETY†
P.O. Box 170, Taunton
Somerset TA1 1HF

The Greenwood Tree

**See *Current Publications by Member Societies* (annual), *List of Family History Project Coordinators*, 6th ed., and *Family History News and Digest* (biennial) — all published by the Federation of Family History Societies; available in the USA from the International Society for British Genealogy and Family History, P.O. Box 20425, Cleveland, OH 44120.

†For additional information send 2 Postal Reply Coupons or 31 pence of English postage for reply to North America; 34 pence to Australia and New Zealand.

STAFFORDSHIRE

Post-1974 Counties of England

The pre-1974 geographical boundaries of Staffordshire included the present county as well as the areas of Walsall, Warley, West Bromwich and Wolverhampton (the southern tip) which are now part of West Midlands County.

Administratively Lichfield was a city with the status of a county from the mid-sixteenth century to 1889, and then a County Borough to 1974. Wolverhampton and Walsall were incorporated Boroughs from the thirteenth and seventeenth centuries, respectively, to 1974. West Bromwich was a Municipal Borough from the nineteenth century to 1974. Warley was made a County Borough in 1965 from the twentieth-century

375

County Borough of Smethwick and the twentieth-century Municipal Boroughs of Oldbury and Rowley Regis.

RECORD OFFICES

LICHFIELD JOINT RECORD OFFICE
Lichfield Library, Bird Street
Lichfield WS13 6PN
Tel. 0543 256787
Hours: M, T, Th, F 10-5:15; W 10-4:30
       No documents produced 12:30-2:30
       (Prior appointment recommended)
Admission free
List of record searchers available upon request[†]

HOLDINGS
Church of England diocesan records (Diocese of Lichfield); Church of England parish records including deposited Parish Registers for churches in Lichfield; some local government records and other resources pertaining to the city of Lichfield.

SOURCES THAT IDENTIFY AN INDIVIDUAL WITH A SPECIFIC LOCATION

City of Lichfield Muniments	14C-20C
Church of England (diocesan)	
Ecclesiastical Court Books[††]	1464-1865
Ecclesiastical Visitations[††]	1558-1900's
Tithe Apportionments	1836-1850's
Church of England (parish)	
Churchwarden's Accounts (Lichfield)	1627-1900's

[†]For additional information send 2 Postal Reply Coupons or 31 pence of English postage for reply to North America; 34 pence to Australia and New Zealand.
[††]Early records in Latin

SOURCES THAT MAY ADDITIONALLY PROVIDE VITAL DATA AND/OR PROVE FAMILY RELATIONSHIPS

City of Lichfield Muniments	14C–20C
Census‡# (Lichfield and environs)	1841–1881
Church of England (diocesan)	
Bishops' Transcripts#	1660–1885
Marriage Licence Bonds	1660–1900's
and Allegations#	
Wills, Admon., Inven.#	1516–1858
Church of England (parish)	
Parish Registers# (Lichfield)	1566–1900's
Parish Register Transcripts*	1538–1837
International Genealogical Index‡##	
(Staffs, Derbys, Shrops, Warws)	
Roman Catholic List	1706
Wills, Register Copies	1858–1928
(Staffs Wills proved at Lichfield)	

PUBLICATIONS†

Staffordshire Record Office Cumulative Hand List Part I, Lichfield Joint Record Office: Diocesan, Probate and Church Commissioners' Records (1978)

---

‡Microfilm/microfiche copies available at above repository

#Microfilm copy available at the LDS Family History Library in Salt Lake City, Utah, and through the LDS Family History Centers.

*Printed or transcribed

##Microfiche copy available at the LDS Family History Library in Salt Lake City, Utah, and through the LDS Family History Centers.

†For additional information send 2 Postal Reply Coupons or 31 pence of English postage for reply to North America; 34 pence to Australia and New Zealand.

STAFFORDSHIRE RECORD OFFICE
County Buildings, Eastgate Street
Stafford ST16 2LZ
Tel. 0785 223121 ext. 8380
Hours: M-Th 9-1, 1:30-5; F 9-1, 1:30-4:30;
By prior appointment S 9:30-1
(Prior appointment necessary to
use microfilm material)
Admission free
List of record agents and details of Record Office genealogical
search service available upon request[†]

HOLDINGS

Church of England parish records including deposited
Parish Registers for approximately 300 churches within the pre-
1974 county of Staffordshire; local government records and
other resources for the pre-1974 division of the county.

(Church of England diocesan records for the Diocese of
Lichfield and Parish Registers of Lichfield parishes are located
at the Lichfield Joint Record Office, Lichfield, Staffs. City and
Borough Records for Lichfield are also at the Lichfield Joint
Record Office.)

SOURCES THAT IDENTIFY AN INDIVIDUAL
WITH A SPECIFIC LOCATION

Borough Records (Stafford)	1528–1940
Freemen's List	
Rates	
Church of England (diocesan)	
Tithe Apportionments[§]	1835–1850

[†]For additional information send 2 Postal Reply Coupons or 31 pence of English
postage for reply to North America; 34 pence to Australia and New Zealand.
[§]Parish copies only; main series located at the Lichfield Joint Record Office.

Church of England (parish)
    Churchwardens' Accounts   late 16C–
Enclosure Awards‡#   18C–19C
Lay Subsidies‡#   1327, 1640
Maps   17C–
Militia Lists   late 18C–
                             early 19C
Poll Books* (some#)   17C–19C
Quarter Sessions
    Judicial Records   17C–19C
    Hearth Tax Assessments*   1665
    Land Tax Assessments   1780–1832
    Lists of Freeholders
    Lists of Jurors   1696–1702,
                           1789,
                           1861–1873
Registration of Papist's Estates   1715–1740
Registers of Electors*   1832–

SOURCES THAT MAY ADDITIONALLY PROVIDE VITAL DATA AND/OR PROVE FAMILY RELATIONSHIPS

Borough Records (Stafford)   1528–1940
    Court
    Title Deeds
Census‡# (post-1974 county area)   1841–1881
Church of England (parish)
    Parish Registers#   1538–20C
Estate and Family Papers   12C–20C
Manorial Records   13C–19C

---

‡Microfilm/microfiche copies available at above repository
#Microfilm copy available at the LDS Family History Library in Salt Lake City, Utah, and through the LDS Family History Centers.
*Printed or transcribed

Nonconformist Registers
Baptist‡#   1793–1837
Independent (Congregational)‡#   1777–1837
Methodist‡#   1830–1837
Society of Friends‡#   1640–1729
Parish Poor Law Records   1662–1834
Apprenticeship Indentures
Examinations
Removal Orders
Settlement Papers
Poor Law Union
Workhouse Records   1834–20C
School Records   late 19C–20C
Title Deeds   12C–20C

PUBLICATIONS†

Leaflets/Lists:
*List of Parish Registers and
Parish Register Transcripts
Information for Readers* (free)
List of Publications (free)

OTHER REPOSITORIES

The sources listed below include only those items reported on the Record Office Survey as located in the specified repositories. Each city and county library should have additional printed materials pertaining to its geographical area.

WILLIAM SALT LIBRARY
Eastgate Street, Stafford ST16 2LZ
Tel. 0785 52276

Hours: T, W, Th 9-1, 2-5; F 9-1, 2-4:30;
       2nd and 4th S/mo 9:30-1

HOLDINGS

An extensive collection of chiefly printed works relating to the local history of Stafford; runs of local Newspapers with an Index of births, marriages and deaths 1795–1840; Directories; published and manuscript Church of England Parish Register Transcripts.

LDS FAMILY HISTORY CENTRE†
P.O. Box 285
The Brampton
Newcastle-under-Lyme ST5 0TV
Tel. 0782 620653

LDS Family History Library Catalog‡##
International Genealogical Index‡##

---

†For additional information send 2 Postal Reply Coupons or 31 pence of English postage for reply to North America; 34 pence to Australia and New Zealand.
‡Microfilm/microfiche copies available at above repository
##Microfiche copy available at the LDS Family History Library in Salt Lake City, Utah, and through the LDS Family History Centers.

LDS FAMILY HISTORY CENTRE†
Purcell Avenue
Lichfield, Staffordshire
Tel. 0543 262621

LDS Family History Library Catalog‡##
International Genealogical Index‡##

GENEALOGICAL AND FAMILY HISTORY SOCIETIES

The societies listed below may have recorded Monumental (tombstone) Inscriptions, compiled an Index to Marriages (from the Parish Registers), an Index to the 1851 Census, and other special indexes, e.g., Strays, Members' Interests, for their geographical areas.** Each Society publishes a quarterly journal (listed in italics) which includes articles on family history, reports on the group's projects, and members' queries.

**BIRMINGHAM AND MIDLAND SOCIETY
FOR GENEALOGY AND HERALDRY†**
Mrs. J. Watkins, Secretary
92 Dimmingsdale Bank
Birmingham, W. Midlands B32 1ST

The Midland Ancestor

---

†For additional information send 2 Postal Reply Coupons or 31 pence of English postage for reply to North America; 34 pence to Australia and New Zealand.
‡Microfilm/microfiche copies available at above repository
##Microfiche copy available at the LDS Family History Library in Salt Lake City, Utah, and through the LDS Family History Centers.
**See *Current Publications by Member Societies* (annual), *List of Family History Project Coordinators*, 6th ed., and *Family History News and Digest* (biennial) — all published by the Federation of Family History Societies; available in the USA from the International Society for British Genealogy and Family History, P.O. Box 20425, Cleveland, OH 44120.

SUFFOLK

Post-1974 Counties of England

The pre-1974 geographical boundaries of Suffolk included the present county, and in addition, the northeastern tip (north of Lowestoft) which became part of Norfolk that year.

Administratively, in 1889 the county was divided into two units, West Suffolk and East Suffolk. Generally this division corresponded to the two ecclesiastical divisions in the county, the Archdeaconry of Sudbury (West Suffolk) and the Archdeaconry of Suffolk (East Suffolk). However, eighteen parishes around Hadleigh were in West Suffolk but not in the Archdeaconry of Sudbury.

In 1974 the two administrative units were reunited to form the present county of Suffolk.

383

Ipswich, an incorporated Borough from the mid-fifteenth century to 1889, became a County Borough between 1889 and 1974. Aldeburgh, Beccles, Bury St. Edmunds, Eye, Lowestoft, Southwold and Sudbury (partly in Essex) were all incorporated Boroughs from the seventeenth century to 1974. Dunwich was an incorporated Borough from the thirteenth century to 1886.

RECORD OFFICES

SUFFOLK RECORD OFFICE:
BURY ST. EDMUNDS BRANCH
Raingate Street, Bury St. Edmunds 1P33 1RX
Tel. 0284 763141 ext. 2522

Hours: M-Th 9-5; F 9-4; S 9-1, 2-5
        Advance booking of documents required for Saturdays
Admission free; system of Reader's Tickets to be introduced
        this year. Write in advance for registration details.
Details of genealogical research service
        available upon request†
List of record searchers available upon request†

HOLDINGS

Church of England diocesan records (Archdeaconry of Sudbury, Diocese of Norfolk to 1837, Diocese of Ely 1837–1914); microfilm copy of Archdeacons' Transcripts and Register Bills for Archdeaconry of Suffolk; Church of England parish records including deposited Parish Registers of approximately 190 churches in the former county of West Suffolk; many local government records and other resources pertaining to the pre-1974 county of West Suffolk.

(Some wills are located in the Norfolk Record Office, Norwich.)

---

†For additional information send 2 Postal Reply Coupons or 31 pence of English postage for reply to North America; 34 pence to Australia and New Zealand.

SOURCES THAT IDENTIFY AN INDIVIDUAL WITH A SPECIFIC LOCATION

Borough Records	13C–20C
(Bury St. Edmunds, Sudbury)	
Freemen's Lists	17C–19C
Rates	17C–19C
Church of England (archidiaconal)	
Ecclesiastical Court Books	17C–18C
Tithe Apportionments	1836–1853
Church of England (parish)	
Churchwardens' Accounts	15C–20C
Directories* (some#)	
Business/Trade	1844–1937
Enclosure Awards	1773–1853
Maps	17C–20C
Parish Poor Law Records	17C–1834
Parish Poor Rates	

SOURCES THAT MAY ADDITIONALLY PROVIDE VITAL DATA AND/OR PROVE FAMILY RELATIONSHIPS

Borough Records (Bury St. Edmunds, Sudbury)	
Court	16C–19C
Title Deeds	13C–20C
Boyd's Marriage Index‡#	1538–1837
Census‡# (W. Suffolk)	1841–1871
(all of Suffolk)	1881
Church of England (archidiaconal)	
Bishops' Transcripts‡#	1560–1860
Marriage Licence Bonds	1683–1839
and Allegations	
Wills, Admon., Inven.#	1354–1858

*Printed or transcribed
#Microfilm copy available at the LDS Family History Library in Salt Lake City, Utah, and through the LDS Family History Centers.
‡Microfilm/microfiche copies available at above repository

385

Church of England (parish)
Parish Registers# (W. Suffolk)   1538–1986
Parish Registers# (Suffolk)   1538–1900
Parish Register Transcripts*#   20C
Estate and Family Papers   13C–20C
International Genealogical Index‡##
(Suffolk, Essex, Norf, Cambs)
Manorial Records   13C–20C
Monumental Inscriptions#   mostly 18C–20C
Nonconformist Registers
Baptist#   1785–1837
Independent (Congregational)#   1689–1975
Methodist#   1800–1954
Presbyterian#   1589–1800
Society of Friends#   1641–1962
Parish Poor Law Records   17C–1834
Apprenticeship Indentures   17C–19C
Examinations   18C–19C
Removal Orders   17C–19C
Settlement Papers   17C–19C
Poor Law Union   1834–
Workhouse Records
School Records   17C–20C
Title Deeds   13C–20C
Wills, Register Copies   1858–1928
(Bury St. Edmunds Probate Registry)

PUBLICATIONS†

Guide to Genealogical Sources in Suffolk (1987)
Notes for Genealogists at Bury St. Edmunds (free)

#Microfilm copy available at the LDS Family History Library in Salt Lake City, Utah, and through the LDS Family History Centers.
*Printed or transcribed
‡Microfilm/microfiche copies available at above repository
##Microfiche copy available at the LDS Family History Library in Salt Lake City, Utah, and through the LDS Family History Centers.
†For additional information send 2 Postal Reply Coupons or 31 pence of English postage for reply to North America; 34 pence to Australia and New Zealand.

SUFFOLK RECORD OFFICE,
IPSWICH BRANCH
County Hall, Ipswich 1P4 2JS
Tel. 0473 230000 ext. 4235

Hours: M-Th 9-5; F 9-4; S 9-1, 2-5

Admission free; system of Reader's Tickets to be introduced
this year. Write in advance for registration details.
Details of genealogical research service
available upon request†
List of record searchers available upon request†

HOLDINGS

Church of England diocesan records (Archdeaconry of Suffolk, Diocese of Norfolk); microfilm copy of Archdeacon's Transcripts for Archdeaconry of Sudbury; Church of England parish records including deposited Parish Registers of more than 300 churches in the former county of East Suffolk; local government records (including Quarter Sessions) and other resources pertaining to the pre-1974 county of East Suffolk.

SOURCES THAT IDENTIFY AN INDIVIDUAL WITH A SPECIFIC LOCATION

Borough Records (Ipswich, Aldeburgh, Dunwich, Eye, Beccles)	16C–1974
Rates	
Church of England (archidiaconal)	
Ecclesiastical Court Books	to 19C
Ecclesiastical Visitations	to 19C
Tithe Apportionments	1838–1852
Church of England (parish)	
Churchwardens' Accounts	15C–

---

†For additional information send 2 Postal Reply Coupons or 31 pence of English postage for reply to North America; 34 pence to Australia and New Zealand.

Directories* (some#)
Business/Trade, Postal, Professional   1844–1937
Enclosure Awards   1787–1880
Lay Subsidies*   1327–1568
Maps   16C–20C
Parish Poor Law Records   17C–1834
Parish Poor Rates
Poll Books* (some#)   1700–1868
Quarter Sessions (some#)   1639–1782
Judicial Records   17C–20C
Hearth Tax Assessment*   1674
Land Tax Assessment   1799,
late 19C–
early 20C

Registers of Electors*
Ipswich Borough and E. Suffolk   1832–
(1982/3–##)

Shipping – Crew Lists   1863–1913
Ipswich and Woodbridge

SOURCES THAT MAY ADDITIONALLY PROVIDE VITAL DATA AND/OR PROVE FAMILY RELATIONSHIPS

Borough Records (Aldeburgh, Beccles,   16C–1974
Dunwich, Eye, Ipswich)
Court
Title Deeds   13C–20C
Boyd's Marriage Index‡#   1538–1837
Cemetery Registers (some*#)   1859–1926
(Ipswich)

---

*Printed or transcribed

#Microfilm copy available at the LDS Family History Library in Salt Lake City, Utah, and through the LDS Family History Centers.

##Microfiche copy available at the LDS Family History Library in Salt Lake City, Utah, and through the LDS Family History Centers.

‡Microfilm/microfiche copies available at above repository

Census‡# (East Suffolk)	1841–1881
(W. Suffolk)	1861
(all of Suffolk)	1881
Church of England (archidiaconal)	
Archdeacons' Transcripts#	1684–1875
Marriage Licence Bonds	1610–1914
and Allegations	
Wills, Admon., Inven.#	1441–1941
Church of England (parish)	
Parish Registers#	1538–
Parish Register Transcripts*#	1538–
Estate and Family Papers	15C–20C
International Genealogical Index‡##	
(Suffolk)	
Manorial Records	13C–20C
Monumental Inscriptions# mostly	18C–20C
Newspapers#	1720–1980
Nonconformist Registers	(# to 1837)
Baptist (some#)	1763–1855
Independent (Congregational) (some#)	1650–1968
Methodist (some#)	1800–1966
Presbyterian (some#)	1689–1929
Society of Friends (some#)	1641–1962
Obituary Notices*	19C
Parish Poor Law Records	17C–1834
Apprenticeship Indentures	
Examinations	
Removal Orders	
Settlement Papers	
Poor Law Union	1834–1929
Workhouse Records	19C–20C

---

‡Microfilm/microfiche copies available at above repository

#Microfilm copy available at the LDS Family History Library in Salt Lake City, Utah, and through the LDS Family History Centers.

*Printed or transcribed

##Microfiche copy available at the LDS Family History Library in Salt Lake City, Utah, and through the LDS Family History Centers.

School Records	19C
Title Deeds	13–20C
Wills, Register Copies	1858–1941

PUBLICATIONS†

Guide to Genealogical Sources in Suffolk (1987)
Notes for Genealogists at Ipswich (free)

SUFFOLK RECORD OFFICE, LOWESTOFT BRANCH
Lowestoft Central Library
Clapham Road, Lowestoft, Suffolk NR32 1DR
Tel. 0502 66325 ext. 3308
Hours: M-Th, S 9:15-5; F 9:15-6
Admission free; system of Reader's Tickets to be introduced
this year. Write in advance for registration details.

HOLDINGS
Resources pertaining to the northeastern part of the county
(Waveney District).

SOURCES THAT IDENTIFY AN INDIVIDUAL
WITH A SPECIFIC LOCATION

Borough Records (Lowestoft)	19C–20C
Rates	
Business Records	18C–20C
Directories* (some#)	19C–20C
Local Histories*	18C–20C

†For additional information send 2 Postal Reply Coupons or 31 pence of English
postage for reply to North America; 34 pence to Australia and New Zealand.
*Printed or transcribed
#Microfilm copy available at the LDS Family History Library in Salt Lake City,
Utah, and through the LDS Family History Centers.

390

Maps	18C–20C
Periodicals*	19C–20C
Poll Books* (some#)	18C–19C
Registers of Electors*	20C

SOURCES THAT MAY ADDITIONALLY PROVIDE VITAL DATA AND/OR PROVE FAMILY RELATIONSHIPS

Borough Records (Lowestoft)	19C–20C
Census‡# (N.E. Suffolk and S.E. Norfolk)	1841–1881
Church of England (parish)	
Parish Registers‡#	16C–20C
Estate and Family Records	18C–20C
International Genealogical Index‡##	
(Suffolk and Norfolk)	
Manorial Records	13C–20C
Newspapers#	19C–20C
Nonconformist Registers	
Independent	17C–20C
Methodist	19C–20C
School Records	19C–20C
Society and Charity Records	19C–20C

PUBLICATIONS†

Guide to Genealogical Sources in Suffolk (1987)

---

*Printed or transcribed

#Microfilm copy available at the LDS Family History Library in Salt Lake City, Utah, and through the LDS Family History Centers.

‡Microfilm/microfiche copies available at above repository

##Microfiche copy available at the LDS Family History Library in Salt Lake City, Utah, and through the LDS Family History Centers.

†For additional information send 2 Postal Reply Coupons or 31 pence of English postage for reply to North America; 34 pence to Australia and New Zealand.

OTHER REPOSITORIES

The sources listed below include only those items reported on the Record Office Survey as located in the specified repositories. Each city and county library should have additional printed materials pertaining to its geographical area.

LDS FAMILY HISTORY CENTRE†
42 Sidegate Lane West
Ipswich, Suffolk IP4 3DB
Tel. 0473 723182

LDS Family History Library Calendar‡##
International Genealogical Index‡##

GENEALOGICAL AND FAMILY HISTORY SOCIETIES

The societies listed below may have recorded Monumental (tombstone) Inscriptions, compiled an Index to Marriages (from the Parish Registers), an Index to the 1851 Census, and other special indexes, e.g., Strays, Members' Interests, for their geographical areas.** Each Society publishes a quarterly journal (listed in italics) which includes articles on family history, reports on the group's projects, and members' queries.

---

†For additional information send 2 Postal Reply Coupons or 31 pence of English postage for reply to North America; 34 pence to Australia and New Zealand.
‡Microfilm/microfiche copies available at above repository
##Microfiche copy available at the LDS Family History Library in Salt Lake City, Utah, and through the LDS Family History Centers.
**See *Current Publications by Member Societies* (annual), *List of Family History Project Coordinators*, 6th ed., and *Family History News and Digest* (biennial) — all published by the Federation of Family History Societies; available in the USA from the International Society for British Genealogy and Family History, P.O. Box 20425, Cleveland, OH 44120.

SUFFOLK GENEALOGY SOCIETY†
Dr. M. Barnett, Secretary
30 Gowers End, Glemsford
Sudbury, Suffolk CO10 7UF

Suffolk Roots

FELIXSTOWE FAMILY HISTORY SOCIETY†
Miss E. Cook, Secretary
5 Marina Gardens
Felixstowe, Suffolk IP11 8HW

Roots and Branches

---

†For additional information send 2 Postal Reply Coupons or 31 pence of English postage for reply to North America; 34 pence to Australia and New Zealand.

EAST SUFFOLK

Pre-1974 Counties of England

The county of East Suffolk was established in 1889 when the county of Suffolk was divided into two administrative units, East Suffolk and West Suffolk. Generally the boundaries of East Suffolk corresponded to those of the Archdeaconry of Suffolk.

In 1974 East Suffolk (except for the tip north of Lowestoft) and West Suffolk were administratively reunited to form the present county of Suffolk.

See Suffolk Record Office, Ipswich Branch, for genealogical resources pertaining to the former county of East Suffolk.

WEST SUFFOLK

Pre-1974 Counties of England

The county of West Suffolk was established in 1889 when the
county of Suffolk was divided into two administrative units,
West Suffolk and East Suffolk. Generally the boundaries of
West Suffolk corresponded to that of the Archdeaconry of Sudbury, with the exception of eighteen parishes around Hadleigh
which were in West Suffolk but not in the Archdeaconry of
Sudbury.

In 1974 West Suffolk and East Suffolk (except for the tip
north of Lowestoft) were administratively reunited to form the
present county of Suffolk.

See Suffolk Record Office, Bury St. Edmunds Branch, for
genealogical resources pertaining to the former county of West
Suffolk.

SURREY

Post-1974 Counties of England

The pre-1889 geographical boundaries of Surrey included the present county, the areas of Deptford (mostly in Kent), Lambeth, Southwark and Wandsworth which became part of the newly formed County of London in 1889, and the areas which became part of Greater London in 1965.

In 1965 local government for London was reorganized and the County of London was abolished. In its place the area of Greater London was created. At the same time the following areas of Surrey were transferred to the new area: Barnes, Beddington and Wallington, Carshalton, Coulsdon and Purley, Kingston upon Thames, Malden and Coombe, Merton and

396

Morden, Mitcham, Richmond, Surbiton, Sutton and Cheam, and Wimbledon. That same year the parishes of Ashford, Laleham, Littleton, Shepperton, Staines, Stanwell, and Sunbury were transferred from Middlesex County to Surrey County. There were only minor boundary changes in Surrey in 1974.

Kingston upon Thames was an incorporated Borough from the thirteenth century. Reigate and Richmond were incorporated as Municipal Boroughs in 1863 and 1890, respectively. Croydon, a Municipal Borough from 1883 to 1889, was a County Borough between 1889 and 1974. It became a part of Greater London in 1965.

Guildford and Godalming were incorporated Boroughs from the thirteenth and sixteenth centuries, respectively, to 1974.

RECORD OFFICES

SURREY RECORD OFFICE
County Hall, Penryhn Road
Kingston-upon-Thames KT1 2DN
Tel. (01) 541 9065

Hours: M, T, W, F 9:30-4:45; closed Th
        By appointment: 2nd, 4th S/mo 9:30-12:30;
Admission free
List of record searchers available upon request†

HOLDINGS

Church of England parish records including deposited Parish Registers for approximately 70 churches located in the pre-1965 area of Surrey; local government records and other resources pertaining to the pre-1965 division of the county.

(Church of England diocesan records for the Archdeaconry of Surrey, Diocese of Winchester are located at the Greater London Record Office.)

---

†For additional information send 2 Postal Reply Coupons or 31 pence of English postage for reply to North America; 34 pence to Australia and New Zealand.

SOURCES THAT IDENTIFY AN INDIVIDUAL
WITH A SPECIFIC LOCATION

Borough Records (Kingston-upon-Thames)		13C–
Freemen's Lists		
Rates		
Church of England (diocesan)		
Tithe Apportionments		1836–
Church of England (parish)		
Churchwardens' Accounts		17C–
Directories* (some#)		
Trade	(periodic)	19C–20C
Enclosure Awards		19C
Maps		18C–
Parish Poor Law Records		17C–1834
Parish Poor Rates		
Quarter Sessions		
Judicial Records#		17C–
Land Tax Assessments#		1780–1832
Lists of Freeholders#		1696–1824
Registers of Electors*#		1832–

SOURCES THAT MAY ADDITIONALLY PROVIDE VITAL
DATA AND/OR PROVE FAMILY RELATIONSHIPS

Borough Records (Kingston-upon-Thames)	13C–
Court	15C–
Guild: Admissions	17C–
Apprenticeship Enrolments	16C–
Title Deeds	13C–
Census‡# (post-1965 county area)	1841–1881
Church of England (parish)	
Parish Registers	1538–

---

*Printed or transcribed
#Microfilm copy available at the LDS Family History Library in Salt Lake City, Utah, and through the LDS Family History Centers.
‡Microfilm/microfiche copies available at above repository

Estate and Family Papers	18C–
International Genealogical Index‡##	
(Surrey)	
Manorial Records‡#	16C–
Nonconformist Registers	
Congregational	late 19C–20C
Methodist	late 19C–20C
Parish Poor Law Records	17C–1834
Apprenticeship Indentures	
Examinations	
Removal Orders	
Settlement Papers	
Poor Law Union	1834–
Workhouse Records	
School Records	19C–20C
Title Deeds	16C–

PUBLICATIONS†

D.L. Powell, *Guide to Surrey Records (1928–1931)*
  I. *Parish Records. Civil and Ecclesiastical* (OOP)
  II. *List of Court Rolls with some note of other Manorial Records*
  III. *Borough Records*
  IV. *Records of Schools and other Endowed Institutions*
  V. *Quarter Sessions Records and Other Records of Justices of the Peace*

Guide to Parish Registers Deposited in Surrey Record Office and Guildford Muniment Room

Parish Records: A Brief Introduction (1977)

---

‡Microfilm/microfiche copies available at above repository

##Microfiche copy available at the LDS Family History Library in Salt Lake City, Utah, and through the LDS Family History Centers.

#Microfilm copy available at the LDS Family History Library in Salt Lake City, Utah, and through the LDS Family History Centers.

†For additional information send 2 Postal Reply Coupons or 31 pence of English postage for reply to North America; 34 pence to Australia and New Zealand.

D.L. Powell, *Surrey Quarter Sessions Records*
(1934–1938, 1952)
  VI. *Order Book and Sessions Rolls* 1659–1661
 VII. *Order Book and Sessions Rolls* 1661–1663
  IX. *Order Book and Sessions Rolls* 1663–1666
  X. *Order Book and Sessions Rolls* 1666–1668
Leaflets:
  Surrey Record Office (free)
  Notes for Family Historians (free)

SURREY RECORD OFFICE,
GUILDFORD MUNIMENT ROOM
Castle Arch, Guildford GU1 3SX
Tel. 0483 573942

Hours: By appointment only: T-Th 9:30-12:30, 1:45-4:45;
       Closed M, F
       1st, 3rd S/mo 9:30-12:30

Admission free
List of record searchers available upon request[†]

HOLDINGS

Church of England parish records including deposited
Parish Registers for approximately 100 churches in southwestern Surrey; local government records and other resources
for the Borough of Guildford and southwestern Surrey.

(Church of England diocesan records for the Archdeaconry
of Surrey, Diocese of Winchester are located at the Greater
London Record Office.)

[†]For additional information send 2 Postal Reply Coupons or 31 pence of English
postage for reply to North America; 34 pence to Australia and New Zealand.

SOURCES THAT IDENTIFY AN INDIVIDUAL WITH A SPECIFIC LOCATION

Borough Records‡# (Guildford)	1514–1974
Freemen's Lists	
Rates	
Church of England (archidiaconal)	
Tithe Apportionments§	1836–1855
Church of England (parish)	
Churchwardens' Accounts	1599–1930
Maps	17C–20C
Parish Poor Law Records	17C–1834
Parish Poor Rates	
Poll Books* (some#)	(periodic) 17C–19C
Registers of Electors* (Guildford)	19C

SOURCES THAT MAY ADDITIONALLY PROVIDE VITAL DATA AND/OR PROVE FAMILY RELATIONSHIPS

Borough Records# (Guildford)	16C–20C
Court	
Title Deeds	
Church of England (parish)	
Parish Registers (some#)	1538–20C
Parish Register Transcripts* (some#)	16C–20C
Estate and Family Papers	
Manorial Records‡#	14C–
	*to early 16C
Nonconformist Registers	
Congregational	1871–1946
Methodist (marriages)	20C

---

‡Microfilm/microfiche copies available at above repository
#Microfilm copy available at the LDS Family History Library in Salt Lake City, Utah, and through the LDS Family History Centers.
§Parish copies only
*Printed or transcribed

Parish Poor Law Records   17C–1834
Apprenticeship Indentures
Examinations   (Guildford)   1797–1836
Settlement Papers
School Records (Guildford)   19C–20C

PUBLICATIONS†

Summary Guide to the Guildford Muniment Room (1967)
(OOP)

OTHER REPOSITORIES

The sources listed below include only those items reported
on the Record Office Survey as located in the specified repositories. Each city and county library should have additional
printed materials pertaining to its geographical area.

LDS FAMILY HISTORY CENTRE†
484 London Road
Mitcham, Surrey
Tel. (01) 769 0160

LDS Family History Library Catalog‡##
International Genealogical Index‡##

†For additional information send 2 Postal Reply Coupons or 31 pence of English
postage for reply to North America; 34 pence to Australia and New Zealand.
‡Microfilm/microfiche copies available at above repository
##Microfiche copy available at the LDS Family History Library in Salt Lake
City, Utah, and through the LDS Family History Centers.

GENEALOGICAL AND FAMILY HISTORY SOCIETIES

The societies listed below may have recorded Monumental (tombstone) Inscriptions, compiled an Index to Marriages (from the Parish Registers), an Index to the 1851 Census, and other special indexes, e.g., Strays, Members' Interests, for their geographical areas.** Each Society publishes a quarterly journal (listed in italics) which includes articles on family history, reports on the group's projects, and members' queries.

EAST SURREY FAMILY HISTORY SOCIETY†
Mrs. M. Brackpool, Secretary
370 Chipstead Valley Road
Coulsdon, Surrey CR3 3BF

East Surrey Family History Society Journal

WEST SURREY FAMILY HISTORY SOCIETY†
Mrs. J. Downham, Secretary
Bradstone Garden Cottage, Christmas Hill
Shalford, Surrey GU4 8HR

Root and Branch

**See *Current Publications by Member Societies* (annual), *List of Family History Project Coordinators*, 6th ed., and *Family History News and Digest* (biennial) — all published by the Federation of Family History Societies; available in the USA from the International Society for British Genealogy and Family History, P.O. Box 20425, Cleveland, OH 44120.

†For additional information send 2 Postal Reply Coupons or 31 pence of English postage for reply to North America; 34 pence to Australia and New Zealand.

SUSSEX

Pre-1974 Counties of England

Prior to 1889 Sussex was one county. That year it was divided into two administrative counties, East Sussex and West Sussex. Their boundaries corresponded approximately to those of the two ecclesiastical subdivisions in the county, the Archdeaconry of Chichester (West Sussex) and the Archdeaconry of Lewes (East Sussex).

Administratively Arundel, Chichester, Hastings, Lewes, Pevensey, Rye, Seaford and Winchelsea were all incorporated Boroughs by the end of the seventeenth century. Except for Hastings, all continued that status to 1974. Brighton, Eastbourne and Worthing became Municipal Boroughs after 1850.

404

From 1889 to 1974 Brighton and Hastings were County Boroughs, with Eastbourne granted that status between 1911 and 1974.

The Cinque Ports, a confederation of port towns formed in Sussex and Kent during the eleventh century, originally provided ships and men for the King's service. Dover, Hastings, Hythe, Romney and Sandwich were the original head ports, with the ancient towns of Rye and Winchelsea added later. Thirty other towns in the two counties were attached to one of the head ports, either as a corporate member (by royal charter) or as a noncorporate member (by private agreement). Corporate members were as follows: Seaford and Pevensy attached to Hastings (Sussex), Tenterden (Kent) attached to Rye (Sussex), Faversham and Folkestone attached to Dover (Kent), and Deal attached to Sandwich (Kent). While the maritime importance of the Cinque Ports declined significantly after the fourteenth century, the head ports and corporate members all had become incorporated Boroughs by the end of the seventeenth century.

See the Record Offices of West Sussex and East Sussex for genealogical resources pertaining to the respective areas.

EAST SUSSEX

Post-1974 Counties of England

Prior to 1889 Sussex was one county. That year it was divided into two administrative counties, East Sussex and West Sussex. Their boundaries corresponded approximately to those of the two ecclesiastical subdivisions in the pre-1889 county, the Archdeaconry of Lewes (East Sussex) and the Archdeaconry of Chichester (West Sussex). Since then several parishes have been transferred from one county to another. In 1974 the following parishes in East Sussex were transferred to West Sussex: Albourne, Ardingly, Balcombe, Bolney, Burgess Hill, Clayton, Cuckfield, Fulking, East Grinstead, Haywards Heath, West Hoathly, Horsted Keynes, Hurstpierpoint, Keymer, Lindfield,

Newtimber, Poynings, Pyecombe, Slaugham, Twineham and Worth.
Administratively Hastings, Midhurst, Pevensey, Rye, Seaford and Winchelsea were all incorporated Boroughs by the end of the seventeenth century. All except for Midhurst, which had ceased to be municipal by the late nineteenth century, and Hastings, continued that status to 1974. Brighton, Eastbourne and Lewes became Municipal Boroughs after 1850. From 1889 to 1974 Brighton and Hastings were County Boroughs, with Eastbourne granted that status between 1911 and 1974.

RECORD OFFICES

EAST SUSSEX RECORD OFFICE
The Maltings, Castle Precincts
Lewes BN7 1YT
Tel. 0273 475400 ext. 12/359

Hours: M-Th 8:45-4:45; F 8:45-4:15

Admission free
List of record searchers available upon request†

HOLDINGS

Church of England diocesan records (Diocese of Chichester) Wills for the Archdeaconry of Lewes; Church of England parish records including deposited Parish Registers for approximately 190 churches within the county; local government records and other resources pertaining to the pre-1974 county of East Sussex.

(Most Church of England diocesan records are located at the West Sussex Record Office, Chichester.)

---

†For additional information send 2 Postal Reply Coupons or 31 pence of English postage for reply to North America; 34 pence to Australia and New Zealand.

SOURCES THAT IDENTIFY AN INDIVIDUAL
WITH A SPECIFIC LOCATION

Borough Records (Lewes, Rye)	16C–19C
Freemen's Lists	
Rates	
Directories* (some#)	19C
Postal	
Enclosure Awards	19C
Church of England (archidiaconal)	
Tithe Apportionment§	19C
Maps	17C–20C
Militia Lists	18C
Parish Poor Law Records	17C–1834
Parish Poor Rates	18C–19C
Poll Books* (some#)	
Quarter Sessions	
Judicial Records#	16C–20C
Hearth Tax Assessments#	1620
(Chichester*)	1670
Land Tax Assessment	1780–1832
Registration of Papist Property	18C
Registers of Electors*	1832–
Shipping – Crew Lists	19C–20C
(Rye and Newhaven)	

SOURCES THAT MAY ADDITIONALLY PROVIDE VITAL
DATA AND/OR PROVE FAMILY RELATIONSHIPS

Borough Records (Lewes, Rye)	
Court	15C–20C
Title Deeds	13C–20C
Census‡# (most of East Sussex)	1841–1881

---

*Printed or transcribed

#Microfilm copy available at the LDS Family History Library in Salt Lake City, Utah, and through the LDS Family History Centers.

§Parish copies only

‡Microfilm/microfiche copies available at above repository

Church of England (archidiaconal)
    Wills, Admon, Inven.#   16C–1858
Church of England (parish)
    Parish Registers#   1538–
    Parish Register Transcripts*#   16C–19C
Estate and Family Papers (some#)   12C–20C
Manorial Records (some#)   13C–20C
Newspapers*   19C–20C
Nonconformist Registers
    Baptist (some#)   18C–20C
    Independent/Congregational (some#)   18C–20C
    Methodist (some#)   18C–20C
    Society of Friends (some#)   17C–20C
    Unitarian (some#)   17C–20C
Parish Poor Law Records   17C–1834
    Apprenticeship Indentures
    Examinations
    Removal Orders
    Settlement Papers
Poor Law Union   1834–20C
    Workhouse Records
School Records   19C
Title Deeds   12C–20C

PUBLICATIONS†

Jacqueline A. Berry, *How to Trace the History of
    Your Family* (1971)
List of Parish Registers Deposited (free)

#Microfilm copy available at the LDS Family History Library in Salt Lake City, Utah, and through the LDS Family History Centers.
*Printed or transcribed
†For additional information send 2 Postal Reply Coupons or 31 pence of English postage for reply to North America; 34 pence to Australia and New Zealand.

OTHER REPOSITORIES

The sources listed below include only those items reported on the Record Office Survey as located in the specified repositories. Each city and county library should have additional printed materials pertaining to its geographical area.

LDS FAMILY HISTORY CENTRE[†]
Old Horsham Road
Crawley, Sussex RH11 8PD
Tel. 0273 516151

LDS Family History Library Catalog[‡##]
International Genealogical Index[‡##]

GENEALOGICAL AND FAMILY HISTORY SOCIETIES

The societies listed below may have recorded Monumental (tombstone) Inscriptions, compiled an Index to Marriages (from the Parish Registers), an Index to the 1851 Census, and other special indexes, e.g., Strays, Members' Interests, for their geographical areas.** Each Society publishes a quarterly journal (listed in italics) which includes articles on family history, reports on the group's projects, and members' queries.

[†]For additional information send 2 Postal Reply Coupons or 31 pence of English postage for reply to North America; 34 pence to Australia and New Zealand.

[‡]Microfilm/microfiche copies available at above repository

[##]Microfiche copy available at the LDS Family History Library in Salt Lake City, Utah, and through the LDS Family History Centers.

**See *Current Publications by Member Societies* (annual), *List of Family History Project Coordinators*, 6th ed., and *Family History News and Digest* (biennial) — all published by the Federation of Family History Societies; available in the USA from the International Society for British Genealogy and Family History, P.O. Box 20425, Cleveland, OH 44120.

SUSSEX FAMILY HISTORY GROUP[†]
Mrs. B. Mottershead, Secretary
44 The Green, Southwick
Brighton, E. Sussex BN4 4FR

Sussex Family Historian

HASTINGS AND ROTHER
FAMILY HISTORY SOCIETY[†]
Mr. S. Tomlin, Secretary
520d Southview Court
Old London Road, Hastings, E. Sussex TN35 5BN

Hastings and Rother Family History Society Quarterly

[†]For additional information send 2 Postal Reply Coupons or 31 pence of English postage for reply to North America; 34 pence to Australia and New Zealand.

WEST SUSSEX

Post-1974 Counties of England

Prior to 1889 Sussex was one county. That year it was divided into two administrative counties, West Sussex and East Sussex. Their boundaries corresponded approximately to those of the two ecclesiastical subdivisions in the county, the Archdeaconry of Chichester (West Sussex) and the Archdeaconry of Lewes (East Sussex). Since then several parishes have been transferred from one county to another. In 1974 the following parishes in East Sussex were transferred to West Sussex: Albourne, Ardingly, Balcombe, Bolney, Burgess Hill, Clayton, Cuckfield, Fulking, East Grinstead, Haywards Heath, West Hoathly, Horsted Keynes, Hurstpierpoint, Keymer, Lindfield,

412

Newtimber, Poynings, Pyecombe, Slaugham, Twineham, and Worth.

Administratively Arundel and Chichester were both incorporated Boroughs from the end of the seventeenth century to 1974.

RECORD OFFICE

WEST SUSSEX RECORD OFFICE
John Edes House, West Street
Chichester PO19 1RN
Tel. 0243 777983 ext. 2770
Hours: M-F 9:15-12:30, 1:30-5
Admission free
List of record searchers available upon request†

HOLDINGS

Church of England diocesan records (Diocese of Chichester): Wills for the Archdeaconry of Chichester (West Sussex), Bishops' Transcripts, Marriage Licence Bonds and Allegations for the whole of Sussex; Church of England parish records including deposited Parish Registers for approximately 240 churches within the county of West Sussex; local government records and other resources which pertain to the pre-1974 county of West Sussex.

SOURCES THAT IDENTIFY AN INDIVIDUAL WITH A SPECIFIC LOCATION

Borough Records
    Electors (Arundel)   1835–1883
    Freemen's Lists (Chichester)   1833–1914

---

†For additional information send 2 Postal Reply Coupons or 31 pence of English postage for reply to North America; 34 pence to Australia and New Zealand.

Church of England (archidiaconal)
Ecclesiastical Court Books   16C–18C
Tithe Apportionments   mid-19C
Church of England (parish)
Churchwardens' Rates   17C–20C
Directories* (some#)
Postal   1845–1938
Enclosure Awards   18C–19C
Maps   18C–19C
Parish Poor Law Records   17C–1834
Parish Poor Rates
Poll Books* (some#)   (periodic) 18C–19C
Quarter Sessions
Judicial Records   17C–20C
Land Tax Assessments   1780–1832
Registration of Papist Property   18C
Registers of Electors*   1832–
Shipping – Crew Lists   1863–1913

*SOURCES THAT MAY ADDITIONALLY PROVIDE VITAL
DATA AND/OR PROVE FAMILY RELATIONSHIPS*

Borough Records (Chichester)
Court   19C
Cemetery Registers   19C–20C
Census‡# (post-1974 West Sussex)   1841–1881
Church of England (diocesan)
Bishops' Transcripts# (all of Sussex)   16C–20C
Marriage Licence Bonds   16C–20C
and Allegations
Wills, Admon., Inven.#   16C–1858

---

*Printed or transcribed
#Microfilm copy available at the LDS Family History Library in Salt Lake City,
Utah, and through the LDS Family History Centers.
‡Microfilm/microfiche copies available at above repository

Church of England (parish)	
Parish Registers#	1538–1900
Parish Register Transcripts*#	16C–19C
Estate and Family Papers	16C–
International Genealogical Index‡##	
(all of Sussex)	
Manorial Records	Medieval–20C
Monumental Inscriptions	18C–20C
Newspapers*	19C–20C
Nonconformist Registers	
Baptist	19C–20C
Independent (Congregational)	18C–20C
Methodist	18C–20C
Parish Poor Law Records	17C–1834
Apprenticeship Indentures	
Bastardy Papers	
Examinations	
Removal Orders	
Settlement Papers	
Poor Law Union	1834–
Workhouse Records	
School Records	19C–20C
Title Deeds	Medieval–20C
Wills, Register Copies	1858–1928

PUBLICATIONS†

Genealogist's Guide to the West Sussex Record Office
(2nd ed., 1983)
List of Emigrants and Transportees from
West Sussex 1778–c. 1874

GENEALOGICAL AND FAMILY HISTORY SOCIETIES

The societies listed below may have recorded Monumental (tombstone) Inscriptions, compiled an Index to Marriages (from the Parish Registers), an Index to the 1851 Census, and other special indexes, e.g., Strays, Members' Interests, for their geographical areas.** Each Society publishes a quarterly journal (listed in italics) which includes articles on family history, reports on the group's projects, and members' queries.

SUSSEX FAMILY HISTORY GROUP†
Mrs. B. Mottershead, Secretary
44 The Green
Southwick, West Sussex BN4 4FR

Sussex Family Historian

---

†For additional information send 2 Postal Reply Coupons or 31 pence of English postage for reply to North America; 34 pence to Australia and New Zealand.
**See *Current Publications by Member Societies* (annual), *List of Family History Project Coordinators*, 6th ed., and *Family History News and Digest* (biennial) — all published by the Federation of Family History Societies; available in the USA from the International Society for British Genealogy and Family History, P.O. Box 20425, Cleveland, OH 44120.

TYNE AND WEAR

Post-1974 Counties of England

Tyne and Wear Metropolitan County was created in 1974. Its geographical boundaries include the areas which previously formed the boundary between County Durham and Northumberland County, i.e. Gateshead, South Shields and Sunderland formerly in County Durham; Newcastle upon Tyne and Tynemouth formerly in Northumberland County.

Administratively Newcastle upon Tyne was a County Corporate from the fifteenth century to 1889 and then a County Borough to 1974. Tynemouth, a Municipal Borough in Northumberland from the mid-nineteenth century to 1904, was a County Borough between 1904 and 1974.

417

Gateshead and Sunderland were both Municipal Boroughs in Durham from the 1835 to 1889 and County Boroughs between 1889 and 1974. South Shields was a Municipal Borough in Durham from the mid-nineteenth century to 1889, and then a County Borough to 1974.

The Tyne and Wear Metropolitan County Council was abolished by Act of Parliament 1 April 1986. At the same time the name of the county was changed to Tyne and Wear County.

(See also the Record Offices in Durham and Northumberland for some sources pertaining to localities in the respective pre-1974 counties.)

(Church of England diocesan records for the Diocese of Durham to 1852 are located at the University of Durham, Department of Palæography and Diplomatic, Durham; those for the Diocese of Newcastle (1852–) are located at the Northumberland Record Office; Church of England parish records including deposited Parish Registers for churches are located in the record offices reflecting the pre-1974 boundaries.)

RECORD OFFICE

TYNE AND WEAR ARCHIVES SERVICE
NEWCASTLE UPON TYNE
Blandford House, Blandford Square
Newcastle upon Tyne NE1 4JA
Tel. (091) 232 6789

Hours: M, W, Th, F 8:45-5:15; T 8:45-8:30; closed S
       Prior appointment required for microfilm reader

Admission free
List of record searchers available upon request[†]

[†]For additional information send 2 Postal Reply Coupons or 31 pence of English postage for reply to North America; 34 pence to Australia and New Zealand.

HOLDINGS

Local government records and other resources pertaining to the present county; microfilm copy of parish records for churches in the county area.

SOURCES THAT IDENTIFY AN INDIVIDUAL WITH A SPECIFIC LOCATION

Borough Records (Newcastle, South Shields, Sunderland, Gateshead, Tynemouth)	(gaps)	17C–19C
Freemen's Lists		1409–
Rates		(1409–1836*)
Directories* (some#)		
Trade	(periodic)	1778–1965
Land Tax Assessments (Newcastle)		1742–1845
Militia Lists		1797–1827
Parish Poor Law Records		17C–1834
Parish Poor Rates		
Poll Books* (some#) (Newcastle, Gateshead)		1741–1860
Registers of Electors* (Newcastle)		1835–1968

SOURCES THAT MAY ADDITIONALLY PROVIDE VITAL DATA AND/OR PROVE FAMILY RELATIONSHIPS

Borough Records (Newcastle)	17C–19C
Court	
Guild: Admissions	17C–1830
Apprenticeship Enrolments	
Title Deeds	
Cemetery Registers	1834–1968

*Printed or transcribed

#Microfilm copy available at the LDS Family History Library in Salt Lake City, Utah, and through the LDS Family History Centers.

Census‡#	1841–1881
Church of England (parish)	
Parish Registers‡#	1558–1970's
Estate and Family Papers	19C–20C
International Genealogical Index‡##	
(Durh, Nthbld)	
Hospital Records§§	19C–20C
Magistrates' Court Records§§	19C–20C
Nonconformist Registers (‡# to 1837)	
Baptist	1753–1946
United Reformed Church	1756–1986
(including Congregational,	
Presbyterian, and Independent)	
Methodist	1778–1837;
	1848–1970's
Society of Friends	1838–1909
Parish Poor Law Records	17C–1834
Apprenticeship Indentures	
Examinations	
Removal Orders	
Settlement Papers	
Poor Law Union	
Workhouse Records	1834–1980
Roman Catholic Records*	1825–1840
School Records	1871–1986

PUBLICATIONS†

North Eastern Ancestors (1987) (Guide to sources in the Tyne and Wear Archives Service, Northumberland Record Office and Durham Record Office)

---

‡Microfilm/microfiche copies available at above repository

#Microfilm copy available at the LDS Family History Library in Salt Lake City, Utah, and through the LDS Family History Centers.

##Microfiche copy available at the LDS Family History Library in Salt Lake City, Utah, and through the LDS Family History Centers.

§§Subject to embargo for 100 years

*Printed or transcribed

†For additional information send 2 Postal Reply Coupons or 31 pence of English postage for reply to North America; 34 pence to Australia and New Zealand.

DISTRICT ARCHIVES AND LIBRARIES

Genealogical resources for metropolitan districts within the county of Tyne and Wear may also be found in the respective repositories in the cities and boroughs listed below.

The sources may vary considerably from one district to another. Those most likely to be found in the Archives Department of a library or record office include Borough Records, Church of England parish records including deposited Parish Registers, Estate and Family Papers, Manorial Records and Title Deeds.

Sources most likely to be in the Local History/Studies Department of a library include transcribed or microfilm copies of Church of England Parish Registers, microfilm copies of Census Records 1841–1881, Postal and Trade Directories, International Genealogical Index, and microfilm copies of Nonconformist Registers for groups within the specific areas.

GATESHEAD METROPOLITAN DISTRICT

(Gateshead, Blagdon, Felling, Ryton, Whickham, pt. Chester-le-Street)

GATESHEAD CENTRAL LIBRARY
(Local Studies)
Prince Consort Road
Gateshead NE8 4LN
Tel. (091) 477 3478, 3482
Contact: Borough Librarian
Hours: M, T, Th, F 9:30-4:30; W 9:30-5; S 9:30-1
Admission free

HOLDINGS

Local government and other resources pertaining to areas now in the Gateshead Metropolitan District.

SOURCES THAT IDENTIFY AN INDIVIDUAL WITH A SPECIFIC LOCATION

Borough Records	
Burgess Rolls	(periodic) 1835–
Directories* (some#)	(gaps) 1778–1939
Local Histories*	
Maps	
Poll Books* (some#)	(few) 19C
(Gateshead, North Durh)	

SOURCES THAT MAY ADDITIONALLY PROVIDE VITAL DATA AND/OR PROVE FAMILY RELATIONSHIPS

Census‡#	1841–1881
Church of England (parish)	
Parish Registers‡# (9 parishes)	1559–1966
Parish Register Transcripts*	16C–19C
(Durh, Nthbld)	
Durham Marriage Bonds*	1594–1815
Marriage Indexes	18C
Newspapers*	18C–20C
Nonconformist Registers	
Congregational‡#	1831–1837
Methodist‡#	1812–1837
Presbyterian‡#	1778–1837
Obituaries‡#	
Roman Catholic Records‡#	1775–1838
Title Deeds	
Wills (some*)	16C–

---

*Printed or transcribed

#Microfilm copy available at the LDS Family History Library in Salt Lake City, Utah, and through the LDS Family History Centers.

‡Microfilm/microfiche copies available at above repository

NEWCASTLE UPON TYNE METROPOLITAN DISTRICT

(Newcastle upon Tyne, Gosforth,
Newburn, pt. Castleward)

NEWCASTLE UPON TYNE CENTRAL LIBRARY
Princess Square
Newcastle upon Tyne NE99 1DX
Tel. (091) 261 0691
Contact: Local Library Historian

Hours: M-Th 9:30-8; F 9:30-5; S 9-5

HOLDINGS

Resources relating primarily to the areas now in Newcastle upon Tyne Metropolitan District. Some indexes for the pre-1974 counties of Durham and Northumberland.

SOURCES THAT IDENTIFY AN INDIVIDUAL WITH A SPECIFIC LOCATION

Burgess Rolls	1835–1880
Directories* (some#)	late 18C–
(Trade, Postal)	
Local Histories*	
Maps	17C–
Periodicals*	
Poll Books* (some#)	1705–1865
(Newcastle, Nthbld, Durh)	
Registers of Electors*	1864–
(Newcastle)	

---

*Printed or transcribed

#Microfilm copy available at the LDS Family History Library in Salt Lake City, Utah, and through the LDS Family History Centers.

SOURCES THAT MAY ADDITIONALLY PROVIDE VITAL DATA AND/OR PROVE FAMILY RELATIONSHIPS

Boyd's Marriage Index‡#	1538–1812
(Durh, Nthbd)	
Census‡# (Newcastle)	1841–1881
Church of England (parish)	
Parish Registers‡#	16C–20C
Parish Register Transcripts*	1538–1812
Durham Marriage Bonds*	1594–1815
Freemen's Lists	1409–1738,
(Newcastle)	1755–1836
Funeral Notices*	1723–1820
(Newcastle Courant)	
International Genealogical Index‡##	
(Durh, Nthbld)	
Marriage Indexes*	1813–1837
(Durh, Nthbld)	
Monumental Inscriptions*	18C–19C
Newspapers (some‡#)	1710–
Obituaries*	1808–
(Newcastle)	
Recusancy Rolls Index*	1591–1691
(Nthbld)	

PUBLICATIONS†

Users' Guides:
- No. 1   *The Local Studies Collection: An Introduction*
- No. 2   *Tracing Your Ancestors in Northeast England*
- No. 3   *Census Records on Microfilm*

---

‡Microfilm/microfiche copies available at above repository

#Microfilm copy available at the LDS Family History Library in Salt Lake City, Utah, and through the LDS Family History Centers.

*Printed or transcribed

##Microfiche copy available at the LDS Family History Library in Salt Lake City, Utah, and through the LDS Family History Centers.

†For additional information send 2 Postal Reply Coupons or 31 pence of English postage for reply to North America; 34 pence to Australia and New Zealand.

No. 5 *Transcripts of Monumental Inscriptions*
No. 6 *Genealogical Sources*
No. 7 *Parish Register Transcripts and Indexes*
No. 8 *Tracing Your Ancestors: A Brief Guide for*
        the Beginner
No. 11 *Electoral Registers and Poll Books*
No. 12 *Local Newspapers*
No. 13 *Notes for Use of the Local Studies Library*

NORTH TYNESIDE METROPOLITAN DISTRICT

(Tynemouth, Wallsend, Longbenton,
pt. Whitley Bay, pt. Seaton Valley)

**TYNE AND WEAR ARCHIVES SERVICE
NORTH TYNESIDE**
Local Studies Centre,
Howard Street, North Shields NE30 1LY
Tel. (091) 258 2811 ext. 17

Hours: M, Th, F 9-1, 2-5; T 9-1, 2-7; W 9-1
        (Prior appointment advised)

Admission free
List of record searchers available upon request†

HOLDINGS

Local government records and other resources pertaining to
the areas now in the North Tyneside Metropolitan District.

---

†For additional information send 2 Postal Reply Coupons or 31 pence of English
postage for reply to North America; 34 pence to Australia and New Zealand.

SOURCES THAT IDENTIFY AN INDIVIDUAL
WITH A SPECIFIC LOCATION

Borough Records (Tynemouth)   1813–1848
   Rates
Directories* (some#)
   Business/Trade, Postal   (periodic) 19C–20C
Maps

SOURCES THAT MAY ADDITIONALLY PROVIDE VITAL
DATA AND/OR PROVE FAMILY RELATIONSHIPS

Cemetery Registers (Tynemouth)   1837–1947
Census‡# (North Tyneside)   1841–1881
Church of England (parish)
   Parish Registers‡#   (few) 16C–
International Genealogical Index‡##
   (Durh, Ntmbd)
Newspapers*   1864–
Nonconformist Registers
   Baptist   1872–1945
Poor Law Union Records   1837–1909

*Printed or transcribed
#Microfilm copy available at the LDS Family History Library in Salt Lake City, Utah, and through the LDS Family History Centers.
‡Microfilm/microfiche copies available at above repository
##Microfiche copy available at the LDS Family History Library in Salt Lake City, Utah, and through the LDS Family History Centers.

SOUTH TYNESIDE METROPOLITAN DISTRICT

(South Shields, Jarrow, The Boldons,
Hebburn, Whitburn, Cleadon, Westoe)

SOUTH TYNESIDE CENTRAL LIBRARY[†]
Local History Library
Prince Georg Square
South Shields, Tyne and Wear NE33 2PE
Tel. Tyneside (091) 456 8841

Hours: M-Th 10-7; F 10-5; S 10-12, 1-4
Prior appointment needed for microfilm
and microfiche readers

HOLDINGS

Resources pertaining primarily to the areas now in the present South Tyneside Metropolitan District.

Cemetery records[‡#§]	16C–
Census[‡#§]	1841–1881
Church of England (parish)	
Parish Registers[‡#§]	16C–
Parish Register Transcripts[‡#§]	16C–19C
International Genealogical Index[‡##§]	
Local Histories[*]	16C–
Marriage Indexes[*§]	16C–
Maps	18C–

[†]For additional information send 2 Postal Reply Coupons or 31 pence of English postage for reply to North America; 34 pence to Australia and New Zealand.

[‡]Microfilm/microfiche copies available at above repository

[#]Microfilm copy available at the LDS Family History Library in Salt Lake City, Utah, and through the LDS Family History Centers.

[§]May provide vital data and/or proof of family relationships.

[##]Microfiche copy available at the LDS Family History Library in Salt Lake City, Utah, and through the LDS Family History Centers.

[*]Printed or transcribed

Newspapers*§	19C–
Periodicals*	19C–
Monumental Inscriptions§	19C–
Poll Books* (some#)	19C
Registers of Electors*	1832–

PUBLICATIONS†

Leaflet: *An Introduction to South Tyneside Libraries*

SUNDERLAND METROPOLITAN DISTRICT

(Sunderland, Hetton, Houghton-le-Spring,
Washington, pt. Chester-le-Street, pt. Easington)

SUNDERLAND CENTRAL LIBRARY, MUSEUM AND ART GALLERY

Borough Road, Sunderland SR1 1PP
Tel. (091) 514 1235
Contact: Local Studies Librarian

Hours: M, W 9:30-6; T, Th, F 9:30-5; S 9:30-4

HOLDINGS

Resources pertaining to the areas now in the Sunderland Metropolitan District.

---

*Printed or transcribed
§May provide vital data and/or proof of family relationships.
#Microfilm copy available at the LDS Family History Library in Salt Lake City, Utah, and through the LDS Family History Centers.
†For additional information send 2 Postal Reply Coupons or 31 pence of English postage for reply to North America; 34 pence to Australia and New Zealand.

SOURCES THAT IDENTIFY AN INDIVIDUAL
WITH A SPECIFIC LOCATION

Borough Records (Sunderland)	19C–20C
Rates	
Directories* (some#)	(gaps) 1827–1963
Local Histories*	
Maps	1737–
Periodicals*	
Poll Books* (some#)	19C
Registers of Electors*	1832–

SOURCES THAT MAY ADDITIONALLY PROVIDE VITAL
DATA AND/OR PROVE FAMILY RELATIONSHIPS

Census‡#	1841–1881
Corder Manuscripts††	
Church of England (parish)	
Parish Register Transcripts* (gaps)	1567–1924
(some Co. Durham, Durham City)	
Durham Marriage Bonds*‡#	1594–1815
Maps	1737–
Newspapers*	1831–
Index	1841–1907,
	1940–
Nonconformist Records	
Society of Friends*	1660–1814

---

*Printed or transcribed

#Microfilm copy available at the LDS Family History Library in Salt Lake City, Utah, and through the LDS Family History Centers.

‡Microfilm/microfiche copies available at above repository

††Thirty-eight manuscript volumes of parish registers, pedigrees of Sunderland families.

PUBLICATIONS[†]

Leaflet: *Genealogical Information Available at the Local Studies Library, Sunderland* (free)

OTHER REPOSITORIES

The sources listed below include only those items reported on the Record Office Survey as located in the specified repositories. Each city and county library should have additional printed materials pertaining to its geographical area.

LDS FAMILY HISTORY CENTRE[†]
Linden Road off Queen Alexandra Road
Sunderland, Tyne and Wear
Tel. (091) 528 5787

LDS Family History Library Index[‡##]
International Genealogical Index[‡##]

[†]For additional information send 2 Postal Reply Coupons or 31 pence of English postage for reply to North America; 34 pence to Australia and New Zealand.
[‡]Microfilm/microfiche copies available at above repository
[##]Microfiche copy available at the LDS Family History Library in Salt Lake City, Utah, and through the LDS Family History Centers.

GENEALOGICAL AND FAMILY HISTORY SOCIETIES

The societies listed below may have recorded Monumental (tombstone) Inscriptions, compiled an Index to Marriages (from the Parish Registers), an Index to the 1851 Census, and other special indexes, e.g., Strays, Members' Interests, for their geographical areas.** Each Society publishes a quarterly journal (listed in italics) which includes articles on family history, reports on the group's projects, and members' queries.

NORTHUMBERLAND AND DURHAM FAMILY HISTORY SOCIETY†

Mr. J.K. Brown, Secretary
33 South Bend, Brunton Park
Newcastle upon Tyne NE3 5TR

Journal of the Northumberland and Durham Family History Society

---

**See *Current Publications by Member Societies* (annual), *List of Family History Project Coordinators*, 6th ed., and *Family History News and Digest* (biennial) — all published by the Federation of Family History Societies; available in the USA from the International Society for British Genealogy and Family History, P.O. Box 20425, Cleveland, OH 44120.

†For additional information send 2 Postal Reply Coupons or 31 pence of English postage for reply to North America; 34 pence to Australia and New Zealand.

WARWICKSHIRE

Post-1974 Counties of England

The pre-1974 geographical boundaries of Warwickshire included the present county, and in addition, the cities of Birmingham and Coventry as well as Solihull and Sutton Coldfield now in West Midlands County.

Administratively Birmingham, Coventry and Sutton Coldfield were County Boroughs from 1889 to 1974 and Solihull from 1964-1974. Coventry was a City and incorporated Borough from the mid-fifteenth century. Stratford upon Avon, Sutton Coldfield, and Warwick were incorporated Boroughs from the mid-sixteenth century to 1974. Birmingham was a Municipal Borough from the mid-nineteenth century to 1889.

RECORD OFFICES

WARWICK COUNTY RECORD OFFICE

Priory Park, Cape Road, Warwick CV34 4JS
Tel. 0926 410410 ext. 2508

Hours: M-Th 9-1, 2-5:30; F 9-1, 2-5; S 9-12:30
Readers' Tickets will be issued and
proof of identity required on first visit.

Admission free

List of record searchers available upon request†

HOLDINGS

Church of England parish records including deposited
Parish Registers for more than 235 churches within the county;
local government records and other resources pertaining to the
pre-1974 division of the county.

(Pre-1837 Church of England diocesan records including
wills for the Diocese of Lichfield – northeastern part of the
county – are located in the Lichfield Joint Record Office, Lichfield, Staffordshire; Pre-1837 Church of England diocesan
records for the Diocese of Worcester – southwestern part of the
county – are located in the Hereford and Worcester Record
Office, Worcester Headquarters. All post-1837 diocesan records are at the latter repository. See separate listings for records
pertaining to Birmingham and Coventry in West Midlands.)

---

†For additional information send 2 Postal Reply Coupons or 31 pence of English
postage for reply to North America; 34 pence to Australia and New Zealand.

SOURCES THAT IDENTIFY AN INDIVIDUAL
WITH A SPECIFIC LOCATION

Borough Records (Warwick)	16C–20C
Freemen's Lists	
Rates	
Church of England (diocesan)	
Tithe Apportionments§#	1838–1851
Church of England (parish)	
Churchwardens' Accounts	16C–20C
Directories* (some#)	19C
Business/Trade, Postal	
Enclosure Awards#	1692–1850
Lay Subsidies#	1332
Maps	16C–20C
Militia Lists#	1790–1797
Parish Poor Law Records#	17C–1834
Protestation Returns#	1641
Poll Books* (some#)	(periodic) 1761–1868
Quarter Sessions††	
Judicial Records#	17C–20C
Hearth Tax Assessments*#	1662–1684
Land Tax Assessments	1782–1832
Lists of Freeholders#	18C
Lists of Jurors#	1696–1849
Recusants' Lists	late 17C
Registration of	(periodic) 1717–1778
Papists' Estates#	
Registers of Electors*#	1838–20C

---

§Parish copies only

#Microfilm copy available at the LDS Family History Library in Salt Lake City, Utah, and through the LDS Family History Centers.

*Printed or transcribed

††Assize Records are not kept locally, but are in the Public Record Office, Chancery Lane, London.

SOURCES THAT MAY ADDITIONALLY PROVIDE VITAL DATA AND/OR PROVE FAMILY RELATIONSHIPS

Borough Records (Warwick)	16C–20C
Court	1545–20C
Title Deeds	13C–20C
Census‡# (Warws)	1841–1881
Church of England (parish)	
Parish Registers#	1538–1970's
Parish Register Transcripts*	16C–20C
Estate and Family Papers#	11C–
International Genealogical Index‡##	
(Warws)	
Manorial Records#	13C–19C
Monumental Inscriptions (some#)	16C–20C
Newspapers*	1806–20C
Nonconformist Registers	
Baptist (some#)	late 18C–20C
Independent/Congregational (some#)	late 18C–20C
Methodist (some#)	19C–20C
Prestyberian (some#)	late 17C–19C
Society of Friends	17C–19C
Unitarian	19C
Parish Poor Law Records	17C–1834
Apprenticeship Indentures	
Examinations	
Removal Orders	
Settlement Papers	
Poor Law Union	1834–1930
Workhouse Records	
Roman Catholic Registers‡#	18C–19C
School Records	1863–20C
Title Deeds#	12C–

---

‡Microfilm/microfiche copies available at above repository

#Microfilm copy available at the LDS Family History Library in Salt Lake City, Utah, and through the LDS Family History Centers.

*Printed or transcribed

##Microfiche copy available at the LDS Family History Library in Salt Lake City, Utah, and through the LDS Family History Centers.

SHAKESPEARE BIRTHPLACE TRUST RECORD OFFICE
Guild Street
Stratford upon Avon CV37 6QW
Tel. 0789 204016

Hours: M-F 9:30-1, 2-5; S 9:30-12:30

Admission free

List of record searchers available upon request[†]

HOLDINGS

Church of England parish records including deposited Parish Registers for the town of Stratford upon Avon; local government records (including Quarter Sessions) and other resources pertaining to the town;

(Most Church of England diocesan records for the Diocese of Worcester are located at the Hereford and Worcester Record Office, Worcester Headquarters.)

SOURCES THAT IDENTIFY AN INDIVIDUAL WITH A SPECIFIC LOCATION

Borough Records (Stratford upon Avon)	1553–1975
Freemen's Lists	1836–1974
Rates	1777–c. 1930
Church of England (diocesan[§])	
Ecclesiastical Court Books[#]	1590–1675
Tithe Apportionments	1836–
Church of England (parish)	
Churchwardens' Accounts	1617–1876

[†]For additional information send 2 Postal Reply Coupons or 31 pence of English postage for reply to North America; 34 pence to Australia and New Zealand.

[§]Parish copies only; most diocesan records are located at the Hereford and Worcester Record Office, Worcester Headquarters.

[#]Microfilm copy available at the LDS Family History Library in Salt Lake City, Utah, and through the LDS Family History Centers.

Directories* (some#)
Postal	(gaps)	1822–1970
Enclosure Awards		1773–1776
Lay Subsidies		1309–1332
Maps		15C–
Militia Lists		1803–1808
Parish Poor Law Records		17C–1834
Parish Poor Rates		
Quarter Sessions		
Judicial Records		17C–1888
Hearth Tax Assessments*	(gaps)	1662–1688
Land Tax Assessments*		1780–1832
Registers of Electors*		1836–

SOURCES THAT MAY ADDITIONALLY PROVIDE VITAL DATA AND/OR PROVE FAMILY RELATIONSHIPS

Borough Records (Stratford upon Avon)	1553–1975
Guild of the Holy Cross, S/A	13C–16C
Guild: Admissions	
Title Deeds	
Census‡# (S/A)	1841–1881
Church of England (parish)	
Parish Registers‡# (S/A)	1558–1976
Parish Register Transcripts*	1538–1812
(South Warws)	
Estate and Family Papers	13C–
International Genealogical Index‡##	
(Warws, Glos, Worcs)	
Manorial Records	13C–

---

*Printed or transcribed
#Microfilm copy available at the LDS Family History Library in Salt Lake City, Utah, and through the LDS Family History Centers.
‡Microfilm/microfiche copies available at above repository
##Microfiche copy available at the LDS Family History Library in Salt Lake City, Utah, and through the LDS Family History Centers.

Monumental Inscriptions*   17C–
(South Warwickshire parishes)
Nonconformist Registers (S/A)
  Independent (Congregational)‡#   1786–1837
  Methodist   1849–1957
Parish Poor Law Records (S/A)
  Apprenticeship Indentures   1606–1843
  Examinations   1740–1843
  Removal Orders   1740–1845
  Settlement Papers   1764–1841
Poor Law Union (S/A Union)   1840's–
  Workhouse Papers
Title Deeds (many Midlands parishes)   12C–20C

PUBLICATIONS†

Leaflets/Lists (free):
  Your Local Records Office
  Sources for Genealogists: Stratford Families
  Parish Register Copies

---

*Printed or transcribed

‡Microfilm/microfiche copies available at above repository

#Microfilm copy available at the LDS Family History Library in Salt Lake City, Utah, and through the LDS Family History Centers.

†For additional information send 2 Postal Reply Coupons or 31 pence of English postage for reply to North America; 34 pence to Australia and New Zealand.

GENEALOGICAL AND FAMILY HISTORY SOCIETIES

The societies listed below may have recorded Monumental (tombstone) Inscriptions, compiled an Index to Marriages (from the Parish Registers), an Index to the 1851 Census, and other special indexes, e.g., Strays, Members' Interests, for their geographical areas.** Each Society publishes a quarterly journal (listed in italics) which includes articles on family history, reports on the group's projects, and members' queries.

BIRMINGHAM AND MIDLAND SOCIETY FOR GENEALOGY AND HERALDRY†
Mrs. J. Watkins, Secretary
92 Dimmingsdale Bank
Birmingham, West Midlands B32 1ST

The Midland Ancestor

**See *Current Publications by Member Societies* (annual), *List of Family History Project Coordinators*, 6th ed., and *Family History News and Digest* (biennial) — all published by the Federation of Family History Societies; available in the USA from the International Society for British Genealogy and Family History, P.O. Box 20425, Cleveland, OH 44120.

†For additional information send 2 Postal Reply Coupons or 31 pence of English postage for reply to North America; 34 pence to Australia and New Zealand.

WESTMORLAND

Pre-1974 Counties of England

The county of Westmorland was abolished in 1974. The area within its boundaries was united with the area in the former county of Cumberland, the Furness area formerly in Lancashire, and the Sedburgh-Dent-Garsdale area formerly in the West Riding of Yorkshire, to establish a new county called Cumbria.

Administratively Kendal was an incorporated Borough from 1575 to 1974. Appleby was a Municipal Borough from the late nineteenth century to 1974.

See the Cumbria Record Office, Kendal, for genealogical resources pertaining to the former county of Westmorland.

440

ISLE OF WIGHT

Post-1974 Counties of England

The Isle of Wight was established as a separate county in 1890. Prior to that year it was part of Hampshire.

Administratively Newport was a Municipal Borough from the sixteenth century to 1974.

RECORD OFFICE

ISLE OF WIGHT RECORD OFFICE
26 Hillside
Newport, Isle of Wight P030 3EB
Tel. 0983 524031 ext. 3820, 3821

Hours: M, T, Th, F 9:30-5; W 9:30-8:30
(Prior appointment advised)

Admission free
List of record searchers available upon request[†]

HOLDINGS

Church of England parish records including deposited Parish Registers for 59 churches on the Isle of Wight. Some local government records and other resources pertaining exclusively to the present county. Complete card index of parish register entries to 1858 (marriages to 1837 only) is also on microfilm.

(Diocesan records for the Diocese of Winchester and some other resources are located at the Hampshire Record Office, Winchester.)

SOURCES THAT IDENTIFY AN INDIVIDUAL WITH A SPECIFIC LOCATION

Borough Records (Newport)	1550–1950
Freemen's Lists	
Rates	
Church of England (diocesan)	
Tithe Apportionments[§]	19C
Church of England (parish)	
Churchwardens' Accounts	1570–

[†]For additional information send 2 Postal Reply Coupons or 31 pence of English postage for reply to North America; 34 pence to Australia and New Zealand.
[§]Parish copies only; main series at Hampshire Record Office, Winchester.

442

Directories* (some#)
  Business/Trade, Postal   (gaps) 1784–
Hearth Tax Assessments*   1664–1674
Maps   16C–20C
Parish Poor Law Records   17C–1834
  Parish Poor Rates
Register of Electors*   1947–

SOURCES THAT MAY ADDITIONALLY PROVIDE VITAL DATA AND/OR PROVE FAMILY RELATIONSHIPS

Borough Records (Newport)
  Title Deeds   1100–
Cemetery Registers   1859–1929
Census‡#†† (county)   1841–1881
Church of England (parish)
  Parish Registers   1538–
Estate and Family Papers   12C–20C
International Genealogical Index‡##
  (British Isles)
Manorial Court Records   15C–18C
Newspapers*   1845–1926
Nonconformist Registers
  Independent#   1739–
  Methodist   19C–20C
Poor Law Union   1834–
  Workhouse Records
School Records   19C–20C
Title Deeds   1100–

---

*Printed or transcribed

#Microfilm copy available at the LDS Family History Library in Salt Lake City, Utah, and through the LDS Family History Centers.

‡Microfilm/microfiche copies available at above repository

††1841–1871 also at Hampshire Record Office.

##Microfiche copy available at the LDS Family History Library in Salt Lake City, Utah, and through the LDS Family History Centers.

PUBLICATIONS†

Education in Hampshire and the Isle of Wight (1977)

P.D.D. Russell, ed., *The Hearth Tax Returns for the Isle of Wight 1664–1674* (1981)

Dom F.F. Hockey, *The Cartulary of Carisbrooke Priory* (1981)

GENEALOGICAL AND FAMILY HISTORY SOCIETIES

The societies listed below may have recorded Monumental (tombstone) Inscriptions, compiled an Index to Marriages (from the Parish Registers), an Index to the 1851 Census, and other special indexes, e.g., Strays, Members' Interests, for their geographical areas.** Each Society publishes a quarterly journal (listed in italics) which includes articles on family history, reports on the group's projects, and members' queries.

ISLE OF WIGHT FAMILY HISTORY SOCIETY†
Mrs. L. Russon, Secretary
Athena House, John Street
Ryde, Isle of Wight PO33 2PZ

Journal of the Isle of Wight Family History Society

---

†For additional information send 2 Postal Reply Coupons or 31 pence of English postage for reply to North America; 34 pence to Australia and New Zealand.

**See *Current Publications by Member Societies* (annual), *List of Family History Project Coordinators*, 6th ed., and *Family History News and Digest* (biennial) — all published by the Federation of Family History Societies; available in the USA from the International Society for British Genealogy and Family History, P.O. Box 20425, Cleveland, OH 44120.

WILTSHIRE

Post-1974 Counties of England

There was no change in the geographical boundaries of Wiltshire during the 1974 reorganization of local government in England.

Administratively Calne, Chippenham, Devizes, Malmesbury, Marlborough, Salisbury, Wilton and Westbury were all incorporated Boroughs from the seventeenth century to 1974.

445

RECORD OFFICE

WILTSHIRE RECORD OFFICE
County Hall, Trowbridge BA14 8JG
Tel. 0225 753641 ext. 3502
Hours: M-F 9-12:30, 1:30-5; W to 8:30; closed S
Admission free
List of record searchers available upon request†

HOLDINGS

Church of England diocesan records (Diocese of Salisbury); Church of England parish records including deposited Parish Registers for over 300 churches within the county; local government records and other resources for the county.

SOURCES THAT IDENTIFY AN INDIVIDUAL WITH A SPECIFIC LOCATION

Borough Records (Calne, Devizes, Marlborough, Wilton, Wootton Bassett)	13C–
Freemen's Lists	18C–
Rates	17C–
Church of England (diocesan)	
Ecclesiastical Court Books	mid-16C–19C
Ecclesiastical Visitations	1662–19C
Tithe Apportionments	1840's
Church of England (parish)	
Churchwardens' Accounts	15C–
Directories* (some#)	
Business/Trade, Postal	1780's–

---

†For additional information send 2 Postal Reply Coupons or 31 pence of English postage for reply to North America; 34 pence to Australia and New Zealand.
*Printed or transcribed
#Microfilm copy available at the LDS Family History Library in Salt Lake City, Utah, and through the LDS Family History Centers.

Enclosure Awards	1730–1880
Maps	1585–
Militia Lists	18C–
Parish Poor Law Records	17C–1834
Parish Poor Rates	
Poll Books* (some#)	late 18C
Quarter Sessions	
Judicial Records	17C–20C
Land Tax Assessments	(gaps) 1773–1830's
Lists of Freeholders	(gaps) 18C–1857
Lists of Jurors	(gaps) 18C–19C
Registration of Papist Property	18C
Registers of Electors*	1832–

SOURCES THAT MAY ADDITIONALLY PROVIDE VITAL DATA AND/OR PROVE FAMILY RELATIONSHIPS

Borough Records (Calne, Chippenham, Devizes, Marlborough, Salisbury, Wilton, Wootton Bassett)	
Court	16C
Guild: Apprentice Enrolments	17C
Admissions	13C–
Title Deeds	mid-19C–
Cemetery Registers	
Census Records‡# (Wilts)	1851
Church of England (diocesan)	
Bishops' Transcripts	1600's–1880
Marriage Licence Bonds and Allegations	1585–1823
Wills, Admon., Inven.#	16C–1928
Church of England (parish)	
Parish Registers#	1538–1800's

---

*Printed or transcribed

#Microfilm copy available at the LDS Family History Library in Salt Lake City, Utah, and through the LDS Family History Centers.

‡Microfilm/microfiche copies available at above repository

447

Estate and Family Papers	17C–
Manorial Records	13C–
Newspapers*	early 18C–
Nonconformist Registers	
Baptist	late 17C–
Independent	18C
Methodist	late 18C–
Presbyterian	19C–
Society of Friends*	mid-17C–
	1837
Unitarian	19C
Poor Law Union	1834–
Workhouse Records	
School Records	18C
Title Deeds	1150–
Wills, Register Copies	mid-16C–
	1928

PUBLICATIONS†

The Wiltshire County Council: Quarter Sessions
Guide to Diocesan Records
Sources for the History of a Wiltshire Family (1981)(free)

OTHER REPOSITORIES

The sources listed below include only those items reported on the Record Office Survey as located in the specified repositories. Each city and county library should have additional printed materials pertaining to its geographical area.

---

*Printed or transcribed

†For additional information send 2 Postal Reply Coupons or 31 pence of English postage for reply to North America; 34 pence to Australia and New Zealand.

WILTSHIRE LIBRARY AND MUSEUM†
(Local Studies)
Bythesea Road, Trowbridge BA14 8BS
Tel. 0225 753641 ext. 2715

Census‡# (Wilts)   1841–1881
International Genealogical Index‡##
(British Isles)

GENEALOGICAL AND FAMILY HISTORY SOCIETIES

The societies listed below may have recorded Monumental (tombstone) Inscriptions, compiled an Index to Marriages (from the Parish Registers), an Index to the 1851 Census, and other special indexes, e.g., Strays, Members' Interests, for their geographical areas.** Each Society publishes a quarterly journal (listed in italics) which includes articles on family history, reports on the group's projects, and members' queries.

WILTSHIRE FAMILY HISTORY SOCIETY†
Richard Moore, President
1 Cambridge Close, Lawn
Swindon, Wiltshire SN3 1JO

Wiltshire Family History Society Journal

---

†For additional information send 2 Postal Reply Coupons or 31 pence of English postage for reply to North America; 34 pence to Australia and New Zealand.
‡Microfilm/microfiche copies available at above repository
#Microfilm copy available at the LDS Family History Library in Salt Lake City, Utah, and through the LDS Family History Centers.
##Microfiche copy available at the LDS Family History Library in Salt Lake City, Utah, and through the LDS Family History Centers.
**See *Current Publications by Member Societies* (annual), *List of Family History Project Coordinators*, 6th ed., and *Family History News and Digest* (biennial) — all published by the Federation of Family History Societies; available in the USA from the International Society for British Genealogy and Family History, P.O. Box 20425, Cleveland, OH 44120.

WORCESTERSHIRE

Pre-1974 Counties of England

The county of Worcestershire was abolished in 1974. Most of the former county was united with the former county of Herefordshire to establish the county of Hereford and Worcester. At the same time the northern tip, including the areas of Dudley, Halesowen and Stourbridge, was transferred to the newly created metropolitan county of West Midlands.

Administratively the city of Worcester was a County Corporate from the seventeenth century to 1889 and a County Borough between 1889 and 1974. Bewdley, Droitwich, Evesham and Kidderminster were all incorporated Boroughs from the seventeenth century to 1974. Dudley was a mid-nineteenth

450

century Municipal Borough and a County Borough during the twentieth century.

Most Worcestershire genealogical material is held at Worcester Headquarters (County Hall, Spetchley Road, Worcester WR5 2NP). Private family collections, artificial collections, diocesan material (excluding Bishops' Transcripts, Probate documents and Marriage Licence material which is held at Headquarters) and the Worcester City archives are at the St. Helen's Branch (Fish Street, Worcester WR1 2HN).

Herefordshire genealogical material is held at the Hereford Branch (The Old Barracks, Harold Street, Hereford HR1 2QX).

YORKSHIRE, EAST RIDING

Pre-1974 Counties of England

The East Riding of Yorkshire was one of three administrative units within the county of Yorkshire. It was abolished
in 1974, and most of the area within its boundaries was
transferred to the newly created county of Humberside. The
north and west border area of the former East Riding were
transferred to the newly created county of North Yorkshire.

Administratively Beverley and Hedon were incorporated
Boroughs in the East Riding from the seventeenth century to
1974.

Kingston upon Hull, geographically located in the East Riding, was a County Corporate from the fourteenth century to 1889 and a County Borough from 1889 to 1974.

See the Humberside Record Office at Beverley, the Kingston upon Hull Record Office, and the North Yorkshire County Record Office for genealogical resources pertaining to the respective pre-1974 areas.

YORKSHIRE, NORTH RIDING

Pre-1974 Counties of England

The North Riding of Yorkshire was one of three administrative units within the county of Yorkshire. In 1974 it was
abolished, and a majority of the area within its boundaries was
transferred to the newly created county of North Yorkshire.
The northwestern tip of the former North Riding was transferred to County Durham and the northeastern border area
(from the Moors to the river Tees) was transferred to the newly
created county of Cleveland.

Prior to 1974 the North Riding included approximately the
northern third of the entire county of Yorkshire.

Scarborough, Richmond and Harrogate were incorporated
Boroughs from the twelfth, sixteenth and nineteenth centuries,
respectively, to 1974.

454

YORKSHIRE, WEST RIDING

Pre-1974 Counties of England

The West Riding of Yorkshire was one of three administrative units within the county of Yorkshire. In 1974 it was
abolished. Approximately the southern third of the area within
its boundaries was transferred to the newly created metropolitan county of South Yorkshire. The northern third and east
central border area were transferred to the newly created county
of North Yorkshire. The remaining area (approximately the
middle third of the former West Riding) was transferred to the
newly created metropolitan county of West Yorkshire.

Administratively Doncaster, Pontefract, Ripon and Leeds
were all incorporated Boroughs from the seventeenth century.
Leeds became a County Borough in 1889 and Doncaster in 1927,

455

which extended to 1974. Ripon and Pontefract remained Municipal Boroughs to 1974.

Barnsley, Bradford, Halifax, Huddersfield, Rotherham, Sheffield and Wakefield were all mid-nineteenth-century Municipal Boroughs and County Boroughs during the twentieth century.

NORTH YORKSHIRE

Post-1974 Counties of England

The county of North Yorkshire was created in 1974. Geographically it includes the former North Riding of Yorkshire, except for the northwestern tip which was transferred to County Durham, and the northeastern border area (from the Moors to the river Tees) which was transferred to the newly created county of Cleveland.

Additionally it includes the city of York, the northern one-third and east central border area of the former West Riding of Yorkshire, and the northern and western border areas of the former East Riding of Yorkshire.

457

Administratively, the city of York was a County Corporate from the fourteenth century to 1889 and then a County Borough to 1974. Scarborough, Richmond and Harrogate were incorporated Boroughs from the twelfth, sixteenth, and nineteenth centuries, respectively, to 1974.

RECORD OFFICES

BORTHWICK INSTITUTE OF HISTORICAL RESEARCH, UNIVERSITY OF YORK

St. Anthony's Hall, York YO1 2PW
Tel. 0904 430000 ext. 274
     0904 642315

Hours: M-F 9:30-12:50, 2-4:50
Prior appointment necessary to view records (up to three months in advance). Three microfilm readers available on first-come, first-serve basis, but this facility is sometimes unavailable due to University teaching commitments. Closed last two weeks of December, short period at Easter, and week preceding and succeeding the August Bank Holiday.

Admission free

HOLDINGS

Church of England: Archbishopric records for the Northern Province (York); Diocesan records (Diocese of York); parish records (Archdeaconry of York) including deposited Parish Registers for approximately 225 churches. Other sources include deeds and manorial records relating primarily to former holdings of the Archbishops and other diocesan officials, as well as some private estate papers.

SOURCES THAT IDENTIFY AN INDIVIDUAL WITH A SPECIFIC LOCATION

Church of England (diocesan)

Ecclesiastical Court Books	14C–19C
and Cause Papers	
Licences of Professionals	16C–19C
Ordinations of Clergy	13C–20C
Ecclesiastical Visitations	16C–20C
Returns of Roman Catholics	18C
Presentments of Nonconformists	17C
and Recusants	
Tithe Apportionments	1837–1850

Church of England (parish)

Churchwardens' Accounts	16C–20C
Poor Law Records	
Parish Poor Rates	16C–20C
Directories* (some#)	1822–1974
Business	
Enclosure Awards	c. 18C–20C
Maps	16C–20C
Periodicals*	

SOURCES THAT MAY ADDITIONALLY PROVIDE VITAL DATA AND/OR PROVE FAMILY RELATIONSHIPS

Church of England (archbishopric)
Wills
(Register copies and originals)

Prerogative Court of York#	1389–1858
Exchequer Court of York#	1389–1858

---

*Printed or transcribed

#Microfilm copy available at the LDS Family History Library in Salt Lake City, Utah, and through the LDS Family History Centers.

Church of England (diocesan)

Bishops' Transcripts#	1600–1643, 1660–mid-19C
Marriage Licence Bonds and Allegations	1660–20C
Wills, Admon., Inven. (original)#	14C–1858

Church of England (parish)

Parish Registers#	1538–20C
Parish Register Transcripts*§	1538–19C
Poor Law Records	17C–20C
Apprenticeship Indentures	17C–19C
Examinations	17C–19C
Removal Orders	17C–19C
Settlement Certificates	17C–19C
Estate and Family Papers	17C–20C
Guild Records	
Apprenticeship Registers (Merchant Taylors' only)	1606–1862
International Genealogical Index‡##§ (Yorkshire)	
Manorial Records	15C–20C
Monumental Inscriptions§	
Schools Records	19C–20C
Title Deeds	18C–20C

#Microfilm copy available at the LDS Family History Library in Salt Lake City, Utah, and through the LDS Family History Centers.

*Printed or transcribed

§Available at the Borthwick Institute Library; no appointment necessary.

‡Microfilm/microfiche copies available at above repository

##Microfiche copy available at the LDS Family History Library in Salt Lake City, Utah, and through the LDS Family History Centers.

PUBLICATIONS†

C.C. Webb, *A Guide to Genealogical Sources in the Borthwick Institute of Historical Research* (1981)

David M. Smith, *A Guide to the Archive Collections in the Borthwick Institute of Historical Research* (1973)

David M. Smith, *A Supplementary Guide to the Archive Collections in the Borthwick Institute of Historical Research* (1980)

Complete list of publications available upon request.†

NORTH YORKSHIRE COUNTY RECORD OFFICE
County Hall, Northallerton
North Yorks DL7 8SG
Tel. 0609 780780 ext. 2455

Hours: M, T, Th 9-4:50; W 9-8:50; F 9-4:20; closed 1-2
　　　 Prior appointment necessary to consult records
　　　 (Consult NYCRO Guides #1 and 5
　　　 before making appointment.)

Admission free

HOLDINGS

　　Church of England parish records including deposited Parish Registers for more than 150 churches; local government and other resources pertaining to the former North Riding of Yorkshire.

　　(Church of England diocesan records for the eastern half of the former North Riding of Yorkshire – Diocese of York – are located at the Borthwick Institute of Historical Research, University of York, York. Those for the western half of the former North Riding – Archdeaconry of Richmond, Eastern Deaneries, Diocese of Chester – are located at the Leeds District Archives, Leeds.)

---

†For additional information send 2 Postal Reply Coupons or 31 pence of English postage for reply to North America; 34 pence to Australia and New Zealand.

SOURCES THAT IDENTIFY AN INDIVIDUAL
WITH A SPECIFIC LOCATION

Borough Records (Richmond, Scarborough)		17C–19C
Freemen's Lists		
Rates		
Church of England (diocesan)		19C
Tithe Apportionments§		
Church of England (parish)		
Churchwardens' Accounts		17C–20C
Enclosure Awards#		19C
(Yorkshire North Riding, West Riding)		
Maps		16C–20C
Parish Poor Law Records	(few)	17C–1934
Parish Poor Rates		
Poll Books* (some#)	(few)	19C
Quarter Sessions		
Judicial Records#		16C–20C
Land Tax Assessments#		1781–1832
Lists of Jurors#		1729–1848
Registration of Papist Estates		1717–1781
Registers of Electors*		1832–20C
		(# to 1875)

SOURCES THAT MAY ADDITIONALLY PROVIDE VITAL
DATA AND/OR PROVE FAMILY RELATIONSHIPS

Borough Records (Richmond, Scarborough)	17C–19C
Court	
Title Deeds	
Census‡# (present county area)	1851

---

§Parish copies only; main series at the Borthwick Institute of Historical Research, University of York, York.

#Microfilm copy available at the LDS Family History Library in Salt Lake City, Utah, and through the LDS Family History Centers.

*Printed or transcribed

‡Microfilm/microfiche copies available at above repository

Church of England (parish)
Parish Registers (some#)   16C–20C
Parish Register Transcripts*#   16C–19C
Estate and Family Papers   13C–20C
Manorial Records (some#)   14C–20C
Nonconformist Registers
Methodist   late 18C–
Society of Friends (some#)   1650–20C
Parish Poor Law Records   (few) 17C–1834
Apprenticeship Indentures
Examinations
Removal Orders
Settlement Papers
Poor Law Union
Workhouse Records   1837–
School Records   1870–
Title Deeds: Register of Deeds
(North Riding of Yorkshire)   1736–1970
                                            (# to 1876)
Wills, Register Copies   19C–20C

PUBLICATIONS†

Guide No. 1: *Calendars, Transcripts and Microfilms in the Record Office*

Guide No. 5: *North Yorkshire Parish Registers – including dates and whereabouts of parish registers, transcripts, microfilms*

Guide No. 6: *North Yorkshire Gazetteer of Townships and Parishes*

#Microfilm copy available at the LDS Family History Library in Salt Lake City, Utah, and through the LDS Family History Centers.

*Printed or transcribed

†For additional information send 2 Postal Reply Coupons or 31 pence of English postage for reply to North America; 34 pence to Australia and New Zealand.

Leaflets/Lists (free):
SR2   *Notes for Enquirers – rules, opening times, etc.*
SR3   *Reproduction Charges*
SR4   *Record Searching Service*
SR9   *North Riding Register of Deeds*
SR11 *Methodist Circuit and Chapel Registers*
       Accommodations in Northallerton
       Map of Northallerton – Plan of County Hall

Complete list of publications available upon request.[†]

YORK CITY ARCHIVES
Art Gallery Building
(entrance around right hand corner of Art Gallery)
Exhibition Square, York YO1 2EW
Tel. 0904 51553

Hours: T, W, Th 9:30-12:30, 2-5:30;
        M, F by prior appointment only

Admission free

HOLDINGS

Resources pertaining to the City and Ainsty (surrounding area) of York.

Apprenticeship Registers[§]	1573–1668, 1721–1945
Boyd's Marriage Index[‡#§] (Yorks)	1539–1837
Cemetery Records[§]	1837–

[†]For additional information send 2 Postal Reply Coupons or 31 pence of English postage for reply to North America; 34 pence to Australia and New Zealand.
[§]May provide vital data and/or proof of family relationships.
[‡]Microfilm/microfiche copies available at above repository
[#]Microfilm copy available at the LDS Family History Library in Salt Lake City, Utah, and through the LDS Family History Centers.

Freemen's Rolls§	1272–
Freedom Claims§	1759–
Lay Subsidies	16C
Hearth Tax Assessments	1665, 1670, 1671, 1674
Militia Lists (Muster Rolls)	16C–19C
Title Deeds	
North Riding Register of Deeds‡#§	1736–1876
Window Tax Assessments	1701
Yorkshire Marriage Index*§	1801–1834

OTHER REPOSITORIES

The sources listed below include only those items reported on the Record Office Survey as located in the specified repositories. Each city and county library should have additional printed materials pertaining to its geographical area.

NORTH YORKSHIRE COUNTY LIBRARY†
Reference Library
Museum Street, York YO1 2DS
Tel. 0904 55631
Hours: M, T, W, F 9-8; Th 9-5:30; S 9-1
Admission free

§May provide vital data and/or proof of family relationships.
‡Microfilm/microfiche copies available at above repository
#Microfilm copy available at the LDS Family History Library in Salt Lake City, Utah, and through the LDS Family History Centers.
*Printed or transcribed
†For additional information send 2 Postal Reply Coupons or 31 pence of English postage for reply to North America; 34 pence to Australia and New Zealand.

HOLDINGS

Resources pertaining primarily to the City and Ainsty of York.

SOURCES THAT IDENTIFY AN INDIVIDUAL WITH A SPECIFIC LOCATION

Directories* (some#)	
Trade	19C
Freemen's Rolls* (York)	1272–1915
Maps	17C–20C
Poll Books* (some#)	
Yorkshire	(periodic) 1741–
York City	(periodic) 1748–
Registers of Electors*	(gaps) 1837–

SOURCES THAT MAY ADDITIONALLY PROVIDE VITAL DATA AND/OR PROVE FAMILY RELATIONSHIPS

Boyd's Marriage Index*# (Yorks)	1539–1877
Census‡# (York area)	1841–1881
Church of England (parish)	
Parish Register Transcripts*	16C–19C
Newspapers*	1729–20C
Serial Publications*	
Surtees Society	
Thoresby Society	
Yorkshire Archaeological Society	
York Marriage Index*	1801–1837

---

*Printed or transcribed

#Microfilm copy available at the LDS Family History Library in Salt Lake City, Utah, and through the LDS Family History Centers.

‡Microfilm/microfiche copies available at above repository

LDS FAMILY HISTORY CENTRE†
West Bank, Acomb
York, North Yorkshire
Tel. 0904 798185

   LDS Family History Library Catalog‡##
   International Genealogical Index‡##

GENEALOGICAL AND FAMILY
HISTORY SOCIETIES

The societies listed below may have recorded Monumental (tombstone) Inscriptions, compiled an Index to Marriages (from the Parish Registers), an Index to the 1851 Census, and other special indexes, e.g., Strays, Members' Interests, for their geographical areas.** Each Society publishes a quarterly journal (listed in italics) which includes articles on family history, reports on the group's projects, and members' queries.

YORK FAMILY HISTORY SOCIETY†
Mrs. J. Denton, Secretary
4 Mount Vale Drive
The Mount, York YO1 2DN

   York Family History Society Newsletter

---

†For additional information send 2 Postal Reply Coupons or 31 pence of English postage for reply to North America; 34 pence to Australia and New Zealand.
‡Microfilm/microfiche copies available at above repository
##Microfiche copy available at the LDS Family History Library in Salt Lake City, Utah, and through the LDS Family History Centers.
**See *Current Publications by Member Societies* (annual), *List of Family History Project Coordinators*, 6th ed., and *Family History News and Digest* (biennial) — all published by the Federation of Family History Societies; available in the USA from the International Society for British Genealogy and Family History, P.O. Box 20425, Cleveland, OH 44120.

SOUTH YORKSHIRE

Post-1974 Counties of England

The Metropolitan County of South Yorkshire was created in 1974. Its geographic boundaries included approximately the southern third of the former West Riding of Yorkshire (including the areas of Doncaster, Barnsley, Sheffield, and Rotherham).

Administratively, Doncaster was an incorporated Borough from the thirteenth century to 1927 and a County Borough from 1927 to 1974. Barnsley, Rotherham and Sheffield all became Municipal Boroughs in the mid-nineteenth century and then were County Boroughs during the twentieth century.

468

The Metropolitan County Council was abolished by Act of Parliament 1 April 1986. At the same time the name of the county was changed to the County of South Yorkshire. The South Yorkshire Record Office was subsequently closed, and its holdings were transferred to the Sheffield Central Library, which is a service of the Sheffield Metropolitan District Council.

The city archives service has been renamed Sheffield Record Office. Enquiries sent to the former County Record Office are being transferred to the Sheffield Record Office.

The Metropolitan District Councils of Barnsley, Doncaster and Rotherham administer an archives service for their respective geographical areas.

(See also the West Yorkshire Archives Service, Headquarters and Wakefield Registry of Deeds, for pre-1974 sources pertaining to the present county of South Yorkshire.)

DISTRICT ARCHIVES AND LIBRARIES

Genealogical resources for metropolitan districts within the county of South Yorkshire may be found in the respective repositories in the cities and boroughs listed below.

The sources may vary considerably from one district to another. Those most likely to be found in the Archives Department of a library or record office include Borough Records, Church of England parish records including deposited Parish Registers, Estate and Family Papers, Manorial Records and Title Deeds.

Sources most likely to be in the Local History/Studies Department of a library include transcribed or microfilm copies of Church of England Parish Registers, microfilm copies of Census Records 1841–1881, Postal and Trade Directories, International Genealogical Index, and microfilm copies of Nonconformist Registers for groups within the specific areas.

SHEFFIELD METROPOLITAN DISTRICT

(Sheffield, Stocksbridge, pt. Wortley)

SHEFFIELD RECORD OFFICE
(Successor to South Yorkshire Record Office, now closed)
Central Library, Surrey Street
Sheffield S1 1XZ
Tel. 0742 734756

Hours: M-F 9:30-5:30;
      By prior appointment S 9-1, 2-4:30

Admission free

HOLDINGS

Microfilm copies of Bishops' Transcripts (Church of England diocesan records); Church of England parish records including deposited Parish Registers for over 100 churches in the Archdeaconry of Sheffield, Diocese of York; microfilm copies and original records of Nonconformist Registers; other resources pertaining to South Yorkshire.

SOURCES THAT IDENTIFY AN INDIVIDUAL WITH A SPECIFIC LOCATION

Enclosure Awards	19C
Lists of Freeholders (Yorkshire)	1784, 1807, 1848
Maps	18C–19C
Militia Lists	17C–19C
Poll Books* (some#)	17C–19C

---

*Printed or transcribed
#Microfilm copy available at the LDS Family History Library in Salt Lake City, Utah, and through the LDS Family History Centers.

SOURCES THAT MAY ADDITIONALLY PROVIDE VITAL DATA AND/OR PROVE FAMILY RELATIONSHIPS

Cemetery Registers#	1835– early 20C
Census‡# (post-1974 county area)	1841–1881
Church of England (diocesan)	
Bishops' Transcripts#§	16C–19C
Church of England (parish)	
Parish Registers (some#)	16C–20C
Estate and Family Papers	13C–20C
Manorial Records	1275–20C
Monumental Inscriptions	19C–20C
Nonconformist Registers	
Baptist‡#	1646–1840
Independent/Congregational/ Presbyterian‡#	1748–1985
Methodist (some‡#)	1786–1981
Marriages for closed churches	1870–
Society of Friends‡#	1646–1940
Unitarian‡#	1681–1983
Poor Law Unions	
Guardians' Minutes and Accounts	1838–1929
Probate	1858–1928
Calendars of Grants of Probates, and Letters of Administration	
School Records	19C–20C
Title Deeds	16C–19C

PUBLICATIONS†

(Various handlists to types of records in preparation)

#Microfilm copy available at the LDS Family History Library in Salt Lake City, Utah, and through the LDS Family History Centers.

‡Microfilm/microfiche copies available at above repository

§Wills, Marriage Licence Bonds and Allegations, Bishops' Transcripts located at the Borthwick Institute in York.

†For additional information send 2 Postal Reply Coupons or 31 pence of English postage for reply to North America; 34 pence to Australia and New Zealand.

BARNSLEY METROPOLITAN DISTRICT

(Barnsley, Cudworth, Darfield, Darton, Dearne,
Dodworth, Hoyland Nether, Penistone, Royston,
Wombwell, Worsbroug, pt. Hemsworth, pt. Wortley)

BARNSLEY CENTRAL LIBRARY
Local Studies Department
Shambles Street
Barnsley, South Yorkshire S70 2JF
Tel. 0226 733241 ext. 41
Contact: Local Studies Librarian
Hours: M-F 9:30-1, 2-6; S 9:30-1, 2-5
         (Prior appointment requested)
Admission free

HOLDINGS

Resources pertaining to the areas now in Barnsley Metropolitan District.

SOURCES THAT IDENTIFY AN INDIVIDUAL
WITH A SPECIFIC LOCATION

Borough Records		1869–
Business Records		19C–
Directories* (some#)		1816/1817–
Local Histories*		19C–20C
Maps		19C–
Periodicals*		19C–
Poll Books* (some#)	(periodic)	1748, 1807–
Rate Books		1825–
Registers of Electors*		1844, 1869–

---

*Printed or transcribed
#Microfilm copy available at the LDS Family History Library in Salt Lake City,
Utah, and through the LDS Family History Centers.

SOURCES THAT MAY ADDITIONALLY PROVIDE VITAL DATA AND/OR PROVE FAMILY RELATIONSHIPS

Cemetery Records	1886–1938
Census‡#	1841–1881
International Genealogical Index‡##	
Monumental Inscriptions	
Newspapers*	mid-19C–
Nonconformist Registers	
Methodist	1816–
United Reformed	1827–
(Congregational/Presbyterian)	
Society and Charity Records	late 19C–20C

DONCASTER METROPOLITAN DISTRICT

(Doncaster, Adwick le Street,
Bentley with Arksey, Conisbrough,
Mexborough, Tickhill, Thorne)

DONCASTER ARCHIVES DEPARTMENT
King Edward Road, Balby,
Doncaster, South Yorkshire DN4 0NA
Tel. 0302 859811

Hours: M-F 9:30-12:30, 2-5; closed S

Admission free

---

‡Microfilm/microfiche copies available at above repository
#Microfilm copy available at the LDS Family History Library in Salt Lake City, Utah, and through the LDS Family History Centers.
##Microfiche copy available at the LDS Family History Library in Salt Lake City, Utah, and through the LDS Family History Centers.
*Printed or transcribed

HOLDINGS

Church of England parish records (Archdeaconry of Doncaster, Diocese of Sheffield) including deposited Parish Registers for approximately 70 churches in the district; other resources pertaining to the Doncaster district.

SOURCES THAT IDENTIFY AN INDIVIDUAL WITH A SPECIFIC LOCATION

Borough Records (Doncaster)	15C–19C
Rates	19C–20C
Business Records	
Church of England (parish)	17C–19C
Churchwardens' Accounts	19C–20C
Magistrates' Court	19C–20C
Trade Union Records	

SOURCES THAT MAY ADDITIONALLY PROVIDE VITAL DATA AND/OR PROVE FAMILY RELATIONSHIPS

Borough Records (Doncaster)	15C–19C
Quarter Sessions	
Title Deeds	
Church of England (parish)	
Parish Registers	16C–
Estate and Family Papers	17C–20C
Nonconformist Registers	19C–20C
Methodist	19C–20C
School Records	19C–20C
Society Records	

PUBLICATIONS†

Guide to Doncaster Archives (2nd ed., 1981)
List: *Parish Registers Deposited in the Diocesan Record Office* (free)

---

†For additional information send 2 Postal Reply Coupons or 31 pence of English postage for reply to North America; 34 pence to Australia and New Zealand.

ROTHERHAM METROPOLITAN DISTRICT

(Rotherham, Maltby, Rawmarsh, Swinton,
Wath upon Dearne, Kiveton Park)

BRIAN O'MALLEY LIBRARY

Archives and Local Studies Section
Walker Place, Rotherham S65 1JH
Tel. 0709 382121 ext. 3583

Hours: M, T, F 10-5; W 1-7; Th 10-7; S 9-5
        (Prior appointment advised for microfilm reader)

Admission free

List of researchers available upon request†

HOLDINGS

Resources pertaining primarily to areas now in the Rotherham Metropolitan District.

SOURCES THAT IDENTIFY AN INDIVIDUAL
WITH A SPECIFIC LOCATION

Directories* (some#)	1822–1974
Enclosure Awards	19C
Local Histories*	19C–20C
Maps	18C–20C
Periodicals*	19C–20C
Rate Books	19C–20C
Society Records	

---

†For additional information send 2 Postal Reply Coupons or 31 pence of English postage for reply to North America; 34 pence to Australia and New Zealand.

*Printed or transcribed

#Microfilm copy available at the LDS Family History Library in Salt Lake City, Utah, and through the LDS Family History Centers.

*SOURCES THAT MAY ADDITIONALLY PROVIDE VITAL
DATA AND/OR PROVE FAMILY RELATIONSHIPS*

Cemetery Records#	19C–
Census‡#	1841–1881
Church of England (parish)	
Parish Registers (some‡#)	16C–19C
Parish Register Transcripts*	16C–19C
Estate and Family Papers	
International Genealogical Index‡##	
(England)	
Newspapers‡#	mid-19C–
Nonconformist Registers	
Congregational	1867–1955
Methodist	c. 1800–20C
Unitarian	18C–19C
Pedigree Records	
Poor Law Union	1834–20C
Workhouse Records	
School Records	19C–20C

#Microfilm copy available at the LDS Family History Library in Salt Lake City,
Utah, and through the LDS Family History Centers.
‡Microfilm/microfiche copies available at above repository
*Printed or transcribed
##Microfiche copy available at the LDS Family History Library in Salt Lake
City, Utah, and through the LDS Family History Centers.

OTHER REPOSITORIES

The sources listed below include only those items reported on the Record Office Survey as located in the specified repositories. Each city and county library should have additional printed materials pertaining to its geographical area.

DONCASTER CENTRAL LIBRARY†
Local History Department
Waterdale, Doncaster DN1 3JE
Tel. 0302 734305

    Census‡#   1841–1881
    Local Histories*
    Maps
    Newspapers‡#

LDS FAMILY HISTORY CENTRE†
Wheel Lane, Grenoside
Sheffield S30 3RN
Tel. 0742 453231

    LDS Family History Library Catalog‡##
    International Genealogical Index‡##

---

†For additional information send 2 Postal Reply Coupons or 31 pence of English postage for reply to North America; 34 pence to Australia and New Zealand.
‡Microfilm/microfiche copies available at above repository
#Microfilm copy available at the LDS Family History Library in Salt Lake City, Utah, and through the LDS Family History Centers.
*Printed or transcribed
##Microfiche copy available at the LDS Family History Library in Salt Lake City, Utah, and through the LDS Family History Centers.

GENEALOGICAL AND FAMILY HISTORY SOCIETIES

The societies listed below may have recorded Monumental (tombstone) Inscriptions, compiled an Index to Marriages (from the Parish Registers), an Index to the 1851 Census, and other special indexes, e.g., Strays, Members' Interests, for their geographical areas.** Each Society publishes a quarterly journal (listed in italics) which includes articles on family history, reports on the group's projects, and members' queries.

**SHEFFIELD AND DISTRICT
FAMILY HISTORY SOCIETY**†
Mrs. Marjorie Dunn, Secretary
359 Baslow Road
Sheffield S17 3BH

Flowing Stream

**See *Current Publications by Member Societies* (annual), *List of Family History Project Coordinators*, 6th ed., and *Family History News and Digest* (biennial) — all published by the Federation of Family History Societies; available in the USA from the International Society for British Genealogy and Family History, P.O. Box 20425, Cleveland, OH 44120.

†For additional information send 2 Postal Reply Coupons or 31 pence of English postage for reply to North America; 34 pence to Australia and New Zealand.

WEST YORKSHIRE

Post-1974 Counties of England

The West Yorkshire Metropolitan County was created in 1974. Its geographical extent covers the largely urban center of the old West Riding of Yorkshire.

Local government reorganization in 1974 abolished all independent Borough, Rural District Council and Urban District Council administrations within the old West Riding. These included the pre-seventeenth-century Boroughs of Pontefract and Ripon, and that of Leeds, which had become a County Borough in the nineteenth century, and also the other County Boroughs of Bradford, Halifax, Dewsbury, Huddersfield and Wakefield.

479

In the place of these superseded authorities five Metropolitan Districts came into existence, namely Bradford, Calderdale (Halifax), Kirklees (Huddersfield and Dewsbury), Leeds and Wakefield.

The West Yorkshire Metropolitan County Council was abolished by Act of Parliament on 1 April 1986. The region continues to bear the title West Yorkshire but administrative functions are vested in the five District Councils (Bradford, Calderdale, Kirklees, Leeds and Wakefield), who carry out their responsibilities either individually districtwide or jointly countywide, via joint boards and joint committees.

The West Yorkshire Archive Service is administered by the West Yorkshire Archives and Archæology Joint Committee, of which Wakefield is the lead authority.

In addition to the offices within each district, the Joint Committee administers the archives held by the Yorkshire Archæological Society in Leeds, founded in 1863.

WEST YORKSHIRE ARCHIVE SERVICE

WAKEFIELD METROPOLITAN DISTRICT

(Wakefield, Castleford, Ossett, Pontefract, Featherstone, Hemsworth, Horbury, Knottingley, Normanton, Stanley, pt. Osgoldcross)

WEST YORKSHIRE ARCHIVE SERVICE HEADQUARTERS AND WAKEFIELD REGISTRY OF DEEDS
(Formerly Yorkshire West Riding Record Office)
Newstead Road, Wakefield WF1 2DE
Tel. 0924 367111 ext. 2352
Contact: Archivist to the Joint Committee

Hours: M 9-8; T-Th 9-5; F 9-1; closed S

Admission free

BRADFORD METROPOLITAN DISTRICT

(Bradford, Keighley, Baildon, Bingley,
Denholme, Ilkley, Shipley, Silsden,
pt. Skipton, pt. Queensbury and Shelf)

WEST YORKSHIRE ARCHIVE SERVICE: BRADFORD
15 Canal Road, Bradford BD1 4AT
Tel. 0274 731931
Contact: District Archivist

Hours: M-W 9:30-1, 2-5; Th 9:30-1, 2-8; F 9:30-1; closed S

Admission free

CALDERDALE METROPOLITAN DISTRICT

(Halifax, Brighouse, Todmorden, Elland,
Hebden Royd, Ripponden, Sowerby Bridge,
Hapton, pt. Queensbury and Shelf)

WEST YORKSHIRE ARCHIVE SERVICE: CALDERDALE
Central Library, Northgate House
Northgate, Halifax HX1 1UN
Tel. 0422 57257 ext. 2636
Contact: District Archivist

Hours: Archives M, T, Th, F 10-5:30; by appointment W 10-12

Admission free

KIRKLEES METROPOLITAN DISTRICT

(Dewsbury, Huddersfield, Batley, Spenborough,
Colne Valley, Denby Dale, Heckmondwike,
Holmfirth, Kirkburton, Meltham, Mirfield)

WEST YORKSHIRE ARCHIVE SERVICE: KIRKLEES
Central Library, Princess Alexandra Walk
Huddersfield HD1 2SU
Tel. 0484 513808 ext. 207
Contact: District Archivist

Hours: M-Th 9-8; F 9-4; By prior appointment S

Admission free

LEEDS METROPOLITAN DISTRICT

(Leeds, Morley, Pudsey, Aireborough,
Garforth, Horsforth, Otley, Rothwell,
pt. Tadcaster, pt. Wetherby, pt. Wharfedale)

WEST YORKSHIRE ARCHIVE SERVICE: LEEDS
Chapeltown Road
Sheepscar, Leeds LS7 3AP
Tel. 0532 628339
Contact: District Archivist

Hours: By prior appointment M-F 9:30-5

Admission free

WEST YORKSHIRE ARCHIVE SERVICE:
YORKSHIRE ARCHÆOLOGICAL SOCIETY
Claremont, 23 Clarendon Road
Leeds LS2 9NZ
Tel. 0532 456362
Contact: Archivist-in-Charge

Hours: Th, F, 2nd and 4th M 9:30-5; T, W 2-8:30;
By prior appointment 1st, 3rd S/mo 9:30-5
Closed 1st, 3rd M; 2nd, 4th S

HOLDINGS‡‡

Resources pertaining to the county of West Yorkshire and the former West Riding, including administrative records at county and district levels.

As records held in the individual districts vary, searchers should write to the Archivist to the Joint Committee for further details about the holdings in each office.

SOURCES THAT IDENTIFY AN INDIVIDUAL WITH A SPECIFIC LOCATION

Borough Records (including Bradford, Leeds, Halifax, Wakefield)	1662–20C
Court	1662–1835
Rates	1713–20C
Business Records	18C–20C
Church of England (diocesan)†† (Ripon and Wakefield dioceses)	
Ecclesiastical Court Books (Ripon)	1543–1896
Ecclesiastical Visitations	1577–1931
Church of England (parish) (Bradford, pt. Ripon and Wakefield dioceses)	
Churchwardens' Accounts	17C–19C
Tithe Apportionments§	1840's
Directories* (some#)	1822–20C
Enclosure Awards	18C–19C

---

‡‡At the request of the Archivist to the Joint Committee, resources for all repositories of the West Yorkshire Archive Service have been consolidated into one list. Contact the Archivist to the Joint Committee, c/o West Yorkshire Archive Service Headquarters, for additional information.

††For pre-1888 diocesan records for Bradford, Calderdale, Kirklees and Wakefield areas and pre-1543 diocesan records for Leeds area see Borthwick Institute, York.

§Parish copies only, main series at the Borthwick Institute, York.

*Printed or transcribed

#Microfilm copy available at the LDS Family History Library in Salt Lake City, Utah, and through the LDS Family History Centers.

Manorial Records

Court Rolls*	13C–20C
Maps	16C–20C
Parish Poor Law Records	17C–19C
Parish Poor Rates	18C–19C
Poll Books*‡ (some#)	19C

Quarter Sessions

Indictment Books	17C–20C
Land Tax Assessment§§	18C–1832
Lists of Jurors	20C
Order Books*	17C–20C
Registration of Papist Property	1717–1737
Registers of Electors*	1840–20C
Sessions Rolls	17C–20C
Trade Union Records	18C–20C
West Riding Registry of Deeds (Wakefield)‡‡	1704–1970

SOURCES THAT MAY ADDITIONALLY PROVIDE VITAL DATA AND/OR PROVE FAMILY RELATIONSHIPS

Cemetery Records	16C–20C
Census‡# (Calderdale and Kirklees only)‡‡	1841–1881
Charity Records	19C

Church of England (diocesan)

Bishops' Transcripts	17C–20C
Marriage Bonds and Allegations	17C–20C
Will, Admon., Inven. (Leeds)‡‡	15C–1858

Church of England (parish)

Parish Registers‡#	16C–20C
Parish Register Transcripts*	16C–19C

---

*Printed or transcribed

‡Microfilm/microfiche copies available at above repository

#Microfilm copy available at the LDS Family History Library in Salt Lake City, Utah, and through the LDS Family History Centers.

§§Duplicate

‡‡Located only at repositories named

Estate and Family Papers	12C–20C
Hospital Records	20C
International Genealogical Index‡##	
(Yorkshire)	
Manorial Records*	12C–20C
Monumental Inscriptions	16C–20C
Nonconformist Registers	
Baptist‡#	17C–20C
Christian Bretheren (Kirklees)‡‡	19C–20C
Congregational‡#	18C–20C
Evangelical Free (Calderdale)‡‡	19C–20C
Independent/Congregational (some#)	17C–20C
Inghamite‡# (Calderdale)‡‡	19C
Methodist‡#	18C–20C
Presbyterian/Unitarian‡#	17C–20C
(Calderdale)‡‡	
Unitarian (some#) (Kirklees)‡‡	19C–20C
Parish Poor Law Records	17C–19C
Apprenticeship Indentures	
Examinations	
Removal Orders	
Settlement Papers	
Poor Law Union	1844–20C
Roman Catholic Registers‡#	1827–1840
(Calderdale)‡‡	
School Records	19C–20C
Society Records	18C–20C
Title Deeds	11C–20C
Wills*	14C–1932

---

‡Microfilm/microfiche copies available at above repository
##Microfiche copy available at the LDS Family History Library in Salt Lake City, Utah, and through the LDS Family History Centers.
*Printed or transcribed
#Microfilm copy available at the LDS Family History Library in Salt Lake City, Utah, and through the LDS Family History Centers.
‡‡Located only at repositories named

PUBLICATIONS†

Guide to the West Yorkshire Archive Service for
Family Historians (1984)

B.J. Barber, Guide to the Quarter Sessions of the West
Riding of Yorkshire 1637–1971 and Other Official
Records (1984)

B.J. Barber and M.W. Beresford, The West Riding County
Council 1889–1974: Historical Studies (1978)

E.W. Crossley, ed., Catalogue of Manuscripts and Deeds in
the Library of the Yorkshire Archæological Society
1867–1931 (1931; reprinted 1986)

S. Thomas, Guide to the Archive Collections of the
Yorkshire Archæological Society 1931–1933 and to
Collections Deposited with the Society (1985)

R.W. Unwin, Search Guide to the English Land Tax (1982)

Leaflets/Lists available upon request:

West Yorkshire Archive Service
West Yorkshire Archive Service: General Information
West Yorkshire Archive Service: Tracing Your
Family Tree – A Beginner's Guide
List of Record Searchers
List of Useful Addresses

Bradford
West Yorkshire Archive Service: Bradford

Calderdale
West Yorkshire Archive Service: Calderdale
Archives on Microfilm: Calderdale Parish Registers
Archives on Microfilm: Summary List
Calderdale Archives in Print (Excluding Parochial
and Non-parochial Registers)
Calderdale Parochial and Non-parochial Registers in
Print

---

†For additional information send 2 Postal Reply Coupons or 31 pence of English
postage for reply to North America; 34 pence to Australia and New Zealand.

Census Returns (on Microfilm) (1985)
Diocesan (Bishops') Transcripts of Parish Registers on Microfilm (1984)
Tombstone Schedules/Transcripts of Graveyard Descriptions (1985)
Calderdale Non-parochial Registers (on microfilm)
Map of the Manor of Wakefield
Map of the Ancient Parish of Halifax

Kirklees

West Yorkshire Archives Service: Kirklees
Local Studies: Kirklees

Leeds

West Yorkshire Archives Service: Leeds
Bishops' Transcripts of Parish Registers Deposited in the Leeds Archives Department
Probate Records in the Leeds Archives Department
Leeds Parish Registers
Deposited Parish Registers

Wakefield Headquarters

West Yorkshire Archives Service: Wakefield Headquarters

Yorkshire Archæological Society

West Yorkshire Archives Service: Yorkshire Archæological Society

OTHER REPOSITORIES

The sources listed below include only those items reported on the Record Office Survey as located in the specified repositories. Each city and county library should have additional printed materials pertaining to its geographical area.

BRADFORD CENTRAL LIBRARY†
Reference Department
Prince's Way, Bradford BD1 1NN
Tel. 0274 758688

Census‡#   1841–1881
Directories*
International Genealogical Index‡##
    (Great Britain)
Monumental Inscriptions*

HUDDERSFIELD CENTRAL LIBRARY†
Local Studies Section
Princess Alexandra Walk
Huddersfield HD1 2SU
Tel. 0484 21356 ext. 206
Contact: Local Studies Librarian

Census‡#   1841–1881
Directories* (some#)   19C
    Trade
Church of England (parish)
    Parish Register Index# (Yorks)   19C–
International Genealogical Index‡##
Newspapers#   19C–
Poll Books* (some#)   19C

---

†For additional information send 2 Postal Reply Coupons or 31 pence of English
postage for reply to North America; 34 pence to Australia and New Zealand.
‡Microfilm/microfiche copies available at above repository
#Microfilm copy available at the LDS Family History Library in Salt Lake City,
Utah, and through the LDS Family History Centers.
*Printed or transcribed
##Microfiche copy available at the LDS Family History Library in Salt Lake
City, Utah, and through the LDS Family History Centers.

LEEDS CENTRAL LIBRARY†
Reference Library
Calverley Street
Leeds LS1 3AB
Tel. 0532 462464
Contact: Local History Librarian

Census‡# (Yorks)	1841–1881
Directories* (some#)	19C
Trade	
Church of England (parish)	
Parish Registers‡#	16C–
Parish Register Transcripts*	16C–19C
International Genealogical Index‡##	
(Yorks)	
Maps	
Periodicals*	

LDS FAMILY HISTORY CENTRE†
Vesper Road
Leeds, West Yorkshire
Tel. 0532 585297

   LDS Family History Library Catalog‡##
   International Genealogical Index‡##

---

†For additional information send 2 Postal Reply Coupons or 31 pence of English postage for reply to North America; 34 pence to Australia and New Zealand.

‡Microfilm/microfiche copies available at above repository

#Microfilm copy available at the LDS Family History Library in Salt Lake City, Utah, and through the LDS Family History Centers.

*Printed or transcribed

##Microfiche copy available at the LDS Family History Library in Salt Lake City, Utah, and through the LDS Family History Centers.

LDS FAMILY HISTORY CENTRE†
12 Halifax Road, Birchencliffe
Huddersfield HD3 8BY
Tel. 0484 20352

LDS Family History Library Catalog‡##
International Genealogical Index‡##

GENEALOGICAL AND FAMILY HISTORY SOCIETIES

The societies listed below may have recorded Monumental (tombstone) Inscriptions, compiled an Index to Marriages (from the Parish Registers), an Index to the 1851 Census, and other special indexes, e.g., Strays, Members' Interests, for their geographical areas.** Each Society publishes a quarterly journal (listed in italics) which includes articles on family history, reports on the group's projects, and members' queries.

FAMILY HISTORY SECTION
YORKSHIRE ARCHÆOLOGICAL SOCIETY†
Mrs. B. Shimmel, Hon. Secretary
Claremont, 23 Clarendon Road
Leeds LS2 9NZ

The Yorkshire Family Historian

---

†For additional information send 2 Postal Reply Coupons or 31 pence of English postage for reply to North America; 34 pence to Australia and New Zealand.
‡Microfilm/microfiche copies available at above repository
##Microfiche copy available at the LDS Family History Library in Salt Lake City, Utah, and through the LDS Family History Centers.
**See *Current Publications by Member Societies* (annual), *List of Family History Project Coordinators*, 6th ed., and *Family History News and Digest* (biennial) — all published by the Federation of Family History Societies; available in the USA from the International Society for British Genealogy and Family History, P.O. Box 20425, Cleveland, OH 44120.

PART III

LONDON BOROUGH

REPOSITORIES

GREATER LONDON

The area of Greater London was created in 1965. It includes the former County of London (created in 1889) and the former County of Middlesex.

Additionally it includes East Ham, a Municipal Borough in Essex between 1904 and 1915, and a County Borough from 1915 and 1965; West Ham, a Municipal Borough in Essex from 1886 to 1889, and a County Borough from 1889 to 1965; and Croydon, a Municipal Borough in Surrey from 1883 to 1889, and a County Borough from 1889 to 1965.

Areas from Essex which were transferred to Greater London include Barking, Chingford, Dagenham, Hornchurch, Ilford, Leyton, Romford, Wanstead and Woodford and Walthamstow. All except Hornchurch became Municipal Boroughs during the twentieth century.

The Urban Districts of Barnet and East Barnet were transferred from Hertfordshire. In Kent the Municipal Boroughs of Beckenham, Bexley, Bromley and Erith were transferred along with the Urban Districts of Chislehurst and Sidcup, Crayford, Orpington, and Penge. From Surrey areas transferred included Barnes, Beddington and Wallington, Carshalton, Coulsdon, Kingston upon Thames, Malden and Coombe, Merton and Morden, Mitcham, Purley, Richmond, Surbiton, Sutton and Cheam, and Wimbledon. Kingston upon Thames (1835) and Richmond (1880) became Municipal Boroughs prior to 1900, while all others except Carshalton, Coulsden, Merton and Morden, and Purley were incorporated during the twentieth century.

The various metropolitan boroughs and urban districts in the areas transferred in 1965 to Greater London were merged at that time into thirty-two larger governmental units known as London Boroughs. A list of the existing London Boroughs, together with names of the areas from which each was formed, is given below.

The Greater London Council was created in 1965 and abolished in 1986.

BARKING AND DAGENHAM

(Essex: pt. Barking, pt. Dagenham)

Post-1965 London Boroughs

VALENCE REFERENCE LIBRARY
Becontree Avenue
Dagenham, Essex RM8 3HT
Tel. (01) 592 6537
Contact: Reference Librarian or Archivist

Hours: M, T, Th, F 9:30-7; W, S 9:30-1

HOLDINGS

Resources pertaining to the areas now in the London Borough of Barking and Dagenham and their administrative predecessors.

SOURCES THAT IDENTIFY AN INDIVIDUAL
WITH A SPECIFIC LOCATION

Church of England (diocesan)
Tithe Records	17C–19C
Vestry Minutes	17C–19C

Church of England (parish)
Churchwardens' Accounts	17C–19C
Rates	18C–19C
Directories* (some#)	late 19C–20C
Local Histories*	
Maps	20C
Periodicals*	19C–20C
Rate Books	
(Barking)	(gaps) 18C–20C
(Dagenham)	20C
Registers of Electors*	
(Barking)	20C
(Dagenham)	1832–1900*,
	1900–1935‡#,
	1936–

SOURCES THAT MAY ADDITIONALLY PROVIDE VITAL
DATA AND/OR PROVE FAMILY RELATIONSHIPS

Census‡#	1841–1881
Charity Records (Barking)	19C–20C
Church of England (parish)	
Parish Registers‡#	1558–20C
Estate and Family Papers	
Hospital Records (Barking)	1893–1936
Manorial Records†† (Barking)	14C–18C
Newspapers‡#	late 19C–20C

---

*Printed or transcribed

#Microfilm copy available at the LDS Family History Library in Salt Lake City, Utah, and through the LDS Family History Centers.

‡Microfilm/microfiche copies available at above repository

††Translation

Poor Law Union
    Guardians' Minute Books‡#   1836–1930
School Records
    (Barking)   late 19C–20C
    (Dagenham)   19C
Society Records (Barking)   19C
Title Deeds   15C–19C

PUBLICATIONS†

Leaflet: *Guide to Local History Resources* (free)

BARKING CENTRAL LIBRARY
Town Square, Barking, Essex 1G11 7NB
Tel. (01) 517 8666
Contact: Reference Librarian
Hours: M, T, Th, F 9:30-7;
    W 9:30-5; S 9:30-1

HOLDINGS

Some printed sources pertaining to the former Borough of Barking and its administrative predecessors.

Church of England (parish)
    Parish Register Transcripts*§   16C–19C
Directories* (some#)
Local Histories*
Maps
Newspapers#§   20C
Periodicals*

---

‡Microfilm/microfiche copies available at above repository
#Microfilm copy available at the LDS Family History Library in Salt Lake City, Utah, and through the LDS Family History Centers.
†For additional information send 2 Postal Reply Coupons or 31 pence of English postage for reply to North America; 34 pence to Australia and New Zealand.
*Printed or transcribed
§May provide vital data and/or proof of family relationships.

BARNET

(Herts: Barnet, E. Barnet, Totteridge)
(Middx: Edgware, Finchley,
Friern Barnet, Hendon)

Post-1965 London Boroughs

LOCAL HISTORY LIBRARY
Hendon Catholic Social Centre
Church Walk, Egerton Gardens
London NW4
Tel. (01) 202 5625 ext. 55

(Postal Address)
LOCAL HISTORY LIBRARY
Ravensfield House
The Burroughs, Hendon NW4 4BE
Attn: The Borough Librarian

497

Hours: M, Th, F 9:30-12:30; T, W 9-5; S 9-4
(Extended hours pending)
Prior appointment necessary

HOLDINGS

Resources pertaining to areas now in the London Borough of Barnet, and their administrative predecessors.

SOURCES THAT IDENTIFY AN INDIVIDUAL WITH A SPECIFIC LOCATION

Business Records	19C
Church of England (diocesan)	
Tithe Maps and Awards§	1840's
Church of England (parish)	
Overseers of the Poor Records	18C–19C
Churchwardens' Accounts (Hendon)	17C–19C
Vestry Minutes (Finchley, Hendon)	18C–20C
Directories* (some#)	20C
Enclosure Awards	1814–1816
Land Tax Assessments	18C–19C
(Barnet, E. Barnet, Totteridge)	
Local Histories*	
Maps	19C–20C
Periodicals* (some#)	
Rate Books	18C–20C
Registers of Electors*	20C

---

§Parish copies only

*Printed or transcribed

#Microfilm copy available at the LDS Family History Library in Salt Lake City, Utah, and through the LDS Family History Centers.

SOURCES THAT MAY ADDITIONALLY PROVIDE VITAL DATA AND/OR PROVE FAMILY RELATIONSHIPS

Census‡#	1841–1881
Census (Hendon)	1801–1821
Charity Records	18C–19C
Estate and Family Papers	19C–20C
Newspapers‡#	19C–20C
Nonconformist Registers	
Congregational (Finchley)	19C–20C
Title Deeds (Hendon, Finchley)	

PUBLICATIONS†

Leaflet: *Archives and Records in the Local History Collection* (free)

CHIPPING BARNET LIBRARY
Church Passage
Barnet, Herts
Tel. (01) 499 0321

Hours: M, T, W, Th 9-8; F 9-5; S 9-4

HOLDINGS

Some printed resources pertaining to the former urban district of Chipping Barnet and its administrative predecessors.

---

‡Microfilm/microfiche copies available at above repository

#Microfilm copy available at the LDS Family History Library in Salt Lake City, Utah, and through the LDS Family History Centers.

†For additional information send 2 Postal Reply Coupons or 31 pence of English postage for reply to North America; 34 pence to Australia and New Zealand.

CHURCH END (FINCHLEY) LIBRARY
24 Hendon Lane
London N3
Tel. (01) 346 5711

Hours: M, T, W, Th 9-8; F 9-5; S 9-4

HOLDINGS

Some printed resources pertaining to the former Borough of Finchley and its administrative predecessors.

BEXLEY

(Kent: Bexley, Erith, Crayford,
pts. Chislehurst and Sidcup)

Post-1965 London Boroughs

THE LOCAL STUDIES CENTRE
BEXLEY LIBRARIES AND MUSEUMS DEPARTMENT
Hall Place, Bourne Road
Bexley, Kent DA5 1PQ
Tel. 0322 526574
Contact: Local Studies Librarian
Hours: M-S 10-4

HOLDINGS

Resources pertaining to the areas now in the London Borough of Bexley and their administrative predecessors.

SOURCES THAT IDENTIFY AN INDIVIDUAL WITH A SPECIFIC LOCATION

Business Records	20C
Church of England (diocesan)	
Tithe Apportionments§ (Bexley)	1840's
Church of England (parish)	18C–20C
Churchwardens' Accounts	late 18C–19C
Parish Poor Rates	18C–19C
Vestry Minutes	18C–20C
Directories* (some#)	1812–
Enclosure Awards	1815, 1819
Local Histories*	
Maps	16C–
Periodicals*	
Poll Books* (some#)	18C–19C
Rate Books	18C–19C

SOURCES THAT MAY ADDITIONALLY PROVIDE VITAL DATA AND/OR PROVE FAMILY RELATIONSHIPS

Census‡#	1841–1881
Charity Records	17C
Church of England (parish)	
Parish Registers#	16C–1812
Parish Register Transcripts* (Bexley)	1565–1812

---

§Parish copies only
*Printed or transcribed
#Microfilm copy available at the LDS Family History Library in Salt Lake City, Utah, and through the LDS Family History Centers.
‡Microfilm/microfiche copies available at above repository

Estate and Family Papers	17C–
International Genealogical Index‡##	
(Essex, Kent, Surrey,	
Sussex and London)	
Manorial Records (Erith)	1659–1901
Newspapers*	1875–20C
Nonconformist Registers	
Baptist (Erith)	1859–1934
School Records	19C–
Society Records	20C
Title Deeds	17C–20C

PUBLICATIONS†

Leaflets:

A Guide to Local History Resources (1983)
Tracing Your Family Tree (1986)
The Local Studies Centre

---

‡Microfilm/microfiche copies available at above repository
##Microfiche copy available at the LDS Family History Library in Salt Lake City, Utah, and through the LDS Family History Centers.
*Printed or transcribed

†For additional information send 2 Postal Reply Coupons or 31 pence of English postage for reply to North America; 34 pence to Australia and New Zealand.

BRENT

(Middx: Wembley, Willesden)

Post-1965 London Boroughs

GRANGE MUSEUM OF LOCAL HISTORY
Neasden Lane, London NW10 1QB
Tel. (01) 908 7432

Hours: M, T, Th, F 12-5; W 12-8; S 10-5

HOLDINGS

Resources pertaining to the areas now in the London Borough of Brent and their administrative predecessors.

SOURCES THAT IDENTIFY AN INDIVIDUAL WITH A SPECIFIC LOCATION

Church of England (diocesan)	
Tithe Apportionments§	1840's
(Willesden, Kingsbury)	
Church of England (parish)	
Parish Poor Rate	18C–19C
Directories* (some#)	late 19C–20C
Enclosure Awards (Willesden)	1823
Local Histories*	
Maps	19C–20C
Periodicals*	
Rate Books	19C–20C
Registers of Electors*	late 19C–20C

SOURCES THAT MAY ADDITIONALLY PROVIDE VITAL DATA AND/OR PROVE FAMILY RELATIONSHIPS

Census (Brent)	1841–1871,*
	1881‡#
Church of England (parish)	
Parish Register Transcripts*	16C–19C

---

§Parish copies only

*Printed or transcribed

#Microfilm copy available at the LDS Family History Library in Salt Lake City, Utah, and through the LDS Family History Centers.

‡Microfilm/microfiche copies available at above repository

Estate and Family Papers
International Genealogical Index‡##
Newspapers*   late 19C–20C
Title Deeds*†† 1709–1869
Wills 19C–20C

PUBLICATIONS†

Leaflet: *Family History: Sources of Information at the
Grange Museum of Local History*

---

‡Microfilm/microfiche copies available at above repository
##Microfiche copy available at the LDS Family History Library in Salt Lake
City, Utah, and through the LDS Family History Centers.
*Printed or transcribed
††Willesden extracts from Middlesex Register of Deeds.
†For additional information send 2 Postal Reply Coupons or 31 pence of English
postage for reply to North America; 34 pence to Australia and New Zealand.

BROMLEY

(Kent: Beckenham, Bromley, Orpington,
Penge, pts. Chislehurst and Sidcup)

Post-1965 London Boroughs

BROMLEY CENTRAL LIBRARY
Local Studies Library
High Street, Bromley BR1 1EX
Tel. (01) 460 9955 ext. 261
Contact: Archivist

Hours: T, Th 9:30-8; W, F 9:30-6; S 9:30-5; closed M
        Prior appointment needed
        to view records and newspapers

HOLDINGS

Resources pertaining to the areas now in the London
Borough of Bromley and their administrative predecessors.

507

SOURCES THAT IDENTIFY AN INDIVIDUAL
WITH A SPECIFIC LOCATION

Church of England (diocesan)
Tithe Apportionments§   1840's
Church of England (parish)
   Churchwardens' Accounts   1806–1833
   Parish Poor Rates   17C–19C
   Vestry Records   c. 1700–1815
Directories* (some#)   late 19C–20C
Local Histories*   18C–20C
Land and Window Tax   (few) 1766–67
Maps   18C–20C
Periodicals*   19C–20C
Poll Books* (some#)   19C
Registers of Electors*   20C

SOURCES THAT MAY ADDITIONALLY PROVIDE VITAL
DATA AND/OR PROVE FAMILY RELATIONSHIPS

Census‡#   1841–1881
Church of England (parish)
   Parish Registers (also some‡#)   16C–20C
   Parish Register Transcripts* (some‡#)   16C–19C
Newspapers*   late 19C–20C
Wills*   15C–18C

PUBLICATIONS†

Leaflets:
Notes on Genealogical Sources
List of Deposited Parish Registers

---

§Parish copies only
*Printed or transcribed
#Microfilm copy available at the LDS Family History Library in Salt Lake City, Utah, and through the LDS Family History Centers.
‡Microfilm/microfiche copies available at above repository
†For additional information send 2 Postal Reply Coupons or 31 pence of English postage for reply to North America; 34 pence to Australia and New Zealand.

CAMDEN

(Middx: Hampstead, Holborn, and St. Pancras)

Post-1965 London Boroughs

SWISS COTTAGE LIBRARY
Local History Library
88 Avenue Road, London NW3 3HA
Tel. (01) 586 5989 ext. 209/234

Hours: M, T, Th 9:30-8; F 9:30-6; S 9:30-5; closed W
        (Prior appointment advised to view
        records or use microfilm reader)

HOLDINGS

Resources pertaining to the former Metropolitan Boroughs of Hampstead and St. Pancras and their administrative predecessors. (Some archives are outstored at Holborn Library – see next entry.)

SOURCES THAT IDENTIFY AN INDIVIDUAL WITH A SPECIFIC LOCATION

Business Records	19C–20C
Church of England (parish)	18C–19C
Parish Poor Rates	
Directories* (some#)	(gaps) mid-19C–20C
Local Histories*	
Maps	17C–20C
Periodicals*	19C–20C
Registers of Electors*	mid-19C–

SOURCES THAT MAY ADDITIONALLY PROVIDE VITAL DATA AND/OR PROVE FAMILY RELATIONSHIPS

Census (LB Camden)	1841–1881‡#
(Hampstead)	1801,1811
Church of England (parish)	
Parish Registers	1560–1842
(St. John Hampstead only)	
Parish Register Transcripts‡	17C–18C
Estate and Family Papers	18C–20C

---

*Printed or transcribed

#Microfilm copy available at the LDS Family History Library in Salt Lake City, Utah, and through the LDS Family History Centers.

‡Microfilm/microfiche copies available at above repository

International Genealogical Index‡##
(London, Middx)
Manorial Records   17C–19C
Monumental Inscriptions   19C–20C
Newspapers* (some‡#)   mid-19C–20C
Society and Charity Records   18C–20C
Title Deeds   18C–20C

HOLBORN LIBRARY
Local History Library
32-38 Theobalds Road, London WC1X 8PA
Tel. (01) 405 2706 ext. 337

Hours: M, Th 9:30-1, 2-8; T, F, S 9:30-5;
Closed W, some S
(Restricted service; prior appointment advised)

HOLDINGS

Resources pertaining to the areas now in the former Metropolitan Borough of Holborn and its administrative predecessors. Some archives pertaining to the areas now in the former Metropolitan Boroughs of St. Pancras and Hampstead are outstored here.

---

‡Microfilm/microfiche copies available at above repository
##Microfiche copy available at the LDS Family History Library in Salt Lake City, Utah, and through the LDS Family History Centers.
*Printed or transcribed
#Microfilm copy available at the LDS Family History Library in Salt Lake City, Utah, and through the LDS Family History Centers.

SOURCES THAT IDENTIFY AN INDIVIDUAL
WITH A SPECIFIC LOCATION

Business Records	19C–20C
Church of England (parish)	17C–19C
Parish Poor Rates (L.B. Camden)	
Vestry Minutes	
Directories* (some#)	(gaps) 19C–20C
Local Histories*	
Maps	16C–20C
Periodicals*	19C–20C
Rate Books (L.B. Camden)	18C–1966
Registers of Electors*	late 19C–20C

SOURCES THAT MAY ADDITIONALLY PROVIDE VITAL
DATA AND/OR PROVE FAMILY RELATIONSHIPS

Cemetery Records	1839–1984
(Highgate Cemetery)	
Church of England (parish)	
Parish Register Transcripts*	18C
Estate and Family Papers	18C–19C
Manorial Records	19C
Monumental Inscriptions	19C
Newspapers*	late 19C–20C
Title Deeds	17C–19C

PUBLICATIONS†

Pamphlet: *The Local History Library: Guide to the Collections* (1987)

---

*Printed or transcribed

#Microfilm copy available at the LDS Family History Library in Salt Lake City, Utah, and through the LDS Family History Centers.

†For additional information send 2 Postal Reply Coupons or 31 pence of English postage for reply to North America; 34 pence to Australia and New Zealand.

CROYDON

(Surrey: Croydon, Coulsdon and Purley)

Post-1965 London Boroughs

CROYDON PUBLIC LIBRARIES
Central Library
Katherine Street, Croydon CR9 1ET
Tel. (01) 760 5570
Contact: Local History Librarian

Hours: M 9:30-7; T-F 9:30-6; S 9-5
Prior appointment necessary

HOLDINGS

Resources pertaining to areas now in the London Borough of Croydon and their administrative predecessors.

513

SOURCES THAT IDENTIFY AN INDIVIDUAL
WITH A SPECIFIC LOCATION

Church of England (parish)

Churchwardens' Accounts		18C–19C
Vestry Minutes		18C–19C
Directories* (some#)	(gaps)	1851–1967
Enclosure Award		1797–1801
Local Histories*		
Maps		late 18C–
Periodicals*		19C–
Poll Books* (some#)	(periodic)	18C–19C
Rate Books		1744–1921
(Including Parish Poor Rates)		
Registers of Electors*		1883–

SOURCES THAT MAY ADDITIONALLY PROVIDE VITAL
DATA AND/OR PROVE FAMILY RELATIONSHIPS

Census‡#	1841–1881
Church of England (parish)	
Parish Registers‡#	1538–
Manorial Records	16C–19C
Newspapers*	1855–
Parish Poor Law Records	
Apprenticeship Indentures	1802–1842
Title Deeds	1329–

---

*Printed or transcribed

#Microfilm copy available at the LDS Family History Library in Salt Lake City, Utah, and through the LDS Family History Centers.

‡Microfilm/microfiche copies available at above repository

514

EALING

(Middx: Acton, Ealing, Southall)

Post-1965 London Boroughs

LOCAL HISTORY LIBRARY
Central Library
103 Ealing Broadway Centre
London W5 5JY
Tel. (01) 567 3656 ext. 37
Contact: Local History Librarian

Hours: T, Th, F 9-7:45; W, S 9-5; closed M

HOLDINGS

Resources pertaining to areas now in the London Borough of Ealing, and their administrative predecessors.

*SOURCES THAT IDENTIFY AN INDIVIDUAL
WITH A SPECIFIC LOCATION*

Church of England (parish)
Parish Poor Rates   17C–18C
Vestry Minutes   18C–20C
Directories* (some#)   (gaps) mid-19C–20C
Local Histories*
Maps   19C–20C
Parish Poor Law Records
Rates* (Ealing)   1696–1835
Periodicals*   20C
Registers of Electors*   late 19C–20C

*SOURCES THAT MAY ADDITIONALLY PROVIDE VITAL
DATA AND/OR PROVE FAMILY RELATIONSHIPS*

Census   1841‡#
                                 1851–1881§
Estate and Family Papers   19C–20C
Newspapers‡#   1866–
Nonconformist Registers
Methodist   1882–1960
School Records   19C–20C
Society and Charity Records   20C

---

*Printed or transcribed
#Microfilm copy available at the LDS Family History Library in Salt Lake City, Utah, and through the LDS Family History Centers.
‡Microfilm/microfiche copies available at above repository
§Photocopies

ENFIELD

(Middx: Edmonton, Enfield, Southgate)

Post-1965 London Boroughs

LOCAL HISTORY UNIT
Southgate Town Hall
Green Lanes, Palmers Green, London N13
Tel. (01) 882 8841 ext. 1145

Hours: M-S 9-5
(Prior appointment advised)

HOLDINGS

Resources pertaining to the areas now in the London Borough of Enfield and their administrative predecessors.

SOURCES THAT IDENTIFY AN INDIVIDUAL
WITH A SPECIFIC LOCATION

Church of England (parish)

Parish Poor Rates	18C–19C
Vestry Minutes	(gaps) 1671–1907
Directories* (some#)	late 19C–20C
Enclosure Awards	1801,1806
Local Histories*	
Maps	18C–
Periodicals*	mid-19C–
Rate Books	18C–19C
Registers of Electors*	late 19C–20C

SOURCES THAT MAY ADDITIONALLY PROVIDE VITAL
DATA AND/OR PROVE FAMILY RELATIONSHIPS

Census‡#	1841–1881
Manorial Records (Enfield)	18C–20C
Newspapers*‡#	mid-19C–20C
School Records	mid-19C–
Society Records (Local)	19C
Title Deeds*‡#	17C–

PUBLICATIONS†

Leaflets/Lists:
A Guide to Local History Resources
Enfield, Edmonton, Southgate: A Local
History Book List

---

*Printed or transcribed

#Microfilm copy available at the LDS Family History Library in Salt Lake City, Utah, and through the LDS Family History Centers.

‡Microfilm/microfiche copies available at above repository

†For additional information send 2 Postal Reply Coupons or 31 pence of English postage for reply to North America; 34 pence to Australia and New Zealand.

GREENWICH

(Kent: Greenwich, pt. Woolwich, Charlton, Kidbrooke,
pt. Blackheath, pt. Deptford, Eltham, Plumstead)

Post-1965 London Boroughs

**GREENWICH LOCAL HISTORY AND
ARCHIVES CENTRE**
Woodlands, 90 Mycenae Road
Blackheath, London SE3 7SE
Tel. (01) 858 4631

Hours: M, T, Th 9-8; S 9-5; closed W, F
        Prior appointment necessary
        for microfilm reader

HOLDINGS

Resources pertaining to the areas now in the London Borough of Greenwich and their administrative predecessors.

SOURCES THAT IDENTIFY AN INDIVIDUAL
WITH A SPECIFIC LOCATION

Business Records	19C–20C
Church of England (diocesan)	
Tithe Apportionments§	19C
Church of England (parish)	
Churchwardens' Accounts	(gaps) 17C–20C
Overseers' Accounts	17C–19C
Parish Poor Rates	17C–19C
Vestry Minutes	
Directories* (some#)	19C–
Enclosure Award	1812
Local Histories*	
Maps	17C–
Militia Books	1763–1828
Periodicals*	
Rate Books	18C–20C
Register of Electors*	20C

---

§Parish copies only
*Printed or transcribed
#Microfilm copy available at the LDS Family History Library in Salt Lake City, Utah, and through the LDS Family History Centers.

SOURCES THAT MAY ADDITIONALLY PROVIDE VITAL DATA AND/OR PROVE FAMILY RELATIONSHIPS

Census[‡][#]	1841–1881
Charity Records	19C
Church of England (parish)	
Parish Registers	17C–
Parish Register Transcripts*	16C–19C
Estate and Family Papers	19C–20C
Manorial Records (some*)	17C
Newspapers*	19C–
Nonconformist Registers	
Presbyterian	19C–
Roman Catholic Registers	1793–1911
School Records	1879–1950
Society Records	20C
Title Deeds	16C–20C

PUBLICATIONS[†]

Leaflet: *Local History in Greenwich: A Guide to Sources* (free)

[‡]Microfilm/microfiche copies available at above repository

[#]Microfilm copy available at the LDS Family History Library in Salt Lake City, Utah, and through the LDS Family History Centers.

*Printed or transcribed

[†]For additional information send 2 Postal Reply Coupons or 31 pence of English postage for reply to North America; 34 pence to Australia and New Zealand.

HACKNEY

(Middx: Hackney, Shoreditch, Stoke Newington)

Post-1965 London Boroughs

HACKNEY ARCHIVES AND
LOCAL HISTORY DEPARTMENT
Rose Lipman Library
De Beauvoir Road, London N1 5SQ
Tel. (01) 241 2886

Hours: M 2-8; T, Th, F 9:30-5; S 9:30-1, 2-5;
          Closed W, and 12-1 some weekdays (depending on
          staff availability)
          Prior appointment necessary

HOLDINGS

Resources pertaining to areas now in the London Borough of Hackney and their administrative predecessors.

SOURCES THAT IDENTIFY AN INDIVIDUAL WITH A SPECIFIC LOCATION

Church of England (parish)	18C–19C
Churchwardens' Accounts	
Parish Poor Rates	
Vestry Minutes	
Directories* (some#)	19C–20C
Land Tax Assessments	18C–19C
Local Histories*	
Maps	17C–
Periodicals*	
Rate Books	18C–19C
Registers of Electors*	19C–20C

SOURCES THAT MAY ADDITIONALLY PROVIDE VITAL DATA AND/OR PROVE FAMILY RELATIONSHIPS

Cemetery, Burial Ground Records	1840–
Census (LB Hackney)	1841–1881‡#
(Hackney)	1811, 1831
Church of England (parish)	
Parish Registers‡#	16C–19C
(some for Shoreditch)	
Estate and Family Papers	18C–20C

---

*Printed or transcribed

#Microfilm copy available at the LDS Family History Library in Salt Lake City, Utah, and through the LDS Family History Centers.

‡Microfilm/microfiche copies available at above repository

International Genealogical Index‡##
(London, Middx)
Monumental Inscriptions   18C–19C
Newspapers* (some‡#)   1857–
Nonconformist Registers
  Congregational   19C–
  Methodist   19C
  Unitarian   18C–19C
School Records
Title Deeds   16C–

PUBLICATIONS†

Leaflets:
L3 *Location of Parish and Nonconformist Registers,
Cemetery Records, Graveyard Inscriptions* (1987)
(free)
L4 *Sources for Family History* (1986) (free)

---

‡Microfilm/microfiche copies available at above repository

##Microfiche copy available at the LDS Family History Library in Salt Lake
City, Utah, and through the LDS Family History Centers.

*Printed or transcribed

#Microfilm copy available at the LDS Family History Library in Salt Lake City,
Utah, and through the LDS Family History Centers.

†For additional information send 2 Postal Reply Coupons or 31 pence of English
postage for reply to North America; 34 pence to Australia and New Zealand.

HAMMERSMITH AND FULHAM

(Middx: Fulham, Hammersmith)

Post-1965 London Boroughs

HAMMERSMITH AND FULHAM ARCHIVES
Shepherd's Bush Library
7 Uxbridge Road, London W12 8LJ
Tel. (01) 743 0910; (01) 748 3020 ext. 3850

Hours: By prior appointment only

HOLDINGS

Resources pertaining to the areas now in the London Borough of Hammersmith and Fulham, and their administrative predecessors.

SOURCES THAT IDENTIFY AN INDIVIDUAL WITH A SPECIFIC LOCATION

Business Records	20C
Church of England (diocesan)	
Tithe Apportionments§	1850
Church of England (parish)	
Churchwardens' Accounts	17C–19C
Parish Poor Rates	17C–1886
Vestry Minutes	17C–1886
Directories* (some#)	19C–20C
Local Histories*	
Maps	18C–
Periodicals*	
Rate Books	17C–20C
Registers of Electors*	1880–

SOURCES THAT MAY ADDITIONALLY PROVIDE VITAL DATA AND/OR PROVE FAMILY RELATIONSHIPS

Census‡#		1841–1881
Church of England (parish)		
Parish Registers		1664–1960
(St. Pauls Hammersmith)		
Estate and Family Papers	(some)	18C–20C
Newspapers*		
Nonconformist Registers		
Methodist	(gaps)	1806–1971
Parish Poor Law Records		17C–19C
Apprenticeship indentures		
Society Records		mid-19C–20C
Title Deeds		15C–20C

---

§Parish copies only
*Printed or transcribed
#Microfilm copy available at the LDS Family History Library in Salt Lake City, Utah, and through the LDS Family History Centers.
‡Microfilm/microfiche copies available at above repository

HARINGEY

(Middx: Hornsey, Tottenham, Wood Green)

Post-1965 London Boroughs

HARINGEY LIBRARIES
Bruce Castle Museum
Lordship Lane, London N17 8NU
Tel. (01) 808 8772

Hours: T-F 10-5; S 10-12:30, 1:30-5; closed M
      Prior appointment essential

HOLDINGS

Resources pertaining to the areas now in the London Borough of Haringey and their administrative predecessors.

SOURCES THAT IDENTIFY AN INDIVIDUAL WITH A SPECIFIC LOCATION

Borough Records	
Rates	1850–1964
Church of England (diocesan)	
Tithe Apportionments§	1840's
Church of England (parish)	
Churchwardens' Accounts	17C–19C
Parish Rates	18C–20C
Vestry Minutes	17C–20C
Directories* (some#)	19C–20C
Enclosure Award	1816
Local Histories*	
Maps	17C–
Periodicals*	20C
Registers of Electors*	1890–1964

SOURCES THAT MAY ADDITIONALLY PROVIDE VITAL DATA AND/OR PROVE FAMILY RELATIONSHIPS

Census‡#	1841–1881
Charity Records	15C–
Church of England (parish)	
Parish Register Transcripts*	1558–1670
Tottenham	

---

§Parish copies only
*Printed or transcribed
#Microfilm copy available at the LDS Family History Library in Salt Lake City, Utah, and through the LDS Family History Centers.
‡Microfilm/microfiche copies available at above repository

Estate and Family Papers	16C–20C
Manorial Records (Tottenham)	(gaps) 1318–1732
Newspapers*	late 19C–20C
Nonconformist Registers	
Methodist	1895–1972
Parish Poor Law Records	
Register of Apprentices	late 18C–19C
School Records	19C–20C
Society Records	19C–20C
Title Deeds	17C–19C

PUBLICATIONS†

Handlist No.1: Deposited Parish Records
Court Rolls of the Manor of Tottenham

---

*Printed or transcribed

†For additional information send 2 Postal Reply Coupons or 31 pence of English postage for reply to North America; 34 pence to Australia and New Zealand.

HARROW

(Middx: Harrow)

Post-1965 London Boroughs

HARROW CIVIC CENTRE LIBRARY
Local History Collection
Box 4, Civic Centre
Station Road, Harrow HA1 2UU
Tel. (01) 863 5611 ext. 2055/2056
Contact: Local History Librarian

Hours: M, T, Th 9-8; F 9-6; S 9-5; closed W

HOLDINGS

Resources pertaining to the former London Borough of
Harrow, and its administrative predecessors.

SOURCES THAT IDENTIFY AN INDIVIDUAL WITH A SPECIFIC LOCATION

Directories* (some#)	19C–20C
Local Histories*	20C
Maps	18C–20C
Periodicals*	19C–
Poll Books* (some#)	1802 only
Registers of Electors*	1890–1914, 1969–

SOURCES THAT MAY ADDITIONALLY PROVIDE VITAL DATA AND / OR PROVE FAMILY RELATIONSHIPS

Cemetery Records	1860–1932
Census‡#	1841–1881
Church of England (parish)	
Parish Register Transcripts*	16C–1837
International Genealogical Index‡##	1978
Manorial Records#	14C–19C
Monumental Inscriptions	19C–20C
Newspapers*	1855–
Nonconformist Registers	
Methodist	19C–20C
School Records	16C–20C
Wills, Register Copies*	14C–19C

PUBLICATIONS†

Leaflet: *Local History Collection* (1984)
Information Sheet 3: *Finding Out About People in the Past* (1979/80)

---

*Printed or transcribed

#Microfilm copy available at the LDS Family History Library in Salt Lake City, Utah, and through the LDS Family History Centers.

‡Microfilm/microfiche copies available at above repository

##Microfiche copy available at the LDS Family History Library in Salt Lake City, Utah, and through the LDS Family History Centers.

†For additional information send 2 Postal Reply Coupons or 31 pence of English postage for reply to North America; 34 pence to Australia and New Zealand.

HAVERING

(Essex: Romford, Hornchurch)

Post-1965 London Boroughs

HAVERING CENTRAL LIBRARY
Reference and Information Library
St. Edward's Way
Romford, Essex RM1 3AR
Tel. 0708 46040 ext. 355
Contact: Reference and Information Librarian

Hours: M-F 9:30-8; S 9:30-5

HOLDINGS

Resources pertaining to the areas now in the London Borough of Havering, and their administrative predecessors.

SOURCES THAT IDENTIFY AN INDIVIDUAL WITH A SPECIFIC LOCATION

Church of England (parish)	1839–1900
Parish Poor Rates	
Directories* (some#)	(gaps) 19C–20C
Local Histories*	
Maps	(gaps) 18C–
Periodicals*	
Registers of Electors*	
(Romford)	1938–1939, 1959
(Hornchurch)	(gaps) 1947–

SOURCES THAT MAY ADDITIONALLY PROVIDE VITAL DATA AND/OR PROVE FAMILY RELATIONSHIPS

Bamford Index*§	17C–
Burial Grounds (Romford)	1888–1953
Census‡#	1841–1881
International Genealogical Index‡##	
(Great Britain)	
Newspapers*	mid-19C–‡#
	1920's–*
Poor Law Union	
Workhouse Records	19C

RELATED PUBLICATIONS†

Romford Record,‡‡ 1– (1969–)

---

*Printed or transcribed

#Microfilm copy available at the LDS Family History Library in Salt Lake City, Utah, and through the LDS Family History Centers.

§Index to church yard burials in Romford

‡Microfilm/microfiche copies available at above repository

##Microfiche copy available at the LDS Family History Library in Salt Lake City, Utah, and through the LDS Family History Centers.

†For additional information send 2 Postal Reply Coupons or 31 pence of English postage for reply to North America; 34 pence to Australia and New Zealand.

‡‡Published by the Romford and District Historical Society; available at above repository.

HILLINGDON

(Middx: Uxbridge, Hayes and Harlingdon,
Ruislip-Northwood, Yiewsley and West Drayton)

Post-1965 London Boroughs

HILLINGDON LOCAL HISTORY COLLECTION
Uxbridge Central Library
High Street, Uxbridge, Middlesex UB8 1JN
Tel. 0895 50600
Contact: Local Studies Librarian

Hours: M-F 9:30-8; S 9:30-5
          (Prior appointment advised)

HOLDINGS

Resources pertaining to the areas now in the London
Borough of Hillingdon, and their administrative predecessors.

SOURCES THAT IDENTIFY AN INDIVIDUAL WITH A SPECIFIC LOCATION

Business Records	mid-19C–
Church of England (parish)	
Churchwardens' Accounts	(gaps) 1749–1872
Vestry Order Books	1806–1894
Directories* (some#)	1840–
Enclosure Awards	1796–1825
Local Histories*	
Maps	17C–
Periodicals*	19C–20C
Registers of Electors*	(gaps) 1838–

SOURCES THAT MAY ADDITIONALLY PROVIDE VITAL DATA AND/OR PROVE FAMILY RELATIONSHIPS

Census‡#	1841–1881
Charity Records	1829–1837
Church of England (parish)	
Parish Register Transcripts* (Marriages)	16C–19C
Estate and Family Papers	mid-17C–
International Genealogical Index‡##	
Monumental Inscriptions	
Newspapers‡#	1854–
Nonconformist Registers	
Congregational	1789–1855
Society Records	20C–

*Printed or transcribed

#Microfilm copy available at the LDS Family History Library in Salt Lake City, Utah, and through the LDS Family History Centers.

‡Microfilm/microfiche copies available at above repository

##Microfiche copy available at the LDS Family History Library in Salt Lake City, Utah, and through the LDS Family History Centers.

HOUNSLOW

(Middx: Bedfont, Brentford, Chiswick, Cranford,
Feltham, Hanworth, Heston, Hounslow, and Isleworth)

Post-1965 London Boroughs

CHISWICK PUBLIC LIBRARY
Duke's Street, Chiswick W4 2AB
Tel. (01) 994 1008
Hours: M-W 9-8; Th 9-1; F 9:30-5; S 9-5

HOLDINGS

Resources pertaining to the areas of Brentford and
Chiswick now in the London Borough of Hounslow, and their
administrative predecessors.

SOURCES THAT IDENTIFY AN INDIVIDUAL WITH A SPECIFIC LOCATION

Borough Records	1859–
Rates	(gaps) early 18C–
	1965
Directories* (some#)	19C–20C
Local Histories*	18C–20C
Maps	17C
Rate Books	1858–1965
Registers of Electors*	(gaps) 1890–

SOURCES THAT MAY ADDITIONALLY PROVIDE VITAL DATA AND/OR PROVE FAMILY RELATIONSHIPS

Census‡#	1841–1881
International Genealogical Index‡## (London, Middx)	
Newspapers* (some#)	1895–
School Records	18C–20C

BRENTFORD PUBLIC LIBRARY
Boston Manor Road
Brentford, Middlesex
Tel. (01) 560 8801

Hours: M-W 9-8; F, S 9-5; closed Th

HOLDINGS

Contains records for New Brentford during the eighteenth century.

---

*Printed or transcribed
#Microfilm copy available at the LDS Family History Library in Salt Lake City, Utah, and through the LDS Family History Centers.
‡Microfilm/microfiche copies available at above repository
##Microfiche copy available at the LDS Family History Library in Salt Lake City, Utah, and through the LDS Family History Centers.

HOUNSLOW PUBLIC LIBRARY††
School Road
Hounslow, Middlesex
Tel. (01) 570 0622
Hours: M, T 9-8; W 9-1; Th 9:30-8; F, S 9-5

HOLDINGS

Resources pertaining to the areas of Heston, Hounslow, Isleworth, and Cranford.

SOURCES THAT IDENTIFY AN INDIVIDUAL WITH A SPECIFIC LOCATION

Borough Records	(gaps) late 17C–
Rates	(gaps) late 17C–1965
Directories* (some#)	19C–20C
Local Histories*	18C–20C
Maps	17C–20C
Rate Books	(gaps) 1890–1965
Registers of Electors*	1926–

SOURCES THAT MAY ADDITIONALLY PROVIDE VITAL DATA AND/OR PROVE FAMILY RELATIONSHIPS

Census‡#	1841–1881
Church of England (parish)	
Parish Registers	1564–c. 1860
Parish Register Transcripts*	1690–1940

---

††Temporary building; Library will move to a new building in the Treaty Center, Hounslow in late spring 1988.
*Printed or transcribed
#Microfilm copy available at the LDS Family History Library in Salt Lake City, Utah, and through the LDS Family History Centers.
‡Microfilm/microfiche copies available at above repository

International Genealogical Index‡##
(London and Middlesex)
Newspapers*   (some) 1870–
School Records   18C–20C

FELTHAM PUBLIC LIBRARY
High Street
Feltham, Middlesex
Tel. (01) 890 3506

Hours: M, T 9-8; W 9-1; Th 9-8; F, S 9-5

HOLDINGS

Resources pertaining to the areas of Feltham, Hanworth and Bedfont. (Borough Records and Rate Books are kept at the Hounslow Library.)

Census‡#§   1841–1881
Local Histories*   18C–20C
Maps   17C–20C
Newspapers#§   1870–
Registers of Electors*   1965–

---

‡Microfilm/microfiche copies available at above repository
##Microfiche copy available at the LDS Family History Library in Salt Lake City, Utah, and through the LDS Family History Centers.
*Printed or transcribed
#Microfilm copy available at the LDS Family History Library in Salt Lake City, Utah, and through the LDS Family History Centers.
§May provide vital data and/or proof of family relationships.

ISLINGTON

(Middx: Finsbury, Islington)

Post-1965 London Boroughs

ISLINGTON CENTRAL LIBRARY
2 Fieldway Crescent, London N5 1PF
Tel. (01) 609 3051 ext. 31
Contact: Local History Librarian

Hours: M-F 9-8; S 9-5
      Prior appointment essential to use
      archive materials and microfilm

HOLDINGS

Resources pertaining to the former Metropolitan Borough of
Islington and its administrative predecessors.

SOURCES THAT IDENTIFY AN INDIVIDUAL WITH A SPECIFIC LOCATION

Church of England (parish)

Churchwardens' Accounts	18C–20C
Vestry Minutes	18C–19C
Directories* (some#)	(gaps) 19C–20C
Local Histories*	18C–
Maps	18C–
Periodicals*	19C–
Rate Books	(gaps) 1729–1960
Registers of Electors*	1860; 1887–
(See also Finsbury)	

SOURCES THAT MAY ADDITIONALLY PROVIDE VITAL DATA AND/OR PROVE FAMILY RELATIONSHIPS

Census‡#	1841–1881
Church of England (parish)	
Parish Registers‡#	1557–1903
(St. Mary's Islington)	
Newspapers* (also‡#)	1856–

PUBLICATIONS†

Leaflet: *Islington Local History Collections* (free)

---

*Printed or transcribed

#Microfilm copy available at the LDS Family History Library in Salt Lake City, Utah, and through the LDS Family History Centers.

‡Microfilm/microfiche copies available at above repository

†For additional information send 2 Postal Reply Coupons or 31 pence of English postage for reply to North America; 34 pence to Australia and New Zealand.

FINSBURY LIBRARY
245 St. John Street, London EC1 V4
Tel. (01) 609 3051 ext. 66
Contact: Reference Librarian

Hours: M, T, Th 9-8; W, F 9-1; S 9-5
Prior appointment essential to
use archive materials or records

HOLDINGS

Resources pertaining to the former Metropolitan Borough of
Finsbury and its administrative predecessors.

SOURCES THAT IDENTIFY AN INDIVIDUAL
WITH A SPECIFIC LOCATION

Church of England (parish)
Vestry Minutes	1567–1900
Directories* (some#)	(gaps) 1804–1855,
(London)	20C
Local Histories*	19C–
Maps	16C–
Periodicals*	18C–
Rate Books	
Parish Rates	1661–1900
Borough Rates	1900–1955, 1960
Registers of Electors*§§	1842, 1873–1885, 1901–

---

*Printed or transcribed
#Microfilm copy available at the LDS Family History Library in Salt Lake City,
Utah, and through the LDS Family History Centers.
§§Arranged by surname

SOURCES THAT MAY ADDITIONALLY PROVIDE VITAL DATA AND/OR PROVE FAMILY RELATIONSHIPS

Census‡#	1841–1881
Church of England (parish)	
Parish Register Transcripts*	1551–1754
Newspapers*	(gaps) 1856–

---

‡Microfilm/microfiche copies available at above repository
#Microfilm copy available at the LDS Family History Library in Salt Lake City, Utah, and through the LDS Family History Centers.
*Printed or transcribed

ROYAL BOROUGH OF KENSINGTON AND CHELSEA

(Middx: Chelsea, Kensington)

Post-1965 London Boroughs

KENSINGTON CENTRAL LIBRARY

Hornton Street, London W8 7RX
Tel. (01) 937 2542

Hours: M, T, Th, F 10-8; W 10-1; S 10-12, 2-5
Prior appointment essential; may be
closed weekdays during lunch hour

HOLDINGS

Resources pertaining to the former Metropolitan Borough of
Kensington and its administrative predecessors.

544

SOURCES THAT IDENTIFY AN INDIVIDUAL WITH A SPECIFIC LOCATION

Business Records	1889–
Church of England (diocesan)	
Tithe Apportionments§	1843
Church of England (parish)	
Churchwardens' Accounts	17C–19C
Parish Poor Rates	18C–19C
Vestry Minutes	18C–
Directories* (some#)	(gaps) 19C–20C
Ecclesiastical Census‡#	1851
Local Histories*	19C–20C
Maps	18C–20C
Periodicals*	20C
Rate Books	20C
Registers of Electors*	1890–

SOURCES THAT MAY ADDITIONALLY PROVIDE VITAL DATA AND/OR PROVE FAMILY RELATIONSHIPS

Borough Records	
Title Deeds	17C–20C
Census‡#	1841–1881
Church of England (parish)	
Parish Register Transcripts*	16C–19C
Estate and Family Papers	19C–20C
International Genealogical Index‡##	
(London)	
Manorial Records	(gaps) 16C–20C

---

§Parish copies only

*Printed or transcribed

#Microfilm copy available at the LDS Family History Library in Salt Lake City, Utah, and through the LDS Family History Centers.

‡Microfilm/microfiche copies available at above repository

##Microfiche copy available at the LDS Family History Library in Salt Lake City, Utah, and through the LDS Family History Centers.

Monumental Inscriptions	
Newspapers[‡][#]	19C–
Parish Poor Law Records	
Examinations	(gaps) 1791–1834
Society and Charity Records	19C–

CHELSEA LIBRARY
Old Town Hall
King's Road, London SW3 5ED
Tel. (01) 352 6056

Hours: M, T, Th 10-8; W 10-1; F, S 10-5
Prior appointment essential; may
be unavailable during lunch hour

HOLDINGS

Resources pertaining to the former Metropolitan Borough of Chelsea and its administrative predecessors.

SOURCES THAT IDENTIFY AN INDIVIDUAL
WITH A SPECIFIC LOCATION

Borough Records	
Rates	17C–20C
Church of England (diocesan)	
Tithe Apportionment[§]	1847
Church of England (parish)	
Parish Poor Rates	1670–1871
Vestry Records	1745–1846

[‡]Microfilm/microfiche copies available at above repository
[#]Microfilm copy available at the LDS Family History Library in Salt Lake City, Utah, and through the LDS Family History Centers.
[§]Parish copies only

Directories* (some#)	1878–1939
Local Histories*	19C–20C
Maps	18C–20C
Periodicals*	20C
Rate Books	1876–1964
Registers of Electors*	19C–20C

SOURCES THAT MAY ADDITIONALLY PROVIDE VITAL DATA AND/OR PROVE FAMILY RELATIONSHIPS

Borough Records	
Title Deeds††	17C–20C
Census‡#	1841–1881
Church of England (parish)	
Parish Register Transcripts*	16C–19C
Estate and Family Papers	19C–20C
International Genealogical Index‡## (London)	
Manorial Records	16C–20C
Monumental Inscriptions	
Newspapers‡#	19C–
Society and Charity Records	19C–

*Printed or transcribed

#Microfilm copy available at the LDS Family History Library in Salt Lake City, Utah, and through the LDS Family History Centers.

††Some records held at the Kensington Library

‡Microfilm/microfiche copies available at above repository

##Microfiche copy available at the LDS Family History Library in Salt Lake City, Utah, and through the LDS Family History Centers.

547

ROYAL BOROUGH OF KINGSTON UPON THAMES

(Surrey: Kingston upon Thames,
Malden and Coombe, Surbiton)

Post-1965 London Boroughs

KINGSTON UPON THAMES HERITAGE SERVICE
Fairfield West, Kingston upon Thames KT1 2PS
Tel. (01) 546 5386
Hours: M-S 10-5

HOLDINGS

Resources pertaining to the former borough of Kingston upon Thames and its administrative predecessors. (See also Surrey Record Office, Kingston upon Thames.)

SOURCES THAT IDENTIFY AN INDIVIDUAL WITH A SPECIFIC LOCATION

Borough Records‡‡	13C–20C
Directories* (some#)	(gaps) 19C;
	1900–1971
Local Histories*	
Maps	19C–
Periodicals*	1900–
Registers of Electors*	1939–40,
	1945–

SOURCES THAT MAY ADDITIONALLY PROVIDE VITAL DATA AND/OR PROVE FAMILY RELATIONSHIPS

Borough Records‡‡	13C–20C
Census‡#	1841–1881
Church of England (parish)	
Parish Register Transcripts*	16C–19C
Newspapers*	1854–

PUBLICATIONS†

Guide to the Borough Archives (1971)

---

‡‡Appointment necessary to view records; contact Surrey Record Office, Kingston upon Thames.

*Printed or transcribed

#Microfilm copy available at the LDS Family History Library in Salt Lake City, Utah, and through the LDS Family History Centers.

‡Microfilm/microfiche copies available at above repository

†For additional information send 2 Postal Reply Coupons or 31 pence of English postage for reply to North America; 34 pence to Australia and New Zealand.

LAMBETH

(Surrey: Lambeth, pt. Wandsworth)

Post-1965 London Boroughs

LAMBETH ARCHIVES DEPARTMENT
Minet Library
52 Knatchbull Road, London SE5 9QY
Tel. (01) 733 3279

Hours: M, T, Th, F 9:30-1, 2-5; closed W
        By prior appointment: alternate S 9-1, 2-4:45

HOLDINGS
Resources pertaining to the areas now in the London Borough of Lambeth and their administrative predecessors.

SOURCES THAT IDENTIFY AN INDIVIDUAL
WITH A SPECIFIC LOCATION

Business Records	mid-19C–20C
Church of England (diocesan)	
Tithe Apportionments§‡‡	1840's
Church of England (parish)	
Churchwardens' Accounts	16C–20C
Vestry Minutes	17C–19C
Directories* (some#)	19C–20C
Enclosure Awards	early 19C
Local Histories*	
Maps	16C–
Periodicals*	16C–
Rate Books	18C–20C
Registers of Electors*	1832–

SOURCES THAT MAY ADDITIONALLY PROVIDE VITAL
DATA AND/OR PROVE FAMILY RELATIONSHIPS

Cemetery Records	1854–1929
Magistrates' Court	1877–1968
Census‡#	1841–1881
Charity Records	17C–20C
Church of England (Parish)	
Parish Register Transcripts*	16C–19C
Estate and Family Papers	18C–20C
Hospital Records§§	18C–19C
Manorial Records (some#)	14C–20C

---

§Parish copies only

‡‡Photocopies

*Printed or transcribed

#Microfilm copy available at the LDS Family History Library in Salt Lake City, Utah, and through the LDS Family History Centers.

‡Microfilm/microfiche copies available at above repository

§§Records subject to embargo for 100 years

Newspapers*	19C–
Nonconformist Registers	
Congregational	18C–20C
Methodist	17C–20C
Poor Law Union	
Workhouse Records	16C–19C
Title Deeds	12C–20C

PUBLICATIONS†

Leaflets:
Guide to London Local History Resources: Lambeth
    (free)
Lambeth Archives Department

---

*Printed or transcribed

†For additional information send 2 Postal Reply Coupons or 31 pence of English postage for reply to North America; 34 pence to Australia and New Zealand.

LEWISHAM

(Kent: pt. Deptford, Lewisham)

Post-1965 London Boroughs

LEWISHAM LIBRARY SERVICE
Lewisham Local History Centre
The Manor House, Old Road, Lee
London SE13 5SY
Tel. (01) 852 5050 / 7087

Hours: M, F, S 9:30-5; T, Th 9:30-8; closed W

HOLDINGS

Resources pertaining to the areas now in the London
Borough of Lewisham and their administrative predecessors.

SOURCES THAT IDENTIFY AN INDIVIDUAL
WITH A SPECIFIC LOCATION

Business Records	19C–20C
Church of England (diocesan)	
Tithe Apportionments§	1840's
Church of England (parish)	
Churchwardens' Accounts	18C–19C
Parish Poor Rates	18C–19C
Vestry Minutes	18C–19C
Directories* (some#)	1790–1939
Enclosure Awards	1810–1819
Local Histories*	
Maps	18C–20C
Periodicals*	20C
Rate Books	18C–20C
Registers of Electors*	1924

SOURCES THAT MAY ADDITIONALLY PROVIDE VITAL
DATA AND/OR PROVE FAMILY RELATIONSHIPS

Census‡#	1841–1881
Church of England (parish)	
Parish Registers	18C–
Parish Register Transcripts#	16C–18C
Estate and Family Papers	18C–20C
Newspapers‡#	19C–20C

---

§Parish copies only

*Printed or transcribed

#Microfilm copy available at the LDS Family History Library in Salt Lake City, Utah, and through the LDS Family History Centers.

‡Microfilm/microfiche copies available at above repository

Nonconformist Registers
   Congregational   1854–1959
   Methodist   1839–1968
School Records   19C–20C
Society and Charity Records   19C–20C
Title Deeds   16C–20C

PUBLICATIONS[†]

Looking Back at Lewisham

[†]For additional information send 2 Postal Reply Coupons or 31 pence of English postage for reply to North America; 34 pence to Australia and New Zealand.

MERTON

(Surrey: Mitcham, Wimbledon, Merton and Morden)

Post-1965 London Boroughs

MITCHAM LIBRARY
London Road
Mitcham, Surrey CR4 2YR
Tel. (01) 648 4070, (01) 648 6516
Hours: M, T, Th, F 9-7; W, S 9-5

HOLDINGS

Resources pertaining to the former borough of Mitcham and its administrative predecessors.

Census*	1841–1881
Church of England (diocesan)	
Tithe Map§	1846
Directories* (some#)	19C–
Local Histories*	
Maps	(gaps) 1746–
Newspapers*	1909–
Periodicals*	20C–
Registers of Electors*	20C–

MORDEN LIBRARY
Morden Road, London SW19 3DA
Tel. (01) 542 1701, (01) 542 2842
Hours: M, T, Th, F 9-7; W 9-1; S 9-5

HOLDINGS
Resources pertaining to the former urban district of Merton and Morden and its administrative predecessors.

Census*	1841–1881
Church of England (diocesan)	
Tithe Maps§	
Morden	1838
Merton	1844
Church of England (parish)	
Parish Register Transcripts*	
(Merton)	16C–1812
Directories*(some#)	late 19C–
Local Histories*	
Maps	(gaps) 1746–
Newspapers*	1935–
Periodicals*	2OC–
Registers of Electors*	20C–

*Printed or transcribed
§Parish copies only
#Microfilm copy available at the LDS Family History Library in Salt Lake City, Utah, and through the LDS Family History Centers.

WIMBLEDON REFERENCE LIBRARY
Wimbledon Hill Road
London SW19 7NB
Tel. (01) 946 1136

Hours: M, T, Th, F 9-7; W 9-1; S 9-5

HOLDINGS

Resources pertaining to the former borough of Wimbledon
and its administrative predecessors.

Census[‡#§]	1841–1881
Church of England (diocesan)	
Tithe Map[§§]	1848
Church of England (parish)	
Parish Register Transcripts*[#§]	16C–1812
Directories* (some[‡#])	19C–
International Genealogical Index[‡##§]	
(Surrey)	
Local Histories*	
Maps	1746–
Newspapers*[§] (some[#])	1880–
Periodicals*	(gaps) 20C
Registers of Electors*	1891–98, 1945–

[‡]Microfilm/microfiche copies available at above repository
[#]Microfilm copy available at the LDS Family History Library in Salt Lake City, Utah, and through the LDS Family History Centers.
[§]May provide vital data and/or proof of family relationships.
[§§]Parish copies only
[*]Printed or transcribed
[##]Microfiche copy available at the LDS Family History Library in Salt Lake City, Utah, and through the LDS Family History Centers.

NEWHAM

(Essex: East Ham, West Ham, pt. Barking)
(Kent: pt. Woolwich)

Post-1965 London Boroughs

LOCAL STUDIES LIBRARY
Stratford Reference Library
Water Lane, London E15 4NJ
Tel. (01) 534 4545 ext. 25662

Hours: M, T, Th, F 9:30-7; W, S 9:30-5
        Prior appointment necessary

HOLDINGS

Resources pertaining to the areas now in the London Borough of Newham and their administrative predecessors.

SOURCES THAT IDENTIFY AN INDIVIDUAL WITH A SPECIFIC LOCATION

Church of England (diocesan)	
Tithe Apportionments§	mid-19C
Church of England (parish)	
Parish Poor Rates (also‡#)	late 18C–19C
Overseers' Accounts	1749–1819
Vestry Minutes	
East Ham	1736–1867#
West Ham	1646–1869
Directories* (some#)	
London	1791, 19C–
Essex	19C–20C
Local Histories*	
Maps	19C
Periodicals*	late 19C–20C
Quarter Sessions (West Ham)	
Judicial Records	1894–1965
Rate Books	late 19C–20C
Registers of Electors*	(gaps) late 19C–

SOURCES THAT MAY ADDITIONALLY PROVIDE VITAL DATA AND/OR PROVE FAMILY RELATIONSHIPS

Census‡#	1841–1881
Charity Records	19C
Church of England (parish)	
Parish Registers‡#	16C–20C
Parish Register Transcripts*	19C
Estate and Family Papers	17C–20C
Manorial Records	18C–20C
Newspapers*‡#	1858–

---

§Parish copies only

‡Microfilm/microfiche copies available at above repository

#Microfilm copy available at the LDS Family History Library in Salt Lake City, Utah, and through the LDS Family History Centers.

*Printed or transcribed

Nonconformist Registers
   Congregational   1806–1970
   Methodist   1826–1970
   Presbyterian   1907–1934
Parish Poor Law Records
   Settlement Certificates   1781–1813
School Records   18C–20C
Society Records   20C
Title Deeds   16C–

PUBLICATIONS†

Leaflets:
   Local History Notes (free)
   Family History Notes (free)
Ordnance Survey Maps Reprints

---

†For additional information send 2 Postal Reply Coupons or 31 pence of English postage for reply to North America; 34 pence to Australia and New Zealand.

REDBRIDGE

(Essex: Ilford, Wanstead and Woodford,
pt. Dagenham, pt. Chigwell)

Post-1965 London Boroughs

REDBRIDGE CENTRAL LIBRARY
Local History Library
Clements Road, Ilford, Essex IG1 1EA
Tel. (01) 478 7145

Hours: T-F 9-8; S 9:30-4; closed M
    (Prior appointment advised)

HOLDINGS

Resources pertaining to the areas now in the London Borough of Redbridge and their administrative predecessors.

SOURCES THAT IDENTIFY AN INDIVIDUAL WITH A SPECIFIC LOCATION

Business Records	20C
Church of England (parish)	
Churchwardens' Accounts	17C–19C
Parish Poor Rates	17C–19C
Directories* (some#)	20C
Local Histories*	
Maps	1863–
Militia Roll (Supplemental)	1803–1804
Periodicals*	mid-19C–20C
Rate Books	20C
Registers of Electors* (some‡##)	late 19C–

SOURCES THAT MAY ADDITIONALLY PROVIDE VITAL DATA AND/OR PROVE FAMILY RELATIONSHIPS

Census‡#	1841–1881
Charity Records	19C–20C
Church of England (parish)	
Parish Register Transcripts*	1558–
Estate and Family Papers	16C–20C
International Genealogical Index‡##	
(United Kingdom)	

---

*Printed or transcribed

#Microfilm copy available at the LDS Family History Library in Salt Lake City, Utah, and through the LDS Family History Centers.

‡Microfilm/microfiche copies available at above repository

##Microfiche copy available at the LDS Family History Library in Salt Lake City, Utah, and through the LDS Family History Centers.

Monumental Inscriptions
Newspapers* (some#)   1900–
Nonconformist Registers
   Baptist   1890, 20C
   Congregational   19C–
   Methodist   20C
Society Records   late 19C–20C
School Records   19C–20C

PUBLICATIONS†

Leaflet: *Local History Library* (free)

RICHMOND UPON THAMES

(Surrey: Barnes, Richmond)
(Middx: Twickenham)

Post-1965 London Boroughs

RICHMOND UPON THAMES
CENTRAL REFERENCE LIBRARY
Old Town Hall, Whittaker Avenue
Richmond, Surrey TW9 1TP
Tel. (01) 940 5529

Hours: T, S 10-12:30, 1:30-5; W 1-8;
         Th, F 10-12:30, 1:30-6; closed M

Researchers advised to apply in writing to Central Reference
   Library first, which will attempt to locate records
   requested and advise of their availability.

HOLDINGS

Resources pertaining to the former boroughs of Barnes and Richmond, now in the London Borough of Richmond upon Thames, and their administrative predecessors.

SOURCES THAT IDENTIFY AN INDIVIDUAL WITH A SPECIFIC LOCATION

Burgess Rolls	1890–1914/15
Church of England (parish)	
Vestry Minutes[tt]	1596–20C
Parish Poor Rates	1726–1924
Directories* (some[#])	(gaps) 19C–
Local Histories*	
Maps	17C–
Periodicals*	(gaps) 19C–
Rate Books	late 19C–20C
Registers of Electors*	1918–1939, 1945–

SOURCES THAT MAY ADDITIONALLY PROVIDE VITAL DATA AND/OR PROVE FAMILY RELATIONSHIPS

Census[‡#]	1841–1881
Manorial Records	1771–1773
Newspapers[‡#]	19C–

[tt]Some Vestry Minutes are located at Richmond Municipal Offices; however, arrangements to consult records should be made at the Central Reference Library.
*Printed or transcribed
[#]Microfilm copy available at the LDS Family History Library in Salt Lake City, Utah, and through the LDS Family History Centers.
[‡]Microfilm/microfiche copies available at above repository

PUBLICATIONS†

Leaflets:
Richmond upon Thames
Local Studies Collections

TWICKENHAM REFERENCE LIBRARY

District Library
Garfield Road, Twickenham, Middlesex TW1 3JS
Tel. (01) 891 7271

Hours: M-F 10-12, 2-6; T 1-8;
W, S 10-12, 2-5; closed Th

HOLDINGS

Resources pertaining to the former borough of Twickenham and its administrative predecessors.

Census‡##§	1841, 1851
Directories* (some#)	19C–
Local Histories*	
Maps	17C–
Newspapers*§ (some#)	19C–
Periodicals*	20C
Registers of Electors*	20C

---

†For additional information send 2 Postal Reply Coupons or 31 pence of English postage for reply to North America; 34 pence to Australia and New Zealand.
‡Microfilm/microfiche copies available at above repository
##Microfiche copy available at the LDS Family History Library in Salt Lake City, Utah, and through the LDS Family History Centers.
§May provide vital data and/or proof of family relationships.
*Printed or transcribed
#Microfilm copy available at the LDS Family History Library in Salt Lake City, Utah, and through the LDS Family History Centers.

SOUTHWARK

(Surrey: Bermondsey, Camberwell, Southwark)

Post-1965 London Boroughs

SOUTHWARK LOCAL STUDIES LIBRARY
211 Borough High Street
London SE1 1JA
Tel. (01) 403 3507
Contact: Local Studies Librarian
Hours: M, Th 9:30-12:30, 1:30-8;
          T, F 9:30-12:30, 1:30-5;
          By prior appointment S 9:30-1; closed W
Staff is not able to undertake any research

HOLDINGS

Resources pertaining to the areas now in the London Borough of Southwark and their administrative predecessors.

SOURCES THAT IDENTIFY AN INDIVIDUAL WITH A SPECIFIC LOCATION

Business Records	19C–20C
Church of England (parish)	
Churchwardens' Accounts	16C–19C
Parish Poor Rates	17C–20C
Vestry Minutes	17C–20C
Directories* (some#)	19C–
Enclosure Maps	1770–19C
Local Histories*	
Maps	16C–
Periodicals*	1870's–
Rate Books	(gaps) 20C
Registers of Electors*	1832–

SOURCES THAT MAY ADDITIONALLY PROVIDE VITAL DATA AND/OR PROVE FAMILY RELATIONSHIPS

Newspapers‡#	1855–
Nonconformist Registers	
Congregational	18C–20C
Methodist	18C–20C
Parish Poor Law Records	mid-17C–19C
Apprenticeship Indentures	
Examinations	18C–19C
Removal Orders	
Settlement Certificates	
School Records	18C–20C
Society Records	19C–
Title Deeds	16C–20C

PUBLICATIONS†

Leaflet: *Southwark Local Studies Library*

---

*Printed or transcribed

#Microfilm copy available at the LDS Family History Library in Salt Lake City, Utah, and through the LDS Family History Centers.

‡Microfilm/microfiche copies available at above repository

†For additional information send 2 Postal Reply Coupons or 31 pence of English postage for reply to North America; 34 pence to Australia and New Zealand.

SUTTON

(Surrey: Beddington and Wallington,
Sutton and Cheam, Carshalton)

Post-1965 London Boroughs

SUTTON CENTRAL LIBRARY
St. Nicholas Way
Sutton SM1 1EA
Tel. (01) 661 5050
Contact: Local Studies Librarian
Hours: T-F 9:30-8; S 9:30-5; closed M
(Prior appointment advised)

HOLDINGS

Local resources pertaining to the areas now in the London
Borough of Sutton and their administrative predecessors.

SOURCES THAT IDENTIFY AN INDIVIDUAL WITH A SPECIFIC LOCATION

Business Records	19C–20C
Church of England (diocesan)	
Tithe Apportionments[§][††]	1840's–1850's
Church of England (parish)	
Churchwardens' Accounts	18C–19C
Parish Poor Rates	(gaps) 18C–19C
Vestry Minutes	18C–19C
Directories* (some[#])	19C–20C
Enclosure Award[††]	19C
Local Histories*	
Maps	17C–20C
Periodicals*	
Rate Books	18C–20C
Registers of Electors*	1841–1871,[#]
	20C–

SOURCES THAT MAY ADDITIONALLY PROVIDE VITAL DATA AND/OR PROVE FAMILY RELATIONSHIPS

Census[‡][#]	1841–1881
Charity Records	1766–1939
Church of England (parish)	
Parish Register Transcripts*	16C–19C
International Genealogical Index[‡][##]	
(Great Britain)	

[§]Parish copies only

[††]Photocopies

*Printed or transcribed

[#]Microfilm copy available at the LDS Family History Library in Salt Lake City, Utah, and through the LDS Family History Centers.

[‡]Microfilm/microfiche copies available at above repository

[##]Microfiche copy available at the LDS Family History Library in Salt Lake City, Utah, and through the LDS Family History Centers.

Manorial Records (early*)	1346–1936
Newspapers* (some#)	19C–20C
Nonconformist Registers	
Congregational	1874–1970
School Records	late 19C–20C
Title Deeds	19C
Wills* (Carshalton)	14C–early 20C

---

*Printed or transcribed

#Microfilm copy available at the LDS Family History Library in Salt Lake City, Utah, and through the LDS Family History Centers.

TOWER HAMLETS

(Middx: Bethnal Green, Poplar, Stepney)

Post-1965 London Boroughs

TOWER HAMLETS CENTRAL LIBRARY
Local History Library
277 Bancroft Road, London E1 4DQ
Tel. (01) 980 4366 ext. 47

Hours: M, T, Th, F 9-8; W, S 9-5

HOLDINGS

Resources pertaining to the areas now in the London Borough of Tower Hamlets, and their administrative predecessors.

SOURCES THAT IDENTIFY AN INDIVIDUAL
WITH A SPECIFIC LOCATION

Business Records	18C–19C
Church of England (parish)	
Churchwardens' Accounts	(gaps) 17C–20C
Parish Rates	(gaps) 18C–19C
Vestry Minutes	(gaps) 18C–20C
Directories* (some#)	1790–1875,
	1889–
Land Tax Assessments	(gaps) 18C–19C
(Bromley)	
Local Histories*	
Maps	late 16C–
Militia	1826–1832
Rate Books	20C
Registers of Electors*	1901–

SOURCES THAT MAY ADDITIONALLY PROVIDE VITAL
DATA AND/OR PROVE FAMILY RELATIONSHIPS

Business Records	
East India Company	18C–19C
Census‡#	1841–1881
Church of England (parish)	
Banns (3 parishes)	18C–20C
Parish Registers‡#	18C–20C
Estate Papers	18C–19C
International Genealogical Index‡##	
(London, Middlesex)	
Jewish Records	20C

---

*Printed or transcribed

#Microfilm copy available at the LDS Family History Library in Salt Lake City, Utah, and through the LDS Family History Centers.

‡Microfilm/microfiche copies available at above repository

##Microfiche copy available at the LDS Family History Library in Salt Lake City, Utah, and through the LDS Family History Centers.

Manorial Records	19C–20C
Marriage Notice Books	19C
Newspapers#	1857–
Nonconformist Registers	
Baptist*	19C
Congregational*	18C–19C
Huguenot*	17C–18C
Methodist*	19C
Parish Poor Law Records (Bow, Bromley)	
Removal Orders	16C–19C
Examinations	
Bow	(gaps) 1739–1861
Bromley	1778–1843
School Records	19C–20C
Society Records	18C–20C
Title Deeds	16C–

PUBLICATIONS†

Archives Deposited in the London Borough of Tower Hamlets, Guide to London Local History Resources, Sect. 11–26

Leaflets:
  Family History
  Parish and Nonconformist Registers Available at the Local History Library

---

#Microfilm copy available at the LDS Family History Library in Salt Lake City, Utah, and through the LDS Family History Centers.
*Printed or transcribed
†For additional information send 2 Postal Reply Coupons or 31 pence of English postage for reply to North America; 34 pence to Australia and New Zealand.

WALTHAM FOREST

(Essex: Chingford, Leyton, Walthamstow)

Post-1965 London Boroughs

VESTRY HOUSE MUSEUM
Vestry Road, London E17 9NH
Tel. (01) 509 1917
Contact: Archivist or Local History Librarian

Hours: By prior appointment only:
      T-F 10:30-1, 2-5:30; S 10:30-1, 2-5; closed M

HOLDINGS

Resources pertaining to the areas now in the London Borough of Waltham Forest, and their administrative predecessors.

SOURCES THAT IDENTIFY AN INDIVIDUAL
WITH A SPECIFIC LOCATION

Business Records	
Rates	late 19C–20C
Church of England (diocesan)	
Tithe Apportionments§	1840's
Church of England (parish)	
Churchwardens' Accounts	
Leyton	1651–1860
Walthamstow	1705–1895
Parish Poor Rates	17C–20C
(Leyton, Walthamstow)	
Vestry Minutes	
Leyton	1618–1904
Walthamstow	1710–1820,
	1899–1938
Directories* (some#)	1823–
(Essex, London)	
Local Histories*	
Maps	17C–
Militia Rolls (S.W. Essex)	1766–1811
Periodicals*	19C–20C
Quarter Sessions (some‡#)	
Judicial Records (Essex)	1651–1938
Land Tax Assessments	1740–
(Walthamstow)	
Rate Books	20C
Registers of Electors*	
Trade Union Records	20C
World War I Roll of Honor	1914–1918

---

§Parish copies only

*Printed or transcribed

#Microfilm copy available at the LDS Family History Library in Salt Lake City, Utah, and through the LDS Family History Centers.

‡Microfilm/microfiche copies available at above repository

SOURCES THAT MAY ADDITIONALLY PROVIDE VITAL DATA AND/OR PROVE FAMILY RELATIONSHIPS

Cemetery Records	
Chingford (also#)	1884–
Census‡##	1811–1831,
	1841–1881‡#
Charity Records	16C–
Church of England (parish)	
Parish Registers (Walthamstow)	16C–
Parish Register Transcripts*	16C–19C
Estate and Family Papers	
International Genealogical Index‡##	
(British Isles)	
Jewish Records	20C
Manorial Records	14C–
Nonconformist Registers	
Baptist	19C–20C
Congregational/Presbyterian	18C–20C
Methodist	19C–20C
Unitarian	18C–19C
Parish Poor Law Records	
Apprenticeship Indentures	mid-18C–early 20C
Examinations	mid-18C–mid-19C
Removal Orders	mid-18C–mid-19C
Settlement Certificates	
Poor Law Union	
Workhouse Admissions	1797–1836
School Records	1890–20C
Society Records	19C–20C

#Microfilm copy available at the LDS Family History Library in Salt Lake City, Utah, and through the LDS Family History Centers.

‡Microfilm/microfiche copies available at above repository

##Microfiche copy available at the LDS Family History Library in Salt Lake City, Utah, and through the LDS Family History Centers.

*Printed or transcribed

WANDSWORTH

(Surrey: Battersea, pt. Wandsworth)

Post-1965 London Boroughs

BATTERSEA DISTRICT LIBRARY
Wandsworth Local History Collection
265 Lavender Hill, London SW11 1JB
Tel. (01) 871 7467

Hours: T 10-1, 2-8; W, F 10-1, 2-5 (Prior appointment advised)
     Other times by prior appointment only

HOLDINGS

Resources pertaining to the areas now in the London Bor–
ough of Wandsworth, and their administrative predecessors.

SOURCES THAT IDENTIFY AN INDIVIDUAL WITH A SPECIFIC LOCATION

Church of England (diocesan)

Tithe Apportionments§	1838–1848

Church of England (parish)

Churchwardens' Accounts	17C–1900
Overseers' Accounts	17C–19C
Parish Poor Rates	18C–19C
Vestry Minutes	17C–1900
Directories* (some#)	(gaps) mid-19C–
Enclosure Award	1820's
Local Histories*	
Maps	17C–
Periodicals*	late 19C–20C
Rate Books	20C
Registers of Electors*	1898–

SOURCES THAT MAY ADDITIONALLY PROVIDE VITAL DATA AND/OR PROVE FAMILY RELATIONSHIPS

Burial Board Minutes	1855–1894
Census‡#	1841–1881
Charity Records	17C–20C
Church of England (parish)	
Parish Register Transcripts*	1555–1876
(4 parishes)	
Estate and Family Papers	1653–1881
International Genealogical Index‡##	
(Surrey)	

---

§Parish copies only

*Printed or transcribed

#Microfilm copy available at the LDS Family History Library in Salt Lake City, Utah, and through the LDS Family History Centers.

‡Microfilm/microfiche copies available at above repository

##Microfiche copy available at the LDS Family History Library in Salt Lake City, Utah, and through the LDS Family History Centers.

ENGLISH REPOSITORIES	LONDON BOROUGHS
Newspapers* (some#)	mid-19C–
Parish Poor Law Records	
Apprenticeship Indentures	18C–19C
Examinations	18C–19C
Removal Orders	18C–19C
School Records	18C–19C
Society Records	19C–20C
Title Deeds	mid- to late 19C
Wills	c. 1650–1900

---

*Printed or transcribed

#Microfilm copy available at the LDS Family History Library in Salt Lake City, Utah, and through the LDS Family History Centers.

CITY OF WESTMINSTER

Post-1965 London Boroughs

WESTMINSTER CITY ARCHIVES DEPARTMENT
Victoria Library, 160 Buckingham Palace Road
London SW1W 9UD
Tel. (01) 798 2180

Hours: M-F 9:30-7; S 9:30-1, 2-5

Admission free

HOLDINGS

Church of England Parish Records including original, transcribed and published Parish Registers for 42 churches in the City of Westminster; local government records and other resources pertaining to the City of Westminster.

SOURCES THAT IDENTIFY AN INDIVIDUAL WITH A SPECIFIC LOCATION

Borough Records	1900–
Church of England (diocesan)	
Tithe Apportionments§	1854–1856
Church of England (parish)	
Churchwardens' Accounts	1460–1888
Directories* (some#)	
Business, Professional#	periodic 1677–
Postal	periodic 1842–
Land Tax Assessments	1689–1833
Lists of Jurors	1826–1889
Maps	1550–
Militia Lists	1803
Poll Books* (some#)	1727–1841
Parish Poor Law Records	
Parish Poor Rates (some#)	1561–1900
Registers of Electors*	1857–

SOURCES THAT MAY ADDITIONALLY PROVIDE VITAL DATA AND/OR PROVE FAMILY RELATIONSHIPS

Census‡# (City of Westminster)	1851–1881
Church of England (diocesan)	
Marriage Licences (special)	1766–1891
Marriage Licence Allegations*	1660–1694
Wills and Administrations#	1504–1858
Church of England (parish)	
Parish Registers (some#)	1550–1983
Parish Register Transcripts*	1539–1837

---

§Parish copies only

*Printed or transcribed

#Microfilm copy available at the LDS Family History Library in Salt Lake City, Utah, and through the LDS Family History Centers.

‡Microfilm/microfiche copies available at above repository

Estate and Family Papers	18C–20C
Hospital Records	1719–1784
Manorial Records	1614–1648
Newspapers*	1757–
Poor Law Records	
Apprenticeship Indentures (some#)	1637–1842
Examinations (some#)	1703–1836
Removal Orders	1694–1867
Settlement Certificates	1694–1867
Workhouse Records	1692–1881

MARYLEBONE LIBRARY
ARCHIVES DEPARTMENT
Marylebone Road
London NW1 5PS
Tel. (01) 798 1030
Contact: Archivist
Hours: M-F 9:30-7; S 9:30-1, 2-5
     Prior appointment necessary to see records

HOLDINGS

Local government records and other resources pertaining to the former Metropolitan Boroughs of St. Marylebone and Paddington, and their administrative predecessors.

SOURCES THAT IDENTIFY AN INDIVIDUAL
WITH A SPECIFIC LOCATION

Business Records	18C–20C
Church of England (diocesan)	
Tithe Apportionments§	1849

---

*Printed or transcribed
#Microfilm copy available at the LDS Family History Library in Salt Lake City, Utah, and through the LDS Family History Centers.
§Parish copies only

Church of England (parish)	
Churchwardens' Accounts	1670–1899
Overseers' Accounts	1670–1900
Parish Poor Rates	17C–1899
Directories* (some#)	(gaps) 1806–
Land Tax Assessments	1801–1885
Local Histories*	
Maps	17C–
Periodicals*	late 19C–
Rate Books (some‡#)	1900–1968/69
Registers of Electors*	(gaps) 1832–
	(# to 1854)

SOURCES THAT MAY ADDITIONALLY PROVIDE VITAL DATA AND/OR PROVE FAMILY RELATIONSHIPS

Census‡#	1851–1881
Church of England (parish)	
Parish Register Transcripts*	17C–19C
Charity Records	1800–20C
Court Records	18C–20C
Estate and Family Papers	18C–20C
Manorial Records	15C–18C
Newspapers*	mid-19C–
Parish Poor Laws	
Apprenticeship Indentures	1689–c. 1850
Society Records	19C–20C
School Records	
Title Deeds	c. 1770–

---

*Printed or transcribed
#Microfilm copy available at the LDS Family History Library in Salt Lake City, Utah, and through the LDS Family History Centers.
‡Microfilm/microfiche copies available at above repository

585

OTHER REPOSITORIES

The sources listed below include only those items reported on the Record Office Survey as located in the specified repositories. Each city and county library should have additional printed materials pertaining to its geographical area.

LDS FAMILY HISTORY CENTRE[†]
41 Kingston Road
Staines, Middlesex TW14 0ND
Tel. 0784 50709

Family History Library Catalogue[‡##]
International Genealogical Index[‡##]

GENEALOGICAL AND FAMILY HISTORY SOCIETIES

The societies listed below may have recorded Monumental (tombstone) Inscriptions, compiled an Index to Marriages (from the Parish Registers), an Index to the 1851 Census, and other special indexes, e.g., Strays, Members' Interests, for their geographical areas.[**] Each Society publishes a quarterly journal (listed in italics) which includes articles on family history, reports on the group's projects, and members' queries.

[†]For additional information send 2 Postal Reply Coupons or 31 pence of English postage for reply to North America; 34 pence to Australia and New Zealand.

[‡]Microfilm/microfiche copies available at above repository

[##]Microfiche copy available at the LDS Family History Library in Salt Lake City, Utah, and through the LDS Family History Centers.

[**]See *Current Publications by Member Societies* (annual), *List of Family History Project Coordinators*, 6th ed., and *Family History News and Digest* (biennial) — all published by the Federation of Family History Societies; available in the USA from the International Society for British Genealogy and Family History, P.O. Box 20425, Cleveland, OH 44120.

EAST OF LONDON FAMILY HISTORY SOCIETY[†]
Mrs. J. Vagg, Secretary
50 Grange Park Road, London E10 5ES

Cockney Ancestor

CENTRAL MIDDLESEX FAMILY HISTORY SOCIETY[†]
Mr. M. Fountain, Secretary
115 Harrow View
Harrow, Middlesex HA1 4SX

Greentrees

NORTH MIDDLESEX FAMILY HISTORY SOCIETY[†]
Miss J. Lewis, Secretary
15 Milton Road, Waltham Stow
London E17 4SF

The North Middlesex Family History Society Journal

WEST MIDDLESEX FAMILY HISTORY SOCIETY[†]
Mr. G. Morgan, Secretary
17 Croft Gardens
Ruislip, Middlesex HA4 8EY

The West Middlesex Family History Society Journal

WALTHAM FOREST FAMILY HISTORY SOCIETY[†]
Mr. J. Bowen, Secretary
1 Gelsthrope Road
Romford, Essex RM5 2NB

Roots in the Forest

[†]For additional information send 2 Postal Reply Coupons or 31 pence of English postage for reply to North America; 34 pence to Australia and New Zealand.

WOOLWICH AND DISTRICT
FAMILY HISTORY SOCIETY†
Ms. S. Highley, Secretary
4 Church Road
Bexleyheath DA7 4DA

Woolwich and District Family History Society Journal

(See also Genealogical and Family History Societies in Essex, Hertfordshire, Kent, and Surrey for areas formerly in those counties.)

---

†For additional information send 2 Postal Reply Coupons or 31 pence of English postage for reply to North America; 34 pence to Australia and New Zealand.

APPENDIX

USEFUL ADDRESSES

ASSOCIATION OF GENEALOGISTS
AND RECORD AGENTS (AGRA)
Mrs. Jean Tooke, B. Com.
1 Woodside Close
Caterham, Surrey CR3 6AU, England

A list of reliable genealogists and record agents can be obtained by sending 60p (UK) or 5 International Reply Coupons (overseas).

BRITISH PHILATELIC BUREAU
20 Brandon Street
Edinburgh EH3 5TT, Scotland

Sells British postage stamps at face value. Accepts checks drawn on any bank worldwide, made out in currency of country of origin and subject to negotiation charges. Also accepts payments by Access, MasterCard and Visa. Allow 28 days for delivery.

ENGLISH TOURIST BOARD
Department D, 4 Bromells Road
London SW4 0BJ, England

Publishes four official accommodation guides:
- Hotels, Motels, Guesthouses and Universities
- Farm Houses, Bed and Breakfast, Inns and Hostels
- Holiday Homes and Holiday Centres
- Camping and Caravan Parks

FAMILY HISTORY LIBRARY
(formerly GENEALOGICAL LIBRARY)

35 North West Temple Street
Salt Lake City, Utah 84150, USA

Lists of Family History Centers (formerly Branch Genealogical Libraries) for various countries and regions of the United States are available free of charge upon request.

FEDERATION OF FAMILY HISTORY SOCIETIES (FFHS)

Mrs. Pauline A. Saul, Administrator
31 Seven Star Road
Solihull, West Midlands B91 2BZ, England

Coordinating body for the Family History Societies in the UK, and associated societies worldwide. List of addresses of all members available upon request.†

GUILD OF ONE NAME STUDIES

Box G, Charterhouse Buildings
Goswell Road, London EC1M 7BA, England

Coordinating body for more than 1,000 one-name societies (groups organized to collect data on a single surname without any limitations). Publishes a booklet, *The Register of One-Name Societies*, available from any society or library which sells FFHS publications.

INTERNATIONAL SOCIETY FOR BRITISH GENEALOGY AND FAMILY HISTORY

P.O. Box 20425, Cleveland, Ohio 44120, USA

Provides members with up-to-date information on resources in the UK, Commonwealth countries and the United States through its quarterly *Newsletter*. Sells British publications of FFHS, Society of Genealogists, and Phillimore and Co., Ltd.

---

†For additional information send 2 Postal Reply Coupons or 31 pence of English postage for reply to North America; 34 pence to Australia and New Zealand.

INDEX

The Index is limited to names of geographical localities, repositories, genealogical and family history societies listed in the text.

Pre-1974 Counties of England

612

Post-1974 Counties of England

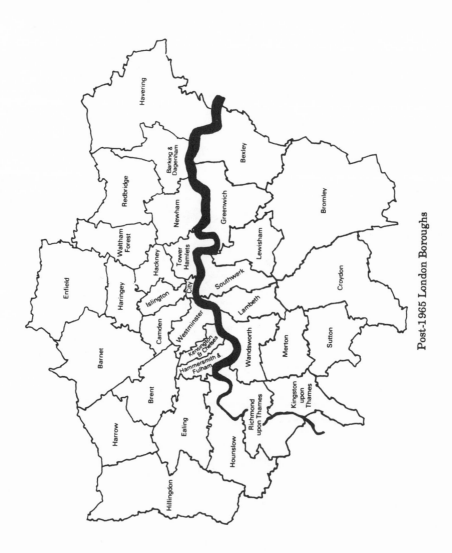

Post-1965 London Boroughs